Artificial Intelligence

Strategies, Applications, and Models Through SEARCH

Second Edition

Christopher Thornton
Benedict du Boulay

AMACOM

New York • Atlanta • Boston • Chicago • Kansas City • San Francisco • Washington, D.C.
Brussels • Mexico City • Tokyo • Toronto

ISBN: 0-8144-0470-7

Printed in the United States of America.

AMACOM

AMERICAN MANAGEMENT ASSOCIATION
1601 Broadway
New York, New York 10019
Visit the American Management Association and
AMACOM on-line at:
http://www.amanet.org

Foreword

This book started out as a set of notes for a POP-11 based course at the University of Sussex on an introduction to Artificial Intelligence. Chris Thornton designed this course around the fundamental idea of search and devised the basic structure of the book. The course expanded to take in Prolog and was then taught by Benedict du Boulay. He added Prolog variants to the POP-11 code. The course is now taught by Steve Easterbrook who made several helpful comments on a draft of the book, as did Mike Sharples. We thank Aaron Sloman and David Hogg for use of their method of writing a simple natural language interface to a blocksworld, and Allan Ramsay and Rosalind Barrett for permission to adapt their "weather rules" in the chapter on expert systems. We also thank various Sussex students who pointed out errors and omissions, particularly Sarah Cole, who carefully proof-read parts of an earlier draft. The programs were developed and the book written using the POPLOG programming environment.

Benedict du Boulay would like to dedicate his contribution to this book to his friend Hugh Noble with whom he started to write a text book not unlike this one but never finished it.

Contents

8 Parsing (search as analysis) 201

9 Expert Systems (probabilistic search) 243

10 Concept learning (description search) 267

Table of Figures

1
Search-Related Techniques in AI

Why search

Almost all artificial intelligence (AI) programs can be said to be doing some form of problem-solving whether it be interpreting a visual scene, parsing a sentence or planning a sequence of robot actions. *Search* is one of the central issues in problem-solving systems. It becomes so whenever the system, through lack of knowledge, is faced with a choice from a number of alternatives, where each choice leads to the need to make further choices, and so on until the problem is solved. Playing chess is a classic example of this situation. Other examples include the attempt to diagnose a malfunction in some complex piece of machinery or determining how best to cut material to make an item of clothing with the minimum of waste. Thus interpreting a visual scene and parsing a sentence can be regarded as searches for a plausible interpretation of possibly ambiguous visual or aural data, and making a plan can be regarded as a search in a space of plans to find one that is internally coherent and achieves the given goals.

Where the number of possibilities is small the program may be able to carry out an exhaustive analysis of them all and then choose the best. In general, however, exhaustive methods will not be possible and a decision will have to be made at each choice-point to examine only a limited number of the more promising alternatives. In chess, for example, there are just too many possibilities for a program (or a person) to imagine every possible move, each of the possible corresponding replies, further moves in response and so on to the anticipated conclusion on the game. But deciding what counts as "promising" is sometimes very hard. A good chess player is good precisely because, among other skills, he or she has an eye for plausible ways to proceed and can concentrate on these. Although it is easy to design problem-solving programs that are good at keeping track of choices made and choices yet to be explored, it is hard to provide a program with the common sense that can cut through such a welter of possibilities to concentrate its main analysis on the small number of critical choices.

Some problems that at first sight require a solution based on blind search, the Rubik's cube for example, turn out on further study to be partially soluble by special purpose methods that are essentially deterministic in character. The degree of search needed in the solution of other problems, such as the travelling salesman problem (i.e. the determination of the shortest circular route linking a given set of cities so that each city is visited once only), can also be enormously reduced by special methods and by relaxing some constraint in the problem, for example that an "acceptable" solution be found rather than the "best" solution.

There is a tension in AI between the investigation of general purpose methods that can be applied across domains and the discovery and exploitation of the special knowledge, heuristics, tricks and shortcuts that can be applied in particular domains to improve performance. This book is largely concerned with general purpose methods. It should be noted, however, that these general purpose methods often provide the framework to which the available domain specific knowledge may be attached.

In many ways the the problem-solvers referred to here are easily outstripped in performance by knowledgeable humans. But this is the state of play at present. What AI has done is to emphasise that even such impoverished tasks as finding one's way using a map or planning how to construct some simple object hide a wealth of issues that belie our apparently effortless human ability to succeed at such tasks.

Objectives

This introductory chapter provides a brief overview of some of the terminology and concepts which are addressed in more detail in the first part of the book, such as *state-space search*.

The book itself is intended to demonstrate how the common thread of *search* binds various topics in AI together. It covers a subset of important AI techniques which can all be understood as variants or generalisations of a basic set of search algorithms. The approach is a practical one in that it includes program code to illustrate the ideas. Code is offered both in POP-11 and in Prolog. Each language has its merits and it is hoped that the dual perspective that the two sets of code examples provide will be helpful. Because POP-11 is not so well known as a language, Appendix A offers some insight into the basic syntax and mechanisms of the language. The "flavour" of the programs derives mainly from the POP-11 and the Prolog code should be read as a kind of annotation to the POP-11. A book devoted to Prolog solely might well have offered Prolog code structured in a different way. In particular, the Prolog code and comments on that code offer a rather procedural view of the language.

We hope that this book will be useful for students with some background in programming who are taking an introductory course in AI. The book was initially written for a first year course in Sussex that leads to a BA in Artificial Intelligence.

Each chapter covers one technique and divides up (roughly) into three sections: a section which introduces the technique (and its usual applications) and suggests how it can be understood as a variant/generalisation of search; a section which develops a POP-11 implementation; and a section which develops a Prolog implementation of the technique. We include brief notes on alternative treatments of the material, further reading and some exercises.

Problem-solving systems

Many problem-solving systems have the following features.

(a) A knowledge base containing information about the current state of the problem in hand.

(b) A set of operators for transforming the knowledge base in some way.

(c) A control strategy or means of deciding which operator to use at any particular point during the solution of the problem, and a way of deciding when the problem is solved or unsolvable.

Consider a robot chef which should plan and then cook a meal. The knowledge base might initially contain the goal to produce dinner. The final state of the knowledge base would be a fully worked out plan for that meal which indicated every ingredient that would be needed and all the necessary cooking and preparation actions. The operators would split the goal to produce some complicated meal into its constituent parts. So the main goal of planning a meal might be split by one operator into the simpler goals of planning a starter and planning a main course and planning a dessert. An alternative operator at this point might ignore the starter, another might ignore the dessert yet another might sub-divide the meal in another way entirely, for example in terms of desirable constituents for a balanced diet. The control strategy would decide between the various operators available at each point, possibly abandoning one putative plan if it lead to an impossible situation, such as the need for an unobtainable ingredient. The control strategy would also ensure that bits of a plan were all coordinated properly.

Consider a program to solve the *8-puzzle* (a favourite in AI books!). This is a puzzle where there are 8 numbered tiles that can slide either sideways or vertically in a 3 by 3 square framework containing 9 spaces. Only one tile can be moved at a time into the single unoccupied space in the framework. In most versions of the puzzle the tiles are set in some disorganised order at the start and the problem is to rearrange them into order by sliding one tile at a time (and not taking them out of the framework).

In a program to solve the 8-puzzle the knowledge base would contain a representation of the tiles in the frame and the operators would be the moves available at the particular point in play. Here a solution would be a completed sequence of tile moves that brought the puzzle to the required state. The control strategy would make sure that in general it was the tiles which were out of place that were moved (though of course it might be necessary to temporarily move tiles that were already in the right place), because it would be these misplaced tiles that would necessarily have to be moved as part of any solution.

The amount of search involved in a problem can be reduced if there is a method of estimating how effective an operator will be in moving the initial problem state towards a solution, e.g. a method for choosing "promising" moves in chess or choosing which tile to slide in the 8-puzzle. A great deal of attention has been given to methods of making such estimates and to the repercussions of such estimates on control strategy.

Occasionally the amount of search can be reduced very dramatically by representing the problem in a new way, that is by looking at it from a different viewpoint (see, e.g. Amarel, 1981). Planning programs, for example, can usually reduce search by first considering only the most important factors of a problem before going on to consider the details once the main issues have been sorted out. In general the representation of the problem by the program is determined by the programmer and even these "hierarchical" planners have their notion of importance built in. Getting a program to decide for itself what counts as important or determine the best way to view a problem is extremely difficult. Getting a program to automatically re-orientate its view of a problem in the way suggested is, alas, beyond the state of the art.

State space search and problem reduction

Many search problems fall into one or other of two classes depending on the action of the operators involved. In some problems each operator takes the problem state or situation and transforms it into a *single* new problem state. For example, in the 8-puzzle each move transforms the arrangement of the tiles to give a new arrangement. Here the problem is to find that sequence of operators (moves) which in total transforms the initial state of the frame of tiles to a concluding state. This is called *State Space Search*.

By contrast *Problem Reduction* involves the use of operators which break down a complex problem possibly into *several* simpler, possibly independent, sub-problems each of which must be solved separately. The meal-planning system alluded to earlier is an example of this kind of system. Each sub-problem may itself be broken down into sub-sub-problems and so on, until "micro-problems" are met which can either be solved immediately without further decomposition or which are seen to be definitely insoluble.

In both State Space approaches and Problem Reduction there may be a variety of operators which in principle can apply at any particular point. Thus in the 8-puzzle (a State Space example) there is always a choice of at least two tiles that could be moved at each stage; in undertaking a mathematical integration (a typical Problem Reduction example) there typically will be a number of methods available, each of which will sub-divide the larger integration problem into smaller ones in a different way.

State space search involves searching what may be thought of as an OR Graph. Here a "graph" should be thought of as a network of nodes linked by arcs, like a road network linking cities. Each node in the graph represents a state of the problem and each arc from a node represents an operator which could be applied to that state. It is called an OR Graph (as opposed to an AND/OR Graph, see below) because the branching paths from each node represent alternatives (hence "or"). The problem for the system is to find a path (possibly the shortest path) linking the node representing the starting state with the node representing the final (or goal) state.

By contrast, problem reduction involves the search of an AND/OR graph where each node now represents only a part of the problem to be solved and each arc links a problem to a sub-problem. Arcs from a node are bunched into groups. Each group of arcs from a node represents a particular way of decomposing the problem by one of the alternative operators which can be applied to that node. As each group is an alternative it can be regarded as the "or" part of the graph. Within each group, the various arcs link to nodes representing the sub-problems that need to be solved using that particular operator. Thus within a group the arcs are in an "and" relation to each other, because all the sub-problems must be solved. The problem for the system in this case is to find the interconnected paths that link the node which represents the starting state with all the nodes that represent the ultimate decomposition of the the problem into its simplest sub-problems.

Blind search and heuristic search

The totality of all possible nodes in a problem is known as its *search space*. It is important to distinguish the complete search space for a problem (i.e. all possible nodes and arcs) from that part of the space that any particular system explores in its attempt to find a solution (i.e. those nodes and arcs actually considered). Usually only a portion of this space is or can be explored. Chess for example has been estimated to have around 10^{120} nodes, and even draughts has around 10^{40}. The reader may care to compute how long such spaces might take to explore even working at the rate of a million nodes per second.

Some control strategies for exploring the search space work *forward* from an initial state towards a solution. Such methods are also sometimes called *data-directed*. An alternative strategy is to work *backward* from a goal or final state towards either soluble sub-problems or the initial state, respectively. Such a control strategy is

A procedural description in POP-11

To search for the path, given a partial path, that ends with a goal state:

1. If the partial path already ends with a goal state, exit with the partial path as the solution.

2. Otherwise, take in turn each extended path, which extends the partial path by one state, and recursively search to see if this extended path can be made to reach the goal; if so exit *immediately* with the resultant path as the solution.

3. If no solution can be found exit with <false> as the solution.

```
define search(partial_path) -> solution;
   if is_goal(last(partial_path)) then partial_path -> solution
   else for extended_path in successors(partial_path) do
           search(extended_path) -> solution;
           if is_path(solution) then return endif
        endfor;
        false -> solution
   endif
enddefine;
```

A declarative description in Prolog

1. The search succeeds with the solution equal to the given partial path, if the last state in the partial path is the goal.

2. Otherwise, the search succeeds with a solution, if the given partial path can be extended by a state to an extended path and the search given this extended path succeeds.

```
search(Partial_path, Solution) :-
   last(Partial_path, Last_state),
   is_goal(Last_state), !,
   Solution = Partial_path.

search(Partial_path, Solution) :-
   successor(Partial_path, Extended_path),
   search(Extended_path, Solution).
```

Figure 1-1 State-space search building the solution, a path

sometimes called *goal directed.* Problem reduction systems often work backward in this way. Sometimes a mixture of both forward and backward strategies is employed, in the hope that working forward and backward will successfully meet in the middle.

Where the search space is small, systematic (but blind) methods can be used to explore the whole search space. These include *depth-first* search where, for each new node encountered, one of the arcs from it is explored. Only if a dead end is reached does the system return to the most recent choice-point and try a different arc. This method is easy to implement but can be dangerous in that the system may spend a long (or infinite!) time fruitlessly exploring a hopeless path. A variation on this method, called *bounded depth first* search, sets a limit on the depth to which exploration is allowed.

Breadth-first search is another systematic but blind method. Here all the arcs from a node are explored before moving on to explore any arcs from the new nodes encountered. The advantage of this method is that it is guaranteed to find a solution consisting of the shortest path (if one exists) but can be computationally expensive on memory especially if each node is bushy, i.e. has many arcs coming out of it. These systematic but blind methods can be applied to either state-space representations or problem reduction.

Problems differ in the form that their goal states take. Sometimes the goal state is known explicitly, such as in the 8-puzzle when all the tiles are to be in correct numerical order. In these cases it may be possible to make a comparison between the current state and the goal state as part of the process of monitoring progress. In other problems, the goal state is not known at the start, but there is a procedure which will decide whether or not a given state conforms with the criterion of being a goal state. An example here might be successfully solving an equation.

Problems also differ in whether the value of the goal state is the real goal of the problem or whether it is the path to that goal which is more important. For instance, route-finding emphasises the path where equation-solving emphasises the goal itself.

Most systems are limited by either time or space constraints to explore only a portion of the search space, choosing only certain of the alternatives available. Such systems depend on knowledge of the problem domain to decide what might be promising lines of development. They will have some measure of the relative merits either of the different nodes or of the available operators to guide them. Search which is so guided is called *heuristic* search. The methods used in such search are called *heuristics*. These terms often carry the connotation of inexactness and fallibility and are contrasted with algorithms which are bound to work. Again both state-space search and problem-reduction search can be conducted using heuristics.

Graphs and trees

Some of the above discussion may give the impression that the search tree of nodes and arcs is a pre-existing artifact which the program explores. Occasionally this is true, but in most cases the problem-solving program explores the space by "growing" a tree as it goes. Thus it is often reasonable to picture a problem-solving program as if it were a driver, without a map but with a notepad, driving around searching for a particular village in a maze of country roads. As the search proceeds the traveller keeps a record of which roads and villages have already been encountered but can have no foreknowledge of what lies ahead.

By choosing one node in the graph as a starting point (whether working forward or backward) and by applying the available operators, the program grows a *tree* rather than a graph. That is, each node explored points back to one node only, the one from which it was produced. The production of a tree rather than a graph makes it straightforward to extract a solution path, traced from the node representing the solution back to the starting node. Depending on the particular problem and on the way the program is implemented this tree may contain the same node at different points or may not. Re-encountering a node on a particular solution path during search indicates that the program has found a loop in the search space. For example, if this happens while solving the 8-puzzle, it means that the program has found a set of moves which takes it to exactly the same position as has been met before.

Organisation of the book

The main division in the book is between the early chapters concerned with variations of state space search and the later chapters which are variations on problem reduction. We start with a simple form of *state space* search where each state has no internal structure. The example is modelled on route-finding from a map. In this case, our *knowledge base* of the current state of the problem is just the name of the location from which we are currently searching. The transforming *operators* are just the *successor* locations that can be reached in one step. The idea of a *state* is developed in the next chapter to include problems where the state itself has component parts. We explain the techniques via the *jugs problem* and also introduce the idea of using an *agenda* to implement exhaustive *breadth* and *depth* first search.

Next we explore *heuristic* search, using the *8-puzzle* as an example and show how the same agenda based search mechanism can be adapted to *hill climbing* and *best first* search. This chapter also deals with heuristic search in the context of two person games (in our case, a variant of *Nim*) and explains *mini-maxing* and *alpha-beta pruning*.

Searching for a solution path in a state space

Throughout the early chapters we introduce variations on a small number of programs. These programs assume that a goal state can be recognised and that it is possible to generate the successors for a given state. The first program deals with sequences of states (i.e. paths) and constructs a path as a solution. The algorithm and code for the first program is given in Figure 1-1.

To search constructing the whole search tree, given a partial path:

1. If the partial path already ends with a goal state, there are no further subtrees to collect.

2. Otherwise, for *every* possible extended path build and collect a new subtree by recursively calling search_tree with the extended path.

3. Exit with a tree built from the last of the given partial path together with either the subtrees built in step 2 or the empty list of subtrees from step 1.

```
define search_tree(partial_path) -> tree;
   if is_goal(last(partial_path))
   then [] -> subtrees
   else [^( for extended_path in successors(partial_path) do
                search_tree(extended_path)
            endfor )] -> subtrees;
   endif;
   [^(last(partial_path)) ^^subtrees] -> tree
enddefine;
```

1. Search_tree succeeds with a tree built solely from the last state of the given partial path, if that last state is the goal.

2. Otherwise, search_tree succeeds with tree built from the last state of the given partial path together with subtrees, if these subtrees are collected through the success of collect_subtrees, itself given a list of extended paths.

```
search_tree(Partial_path, Tree) :-
   last(Partial_path, Last_state),
   is_goal(Last_state), !,
   Tree = [Last_state | []].

search_tree(Partial_path, Tree) :-
   last(Partial_path, Last_state),
   successors(Partial_path, Extended_paths),
   collect_subtrees(Extended_paths, Subtrees),
   Tree = [Last_state | Subtrees]).

collect_subtrees([],[]).

collect_subtrees([Extended_path | Extended_paths], [Subtree | Subtrees]) :-
   search_tree(Extended_path, Subtree),
   collect_subtrees(Extended_paths, Subtrees).
```

Figure 1-2 State-space search building the search tree, an OR tree

Note that this particular function and predicate are not intended to be directly runnable, as we are not offering definitions of the subsidiary functions at this early stage of the book, so the code is really a kind of schema that will be fleshed out later. Also we have glossed over various details, e.g. local variables, how to terminate the search properly and avoid loops — all of which are covered in detail in the body of the book. The algorithm and programs are given here to set the scene for what is to come.

The second general purpose state-space program schema constructs a search tree (an OR tree), see Figure 1-2. In Prolog we use a subsidiary predicate (i.e. **`collect_subtrees/2`**) to do the work which the POP-11 built-in looping mechanism handles.

Search is applied to game-playing programs and even *minimaxing* and *alpha-beta pruning* are shown to be a variant on the same theme.

Problem reduction

The second half of the book concentrates on *problem reduction* and again offers variants on a basic program theme. The main theme, started in Chapter 6, concerns reasoning with a set of rules each of which associates a goal with its related subgoals. We show how the search tree in this case is an *and/or* tree and distinguish *forwards* from *backwards* search of this tree.

Chapter 7 develops the idea of problem reduction in the context of planning via a specialised set of rules called *operators*, each of which can transform the current state of a world description in some way. The planning system forms the chosen operators into a sequence to make the plan. As the operators have to be chosen to fit together sensibly, this process involves search.

Parsing sentences according to a grammar (viewed as a set of rules) is shown to be yet another variant on the same theme, except that here there is an extra constraint that the words in the sentence may be "used up" once only. Parsing is used to distinguish *top down* from *bottom up* search and to examine their relative merits. Using one of these parsers, we provide a very simple *blocksworld* interrogation program.

The topic of reasoning is further developed in the special case where the reasoning rules themselves are associated with a degree of uncertainty, as is often the situation in *expert systems*. The same search programs as already developed are extended to deal with *certainty factors*. To conclude the main section of the book, the topic of learning is explained in terms of search in a *description space* and the basic set of search programs are again adjusted. The concluding chapter offers an implementation of Prolog *in* POP-11 to show how the built-in search capabilities of Prolog can be implemented. Some of the search programs developed in earlier parts of the book are themselves then run using this implementation of Prolog.

The algorithm studied in these later chapters is one which searches to satisfy a list of goals, given a set of rules which associate each goal with one or more lists of

---

To search through a list of goals to see if they can all be satisfied, returning true if they can, false otherwise:

1. If the list of goals is empty, exit with <true>.

2. Otherwise, take the first goal from the list, leaving other goals for step 4.

3. Take each rule in turn that relates to this first goal and collect its list of subgoals, and recursively search the list of subgoals. If this is successful, goto step 4, otherwise find the next applicable rule. If none of the rules work, exit with <false>.

4. Search the "other goals" from step 2. If this is successful, exit with <true>, otherise exit with <false>.

```
define search(goals) -> result;
   if null(goals) then true -> result
   else goals --> [?first_goal ??other_goals];
        foreach [^first_goal ??subgoals] in rules do
            search(subgoals) and search(other_goals) -> result;
            if result = true then return endif
        endforeach;
        false -> result
   endif
enddefine;
```

---

1. Search succeeds if the given list of goals is empty.

2. Otherwise, search succeeds if there is a rule that associates the first of the given goals with subgoals and search succeeds for these subgoals as well as search succeeding with the other remaining given goals for step 4.

```
search([]).

search([First_goal | Other_goals]) :-
   rule([First_goal | Subgoals]),
   search(Subgoals),
   search(Other_goals).
```

Figure 1-3 Problem reduction search

To search through a list of goals and construct the solution tree:

1. If the list of goals is empty, exit with the empty tree.

2. Otherwise, take the first goal from the list, leaving other goals for step 4.

3. Take each rule in turn that relates to this first goal and collect its list of subgoals, and recursively search the list of subgoals. If this is successful, keep the resultant subtrees and this first goal, otherwise find the next applicable rule. If none of the rules work, exit with <false>.

4. Recursively search the other goals from step 2. If this is successful, collect its other trees and exit with them together with the first goal and subtrees from step 3, otherwise exit with <false>.

```
define search_tree(goals) -> solution_tree;
   if null(goals) then [] -> solution_tree
   else goals --> [?first_goal ??other_goals];
        foreach [^first_goal ??subgoals] in rules do
            search_tree(subgoals) -> subtrees;
            if is_tree(subtrees)
            then search_tree(other_goals) -> other_trees;
                 if is_tree(other_trees)
                 then [[^first_goal ^^subtrees] ^^other_trees]
                      -> solution_tree; return
                 endif
            endif
        endforeach;
        false -> result
   endif
enddefine;
```

1. Search_tree succeeds with an empty tree if the given list of goals is empty.

2. Otherwise, search_tree succeeds with a tree built from the first goal and its subtrees together with the other trees, if a rule can be found for the first goal and search succeeds in building the subtrees associated with subgoals of that rule, and search also succeeds in building the other trees for the other remaining given goals.

```
search_tree([], []).

search_tree([First_goal | Other_goals], [[First_goal | Subtrees] | Other_trees])
   :-
   rule([First_goal | Subgoals]),
   search_tree(Subgoals, Subtrees),
   search_tree(Other_goals, Other_trees).
```

Figure 1-4 Problem reduction search building the solution, an AND tree

subgoals. Figure 1-3 gives the algorithm and the general form of the programs.

The related algorithm is one which constructs the solution AND tree (not a path, as in state-space search) as a product of its search. Figure 1-4 gives the general form of the programs. Both sentence parsers and expert systems can be built out of variations of the programs in Figure 1-4.

A very brief comparison of POP-11 and Prolog

Most of the definitions in POP-11 in the book are of functions, i.e. self-contained, named segments of code which return a result given a number of arguments. In Figure 1-5 function **foo** takes arguments **arg1** to **argN** and computes the result **result**. Many of the definitions are recursive, so the the body of the function is made up of a conditional statement that deals with the base case and the recursive case. The corresponding definition in Prolog is a procedure **foo/N** that is used like a function. That is, the procedure succeeds given instantiated arguments **Arg1** to **ArgN** and as a result binds **Result** to some value. Typically the clauses of the procedure deal with the base and the recursive cases. We indicate the modes of the Prolog clause arguments by "+" (for instantiated) and "-" (to be instantiated).

Where the function in POP-11 contains a loop, the corresponding procedure in Prolog typically involves a call to second procedure which implements the loop as a recursion.

POP-11 function	Prolog procedure
define foo(arg1...argN) **-> result;**	**foo**(+Arg1...+ArgN, -Result) :- <body of base case>
<conditional deals with base case(s) and recursive case(s)>	**foo**(+Arg1...+ArgN, -Result) :- <body of recursive case>
enddefine;	

Figure 1-5 Comparison of POP-11 and Prolog

Further reading

For those who wish to explore the issue of search more deeply the best single reference is probably Pearl (1984). Less technical, but comprehensive overviews can be found in Nilsson (1980) and in Barr and Feigenbaum (1981). Text-books on AI that have sections on search include Winston (1984), Rich (1983), Rich and Knight (1991) and Charniak and McDermott (1985). Bratko (1990) is both an excellent introduction to Prolog as well as providing a good section on search containing Prolog code. Those interested in a comparison of human and artificial problem-solving (including search behaviour) are referred to Gilhooly (1989). Finally, for a very readable and up-to-date overview of current results in search, the reader is referred to Korf (1988).

There are lots of books on Prolog including, for example, Bratko (1990), Clocksin and Mellish (1987), Sterling and Shapiro (1986), O'Keefe (1990), Scott and Nicolson (1991).

Books on POP-11 are thinner on the ground but include Sharples *et al.* (1988), Barrett, Ramsay and Sloman (1985), Laventhol (1987), Burton and Shadbolt (1987) as well as Gazdar and Mellish (1989a). This latter also exists in a Prolog version, and Sharples *et al.* is about to come out as a Prolog version, so these both give further possibilities of comparison of POP-11 and Prolog code.

2
Simple State Space Search

Path-finding

We will begin our review of search-related techniques by looking at the simplest form of search of all, namely *state space* search, where each state has no internal structure and is represented simply by a token. This process is subsumed in the general class of *OR-tree* search and is dealt with more generally in the next chapter. We will use the example of finding a path using a map. It is easy to describe and corresponds fairly closely to the non-technical meaning of the word "search". It is just the process of looking around systematically for a given location or object. In a sense, path-finding search is just ordinary, common-or-garden search, but cast in a computational framework.

Imagine that you are stranded in some unfamiliar town -- Brighton, say -- and you need to get to a specific place, e.g. the Palace Pier. One way to proceed is to start systematically exploring the immediate vicinity looking for a pier. (To make this seem a little more realistic, assume that it is a Sunday morning, there is no-one about, and you have no road map so you can get no overall strategic, birds-eye view of the town.)

If you keep going long enough (and the pier has not yet been demolished) then eventually you will find it. If you are being systematic you will explore every possibility and you will not look in any particular place more than once. There are a finite number of places in Brighton so eventually you *must* come across the one you are looking for. This is a logical necessity. Of course, if you get lost and start being unsystematic you may go on forever.

Once you have found the place you are looking for, you will have discovered a route (i.e. a *path*) which connects the place you started from to the place for which you were looking. Anyone following this path will always arrive at the desired location, though there is no guarantee that the route is a direct one. Of course, if you had known the path to begin with you could have gone directly to it without doing any searching around.

This is where the computational process of path-finding search comes in. By programming a computer to carry out this process of "looking around" it can discover the path which connects the starting location to the desired location without us doing any searching ourselves. Once we have the path, we can go directly to the desired location. The trick here is to let the computer do the walking.

But how can we program a computer to produce this sort of behaviour? The basic idea is to write a program which will imitate the process that someone goes through when they are physically searching for a location. This involves two main tasks: firstly, we have to write a bit of code which will simulate the process of "looking around"; secondly we have to write some code which will enable the first bit of code to know *where* it is able to look starting from any given location. Since the second task is the easier of the two this is the one we will tackle first.

Setting up the database

It is important to realise that the search programs described in this chapter will not be able to view the map of Brighton in Figure 2-1 as a whole, i.e. as a map. They will have a "ground level" rather than an overall view and be able to follow the connections indicated in the representation of the map but not "see" the general way to go.

To build a program which will find paths in Brighton we need to write some code which will show where you can go starting from any given location in Brighton. But this raises a question; namely, where *can* you go starting from any given location in Brighton? The basic locations and interconnecting roads will be taken to be as depicted in Figure 2-1. Thus, we will assume that there are only nine named locations

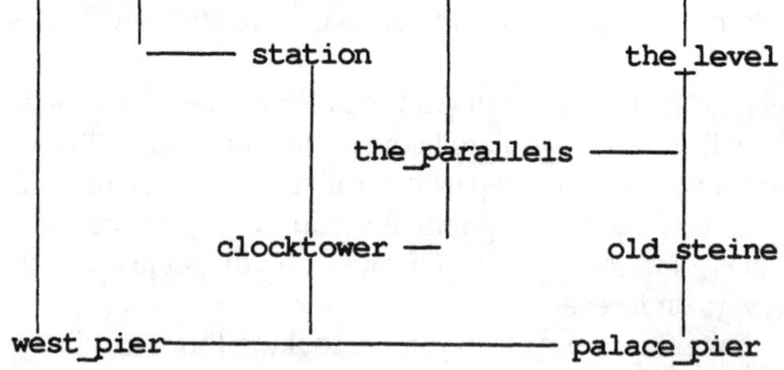

Figure 2-1 Map of Brighton

and that you can get from one to another if and only if there is a line (i.e. a road) connecting them in Figure 2-1. This means, for instance, that (by assumption) you cannot get from the Palace Pier to the Parallels without going via an intermediate location such as the Old Steine.

How can we express this road map as POP-11 code? The easiest way is to set up a database which is just a big list of connecting roads. A given connecting road can be represented as a list of two elements, these being the two connected locations. Thus the connecting road between the palace pier and the clocktower could be represented as:

```
[palace_pier clocktower]
```

Note that we have joined the words "palace" and "pier" together using the underscore character so as to show that we are talking about a single place rather than two places called "palace" and "pier". We can construct the desired database by writing list expressions for all the connecting roads and enclosing them all in a big list which we then assign to the variable "database". Each pair of linked locations is mentioned twice (once in each order) to represent explicitly that one can traverse each link in either direction, i.e. that there are no one-way streets in this map.

```
vars brighton;

[[seven_dials preston_circus]
 [seven_dials station]
 [seven_dials west_pier]
 [preston_circus seven_dials]
 [preston_circus the_level]
 [preston_circus the_parallels]
 [the_level preston_circus]
 [the_level the_parallels]
 [the_level old_steine]
 [old_steine the_level]
 [old_steine the_parallels]
 [old_steine palace_pier]
 [palace_pier old_steine]
 [palace_pier west_pier]
 [palace_pier clocktower]
 [west_pier palace_pier]
 [west_pier clocktower]
 [west_pier seven_dials]
 [station seven_dials]
 [station clocktower]
 [the_parallels preston_circus]
```

```
[the_parallels the_level]
[the_parallels old_steine]
[the_parallels clocktower]
[clocktower station]
[clocktower the_parallels]
[clocktower palace_pier]
[clocktower west_pier]] -> brighton;
```

This database looks large and complicated but it makes the job of writing some POP-11 code which can work out where you can look (i.e. go) starting from any given location very easy. We just need to write a function which takes as input a given location (e.g. **clocktower**) and returns a list of all the places that you can get to in one hop (e.g. **[station the_parallels palace_pier west_pier]**).

This function will be called the **successors1** function for reasons that will be explained below. Given the availability of the database, it can be implemented very easily using a **foreach** loop. In the definition, the command finds all the entries in the database which match a pattern consisting of the given location followed by a match-variable (e.g. **[^location ?successor]**). Any word appearing as second element in one of these lists must represent a place you can get to in one hop. Therefore a list of all the second elements is the required result. The definition of the function is given in Figure 2-2.

search can be tested as follows:

```
brighton -> database;

successors1("old_steine") ==>
** [the_level the_parallels palace_pier]
```

```
/* successors1 takes a location and returns a list
   of the places directly linked to it. */

define successors1(location) -> result;
   vars successor;
   [^( foreach [^location ?successor] do successor endforeach)]
   -> result
enddefine;
```

Figure 2-2 Computing successors

```
successors1("station") ==>
** [seven_dials clocktower]
```

Note that below we will refer to the list of elements returned by the **successors1** function for a given input L as the *successors* of L. In most cases, following normal practice, the **successors** function will just be called *the successor function*.

Setting up the path-finding function

Now that we have set up a database and a function which lets us find out where we can get to from any given location we can concentrate on writing the code which will actually try out different paths. Imagine we are at some location S and we want to get to some desired location (which will be called the *goal* below). We can easily find out where we can get to in one hop from S (by calling the successor function) so a reasonable strategy would be to first check whether we are already at the goal location and, if not, test to see whether we can get to the goal starting from any one of the successors of S.

So, we want a function which will

- take as input a current location S
- test whether S is the goal
- if not, test to see whether the goal can be reached from any successor of S.

Notice that the task involved in the last step of this function is basically just the same task that we were trying to solve to begin with, i.e. find a way of getting from some arbitrary location to some other arbitrary location. This means that we can write the function *recursively*. In the case where it finds that the current location is not the goal, the function can use itself to see whether there is a path to the goal from any of the successors of the current location. A definition of this function is shown in Figure 2-3. The **search** function calls **is_goal** which tests whether the current location matches the goal.[1] If it does, the function returns <true>. If it does not, the function uses a **for** loop to work through all the successors of the current location. If it finds that there is a path from any of these locations to the goal it immediately returns <true>. If all possibilities are exhausted it returns <false>.

Thus if we make the following call on **search**, having ensured that **search** makes use of **successors1**:

---

[1] For the examples here, **is_goal** merely matches the location against a pre-specified goal location. In principle it could be defined as a recogniser of a goal without being given any specific goal e.g. returning true if the location starts with "f", say, or contains exactly five letters. In this latter case the second argument would be a dummy (as would the second argument of **search**).

```
/* search takes the current location and the goal location and returns
   true if a path can be found to link them and false otherwise. */

define search(current_location, goal) -> boolean;
   vars successor;
   if is_goal(current_location, goal) then
      true -> boolean
   else
      for successor in successors(current_location) do
         if search(successor, goal) then
            true -> boolean; return
         endif
      endfor;
      false -> boolean
   endif;
enddefine;

define is_goal(location, goal) -> boolean;
   location matches goal -> boolean
enddefine;
```

Figure 2-3 A true/false search function

```
successors1 -> successors;

search("clocktower", "seven_dials") ==>
** <true>
```

it returns the value <true>.

We can find out how it arrived at this result by tracing the **search** and **successors** functions:

```
trace search successors;

search("clocktower", "seven_dials") ==>

>search clocktower seven_dials
!>successors clocktower
!<successors [station the_parallels palace_pier west_pier]
!>search station seven_dials
!!>successors station
!!<successors [seven_dials clocktower]
```

```
!!>search seven_dials seven_dials
!!<search <true>
!<search <true>
<search <true>

** <true>
```

In the initial call of the function, the first input is **clocktower**. This is not equal to the goal **seven_dials**. Thus, the function starts working through the successors of **clocktower**. The first successor is **station** so the recursive call on **search** has this item as the main input. The recursive call tests whether **station** is equal to **seven_dials** and finding that it is not, starts working through the successors of this item. The first successor is **seven_dials** which obviously *is* equal to the goal. Thus the third recursive call returns <true> immediately. This causes both of the enclosing calls to return <true>.

Unfortunately, it turns out that for some problems the search function we have implemented will not always work in the way we expect. Frequently, it will go into a never-ending loop. We can see an example of a loop if we test the function on a different pair of inputs:

```
untrace successors;

search("old_steine", "station") ==>

>search old_steine station
!>search the_level station
!!>search preston_circus station
!!!>search seven_dials station
!!!!>search preston_circus station
!!!!!>search seven_dials station
!!!!!!>search preston_circus station
!!!!!!!>search seven_dials station
!!!!!!!!>search preston_circus station
!!!!!!!!!>search seven_dials station
!!!!!!!!!!>search preston_circus station
!!!!!!!!!!!>search seven_dials station
```

... ad infinitum

The trace output makes the nature of the problem fairly obvious. The computer is doing exactly what the definition of **search** tells it to do. To find a path from **old_steine** to **station** it found out all the places it could get to in one hop from **old_steine**. One of these was **the_level**. It tested if this was the goal location; it was not, so it then tested to see whether a path could be found from **the_level** to the goal (see the second line of the trace output).

It then went through exactly the same process but this time it found that from **the_level** it could get to **preston_circus**. And from **preston_circus** it found it could get to **seven_dials**; and from **seven_dials** it found it could get to **preston_circus**, and from **preston_circus** it found it could get to **seven_dials** and so on, *ad infinitum*.

The problem is that our program is not keeping track of where it has already been. It therefore quite happily "visits" the same locations over and over again, if the search space makes this possible as in this case. Where the search space itself precludes loops the program works fine. To stop this happening we need to make sure that any given call of the search function knows which locations have already been visited; i.e. we need to make the program *systematic* in its searching strategy.

One way to achieve this is to change the **search** function so that it can be given a list of the locations which have already been visited as an extra input. But if we do this it is a bit silly providing the input which specifies the current location. This is always going to appear as the final element of the list of locations already visited. So, we can get away with using just one main input; namely, the list of locations already visited. We will, of course, need to change the function so that it digs out the name of

```
/* search_path takes a path so far and a goal and returns a solution
   path that links them or false if no path can be found. */

define search_path(path_so_far, goal) -> solution_path;
   vars current_location, successor;
   last(path_so_far) -> current_location;
   if is_goal(current_location, goal) then
      path_so_far -> solution_path
   else
      for successor in successors(current_location) do
         unless member(successor, path_so_far) then
            search_path([^^path_so_far ^successor], goal)
            -> solution_path;
            if islist(solution_path) then return endif
         endunless
      endfor;
      false -> solution_path;
   endif;
enddefine;
```

Figure 2-4 Searching for a solution path

the current location by accessing the last element of this list.

The definition of the new version of the function, **search_path** is shown in Figure 2-4. Its first input is the list of already-visited locations but since, in some sense, this list forms a *path* which the function is trying to "extend" towards the goal, we have named the corresponding variable **path_so_far**. Notice how the location that is currently being visited is effectively glued onto the end of the list by the expression

```
[^^path_so_far ^successor]
```

which forms the first input in the recursive call. This function has as its result either a list representing a path or "false" if no such list can be found.

To test this function we have to remember to give it as its first argument a dummy path which just has the starting location in it. This is because the function works on the basis that the first argument will be a **path_so_far**. Thus:

```
trace search_path;

search_path([old_steine], "station") ==>

>search_path [old_steine] station
!>search_path [old_steine the_level] station
!!>search_path [old_steine the_level preston_circus] station
!!!>search_path [old_steine the_level preston_circus seven_dials]
    station
!!!!>search_path [old_steine the_level preston_circus seven_dials
     station] station
!!!!<search_path [old_steine the_level preston_circus seven_dials
     station]
!!!<search_path [old_steine the_level preston_circus seven_dials
    station]
!!<search_path [old_steine the_level preston_circus seven_dials
   station]
!<search_path [old_steine the_level preston_circus seven_dials
  station]
<search_path [old_steine the_level preston_circus seven_dials
 station]

** [old_steine the_level preston_circus seven_dials station]
```

The function works but if we test it on some other inputs, we find that it is capable of producing tortuous paths. (Tracing of the search_path function is turned off since the call in question produces a huge amount of trace output.)

```
untrace search_path;

search_path([west_pier], "station") ==>
** [west_pier palace_pier old_steine the_level preston_circus
     seven_dials station]
```

If you look at the map you will see that this is not exactly the most direct path from `west_pier` to `station`.

The generality of search

It appears that the POP-11 program we have written fulfils its purpose quite adequately. We could use it to find out what the best path is from one location in Brighton to another without doing any walking. If we wanted to make the program more realistic we would only have to alter the database so as to introduce more locations and connecting roads.

The program works by directly simulating the actions of a person systematically looking around a physical environment. This would seem to be a process which is really only of relevance in the case where we are trying to find a path from one location to another. However, as we shall see, it turns out that the process has a range of applications.

The following chapters will attempt to show some of the dimensions of this generality. In order to make life easier, the rest of the current chapter will introduce a slightly more abstract view of the path-finding process we have described. Although, in the current context, it is quite satisfactory to talk about "visiting locations" and getting from one place to another "in one hop", this approach is not so helpful when considering more advanced applications.

Search spaces and search trees

Figure 2-1 represented as a graph the totality of possible places and their links in our map of Brighton. As such the graph represents a bird's-eye view of the *search space* for our programs.

Search is hard just because the program does *not* have this bird's-eye view. Thus any particular program will search the locations in some order and may (in principle) only search through *some* of the locations. As a program searches it effectively (and sometimes actually) constructs a tree whose root is the starting location and whose branches represent locations covered so far. This tree is called a *search tree*.

Our check that any particular path does not contain two copies of the same location prevents the search program being caught in cycles in the search space. However it is still possible for it to undertake some part of the search more than once.

Without a global check (rather than simply a check along the current path) on re-visiting the same location twice such a tree may contain duplicated subtrees. Such duplicated parts of the *search tree* represent the possibility that the same location can be reached by more than one path and, having got there, the same subsequent possibilities obtain.

We can remove duplications in the *search tree* by leaving a single copy of each duplicated tree and adding extra links to it, thus turning the search tree into a *search graph*. But even so the *search graph* represents that part of the overall *search space* that has been searched by the program. Thus the *search space* is really a property of the situation or problem and the *search tree* or *search graph* is a property of the search mechanism applied to the situation. Of course, if the search mechanism is systematic and exhaustive (and there is no solution) it will *eventually* explore the whole space and at that point the search tree or graph will include every location and connection from the search space.

Imagine that we select some arbitrary location in the hypothetical version of Brighton (**old_steine** say) and construct a list of all its successors. Then, for each successor we set up a new list of all *its* successors. Then, for each successor in each one of these successor lists we set up a list of all its successors, and so on. If we recursively substitute location names with lists featuring the name itself followed by the successors then we will end up with a structure of lists-inside-lists (i.e. nested lists), the first part of which looks like this:

```
[old_steine
   [the_level
      [preston_circus]
      [the_parallels]]
   [the_parallels
      [preston_circus]
      [the_level]
      [clocktower]]
   [palace_pier
      [west_pier]]]
```

These lists form a tree structure, although as printed above, the tree is upside-down and leaning to the left. The word **old_steine** forms the root of the tree; this splits into three main branches corresponding to **the_level**, **the_parallels** and **palace_pier**; then the first of these branches itself splits into two sub-branches corresponding to **preston_circus** and **the_parallels** etc.

The tree forms an explicit representation of the structure of choices in this particular search problem; i.e. the information which is implicitly represented in the combination of the database and the successors function. It effectively maps out the transitions which the search function goes through as it searches for a solution path and therefore forms a *search tree* for the problem.

```
vars tree;

[old_steine
   [the_level
      [preston_circus]
      [the_parallels]]
   [palace_pier
      [west_pier]]] -> tree;

showtree(tree);
```

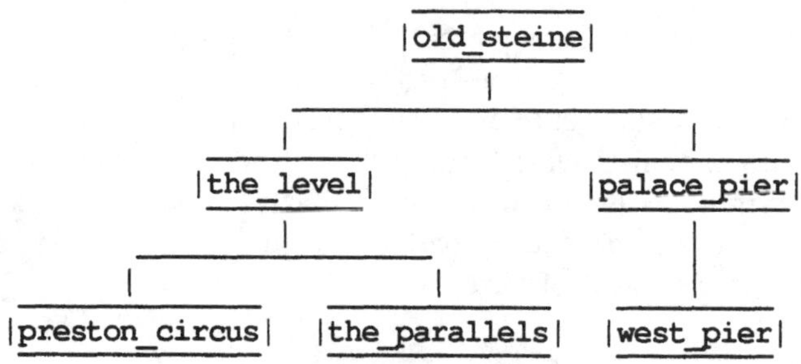

Figure 2-5 A search tree

Technically, this is an *OR-tree* since branches always indicate choices between alternatives in the search. For instance, the branch:

```
[the_level
   [preston_circus]
   [the_parallels]]
```

represents the fact that from **the_level** you can go *either* to **preston_circus** *or* to **the_parallels**. Later on we will meet a different type of search in which tree branches are *conjunctive* rather than *disjunctive*. At that point, calling the type of search we are dealing with here an "OR-tree" will make more sense.

As is noted in appendix A, the POP-11 library function **showtree** is capable of constructing representations of tree-structured lists which make the branching structure easier to see. As we have seen, **showtree** actually draws trees upside-down. Thus if we call it giving it an abbreviated version of the list structure shown above, the function would construct a representation as in Figure 2-5.

Constructing an explicit representation of the search-tree

If we want, we can write a POP-11 function which will *construct* the explicit tree-representation of the search tree from a database of connections such as we defined above. The structure of this function is quite similar to the structure of the search function. The reason for this is straightforward. The task of constructing the search tree is virtually identical to the task of searching it. Both tasks involve working out what the choices are at every given location (node).

To keep things manageable we will set up a new database describing a simpler set of connections. These are depicted in Figure 2-6. Note that, unlike the previous case, all connections are one-way streets (i.e. a *directed* graph) and their direction is indicated by the arrow symbols. The database corresponding to these connections is constructed as follows:

```
vars toytown;

[[A B][A C][C F][B E][B D]  [D X][E X][X Z][Z Y]] -> toytown;
```

The function which constructs the explicit representation of the search tree might be defined as in Figure 2-7. It returns a representation of the search tree for the problem of finding a path from the current location to the goal location working in basically the same way as the **search** function.

First of all it checks if the current location is the location being sought. If it is, or if the current location represents a dead-end with no successors, it simply returns a tree made from the current location. Otherwise, it constructs a list which begins with the name of the current location and contains, for each successor of the current location, a representation of the search subtree for finding a path from that successor to the goal. It obtains these subtrees via recursive calls in the familiar fashion.

To watch the behaviour of this function we need to trace it and then call it with an appropriate set of inputs:

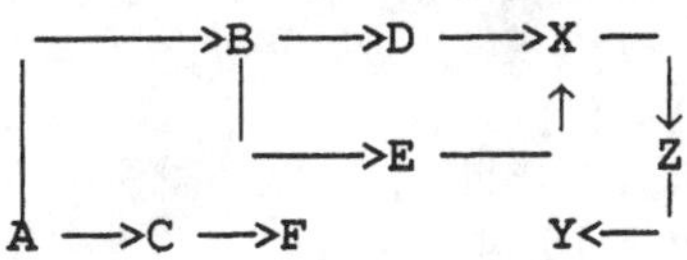

Figure 2-6 A map of toytown

```
/* search tree takes a path so far and a goal and returns the
   corresponding search tree. */

define search_tree(path_so_far, goal) -> tree;
   vars successor, subtree, current_location;
   last(path_so_far) -> current_location;
   [^current_location] -> tree;
   unless is_goal(current_location, goal) then
      for successor in successors(current_location) do
         unless member(successor, path_so_far)
         then search_tree([^^path_so_far ^successor], goal)
                -> subtree;
                [^^tree ^subtree] -> tree
         endunless
      endfor
   endunless
enddefine;
```

Figure 2-7 Computing the search tree

```
trace search_tree;

toytown -> database;

search_tree([A], "Z") ==>

> search_tree [A] Z
!> search_tree [A B] Z
!!> search_tree [A B E] Z
!!!> search_tree [A B E X] Z
!!!!> search_tree [A B E X Z] Z
!!!!< search_tree [Z]
!!!< search_tree [X [Z]]
!!< search_tree [E [X [Z]]]
!!> search_tree [A B D] Z
!!!> search_tree [A B D X] Z
!!!!> search_tree [A B D X Z] Z
!!!!< search_tree [Z]
!!!< search_tree [X [Z]]
!!< search_tree [D [X [Z]]]
!< search_tree [B [E [X [Z]]] [D [X [Z]]]]
```

```
!> search_tree [A C] Z
!!> search_tree [A C F] Z
!!< search_tree [F]
!< search_tree [C [F]]
< search_tree [A [B [E [X [Z]]] [D [X [Z]]]] [C [F]]]

** [A [B [E [X [Z]]] [D [X [Z]]]] [C [F]]]
```

If we want we can use **showtree** to construct a graphical representation of the tree constructed by this function. The output produced is shown in Figure 2-8.

Search graphs

Note that in some cases, the search tree has *duplicate* identical subtrees (see the subtrees starting at the nodes labelled "X" in Figure 2-8). This is because given locations (i.e. the nodes labelled X in this case) can be reached in different ways (from E and from D). These duplicate subtrees occur because the test embedded in **search_tree** checks only that a given path does not contain the same location twice and makes no *global* check to ensure that the same location is never visited explored twice in any part of the search.

```
showtree(search_tree([A], "Z"));
```

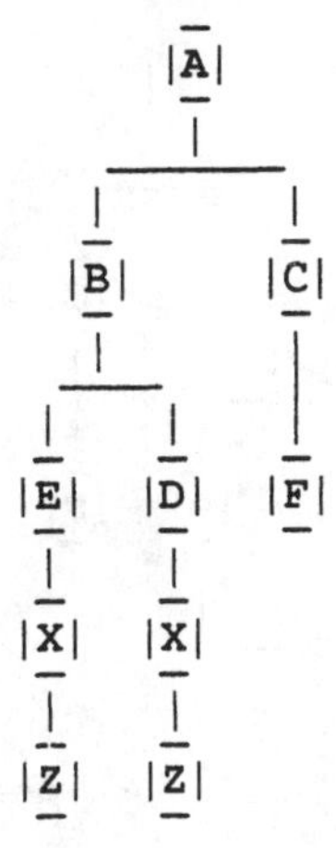

Figure 2-8 The search tree for Z from A

We could construct a representation of the search tree which has only one node for any given location. This is called a *search graph.* The search graph representation of a search tree is derived by merging nodes which have the same label. The search graph corresponding to the search-tree depicted in Figure 2-8 is shown in Figure 2-9. This graph has been drawn by hand and cannot be produced by **showtree**.

A version **search_tree** which omits duplicates would check to see whether a particular location had *ever* been visited before. To implement this we require a variable, global with respect to the search, which accumulates a list of *all* locations visited. A version of the search program which does this is given in Figure 2-10. This program makes use of a simplified version of the previous definition of **search_tree** named **simple_search_tree**, which works with locations rather than paths and does all its checking for duplicates against the variable **visited**. There is no need to store paths and check for cycles in them since the global check covers this.

Note that the tree returned by **search_tree_no_dups** contains no duplicates and that both its arguments are simply the names of locations:

```
search_tree_no_dups("A","Z") ==>
** [A [B [E [X [Z]]] [D]] [C [F]]]
```

By offering an impossible goal we can force the program to search the whole search space (e.g. also beyond Z):

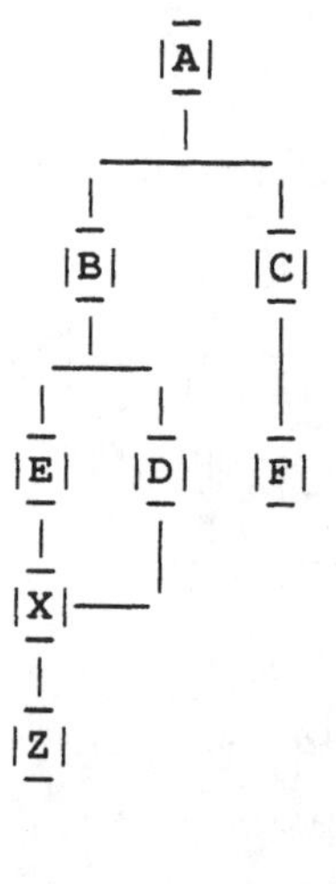

Figure 2-9 The search graph for Z from A

```
/* search_tree_no_dups takes a location and a goal and returns
   the corresponding search tree without duplicates. */

define search_tree_no_dups(current_location, goal) -> tree;
   vars visited;
   [] -> visited;
   simple_search_tree(current_location, goal) -> tree
enddefine;

define simple_search_tree(current_location, goal) -> tree;
   vars successor, subtree;
   [^current_location ^^visited] -> visited;    /* SIDE EFFECT */
   [^current_location] -> tree;
   unless is_goal(current_location, goal) then
      for successor in successors(current_location) do
         unless member(successor, visited) then
            simple_search_tree(successor, goal) -> subtree;
            [^^tree ^subtree] -> tree
         endunless
      endfor
   endunless
enddefine;
```

Figure 2-10 Searching with no location visited more than once

```
search_tree_no_dups("A","T") ==>
** [A [B [E [X [Z [Y]]]] [D]] [C [F]]]
```

We can try this program out on the brighton database as before to see that it does not loop:

```
search_tree_no_dups("old_steine", "station") ==>
** [old_steine
     [the_level
      [preston_circus
       [seven_dials
        [station]
        [west_pier [palace_pier [clocktower [the_parallels]]]]]]]]
```

The shape of the tree not containing duplications is dependent very much on the order in which potentially duplicated nodes are encountered during the search process. As the search is conducted *depth first* and *left to right*, it is the right-most subtree rooted at "X" which is omitted in this case.

Node terminology

Trees and graphs are built from *nodes* linked together by *arcs*. Nodes can have a variety of relationships with each other. The conventional labels used for these relationships exploit the analogy with family trees. Thus, in Figure 2-11, C and D would be said to be B's *children* or *successors*. This is why we called the function which would return C and D, given B as input, the successor function. B, C and D are also said to be the *descendants* of A.

Similarly, F would be said to be G's *parent* while E and F are said to be *ancestors* or *predecessors* of G. C, D, G and H would all be said to be *leaf*, *tip*, or *terminal* nodes while all other nodes are *internal* nodes. Internal nodes always form the root of a embedded tree structure. This is said to be the *subtree* of the node.

Backwards v. forwards searching

Construing the structure of choices inherent in the databases defined above in terms of a search space made up from internal nodes and leaf nodes enables us to gain a more abstract perspective on the basic path-finding process. It allows us to see that a given *search problem* consists of just three components: a successor function, a description of the starting location (called the *start node* below) and a description of the goal location (called the *goal node* below).

The successor function provides a *virtual* representation of the search tree. The representation is virtual because it -- or any part of it -- can always be constructed but, otherwise, does not actually exist. The start node gives us the root of the tree and the goal node tells us which node the search is looking for. A solution can then be found simply by calling the search function defined earlier, giving it a path containing the start node as first input and the goal node as second input.

Used in this way the search function tries to extend a path from the start node to the goal node. Of course, if we wanted, we could use the function in reverse. That is to say, we could give it a path containing the goal node as first input and the start node as second input. In this case it would try to extend a path from the goal node to the start node. The result would be a perfectly good solution path, but it would be back-to-front. To get an ordinary solution we would need to reverse it.

In later chapters we will see that in some cases, depending on the way the successor function behaves, it is easier to find a back-to-front path and then reverse it, than it is to construct a path in the correct sequence. For the present we will just note that the strategy of searching forwards from the start node to the goal node is referred to as *forwards search*; while the complimentary strategy is referred to as *backwards search*.

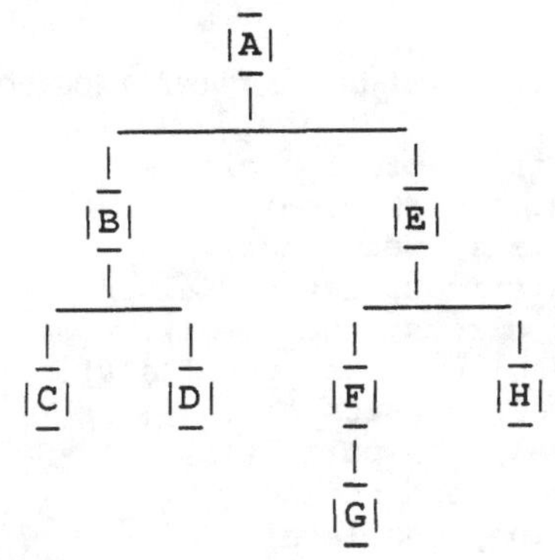

Figure 2-11 A tree

OR-tree search in Prolog

This section provides Prolog versions of some of the POP-11 programs already introduced. The central search ideas have already been covered so the Prolog code just offers an alternative runnable representation of what has already been explained.

The basic map of Brighton can be stored as a collection of facts, as follows. This corresponds to the assignment to the database in POP-11. For consistency we have chosen the name **`successor`** for this procedure, though it could as well be anything one likes, see Figure 2-12. In POP-11 we will define a number of different *successor* functions **`successors1`**, **`successors2`** and so on, and we defined a number of global variables to hold the maps such as **`brighton`** and **`toytown`**. In Prolog we can simplify matters and just use a single predicate name **`successor`** since we can rely on the value of the first argument to select the appropriate clauses.

As we have already demonstrated the need to work with paths rather than locations in order to avoid loops, we will start with a definition of **`search_path/3`**. Finding a path can be construed in much the same terms as in POP-11. The procedure **`search_path/3`** has three arguments, the given path so far, the given goal being sought and the resultant (possibly extended) path. This procedure, in Figure 2-13, corresponds to the POP-11 procedure **`search_path`**, in Figure 2-4, which checked for loops.

There are two cases to consider. One is where the path so far already has the goal as its final location. In this case the search is over and the resultant path is the one given. We could have avoided the explicit call to "=" in the first clause but included it to make the code more similar to the POP-11 version. The other case is

```
/* successor(+Here, -Next)
   Successor embodies the relation between a location and its successor. */

successor(seven_dials, preston_circus).
successor(seven_dials, station).
successor(seven_dials, west_pier).
successor(preston_circus, seven_dials).
successor(preston_circus, the_level).
successor(preston_circus, the_parallels).
successor(the_level, preston_circus).
successor(the_level, the_parallels).
successor(the_level, old_steine).
successor(old_steine, the_level).
successor(old_steine, the_parallels).
successor(old_steine, palace_pier).
successor(palace_pier, clocktower).
successor(palace_pier, old_steine).
successor(palace_pier, west_pier).
successor(west_pier, palace_pier).
successor(west_pier, clocktower).
successor(west_pier, seven_dials).
successor(station, seven_dials).
successor(station, clocktower).
successor(the_parallels, preston_circus).
successor(the_parallels, the_level).
successor(the_parallels, old_steine).
successor(the_parallels, clocktower).
successor(clocktower, station).
successor(clocktower, the_parallels).
successor(clocktower, palace_pier).
successor(clocktower, west_pier).
```

Figure 2-12 The map of Brighton in Prolog

where it does not, so a **Successor** is added to the given path so far and a recursive search is conducted for the goal from this **Successor**. We can avoid the **foreach** and **for** loops of the Pop-11 version of **successors** and **search_path** by exploiting the built-in backtracking in Prolog to automatically work through possible successors if desired. Note that the function in POP-11 of two arguments and one result is transformed into a procedure in Prolog of three arguments, where the third argument plays the same role of the result and the first two arguments play the role of input. The cut in the first clause of **search_path/3** is to ensure that once the goal is found along a particular path, no attempt is made to search beyond the goal on that path. The program would be more efficient by avoiding the call to **append/3** and building the paths in the reverse order. We have chosen explicitness over efficiency here.

```
/* search_path(+Path_so_far, +Goal, -Solution_path)
   Given a Path_so_far and a Goal, search_path succeeds
   with a Solution_path that extends the Path_so_far to the Goal. */

search_path(Path_so_far, Goal, Solution_path) :-
    last(Path_so_far, Current_location),
    is_goal(Current_location, Goal), !,
    Path_so_far = Solution_path.

search_path(Path_so_far, Goal, Solution_path) :-
    last(Path_so_far, Current_location),
    successor(Current_location, Successor),
    not(member(Successor, Path_so_far)),
    append(Path_so_far, [Successor], New_path),
    search_path(New_path, Goal, Solution_path).

/* is_goal(+Location, +Goal)
   is_goal succeeds if the Location is equal to the Goal. */

is_goal(Goal, Goal).

/* last(+List, -Element)
   last succeeds if Element is the final element of List. */

last([X], X) :- !.
last([_ | L], X) :- last(L, X).

/* append(+List1, +list2, -List3)
   append succeeds if List1 and list2 together form List3. */

append([], L, L).
append([X | L1], L2, [X | L3]) :- append(L1, L2, L3).

/* member(+Element, +list)
   member succeeds if Element is a member of List. */

member(X, [X | _]).
member(X, [_ | L]) :- member(X, L).
```

Figure 2-13 Computing a search path in Prolog

Running **search_path/3** gives the same answer as **search_path** did in POP-11:

```
?- search_path([old_steine], station, S).
S = [old_steine, the_level, preston_circus, seven_dials,
      station] ?
```

One of the benefits of Prolog is that we can ask for further solutions by typing ";" in response to the "?", as follows:

```
S = [old_steine, the_level, preston_circus, seven_dials,
      west_pier, palace_pier, clocktower, station] ? ;
S = [old_steine, the_level, preston_circus, seven_dials,
      west_pier, clocktower, station] ? ;
S = [old_steine, the_level, preston_circus, the_parallels,
      clocktower, station] ?
yes
```

However, the program, like its POP-11 equivalent, does have one piece of slightly non-intuitive behaviour because of the way it is defined:

```
?- search_path([station],station,S).
S = [station] ? ;
no
?- search_path([bombay],bombay,S).
S = [bombay];
no
```

In this example, it can find the trivial path from Bombay to Bombay even though this city is not mentioned in the database. Note also that **search_path/3** is designed to be called with its first two arguments already instantiated.

Constructing search trees (possibly containing duplicate sub-trees) is also straightforward. First we encode in Figure 2-14 the simplified "toytown" map given in Figure 2-6 in the same way as earlier using the **successor/2** clauses. Predicate **successors/2** in Figure 2-14 uses the built-in procedure **bagof/3** to collect up in the variable **Successors** all the successors following on from the current location, just as for POP-11 function of the same name. We need to collect up all the successors so that we can assemble together all the subtrees of any particular node. There are two clauses for **successors/2** because we want an empty list of successors if there are no successors but **bagof/3** fails if it finds no instances. The cut in the first clause is to ensure that we get only a single solution from **successors/2**.

We can try out **successor/2** and **successors/2** as follows, assuming that the "toytown" version of **successor** is loaded:

```
/* successor(+Location, -Successor)
   The toytown map. */

successor(a, b).
successor(a, c).
successor(c, f).
successor(b, e).
successor(b, d).
successor(d, x).
successor(e, x).
successor(x, z).
successor(z, y).

/* successors(+Location, -Successors)
   successors succeeds when Successors is a list of the successors
   of Location, or is an empty list when there are none. */

successors(Location, Successors) :-
    bagof(Successor, successor(Location, Successor), Successors), !.

successors(_, []).
```

Figure 2-14 Computing successors in Prolog

```
?- successor(x, Next).
Next = z ? ;
no
?- successor(b, Next).
Next = e ? ;
Next = d ? ;
no
?- successors(b, Next).
Next = [e, d] ?
yes
?- successors(bombay, Next).
Next = [] ?
yes
```

Procedure **search_tree/3** in Figure 2-15 corresponds to the earlier POP-11 function **search_tree** in Figure 2-7. It takes three arguments. The first is the path so far (initially containing the starting node), the second is the goal being sought and the third argument holds the tree being built.

```
/* search_tree(+Path_so_far, +Goal, -Tree)
   Given a Path_so_far and a Goal, search_tree succeeds if Tree is the search
   tree starting from the path so far which either reaches the goal or reaches
   a dead ends.  */

search_tree(Path_so_far, Goal, Tree) :-
    last(Path_so_far, Current_location),
    is_goal(Current_location, Goal), !,
    [Current_location] = Tree.

search_tree(Path_so_far, Goal, Tree) :-
    last(Path_so_far, Current_location),
    successors(Current_location, Successors),
    sub_trees(Path_so_far, Successors, Goal, Subtrees),
    [Current_location | Subtrees] = Tree.

/* sub_trees(+Path_so_far, +Successors, +Goal, -Subtrees)
   sub_trees takes a Path_so_far, a list of immediate Successors
   and a Goal, and succeeds with a list of Subtrees corresponding to
   the list of Successors. */

sub_trees(_, [], _, []).

sub_trees(Path_so_far, [Succ | Succs], Goal, Subtrees) :-
    member(Succ, Path_so_far),
    sub_trees(Path_so_far, Succs, Goal, Subtrees).

sub_trees(Path_so_far, [Succ | Succs], Goal, [Subtree | Subtrees]) :-
    append(Path_so_far, [Succ], New_path_so_far),
    search_tree(New_path_so_far, Goal, Subtree),
    sub_trees(Path_so_far, Succs, Goal, Subtrees).
```

Figure 2-15 Computing the search tree in Prolog

Similar output to the POP-11 version can be produced as follows:

```
?- search_tree([a], z, Tree).
Tree = [a, [b, [e, [x, [z]]], [d, [x, [z]]]], [c, [f]]]
```

In POPLOG Prolog **showtree/1** will work as in POP-11 to produce identical diagrams as shown earlier.

The procedure **search_tree/3** has two cases to deal with. If the **Path_so_far** reaches the goal, the resultant tree is just that goal (in list brackets). Otherwise, the list of successors is constructed and a tree is built which consists of the current location followed by the subtrees corresponding to each of these successors.

Procedure **sub_trees/4** works its way through the list of successors until it is empty, calling **search_tree/3** on each one with an appropriately augmented path so far. It has three clauses. The first is the stopping case when the list of successors is empty. The second clause deals with the case where the first of the successors is already on the **Path_so_far** by ignoring it and just dealing with the remaining successors.

The third clause does the real work. As in the POP-11 version, the new location is added onto the right-hand end of the path so far, though a more succinct Prolog program would build this path the other way round since lists are more easily accessed at the front.

In the POP-11 version of **search_tree** there is both a recursive call to **search_tree** as well as an embedded **for** loop. The recursion delves deeper "down" the tree and the loop works its way "along" through all the successors of a given node. The Prolog version achieves the same ends using much the same division of labour. Procedure **sub_trees/4** corresponds to the POP-11 **for** loop containing the embedded recursive call to **search_tree**.

By examining the trace of either the POP-11 **search_tree** or the Prolog version one can see the *depth first, left to right order* in which the search tree is built. This topic will be returned to later:

```
?- spy search_tree.
?- search_tree([a], z, Tree).
** (1) Call : search_tree([a], z, _1)?
** (2) Call : search_tree([a, b], z, _2)?
** (3) Call : search_tree([a, b, e], z, _3)?
** (4) Call : search_tree([a, b, e, x], z, _4)?
** (5) Call : search_tree([a, b, e, x, z], z, _5)?
** (5) Exit : search_tree([a, b, e, x, z], z, [z])?
** (4) Exit : search_tree([a, b, e, x], z, [x, [z]])?
** (3) Exit : search_tree([a, b, e], z, [e, [x, [z]]])?
** (6) Call : search_tree([a, b, d], z, _6)?
** (7) Call : search_tree([a, b, d, x], z, _7)?
** (8) Call : search_tree([a, b, d, x, z], z, _8)?
** (8) Exit : search_tree([a, b, d, x, z], z, [z])?
** (7) Exit : search_tree([a, b, d, x], z, [x, [z]])?
** (6) Exit : search_tree([a, b, d], z, [d, [x, [z]]])?
** (2) Exit : search_tree([a, b], z, [b, [e, [x, [z]]],
                                     [d, [x, [z]]]])?
** (9) Call : search_tree([a, c], z, _9)?
** (10) Call : search_tree([a, c, f], z, _10)?
** (10) Exit : search_tree([a, c, f], z, [f])?
```

```
** (9) Exit : search_tree([a, c], z, [c, [f]])?
** (1) Exit : search_tree([a], z, [a, [b, [e, [x, [z]]],
                         [d, [x, [z]]]], [c, [f]]])?
Tree = [a, [b, [e, [x, [z]]], [d, [x, [z]]]], [c, [f]] ?
yes
```

Reading

In this chapter we have looked at simple state space search, otherwise known as OR-tree search, and seen the way in which it can be used to solve simple routing problems. Each state in the search space is merely a token without internal structure and the test for a goal is that it simply corresponds to a particular token. We have also considered the way in which we can adapt a search function so as to make it construct a representation of the search tree for a given search problem. Most AI texts which deal with search do not restrict the discussion to the area we have covered in this chapter, i.e. state space search where the states have no internal structure. These books are therefore probably best consulted once the material to be presented in the Chapter 3 has been covered. However, Winston (1984, pp. 87-90) covers some of the concepts introduced above and goes over the terminology for search space nodes. Charniak and McDermott (1985, p. 257) may also be of interest. The most substantial reference of real relevance is Sharples *et al.* (1988, Sections 1 to 2.2 inclusive).

Exercises

1. Construct a database of lists representing links between locations in some physical environment with which you are familiar. Use either language version of **search_tree** together with **showtree** to construct a representation of the search tree for the problem of getting between two locations.

Don't forget to type, in POPLOG POP-11

```
lib showtree;
```

or in Prolog

```
library(showtree).
```

before trying to use **showtree**.

2. Write a Prolog version of **search_tree_no_dups** which omits *all* duplicates. One method would be to include an extra argument which stores a list of all nodes visited

throughout the search.

3. Examine the behaviours of `search_path/2` and `search_tree/3` when in each case the cut is removed from clause 1.

3
State Space Search

Introduction

In the previous chapter, we saw that we can write a program consisting of a search function and a successor function which will search a representation of a physical environment to find a path from a start node to a goal node. This sort of program obviously has uses for any task which involves route planning (e.g. programming mobile robots). But in fact the program we have constructed has many other possibilities.

Any problem which can be construed in terms of a start node, a goal node recogniser and a successor function (i.e. any problem which can be construed as a *search problem* through states) can, in principle, be solved using the search function we defined in the previous chapter. In the present chapter we will look at an example of such a problem in which the successor function represents connections between abstract states in a problem rather than physical locations in a town. States will now contain internal structure rather than simply being tokens, such as the names of locations. In this scenario the successors of any given node are effectively the states which can be achieved in one move rather than the locations which can be reached in one hop; and the search space is said to be a *state space* or *problem space.* Choices at each node are still "OR" choices, so the search trees that get built are still "OR Trees" as in the previous chapter and solutions are still *paths* from the root node of the OR Tree to the goal node.

The water jugs problem

Imagine that you have two jugs called X and Y. Initially, both are empty. You are allowed to fill either jug X or jug Y from a tap but if you do, you have to fill it completely. You are also allowed to fill jug X from jug Y, or jug Y from jug X, and to empty either jug on the ground. Jug X can hold 4 pints and jug Y can hold 3 pints.

The problem is simply this: given the allowed actions, can you manage to reach a state where you have exactly 2 pints in jug X.

This problem is known as the *water jugs problem* and it has no easy solution. If we just fill X from the tap we end up with 4 pints in X, not 2. If we fill Y from the tap and empty it into X, we end up with 3 pints in X. The only way to find a solution to this problem is to consider systematically the effects achieved by performing *sequences* of actions. But how can we go about this?

Systematically considering all possible sequences of actions is just like systematically considering all possible sequences of locations (i.e. all possible routes). So the water jugs problem can be construed as a sort of search problem. Of course, if we *are* going to construe the water jugs problem as a search problem, nodes in the search space will have to represent *states* of the two jugs rather than locations in a physical environment. The start node will have to be a representation of the initial state (e.g. 0 pints in both jugs); the goal node will have to be a representation of the goal state (e.g. 2 pints in X, any amount in Y), and the successor function will have to return that set of new states which can be reached from any given state by performing exactly one allowed action. So the main difference between this example and the one used in the previous chapter is that each state now contains some components (e.g. the contents of the two jugs) rather than just being an atomic value (e.g. **clock_tower**).

Constructing successor nodes

We can represent states in the water jugs problem as two-element lists in which the first element is an integer representing the number of pints in the jug called X, and the second element is an integer representing the number of pints in Y. Thus, the state in which X has 3 pints in it and Y has 2 would be represented by the list expression:

```
[3 2]
```

We could implement the successor function using the approach that we took with the path-finding problem, i.e. we could construct a database showing the connections between states and then use a **foreach** loop to dig out the states we can achieve in one move. The beginning of the database might look something like this:

```
[ [[0 0] [4 0]]
  [[0 0] [0 3]]
      ...
      ...

] -> database;
```

These first two elements represent the fact that from the state `[0 0]` you can either fill X to achieve `[4 0]` or fill Y to achieve `[0 3]`. Note that the *complete* database will be large. There are 5 × 4 possible states and there are normally 6 possible actions. So the database will have roughly 5 × 4 × 6 = 120 entries. It will not be exactly 120 because, for some states, two different actions can lead to an identical new state. Nevertheless this multiplicity leads us to wonder whether there might be an easier way to implement the successor function.

Note that our state representations are structures with two separate components. The successors of any given state can be derived (i.e. computed) by looking at the components of any state representation and making some substitutions. For example, imagine that we wish to work out what the successors of the state `[4 2]` are. We know that one possible action is to empty X into Y; thus one successor is just the state which is reached by carrying out this action. But what is this state?

We can construct it quite easily. Y can hold 3 pints. So if we empty X into Y (which already has 2 pints in it), exactly 1 pint will flow from X to Y. X will have 3 pints left in it and Y will have 3 pints in it. It is quite easy to turn this bit of computation into POP-11 code. In fact we can write POP-11 rules to take care of every allowable action. If we put them all together, we get a function which produces the successors of any given state. This program obviously implements the desired successor function. But it does not do so in the same way that our previous program did — by scanning a database. It produces the successors by operating on the components of structured state descriptions.

A simple version of the successor function might be defined as in Figure 3-1. This version of the function only takes account of the single action whereby one jug is emptied on the ground. Either X can be emptied or Y can be emptied; so the successors of any state include one state in which X has 0 pints (regardless of what it had before) and one state in which Y has 0 pints. The number of pints in the other jug remains the same in either case.

```
/* successors2 takes a state and returns a list of successor states. */

define successors2(state) -> result;
    vars X Y;
    state --> [?X ?Y];
    [[^X 0] [0 ^Y]] -> result;
enddefine;
```

Figure 3-1 Partial successor function for the jugs problem

The function digs out the components of the input state description using the matcher arrow. This, effectively, puts the number of pints in the jug X in to the variable called "X", and the number of pints in the jug Y in to the variable called "Y". It then constructs a list of lists (i.e. a list of states), one of which substitutes the original X with 0 and the other of which substitutes the original Y with 0. These are just the successor states of the original state resulting from the action of emptying either X or Y on the ground.

To implement the complete successor function for this problem we need to take account of the other possible actions. Note that in the case of actions involving the emptying of one jug into another, the generation of a successor state entails doing a little bit of arithmetic. For example, to work out how much water flows from X to Y when we empty X into Y, we have to work out how much space Y has in it (by subtracting 3 from Y) and how much water is transferred by subtracting this from the current value of "X". The complete function might be defined as in Figure 3-2. Note the use of comments.

```
/* successors3 takes a state and returns a list of successor states. */

define successors3(state) -> result;
   vars X Y result;
   state --> [?X ?Y];
   [^(
      /* FILL X COMPLETELY FROM Y WITH SOME LEFT OVER */
         if Y /= 0 and X /= 4 and X+Y > 4 then [4 ^(X+Y-4)] endif;
      /* EMPTY Y COMPLETELY INTO X */
         if Y /= 0 and X /= 4 and X+Y =< 4 then [^(X+Y) 0] endif;
      /* FILL Y COMPLETELY FROM X WITH SOME LEFT OVER */
         if Y /= 3 and X /= 0 and X+Y > 3 then [^(X+Y-3) 3] endif;
      /* EMPTY X COMPLETELY INTO Y */
         if Y /= 3 and X /= 0 and X+Y =< 3 then [0 ^(X+Y)] endif;
      /* EMPTY OUT X */
         if X /= 0 then [0 ^Y] endif;
      /* EMPTY OUT Y */
         if Y /= 0 then [^X 0] endif;
      /* FILL X UP FROM THE TAP */
         if X /= 4 then [4 ^Y] endif;
      /* FILL Y UP FROM THE TAP */
         if Y /= 3 then [^X 3] endif;
      )] -> result;
enddefine;
```

Figure 3-2 Successor function for the jugs problem

This function has eight parts to it corresponding to the eight actions which can be carried out. Each part constructs a state representation for the successor state. Thus:

```
successors3([0 0]) ==>
** [[4 0] [0 3]]

successors3([4 0]) ==>
** [[1 3] [0 0] [4 3]]

successors3([1 3]) ==>
** [[4 0] [0 3] [1 0] [4 3]]
```

We can easily confirm that this behaviour corresponds to the rules of the puzzle by working out what the real successors of any state are and checking that the successor function returns exactly this set. This task is left as an exercise for the reader.

```
/* limited_search_tree takes a path so far, a goal and a depth and returns
   the corresponding search tree within given depth limit. */

define limited_search_tree(path_so_far, goal, depth) -> tree;
   vars successor, subtree, current_location;
   last(path_so_far) -> current_location;
   [^current_location] -> tree;
   unless is_goal(current_location, goal) or depth =< 0 then
      for successor in successors(current_location) do
          unless member(successor, path_so_far)
          then limited_search_tree([^^path_so_far ^successor], goal,
                                                     depth-1) -> subtree;
               [^^tree ^subtree] -> tree
          endunless
      endfor
   endunless
enddefine;
```

Figure 3-3 Computing a search tree with depth limited depth-first search

The problem space

Now that we have implemented the successor function for the water jugs problem we can solve the problem by application of the `search` function defined in the previous chapter. We can also construct an explicit representation of the search tree for this problem by applying the `search_tree` function. In the current case, a goal node corresponds to any state in which Y has 2 pints regardless of what X has in it. Thus a state is a *goal state* provided that it matches the pattern `[= 2]`.

In our definition of `is_goal` we used a "matches" expression rather than a straight equality test to find out whether the current node constituted a goal node. This means, that provided the goal description provided as input is a match pattern such as `[= 2]` or `[3 3]`, the function will work in exactly the way we want:

```
successors3 -> successors;

search_tree([[0 0]], [= 2]) ==>

** [[0 0]
    [[4 0]
     [[1 3]
      [[0 3] [[3 0] [[3 3] [[4 2]] [[4 3]]]]] [[4 3]]]
      [[1 0]
       [[0 1]
        [[4 1]
         [[2 3]
          [[0 3] [[3 0] [[3 3] [[4 2]] [[4 3]]]]] [[4 3]]]
          [[2 0] [[0 2]]]
          [[4 3] [[0 3] [[3 0] [[3 3] [[4 2]]]]]]]
         [[4 3] [[0 3] [[3 0] [[3 3] [[4 2]]]]]]]
        [[0 3] [[3 0] [[3 3] [[4 2]] [[4 3]]]]] [[4 3]]]]]
      [[4 3] [[0 3] [[3 0] [[3 3] [[4 2]]]]]]]
     [[4 3] [[0 3] [[3 0] [[3 3] [[4 2]]]]]]]
    [[0 3]
     [[3 0]
      [[4 0]
       [[1 3]
        [[1 0] [[0 1] [[4 1] [[2 3] [[2 0] [[0 2]]] [[4 3]]] [[4 3]]]]]
        [[4 3]]]
       [[4 3]]]
      [[3 3]
       [[4 2]]
       [[4 3]
        [[4 0] [[1 3] [[1 0] [[0 1] [[4 1] [[2 3] [[2 0] [[0 2]]]]]]]]]]]]
     [[4 3]
      [[4 0] [[1 3] [[1 0] [[0 1] [[4 1] [[2 3] [[2 0] [[0 2]]]]]]]]]]]
```

This result has the usual upside-down and sloping-to-the-left tree structure. Unfortunately, if we try to use **showtree** to construct a better representation we will not get the effect that we want, and the tree is very large. The scheme we are using represents a state as a list of two elements. But **showtree** normally interprets a list of two elements as a representation of a "tree" consisting of a root (the first element of the list) and one branch (the second element of the list). To get around this problem we redefine how **showtree** recognises and prints root nodes (see Notes at the end of this chapter). For convenience we have changed the **search_tree** function from the previous chapter so that it takes a third input (an integer) denoting the depth to which the search tree should be constructed. In each recursive call of **limited_search_tree**, this integer is decremented. Thus any call of **limited_search_tree** which finds that its **depth** input is less than 0 can assume that it should not generate any more recursive calls, i.e. it should cause the tree-growing process to "bottom-out". Putting these modifications together leads to the definition shown in Figure 3-3. With this new definition, we can safely use showtree to display the structure of the search tree (containing duplicate nodes); see Figure 3-4.

```
showtree(limited_search_tree([[0 0]], [= 2], 5));
```

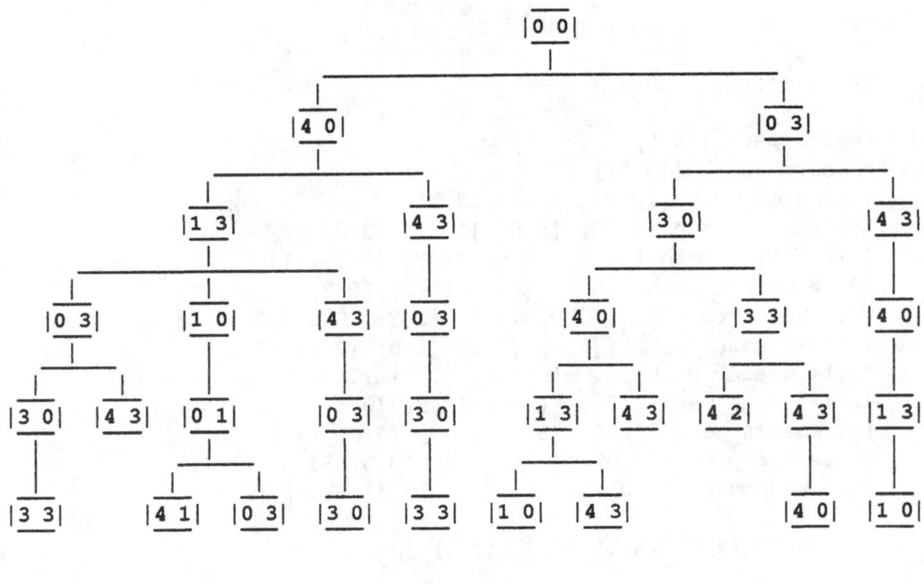

Figure 3-4 Search tree for the jugs problem

Another way to simplify the tree without using a depth bound, as in Figure 3-5, is to use the **search_tree_no_dups** function from the previous chapter. This explores the search space but never computes the successors of the same node twice,

Note that the actual shape of the tree generated depends very much on the order in which nodes are encountered, since no node is visited twice. The search method is depth-first and node [3 3] is encountered in the left hand path. This means that [3 3] will not occur in any other part of the tree and therefore can never be part of any other solution in this case. Of course, a successor function that generated nodes in a different order or a different search method might well include this node in some other solution path.

Searching for a solution path

We have already noted that a solution to the water jugs problem is just a sequence of actions which transform the starting state (assumed to be [0 0]) into the goal state. We can search for such a sequence in exactly the same way as we searched for a sequence of locations which connected a starting location to a goal location. In other words, we can find a solution (or "solution path") for the water jugs problem by running the **search_path** function we constructed in the previous chapter.

Thus, searching for the new goal [3 3] gives:

```
trace search_path;

search_path([[0 0]], [3 3]) ==>
> search_path [[0 0]] [3 3]
!> search_path [[0 0] [4 0]] [3 3]
!!> search_path [[0 0] [4 0] [1 3]] [3 3]
!!!> search_path [[0 0] [4 0] [1 3] [0 3]] [3 3]
!!!!> search_path [[0 0] [4 0] [1 3] [0 3] [3 0]] [3 3]
!!!!!> search_path [[0 0] [4 0] [1 3] [0 3] [3 0] [3 3]] [3 3]
!!!!!< search_path [[0 0] [4 0] [1 3] [0 3] [3 0] [3 3]]
!!!!< search_path [[0 0] [4 0] [1 3] [0 3] [3 0] [3 3]]
!!!< search_path [[0 0] [4 0] [1 3] [0 3] [3 0] [3 3]]
!!< search_path [[0 0] [4 0] [1 3] [0 3] [3 0] [3 3]]
!< search_path [[0 0] [4 0] [1 3] [0 3] [3 0] [3 3]]
< search_path [[0 0] [4 0] [1 3] [0 3] [3 0] [3 3]]

** [[0 0] [4 0] [1 3] [0 3] [3 0] [3 3]]
```

The list returned by our call on **search_path** is a sequence of states. Each state can be reached by applying one action to the previous state. The first state in the sequence is the starting state and the last state is a goal state. Thus the sequence constitutes a solution to the water jugs problem.

```
showtree(search_tree_no_dups([0 0], [= 2]));
```

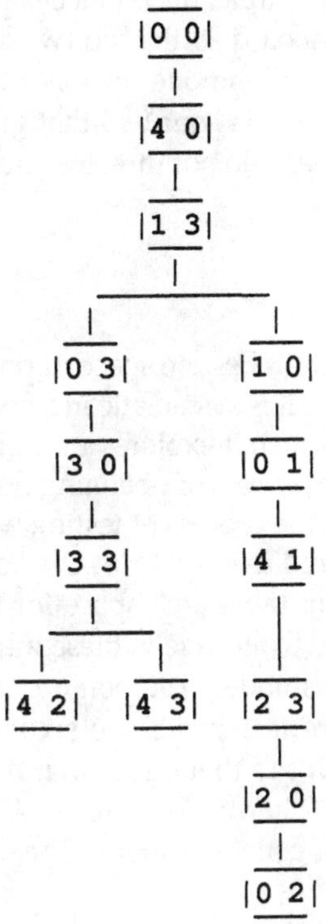

Figure 3-5 Search tree for the jugs problem without duplicated nodes

We might translate the solution, involving six states and hence five actions, into English as follows. To reach the state `[3 3]` starting from `[0 0]` using only allowed actions, do the following: fill X, empty X into Y, empty X, fill X from Y and finally fill Y. Note that this solution is not very sensible — the initial actions of filling X and moving its contents into Y are completely redundant. However, it *is* a solution.

A great many problems can be solved using the **search_path** function. The classic examples are the 8-puzzle, the Tower of Hanoi problem, and the Missionaries and Cannibals problem. But *any* problem whose instantaneous state can be represented precisely, and whose solution involves finding a sequence of moves connecting a starting state to a goal state can, in principle be solved through search. Of course, there are many search problems for which finding a solution using ordinary search will take an astronomical amount of time in practice, e.g. chess.

In some problems the goal state is explicitly known at the start and the search process looks for it specifically. In other problems the goal state may not be known at the start but can be *recognised* if found. For example, the 8-Queens problem. Here the problem is to place eight queens on a chessboard so that no two share the same row, column or diagonal. At the start of the problem one does not know how the queens will be arranged but it is possible to define **`is_goal`** so that given any configuration it returns <true> if, and only if, the queens do not threaten each other.

Problem space exploration strategies

The search function we have been using so far searches the space of possible states in a systematic fashion. But it is not just systematic, it is systematic in a specific way. We can bring this out by considering the order in which it explores states in the problem space for the water jugs problem. Note that the process of obtaining the successors of a node is referred to as *expanding* the node; and the process of testing whether a given node is, or lies on a path to, a goal node is referred to as *exploring* the node.

Figure 3-6 shows the first few branches in the search space for the water jugs problem. Each node has a number beside it and, collectively, these numbers indicate the order in which our search function expands nodes. The point to note is that the function expands the children of `[4 0]` before it expands the second child of the starting state, namely `[0 3]`. In general we can say that our search function always explores nodes at level N+1 before exploring further nodes at level N. That is to say, it always explores successor nodes as soon as it generates them. The diagram shows

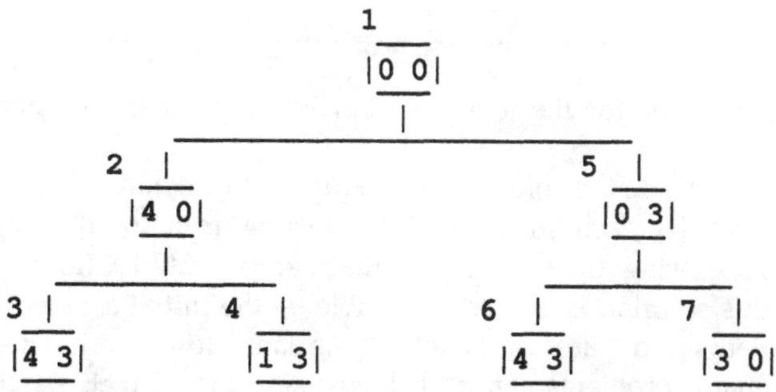

Figure 3-6 Depth-first search

depth-first search with backtracking. That is when the search reaches as far down the tree as it can (e.g. because a node is a dead end) it backs up to the most recent node where there was a choice and continues the search downwards from there (hence the node labelled 5 after the node labelled 4). This particular type of search behaviour is called *depth-first search.* It is very easy to implement using a recursive function because, at any point in the search process, the *recursion stack* provides a complete record of the current state of the search. But why is this so important?

When a function calls itself (i.e. makes a recursive call) in POP-11, mechanisms which are built in to the language serve to keep a record of the current state of the calling function. This means that when the *called* function finishes, the original function can continue executing. In the case where we have a whole set of function calls (one function which has called another, which has called another, which has called another...) then the built-in language mechanisms keep track of the states of all these functions.

In the case of our search function, this information (which is called the *recursion stack*) plays a very important role: it provides an implicit representation of the search space which is being explored. In effect, it makes sure that the search function does not start searching some portion of the tree which it has already looked at.

What this means is that when we write a recursive search function in a language such as POP-11, we are effectively making a feature of the language do an important subtask in the search process; namely, the task of keeping track of exactly where in the space the search has got to at any one moment. The fact that we are able to do this means that we can write depth-first search programs — which implement a very complex form of processing — using just a few lines of code. This issue comes out more clearly in Prolog, where the built-in mechanisms provide exactly what is needed for depth-first search.

Depth-first search that simply plunges down the tree may fruitlessly explore a very deep (or infinite) part of the tree and never find a solution, though this can be circumvented by imposing a depth bound. However depth-first search is efficient in storage space terms. If we use the recursion stack to keep track of where we are, then we do not need to store the explored nodes explicitly. Even if we do store explored nodes explicitly we only need to keep track of those nodes between the start and where the search has currently reached (and perhaps their immediate siblings) so the amount of storage consumed is roughly proportional to the depth explored.

Breadth-first search

Depth-first search always explores nodes at level N+1 before exploring any (more) at level N. But what happens if we implement a different strategy which does just the opposite of this, i.e. always explores nodes at level N before exploring any (more) nodes at level N+1? In fact this strategy is a perfectly good way of systematically searching a given problem space. It is called *breadth-first search* in view of the fact that it works down the tree expanding nodes in a breadth-first fashion. The sequence in which nodes would be expanded by a breadth-first search process applied to the water jugs problem is shown in Figure 3-7. By contrast with depth-first search the amount of storage consumed by breadth-first search is large since it needs to store all the nodes explored so far. Its advantage is that it will always find the shortest possible solution (if one exists) since it explores downwards from the start node one complete layer at a time.

But how could we implement the breadth-first strategy? Given the comments that have just been made with respect to recursion, we might expect that implementing breadth-first search will not be quite so easy. This is in fact the case; however, the task is well within our reach. A convenient way to implement breadth-first search involves making use of a data structure called an *agenda*.

Agendas

An agenda is a list of the jobs which a search function is going to do next. These "jobs" are just nodes (states) which are going to be expanded as the search continues. By arranging things such that the function always adds new jobs into the agenda in a specific way we can obtain the breadth-first searching behaviour that we want.

Let us imagine that we provide a search function with an agenda which initially contains just the starting state. The function can then execute a search by repeatedly executing a sequence of three steps.

- Take the first job off the *front* of the agenda;

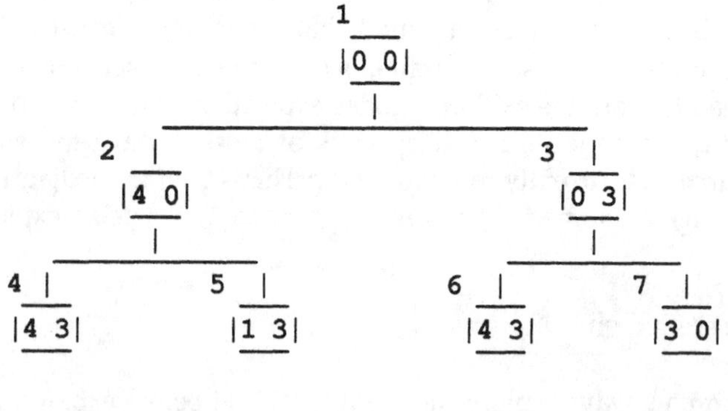

Figure 3-7 Breadth-first search

- if it is a goal node, exit;
- otherwise, obtain its successors and add them onto the *end* of the agenda

By taking jobs off the *front* of the agenda and adding successors onto the *end* of the agenda, we ensure that the sequence in which this function expands nodes is breadth-first rather than depth-first. The nodes at level N+1 will always be added to the end of the agenda *behind* any nodes at level N. Thus they will never be expanded before any nodes at the current level.

If we want to make sure that the **agenda_search** function does not construct (explore) paths which have loops in them (i.e. go through one node more than once) then we need to arrange for the agenda to contain not just "nodes to be expanded", but "paths to be extended". This way, the function **new_paths** could always check to see whether a particular successor of the current node has already been considered, i.e. is already in the path that needs to be extended. We have stored paths explicitly as lists of states. A more efficient method would have been to store paths implicitly as pointers between states. The function simply needs to test whether the node is already a member of the path and if so, to ignore it. Because the agenda is storing paths, we can also cease searching if the current path being considered exceeds a given length (i.e. depth in the search tree). This will be useful, especially in depth-first search to conserve search effort. Functions with the desired features are defined in Figure 3-8. The function also keeps a record, in **visited**, of every path that has been expanded. This is not used at this stage, but will be used in later versions of the program.

So far we have been representing a path as a list of states starting at the first state and terminating at the final state. This is intuitively clear but rather inefficient as our programs have to traverse each path along its length to get to the "current_location". From now on we will internally represent paths in the opposite order, thus making access faster, but print paths out by using the built in function **rev**.

Because the processing which we achieve with this function does not exploit recursive sub-procedure calls, tracing does not tell us much about the way it works. However, by including a command which has the effect of printing out the number of paths on the agenda and the current path that is being extended (**if chatty then ... endif**) we can see what is going on. If we test this function on the water jugs problem we get the following behaviour, choosing "10" as the depth bound:

```
true -> chatty;

successors3 -> successors;

extend_agenda1 -> extend_agenda;

agenda_search([0 0], [2 =], "breadth", 10) ==>
```

```
/* agenda_search takes an initial state, a goal, a word denoting a
   search method and a depth limit. It returns a path from the initial
   state to the goal using the specified search method.  If no path can
   be found it returns false. */

define agenda_search(initial_state, goal, search_type, depth) -> path;
   vars agenda paths visited;
   [ [^initial_state] ] -> agenda;
   [] -> visited;
   until agenda = [] do
      agenda --> [?path ??paths];
      if chatty then pr(length(agenda)); sp(1); pr(rev(path)); nl(1)
      endif;
      if is_goal(hd(path), goal)
      then rev(path) -> path; return
      elseif length(path) > depth then paths -> agenda
      else [^path ^^visited] -> visited;
           extend_agenda(paths, path, search_type) -> agenda;
      endif;
   enduntil;
   false -> path;
enddefine;

/* new_paths takes a path and uses the successor function to return a
   list of all extended paths which exclude duplicated nodes. */

define new_paths(path) -> extended_paths;
    vars state;
    [^( for state in successors(hd(path)) do
            unless member(state, path)
            then [^state ^^path]
            endunless
        endfor
      )] -> extended_paths
enddefine;

/* extend_agenda1 takes an agenda of paths, a path and a search method
   and returns a new agenda that incorporates the new extended paths. */

define extend_agenda1(agenda, path, search_type) -> new_agenda;
    vars extended_paths;
    new_paths(path) -> extended_paths;
    if search_type = "breadth"
    then [^^agenda ^^extended_paths] -> new_agenda
    elseif search_type = "depth"
    then [^^extended_paths ^^agenda] -> new_agenda
    endif
enddefine;
```

Figure 3-8 Agenda-based search

```
1 [[0 0]]
2 [[0 0] [4 0]]
3 [[0 0] [0 3]]
4 [[0 0] [4 0] [1 3]]
6 [[0 0] [4 0] [4 3]]
6 [[0 0] [0 3] [3 0]]
7 [[0 0] [0 3] [4 3]]
7 [[0 0] [4 0] [1 3] [0 3]]
8 [[0 0] [4 0] [1 3] [1 0]]
8 [[0 0] [4 0] [1 3] [4 3]]
8 [[0 0] [4 0] [4 3] [0 3]]
8 [[0 0] [0 3] [3 0] [4 0]]
9 [[0 0] [0 3] [3 0] [3 3]]
10 [[0 0] [0 3] [4 3] [4 0]]
10 [[0 0] [4 0] [1 3] [0 3] [3 0]]
10 [[0 0] [4 0] [1 3] [0 3] [4 3]] /* SEE TEXT */
9 [[0 0] [4 0] [1 3] [1 0] [0 1]]
10 [[0 0] [4 0] [1 3] [4 3] [0 3]]
10 [[0 0] [4 0] [4 3] [0 3] [3 0]]
10 [[0 0] [0 3] [3 0] [4 0] [1 3]]
11 [[0 0] [0 3] [3 0] [4 0] [4 3]]
10 [[0 0] [0 3] [3 0] [3 3] [4 2]]
12 [[0 0] [0 3] [3 0] [3 3] [4 3]]
12 [[0 0] [0 3] [4 3] [4 0] [1 3]]
12 [[0 0] [4 0] [1 3] [0 3] [3 0] [3 3]]
13 [[0 0] [4 0] [1 3] [1 0] [0 1] [4 1]]
14 [[0 0] [4 0] [1 3] [1 0] [0 1] [0 3]]
15 [[0 0] [4 0] [1 3] [4 3] [0 3] [3 0]]
15 [[0 0] [4 0] [4 3] [0 3] [3 0] [3 3]]
15 [[0 0] [0 3] [3 0] [4 0] [1 3] [1 0]]
15 [[0 0] [0 3] [3 0] [4 0] [1 3] [4 3]]
14 [[0 0] [0 3] [3 0] [3 3] [4 2] [0 2]]
14 [[0 0] [0 3] [3 0] [3 3] [4 2] [4 0]]
15 [[0 0] [0 3] [3 0] [3 3] [4 2] [4 3]]
15 [[0 0] [0 3] [3 0] [3 3] [4 3] [4 0]]
15 [[0 0] [0 3] [4 3] [4 0] [1 3] [1 0]]
15 [[0 0] [4 0] [1 3] [0 3] [3 0] [3 3] [4 2]]
16 [[0 0] [4 0] [1 3] [0 3] [3 0] [3 3] [4 3]]
15 [[0 0] [4 0] [1 3] [1 0] [0 1] [4 1] [2 3]]

** [[0 0] [4 0] [1 3] [1 0] [0 1] [4 1] [2 3]]
```

Notice how the paths being considered gradually increase in length. Since the function works breadth-first it is guaranteed to find a solution path which is at least as short as any other solution path, i.e. it is guaranteed to find a solution path which is as short as possible. The path marked with a comment is not expanded past the node `[4 3]` because to do so would necessarily produce a node that has been visited before on that path, i.e. either `[4 0]` or `[0 3]`, hence the reduction in agenda length from 10 to 9. The size of the agenda generally increases fairly speedily, so that at the point where paths containing seven states are considered, there are already fifteen paths on the agenda. By counting the number of lines of "trace" output, namely 38, we can determine how many nodes were expanded prior to finding the solution.

Implementing depth-first search using an agenda

One of the advantages of the agenda-based search function is that it can very easily be modified so as to implement the more familiar depth-first search strategy. We simply arrange that instead of adding new nodes to the *end* of the agenda, the function **extend_agenda1** always adds them to the *beginning*. This means that the successors of some node at some level N+1 of the tree will always be added to the front of the agenda and get expanded before any (more) nodes at level N. This ensures that the strategy is depth-first. The definition of **extend_agenda1** already includes this possibility, so all that needs to be done is to call **agenda_search** with "depth" as its third argument, namely the value of **search_type** and again "10" as the depth bound:

```
agenda_search([0 0], [2 =], "depth", 10) ==>

 1 [[0 0]]
 2 [[0 0] [4 0]]
 3 [[0 0] [4 0] [1 3]]
 5 [[0 0] [4 0] [1 3] [0 3]]
 6 [[0 0] [4 0] [1 3] [0 3] [3 0]]
 6 [[0 0] [4 0] [1 3] [0 3] [3 0] [3 3]]
 7 [[0 0] [4 0] [1 3] [0 3] [3 0] [3 3] [4 2]]
 8 [[0 0] [4 0] [1 3] [0 3] [3 0] [3 3] [4 2] [0 2]]
 8 [[0 0] [4 0] [1 3] [0 3] [3 0] [3 3] [4 2] [0 2] [2 0]]

 ** [[0 0] [4 0] [1 3] [0 3] [3 0] [3 3] [4 2] [0 2] [2 0]]
```

Notice how each path being considered is simply an extension of the previous path with one more node added and that the solution is non-optimal and that the size of the agenda increases much more slowly than in the breadth-first case. In this case the number of nodes expanded is eight. If we reduce the depth bound so as to preclude the nine state solution above, we can force depth-first search to find (eventually) the shorter solution (found first by breadth-first search):

```
agenda_search([0 0], [2 =], "depth", 7) ==>

1 [[0 0]]
2 [[0 0] [4 0]]
3 [[0 0] [4 0] [1 3]]
5 [[0 0] [4 0] [1 3] [0 3]]
6 [[0 0] [4 0] [1 3] [0 3] [3 0]]
6 [[0 0] [4 0] [1 3] [0 3] [3 0] [3 3]]
7 [[0 0] [4 0] [1 3] [0 3] [3 0] [3 3] [4 2]]
8 [[0 0] [4 0] [1 3] [0 3] [3 0] [3 3] [4 2] [0 2]] /* BOUNDED */
7 [[0 0] [4 0] [1 3] [0 3] [3 0] [3 3] [4 2] [4 3]]
6 [[0 0] [4 0] [1 3] [0 3] [3 0] [3 3] [4 3]]
5 [[0 0] [4 0] [1 3] [0 3] [4 3]]
4 [[0 0] [4 0] [1 3] [1 0]]
4 [[0 0] [4 0] [1 3] [1 0] [0 1]]
5 [[0 0] [4 0] [1 3] [1 0] [0 1] [4 1]]
6 [[0 0] [4 0] [1 3] [1 0] [0 1] [4 1] [2 3]]

** [[0 0] [4 0] [1 3] [1 0] [0 1] [4 1] [2 3]]
```

```
agenda_search([0 0], [2 =], "depth", 2) ==>

1 [[0 0]]
2 [[0 0] [4 0]]
3 [[0 0] [4 0] [1 3]]
2 [[0 0] [4 0] [4 3]]
1 [[0 0] [0 3]]
2 [[0 0] [0 3] [3 0]]
1 [[0 0] [0 3] [4 3]]

** <false>
```

Iterative deepening

The trade-off between depth- and breadth-first search is in terms of the maximum storage space needed by the agenda against the shortness of the first solution found. In addition either case may have to expand a large number of nodes before finding a solution. Given that the water jugs problem has relatively small search space, the differences between the methods do not show up very strongly, though a more complex problem is tackled in the next chapter. A compromise between the two methods is a technique called *iterative deepening*. Here the idea is to use depth-first search (with its relatively efficient maximum storage requirements) but place ever increasing depth bounds on it, starting with one and increasing as far as necessary. This constraint will cause the method to find the shortest solution (if one exists) at the cost of re-exploring the whole tree from the start at ever increasing depths. Of course this is inefficient but as most of the nodes of the tree are generally in the final layer, the inefficiency is not as bad as it sounds. Although many nodes may be expanded (and re-expanded) the maximum agenda size is essentially a function of the length of the solution. Figure 3-9 shows the code which makes use of **agenda_search** inside a loop.

We have arranged that **iterative_deepening_search** now has an overall maximum depth below which it will not search. Within that limit it successively searches depth-first initially with a temporary depth limit of one, then of two and so on until either the solution is found or the overall maximum depth limit is reached.

We can see how this behaves as follows:

```
false -> chatty;

iterative_deepening_search([0 0], [2 =], 20) ==>
** [[0 0] [4 0] [1 3] [1 0] [0 1] [4 1] [2 3]]
```

Notice that, although it is working depth-first, it finds the same short solution as breadth-first given earlier. With "chatty" switched on one can observe the number of nodes expanded (96) and the maximum size of the agenda (7).

Water jugs in Prolog

The simple state space search considered in the previous chapter is just a special case of general state space search. The main difference is that in the example used of path finding search we did not "look inside" the representation of a location, e.g. **seven_dials**, and treated it as an atomic entity. In state space search the same

---

```
/* iterative deepening takes an initial state, a goal and a maximum depth
   and repeatedly calls agenda_search in depth-first mode with an ever
   increasing depth bound. It returns the solution path or false. */

define iterative_deepening_search(initial_state, goal, maxdepth) -> path;
    vars depth;
    for depth from 1 to maxdepth do
        agenda_search(initial_state, goal, "depth", depth) -> path;
        if path then return endif;
    endfor
enddefine;
```

Figure 3-9 Iterative deepening search

general OR trees are grown but the states themselves have inner structure, e.g. `[3 0]` for the water jugs problem. It is not surprising then that the Prolog programs from previous chapter need very little adaptation.

In Prolog the successors relation for the water jug problem could be stored as roughly 120 entries as follows. This is open to the same criticism as was made for POP-11 that it would be an inelegant way to represent this information:

```
successor([0,0],[4,0]).
successor([0,0],[3,0]).
```

....and so on.

By doing much the same analysis of cases as earlier we can define a procedure **successor/2**, see Figure 3-10, which defines the relation between a state and its successor. The first argument of **successor/2** is the current state and the second argument is the next state. One disadvantage of this compact "procedural" representation of successors is that one cannot use it to compute the *previous* state from a given state (nor can one in the POP-11 procedure). Representing the 120 POP-11 database sublists or the 120 Prolog **successor/2** predicates would have allowed this.

The **successor/2** procedure includes the same checks as the POP-11 version so that it does not produce duplicate states when forced to backtrack. **successors/2** was defined in the previous chapter:

```
?- successor([4,0],S).
S = [1, 3] ? ;
```

```
/* successor(+This_state, -Next_state)
   successor succeeds with This_state of the water jugs problem if
   Next_state is a succeeding state. */

successor([X,Y],[4,Z]) :- not(Y=0), not(X=4), X+Y > 4, Z is X+Y-4.
successor([X,Y],[Z,0]) :- not(Y=0), not(X=4), X+Y =< 4, Z is X+Y.
successor([X,Y],[Z,3]) :- not(X=0), not(Y=3), X+Y > 3, Z is X+Y-3.
successor([X,Y],[0,Z]) :- not(X=0), not(Y=3), X+Y =< 3, Z is X+Y.
successor([X,Y],[0,Y]) :- not(X=0).
successor([X,Y],[X,0]) :- not(Y=0).
successor([X,Y],[4,Y]) :- not(X=4).
successor([X,Y],[X,3]) :- not(Y=3).
```

Figure 3-10 Successor function for the jugs problem in Prolog

```
S = [0, 0] ? ;
S = [4, 3] ? ;
no

?- successors([4,0], Successors).
Successors = [[1, 3], [0, 0], [4, 3]] ?
```

Finding a sequence of states (i.e. a path) from an initial state to a goal state can make use of procedure **search_path/3** from the previous chapter. This procedure searches *depth-first* just like the POP-11 procedure **search_path**. This procedure also represented paths in the inefficient manner of start to finish. As before, one can force Prolog to produce all the solutions via backtracking. Note that we have used the anonymous variable "_" to do the same work as the "=" in the POP-11 version, so the following represents a search to get 2 pints in X and an undefined amount in Y:

```
?- search_path([[0,0]], [2,_], R).

R = [[0, 0], [4, 0], [1, 3], [0, 3], [3, 0], [3, 3], [4, 2],
     [0, 2], [2, 0]] ? ;
R = [[0, 0], [4, 0], [1, 3], [1, 0], [0, 1], [4, 1], [2, 3]] ? ;
R = [[0, 0], [4, 0], [1, 3], [1, 0], [0, 1], [4, 1], [4, 3],
     [0, 3], [3, 0], [3, 3], [4, 2], [0, 2], [2, 0]] ? ;
R = [[0, 0], [4, 0], [1, 3], [1, 0], [0, 1], [0, 3], [3, 0],
     [3, 3], [4, 2], [0, 2], [2, 0]] ? ;
R = [[0, 0], [4, 0], [1, 3], [4, 3], [0, 3], [3, 0], [3, 3],
     [4, 2], [0, 2], [2, 0]] ? ;
R = [[0, 0], [4, 0], [4, 3], [0, 3], [3, 0], [3, 3], [4, 2],
     [0, 2], [2, 0]] ?
yes
```

There are further solutions but they have not been printed here. Recall that **search_path/3** checks for loops in each path but does not implement a stringent check about expanding *any* node more than once.

Agendas in Prolog

Both depth and breadth-first search can be produced in Prolog by differentially extending an explicit agenda of paths to be explored just as in POP-11. As in the POP-11 program earlier, we will take this opportunity to change the representation of paths so that they are stored from finish to start in order to make access to the "current location" faster. The main procedure, see Figure 3-11 is named **agenda_search/5** and corresponds to the POP-11 agenda version of **agenda_search** given earlier in Figure 3-8, except that it make no reference to a list of visited nodes (which will be introduced in the next chapter).

The agenda searching mechanism makes use of a subsidiary procedure **extend_agenda/4**, see Figure 3-12, which computes new paths and adds them either onto the front (depth-first search) or back (breadth-first search) of the given agenda to form a new agenda. The agenda is just a list of paths, and each path is just a sequence of states. Thus the initial value of the agenda is a single path containing a single state, the initial state.

Procedure **agenda_search/5** does the actual search and has three cases to deal with. Each clause includes a call to **chatty_print/1** for possible tracing purposes. This behaves like the "chatty" mechanism in the POP-11 version except that the size of the agenda is not printed out at each stage. The first clause copes with the case where the path at the start of the agenda already contains the goal state. The second clause checks whether the path to be extended is already longer than the depth bound, in which case it is ignored. The third clause of **agenda_search/5** does the work. It calls **new_paths/3** to compute the new paths from the given path and then calls **extend_agenda/4** to extend the agenda with these new paths according to the search type, breadth or depth. Finally it calls itself recursively with the new agenda.

extend_agenda has two clauses, one for depth-first search, the other for bread first search. The difference between them is the order of the arguments to **append/3** which produces the new agends. Procedure **new_paths/3** takes a path and a list of successors and forms a list of new paths, each new path made up of the original path plus one of the successors.

In the example below the variable S is bound to the solution path. The initial agenda is a list containing a single path containing a single state, hence `[[[0,0]]]` and the inital value of the visited nodes is `[]`:

```
?- assert(chatty).
?- agenda_search([[[0,0]]], [2,_], breadth, 10, S).

[[0, 0]]
[[0, 0], [4, 0]]
[[0, 0], [0, 3]]
[[0, 0], [4, 0], [1, 3]]
[[0, 0], [4, 0], [4, 3]]
[[0, 0], [0, 3], [3, 0]]
[[0, 0], [0, 3], [4, 3]]
[[0, 0], [4, 0], [1, 3], [0, 3]]
[[0, 0], [4, 0], [1, 3], [1, 0]]
[[0, 0], [4, 0], [1, 3], [4, 3]]
[[0, 0], [4, 0], [4, 3], [0, 3]]
[[0, 0], [0, 3], [3, 0], [4, 0]]
[[0, 0], [0, 3], [3, 0], [3, 3]]
```

/* agenda_search(+Agenda, +Goal, +Search_type, +Depth, -Solution)
agenda_search takes an Agenda of paths, a Goal, a Search_type, either depth or breadth, and a maximum Depth, and succeeds when path is a Solution path. */

```
agenda_search([Path | _], Goal, _, _, Solution) :-
    Path = [Current_location | _],
    is_goal(Current_location, Goal), !,
    rev(Path, [], Solution),
    chatty_print(Path).

agenda_search([Path | Paths], Goal, Search_type, Depth, Solution) :-
    length(Path, Length),
    Length > Depth, !,
    chatty_print(Path),
    agenda_search(Paths, Goal, Search_type, Depth, Solution).

agenda_search([Path | Paths], Goal, Search_type, Depth, Solution) :-
    chatty_print(Path),
    Path = [Current_location | _],
    successors(Current_location, Successors),
    new_paths(Path, Successors, New_paths),
    extend_agenda(Paths, New_paths, Search_type, New_agenda),
    agenda_search(New_agenda, Goal, Search_type, Depth, Solution).
```

/* chatty_print(+Path)
chatty_print prints a path for tracing purposes. */

```
chatty_print(Path) :-
   chatty, !,
   rev(Path, [], Reversed_path),
   write(Reversed_path), nl.

chatty_print(_).
```

/* rev(+List, +Sofar, -Reversed_list)
rev is true when Reversed_list is the reverse of List */

```
rev([], Sofar, Sofar).

rev([H | T], Sofar, Reversed_list) :-
   rev(T, [H | Sofar], Reversed_list).
```

Figure 3-11 Agenda-based search in Prolog

```
/* extend_agenda(+Agenda, +New_paths, +Search_type, -New_agenda)
   extend_agenda takes an Agenda of paths, and New paths, a search type
   and succeeds with a new agenda containing the new paths
   in a position according to the search type. */

extend_agenda(Agenda, New_paths, depth, New_agenda) :-
    append(New_paths, Agenda, New_agenda).

extend_agenda(Agenda, New_paths, breadth, New_agenda) :-
    append(Agenda, New_paths, New_agenda).

/* new_paths(+Path, +Successors, -New_paths)
   new_paths succeeds with New_paths made from an existing Path and a
   list of Successors, omitting any new path that contains the same
   state twice. */

new_paths(_, [], []).

new_paths(Path, [Succ | Succs], New_paths) :-
     member(Succ, Path), !,
     new_paths(Path, Succs,  New_paths).

new_paths(Path, [Succ | Succs], [[Succ | Path] | New_paths]) :-
     new_paths(Path, Succs, New_paths).
```

Figure 3-12 Agenda mechanism in Prolog

```
[[0, 0], [0, 3], [4, 3], [4, 0]]
[[0, 0], [4, 0], [1, 3], [0, 3], [3, 0]]
[[0, 0], [4, 0], [1, 3], [0, 3], [4, 3]]
[[0, 0], [4, 0], [1, 3], [1, 0], [0, 1]]
[[0, 0], [4, 0], [1, 3], [4, 3], [0, 3]]
[[0, 0], [4, 0], [4, 3], [0, 3], [3, 0]]
[[0, 0], [0, 3], [3, 0], [4, 0], [1, 3]]
[[0, 0], [0, 3], [3, 0], [4, 0], [4, 3]]
[[0, 0], [0, 3], [3, 0], [3, 3], [4, 2]]
[[0, 0], [0, 3], [3, 0], [3, 3], [4, 3]]
[[0, 0], [0, 3], [4, 3], [4, 0], [1, 3]]
[[0, 0], [4, 0], [1, 3], [0, 3], [3, 0], [3, 3]]
[[0, 0], [4, 0], [1, 3], [1, 0], [0, 1], [4, 1]]
[[0, 0], [4, 0], [1, 3], [1, 0], [0, 1], [0, 3]]
[[0, 0], [4, 0], [1, 3], [4, 3], [0, 3], [3, 0]]
[[0, 0], [4, 0], [4, 3], [0, 3], [3, 0], [3, 3]]
```

```
[[0, 0], [0, 3], [3, 0], [4, 0], [1, 3], [1, 0]]
[[0, 0], [0, 3], [3, 0], [4, 0], [1, 3], [4, 3]]
[[0, 0], [0, 3], [3, 0], [3, 3], [4, 2], [0, 2]]
[[0, 0], [0, 3], [3, 0], [3, 3], [4, 2], [4, 0]]
[[0, 0], [0, 3], [3, 0], [3, 3], [4, 2], [4, 3]]
[[0, 0], [0, 3], [3, 0], [3, 3], [4, 3], [4, 0]]
[[0, 0], [0, 3], [4, 3], [4, 0], [1, 3], [1, 0]]
[[0, 0], [4, 0], [1, 3], [0, 3], [3, 0], [3, 3], [4, 2]]
[[0, 0], [4, 0], [1, 3], [0, 3], [3, 0], [3, 3], [4, 3]]
[[0, 0], [4, 0], [1, 3], [1, 0], [0, 1], [4, 1], [2, 3]]

S = [[0, 0], [4, 0], [1, 3], [1, 0], [0, 1], [4, 1], [2, 3]] ?
yes
```

As expected for breadth-first search, paths are searched in increasing order of length, so the first solution found is as short as it can be. Because **agenda_search/5** contains a cut in clause 1, our program will not generate any further solutions.

Running **agenda_search/5** in depth-first mode with a depth bound of "10" is just as simple:

```
?- agenda_search([[[0,0]]], [2,_], depth, 10, S).

[[0, 0]]
[[0, 0], [4, 0]]
[[0, 0], [4, 0], [1, 3]]
[[0, 0], [4, 0], [1, 3], [0, 3]]
[[0, 0], [4, 0], [1, 3], [0, 3], [3, 0]]
[[0, 0], [4, 0], [1, 3], [0, 3], [3, 0], [3, 3]]
[[0, 0], [4, 0], [1, 3], [0, 3], [3, 0], [3, 3], [4, 2]]
[[0, 0], [4, 0], [1, 3], [0, 3], [3, 0], [3, 3], [4, 2], [0, 2]]
[[0, 0], [4, 0], [1, 3], [0, 3], [3, 0], [3, 3], [4, 2], [0, 2],
 [2, 0]]

S = [[0, 0], [4, 0], [1, 3], [0, 3], [3, 0], [3, 3], [4, 2],
      [0, 2], [2, 0]] ? ;
yes
```

The solution above is the first one found. Notice that it is not the same as the solution found by breadth-first search. This is because of the different way in which the search space is explored. However no more solutions will be presented if we type ";" because of the cut in the first clause of **agenda_search/5**, see Figure 3-11. This cut prevents any further solutions and makes the Prolog program behave in much the same way as the POP-11 version.

Of course, if we impose a smaller depth bound then even depth-first search will find the shorter solution:

```
?- retractall(chatty).
yes
?- agenda_search([[[0,0]]], [2,_], depth, 7, S).

S = [[0, 0], [4, 0], [1, 3], [1, 0], [0, 1], [4, 1], [2, 3]] ?
yes
```

Iterative deepening in Prolog

The same arguments about the number of nodes explored, the maximum size of the agenda and the length of the solution found apply to the Prolog versions as to the POP-11 versions of the above programs. We can compromise between a small maximum agenda size and finding a shortest solution via a Prolog version of iterative deepening, see Figure 3-13.

The first clause of `iterative_deepening_search/5` ensures that search does not go deeper than Maxdepth. The second clause calls the depth-first version of `agenda_search/5` (constructing an initial path as its first argument). The third clause increments the depth bound and recursively calls itself:

```
/* iterative_deepening_search(+Initial_state, +Goal, +Depth, +Maxdepth, -S)
   iterative deepening search succeeds with a solution S, given an
   Initial_state, a Goal, a Depth and an overall Maxdepth. */

iterative_deepening_search(_, _, Depth, Maxdepth, _) :-
    Depth > Maxdepth,
    !, fail.

iterative_deepening_search(Initial_state, Goal, Depth, Maxdepth, S) :-
    agenda_search([[Initial_state]], Goal, depth, Depth, S), !.

iterative_deepening_search(Initial_state, Goal, Depth, Maxdepth, S) :-
    New_depth is Depth + 1,
    iterative_deepening_search(Initial_state, Goal, New_depth, Maxdepth, S).
```

Figure 3-13 Iterative deepening in Prolog

```
?- iterative_deepening_search([0, 0], [2, _], 1, 20, Solution).
Solution = [[0, 0], [4, 0], [1, 3], [1, 0], [0, 1], [4, 1],
            [2, 3]] ? ;
no
?- iterative_deepening_search([0, 0], [9, 9], 1, 20, Solution).
no
```

The second goal above attempts to find an impossible solution while the first goal finds the same solution as the POP-11 version shown earlier.

Reading

There is a considerable amount of material in the AI literature which discusses the ideas covered in this chapter. The AI Handbook (volume 1) discusses problem spaces and the two main search strategies (Barr and Feigenbaum 1981, pp. 32-57). Winston also deals extensively with all aspects of state-space search (Winston, 1984, pp. 87-100); see also Rich (1983, Chapters 2 and 3). Bundy *et al.* (1980, chapter 1) provide a discussion using sample algorithms in LOGO. The topic of iterative deepening is covered by Korf (1988).

Charniak and McDermott's discussion of search issues (1985, Chapter 5) is comprehensive and makes quite extensive use of LISP code. They provide some background material concerning the development of chess playing programs which is well worth looking at (see Box 5.2). Nilsson's text (Nilsson, 1980) covers search strategies from a fairly formal perspective using pseudo-code rather than LISP. Nilsson pays quite a lot of attention to the topic of *graph search*.

For a discussion which considers the implementation of search procedures in POP-11, see Burton and Shadbolt (1987, Chapter 7). Sterling and Shapiro (1986) deal with state-space search in Prolog, including the jugs problem, as do O'Keefe (1990) and Bratko (1990).

Exercises

1. Bundy *et al.* (1980) provide the following description of the Missionaries and Cannibals problem.

> Three missionaries and three cannibals seek to cross a river from the left bank to the right bank. A boat is available, which will hold two people and which can be navigated by any combination of missionaries and cannibals involving one or two people. If the missionaries on either bank of the river are outnumbered at any time by cannibals, the cannibals will eat them. When the boat is moored at a bank it is counted as part of the bank for these purposes. (p. 7)

Devise a way of representing states in this scenario and implement an appropriate successor function. Construct a solution to the problem by using one of the "search" functions provided above.

2. Remove the **!** from the first clause of **agenda_search/5** in Figure 3-11 and observe the alternative breadth and depth-first solutions produced on typing ";".

3. Augment the definition of **chatty_print/1** so that it prints out the size of the agenda, as in the POP-11 version.

4. Generalise the successor function for the two jugs problem to cope with jugs of arbitrary capacity and examine the behaviour of depth, breadth and iterative deeping in either Prolog or POP-11. Compare the numbers of nodes expanded, the maximum sizes of the agenda and the solution lengths.

5. Write a three jugs version of the problem-solver.

Notes

The following adjustment is needed to make **showtree** display water jug states.

```
/* root is called by showtree. It returns the string to be printed
   as the name of root of the tree it is given. */

define root(tree) -> root_name;
   vars x y subtrees;
   tree --> [[?x ?y] ??subtrees];
   x >< ' ' >< y -> root_name
enddefine;
```

4
Heuristic State Space Search

Introduction

The two basic search strategies discussed in the previous chapter (depth-first and breadth-first) are said to be *exhaustive*. This means that they explore the search space systematically but with no inkling of where a goal node is likely to be found. Recall that the programs have a "worm's-eye" rather than a "bird's-eye" view of the space. They just work through the space, methodically checking out every single possibility. For simple problems (small search spaces) such as the water jugs problem this strategy is perfectly adequate. However, if the search space is particularly big, then exploring it exhaustively may take too much time. As it turns out, most interesting problems have *huge* search spaces.

The 8-puzzle

A problem which demonstrates just how easy it is for a search space to get unmanageably large is the 8-puzzle. Most people will be familiar with this game. It consists of a little 3 by 3 plastic tray with eight tiles on it (hence the name). The tiles are numbered and can be slid horizontally or vertically. The objective is to slide the tiles around so as to get the numbers into some given sequence. We can informally represent a particular configuration of tiles as a 2-dimensional array of numbers, e.g.

```
1 3 4
6 8 7
  5 2
```

Each number represents the tile with that digit printed on it and the position of the number in the diagram indicates the position of that tile. So the tile labelled 3 is in the middle of the top row.

Starting from this configuration we can slide tile 5 leftwards into the hole to get:

```
1 3 4
6 8 7
5   2
```

Or we can slide tile 6 down into the hole to get:

```
1 3 4
  8 7
6 5 2
```

The original state therefore has exactly two successors. If, in the original state, the hole had been in the centre position there would have been four possible actions (four successors) whereas if it had been at a non-corner position there would have been three.

Constructing 8-puzzle successors

We can represent states in the 8-puzzle problem as a list of numbers, e.g.

```
[ 1 3 4
  6 8 7
  5 2 hole ]
```

If we write out this list expression on one line it looks like this:

```
[1 3 4 6 8 7 5 2 hole]
```

In this representation a given position on the tray corresponds to a particular position in the list. Thus the top, right hand position corresponds to the first position in the list; the top, middle position corresponds to the second position in the list, and so on.

A given tile is just represented as the number which appears on its surface. In the representation shown, the number 4 appears in the third position in the list. This represents tile number 4 being in the top, right position on the tray. The word "hole" which appears in the ninth position in the list shows that, in the state represented, the hole is in the bottom, right position. Note that from a given state of the 8-puzzle we can always construct the corresponding representation just by reading off the sequence of numbers working left-to-right and top-to-bottom; cf. Figure 4-1.

Given this representational scheme, we can implement the successor function in much the same way as we implemented it for the water jugs problem. We construct a function which takes an input state representation and constructs representations for

1	4	3
2	8	
7	5	6

`= [1 4 3 2 8 hole 7 5 6]`

State **Representation**

Figure 4-1 8-puzzle state representation

all the successors. Unfortunately, by choosing such a simple representation we have given ourselves some implementation problems. States resulting from the movement of a tile upwards or downwards into a hole can be very easily constructed. A downwards movement of a tile corresponds to a number moving exactly three positions to the right in the representation and swapping places with the "hole", e.g. moving tile 3 downwards in the state:

```
[1 2 3 4 5 hole 6 7 8]
```

produces

```
[1 2 hole 4 5 3 6 7 8]
```

An upwards movement of a tile corresponds to a number being switched with the word "hole" appearing three positions to the left.

A leftwards movement of a tile corresponds to a number being switched with the word "hole" appearing one position to the left and a rightwards movement corresponds to a number being switched with the word "hole" appearing one position to the right. So it seems as if we might implement leftwards and rightwards just by switching the word "hole" with neighbouring tiles. Unfortunately, this will not work in general. Consider the state:

```
[1 2 hole 4 5 3 6 7 8]
```

If we switch the word "hole" with the number "4" which appears immediately to its right, with the idea of implementing a leftwards tile-movement, we effectively implement an *illegal* move; namely, a move in which a tile is moved off the left-hand edge of the board, around the back and into the hole appearing on the right hand edge! We could solve this problem by changing the representation. But a simpler approach

```
/* up takes a state and returns the state corresponding to moving a
   tile up or false if it cannot be moved. */

define up(node) -> new;
   vars a b c d x;
   if node matches [??a hole ?b ?c ?x ??d]
   then [^^a ^x ^b ^c hole ^^d] -> new
   else false -> new;
   endif;
enddefine;

/* down takes a state and returns the state corresponding to moving a
   tile down or false if it cannot be moved. */

define down(node) -> new;
   vars a b c d x;
   if node matches [??a ?x ?b ?c hole ??d]
   then [^^a hole ^b ^c ^x ^^d] -> new
   else false -> new
   endif;
enddefine;

/* exchange takes a state and returns a new state with the rows and
   columns exchanged. */

define exchange(node) -> new_node;
   vars a b c d e f g h i;
   node --> [?a ?b ?c ?d ?e ?f ?g ?h ?i];
   [^a ^d ^g ^b ^e ^h ^c ^f ^i] -> new_node
enddefine;

/* successors4 takes a state and returns a list of the successor states. */

define successors4(node) -> result;
   vars move turned;
   [^(
      down(node) -> move; if move then move endif;
      up(node) -> move; if move then move endif;
      exchange(node) -> turned;
      down(turned) -> move; if move then exchange(move) endif;
      up(turned) -> move; if move then exchange(move) endif;
    )] -> result
enddefine;
```

Figure 4-2 Successor function for the 8-puzzle

involves realising that if we exchange the rows and columns of the representation, moving a tile leftwards is just like moving it up and moving a tile rightwards is just like moving a tile down. The function **exchange** exchanges rows and columns:

```
exchange([1 2 hole 4 5 3 6 7 8]) ==>
** [1 4 6 2 5 7 hole 3 8]
```

The result is organised by columns rather than rows, e.g. 1,4,6 is the first column. Note that exchanging twice leaves the state as it is:

```
exchange(exchange([1 2 hole 4 5 3 6 7 8])) ==>
** [1 2 hole 4 5 3 6 7 8]
```

The **successors4** function simply accumulates possible new states by trying a **down** move, an **up** move and the same again with the **exchange**d board (but we have to call **exchange** again to put the state back to normal afterwards).

We can test the **successors4** function by calling it on a example starting state corresponding to the configuration depicted in Figure 4-3. Thus:

```
successors4([2 3 4 1 5 6 hole 7 8]) ==>
 ** [[2 3 4 hole 5 6 1 7 8]          /* MOVED 1 DOWN */
      [2 3 4 1 5 6 7 hole 8]]        /* MOVED 7 LEFT */
```

We can apply our **limited_search_tree** function (with the depth bound) to a given state representation so as to see what the first few branches of the search tree for this problem look like. We have modified the **showtree** function so that it prints states sensibly (see Notes at the end of this chapter). Figure 4-4 shows the first few layers.

In this search space nodes always have between one and three successors. On average, the number of new successors is just under two. This "average number of

2	3	4
1	5	6
	7	8

= [2 3 4 1 5 6 hole 7 8]

State | Representation

Figure 4-3 Example of 8-puzzle starting state

```
vars tree;
successors4 -> successors;
limited_search_tree([[1 3 4 6 8 7 5 2 hole]],
                    [1 2 3 4 5 6 7 8 hole], 4) -> tree;
showtree(tree);
```

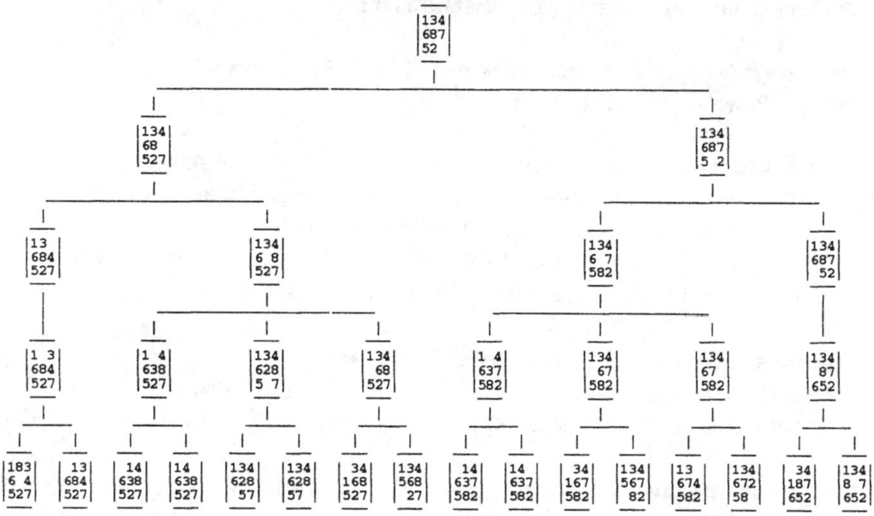

Figure 4-4 First four layers of an 8-puzzle search tree

successors" is referred to as the *branching factor* for the search space in question. By computing the branching factor of the search space for a given problem we can estimate how many nodes it has in total, and therefore how long it will take, in general, to solve the problem using exhaustive search (i.e. search which, in the worst case, looks at every node in the space).

The relationship between the branching factor and the total number of nodes is quite straightforward. If the branching factor is N, every node in a given layer of the search space has N successors. Thus, the number of nodes in each *new* layer of the search space is just the number of the nodes in the previous layer multiplied by the branching factor. So to work out the total number of nodes in a layer we simply need to raise the branching factor to a power equal to the depth of that layer in the search space. The total number of nodes will be the sum of subtotals of the nodes in all the layers.

In the current case, the branching factor ranges between 1 and 3. Thus, if a solution to the 8-puzzle normally involves more than 30 moves, the problem space contains more than 30 layers and the total number of nodes might be about 2^{30} = 1073741824, because this is the number of nodes in the 30th layer. In fact this an over-estimate because it takes no account of duplicated nodes. Perhaps a better estimate of the total number of different nodes in the search space for the 8-puzzle is to compute 9!/2 (i.e. the number of reachable permutations of the tiles in the frame). This number comes out to the more manageable 181440.

Nevertheless solving even a very simple problem like the 8-puzzle using exhaustive search is not particularly practical. Most interesting problems (e.g. chess) are *much* more complex than the 8-puzzle.[1] This means that, in general, they will have much bigger search spaces and therefore be effectively unsolvable using exhaustive search. Does this mean that search is not really such an effective way of solving problems? Not necessarily. There is a way of improving the performance of the search function. This involves the use of heuristics.

Heuristic search

To improve on exhaustive search we need to provide the searching mechanism with some way of moving more *directly* towards a goal node, i.e. we need to give the search function some clue as to where a goal node might be. Technically, this sort of "clue" is called a *heuristic* for the search problem in question.

A simple heuristic for the 8-puzzle can be constructed quite easily. The goal is to get the tiles into certain positions. Therefore we can estimate how close to the goal any given state is (i.e. how much work will be needed to transform it into the goal state) simply by working out how far tiles are from their desired positions both up or down and let or right. This distance measure is known as the "Manhattan" distance. Of course, this heuristic does not measure the consequential difficulty of shifting other tiles out of the way since it treats the distance of each tile from its goal position as an independent sub-problem. The heuristic tends to under-estimate the work to be done. More importantly, it never over-estimates since there is no quicker route than the direct one.

There are three rows and three columns in the puzzle, so a tile can be at most two moves away from the correct column and two moves away from the correct row. So in the following state the "1" tile and the "6" tile are both one row and 2 columns away from their ideal positions of first and sixth in the list:

```
[6 2 3 4 5 1 7 8 hole]
```

The desired position of tile number 3 is position 3; the desired position for tile

[1] It has been estimated that the search space for chess contains on the order of 10^{120} nodes.

number 7 is position 7, and so on. Functions **rowdist** and **columndist** compute the row and column distance of a tile from its ideal position, assuming that the tile "hole" has value "9" and should be ninth. That is they each return a value of zero, one or two depending on how many rows or columns the tile is away from where it should be. The built in functions **abs, mod** and **div** compute the absolute value of a number, the remainder after division and the quotient ignoring the remainder.

The function **distance_to_goal** works out the total out-of-position value by iterating over the sequence of possible positions (i.e. 1 to 9) keeping a running total of the out-of-position manhattan values for each tile; cf. the definition of "distance_to_goal" in Figure 4-5. The total excludes the cost of moving the hole as that is already computed in the movements of the tiles.

Once we have a function which computes an estimate of **distance-to-goal** we can define a function which forms (and returns) an estimate of **closeness-to-goal** by subtracting the distance-to-goal value from a maximum distance value (here arbitrarily assumed to be 100). This **closeness_to_goal** function provides an inverse estimate of the amount of work needed to transform the current node into the goal node. Note that it is *only* an estimate, and it is only intended to be *proportional* to the number of moves required. Due to the structure of the problem, it is difficult to tell for sure how many steps it will take to transform any given state into the goal state. This function just assumes that the closeness-to-goal decreases linearly with the degree to which tiles are out of position. We can show the function works by seeing what values it returns for different states, e.g.

```
closeness_to_goal([1 3 2 4 5 6 7 8 hole]) ==>
** 98
closeness_to_goal([7 8 3 2 1 hole 4 5 6]) ==>
** 89
```

Given this **closeness_to_goal** function we can provide our search program with a mechanism for deciding where the goal is likely to be. This mechanism takes the form of a function called **closer_to_goal** which takes, as input, two states (e.g. two successors) and decides whether or not the first one is closer to the goal than the second one. The boolean value returned shows whether or not the goal node is likely to be found down a given branch of the search space. The definition of the function is shown in the lower part of Figure 4-5.

In order to make the ordinary, depth-first search function exploit this function we need to change it so that instead of expanding the successors of a node in the order that they are returned by the successor function, it always expands the best (i.e closest-to-goal) node *first*. If we arrange things such that it *always* does this then we can be sure that it will explore that particular path in the search space which is most likely (given our heuristic) to lead to a goal node. In other words, we can be sure that it will always look in the most sensible places first.

```
/* columndist takes tile value and a position and computes how many
   columns away it is from its home column. */

define columndist(tile,pos) -> dist;
   abs(((tile - 1) mod 3) - ((pos - 1) mod 3)) -> dist
enddefine;

/* rowdist takes tile value and a position and computes how many rows
   away it is from its home row. */

define rowdist(tile,pos) -> dist;
   abs(((tile - 1) div 3) - ((pos - 1) div 3)) -> dist
enddefine;

/* distance_to_goal takes a state and computes the minimum number of
   moves to get all the tiles in their goal positions. */

define distance_to_goal(node) -> num;
    vars tile;
    0 -> num;
    for pos from 1 to 9 do
        node(pos) -> tile;
        unless tile = "hole"
        then num + columndist(tile,pos) + rowdist(tile,pos) -> num;
        endunless;
    endfor;
enddefine;

/* closeness_to_goal takes a state and computes numerically how close
   it is to the goal state, with 100 the arbitrary maximum possible value. */

define closeness_to_goal(node) -> value;
   100 - distance_to_goal(node) -> value
enddefine;

/* closer_to_goal takes two states and returns true if the first is
   nearer to the goal than the second. */

define closer_to_goal(node1, node2) -> boolean;
   closeness_to_goal(node1) > closeness_to_goal(node2) -> boolean
enddefine;
```

Figure 4-5 Estimating closeness to goal in the 8-puzzle

To make sure that our search function expands nodes in the correct sequence (i.e. closest-to-goal nodes first) we need to insert into the search function a call on the built-in sorting function **syssort**. As is explained in Appendix B, this function takes a list and a function which compares two items and returns <*true*> if the first item should come before the second item in the sorted list. Our function **closer_to_goal** is, of course, exactly such a function.

Note that we have made the function (see Figure 4-6) check that the closeness-to-goal of the successor node being considered is greater than the closeness-to-goal of the current node. Expanding a node which has a lower closeness-to-goal than the current node would correspond to moving away from the goal.

We can test the new function on a simple problem as follows:

```
trace heuristic_search;

successors4 -> successors;
```

```
/* heuristic_search uses the recursion stack to give backtracking hill
   climbing search. It takes a path so far and a goal and returns a
   solution path. */

define heuristic_search(path_so_far, goal) -> path;
   vars current_node, path, successor;
   hd(path_so_far) -> current_node;
   if is_goal(current_node, goal) then
      rev(path_so_far) -> path
   else
      for successor in syssort(successors(current_node),
                                                    closer_to_goal) do
         unless member(successor, path_so_far) or
               closer_to_goal(current_node, successor)
         then heuristic_search([^successor ^^path_so_far], goal)
               -> path;
               if islist(path) then return endif
         endunless
      endfor;
      false -> path;
   endif;
enddefine;
```

Figure 4-6 Backtracking hill-climbing search

```
heuristic_search([[1 2 hole 4 5 3 7 8 6]], [1 2 3 4 5 6 7 8 hole])
==>

>heuristic_search [[1 2 hole 4 5 3 7 8 6]] [1 2 3 4 5 6 7 8 hole]
!>heuristic_search [[1 2 hole 4 5 3 7 8 6] [1 2 3 4 5 hole 7 8 6]]
                   [1 2 3 4 5 6 7 8 hole]
!!>heuristic_search [[1 2 hole 4 5 3 7 8 6] [1 2 3 4 5 hole 7 8 6]
                    [1 2 3 4 5 6 7 8 hole]] [1 2 3 4 5 6 7 8 hole]
!!<heuristic_search [[1 2 hole 4 5 3 7 8 6] [1 2 3 4 5 hole 7 8 6]
                    [1 2 3 4 5 6 7 8 hole]]
!<heuristic_search [[1 2 hole 4 5 3 7 8 6] [1 2 3 4 5 hole 7 8 6]
                   [1 2 3 4 5 6 7 8 hole]]
<heuristic_search [[1 2 hole 4 5 3 7 8 6] [1 2 3 4 5 hole 7 8 6]
                  [1 2 3 4 5 6 7 8 hole]]

** [[1 2 hole 4 5 3 7 8 6] [1 2 3 4 5 hole 7 8 6]
    [1 2 3 4 5 6 7 8 hole]]
```

Hill-climbing search

The search strategy implemented by this new function is a variant on *hill-climbing* that backtracks. The logic for this terminology is quite straightforward. If we imagine that we arrange all the nodes in the search space along the horizontal dimension of a graph, and then plot the closeness-to-goal values for each state in the vertical dimension, we produce a kind of landscape, cf. Figure 4-7. The objective of the search is to try to get closer and closer, and ultimately to reach, the goal node. In

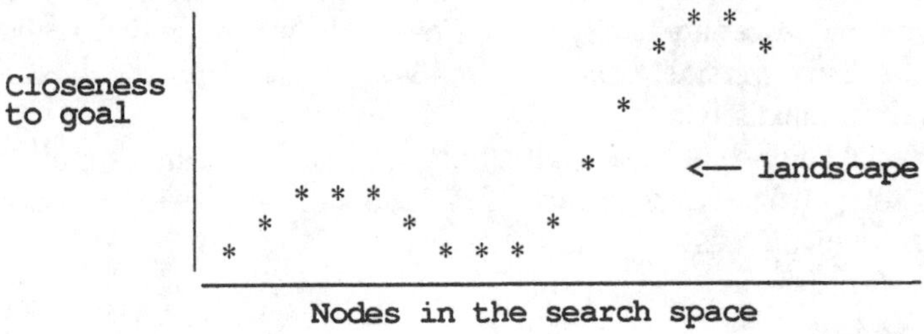

Figure 4-7 Two-dimensional view of hill-climbing

terms of the landscape shown this corresponds to trying to get higher and higher, and ultimately to reach the *highest* hilltop. This spatial analogy is quite helpful. It lets us see that our heuristic search function is going to face at least two difficulties.

Firstly, it may be the case that there is a *foothill*, i.e. a region of the landscape which is higher than any of the points which immediately surround it but lower than some other hill which is in the distance. Given the way in which we have defined our search function, the search will get stuck if ever it comes across one of these foothills. It will effectively "refuse" to move downhill, i.e. to expand any node which is further away from the goal (i.e. lower) than the current one. One way out of this might be to change the function so that it does not mind going downhill. However, if we do this, the function will obviously not hill-climb so effectively.

Another problem occurs when there is a *plateau* in the landscape, i.e. a region in which points are exactly the same height as all their immediate neighbours. If our search mechanism meets a plateau it may either get stuck completely or wander about at random. It all depends whether we arrange things such that the function does not mind expanding a node which is at the same level (i.e. is equally close to the goal) as the current node. As we have defined the function, a successor node is expanded unless the value of **closer_to_goal(current_node, successor)** is **<false>**. This means that the function will refuse to expand a successor which is no "higher" than the current node.

True hill-climbing search does not offer the possibility of backtracking, but merely selects the best child of any node and forgets the others and so can never return to an earlier node and re-continue. This means that it is easy to implement, consumes very little storage space (as it does not store alternative nodes) but may well get stuck as described above.

In the previous chapter we showed how depth-first search could be produced using an agenda mechanism. This procedure can be adjusted to give *irrevocable* (i.e. in the sense that certain choices are never considered) hill climbing search by arranging that new states are sorted (using **syssort**) and only the best one (so long as it is better than its parent) is made the sole member of the agenda, as in Figure 4-8. The **agenda_search** procedure itself does not need adjustment, only the **extend_agenda** mechanism. This version, **extend_agenda2**, uses a function **better_path_h** described in the next section.

We can examine successful hill-climbing behaviour with a simple example. As **chatty** is set to true, we get a trace of the path currently being considered and the agenda size (which necessarily stays at one):

```
true -> chatty;

extend_agenda2 -> extend_agenda;

agenda_search([hole 1 2 4 5 3 7 8 6],[1 2 3 4 5 6 7 8 hole],
              "hill_climbing", 10) =>
```

```
1 [[hole 1 2 4 5 3 7 8 6]]
1 [[hole 1 2 4 5 3 7 8 6] [1 hole 2 4 5 3 7 8 6]]
1 [[hole 1 2 4 5 3 7 8 6] [1 hole 2 4 5 3 7 8 6]
   [1 2 hole 4 5 3 7 8 6]]
1 [[hole 1 2 4 5 3 7 8 6] [1 hole 2 4 5 3 7 8 6]
   [1 2 hole 4 5 3 7 8 6] [1 2 3 4 5 hole 7 8 6]]
1 [[hole 1 2 4 5 3 7 8 6] [1 hole 2 4 5 3 7 8 6]
   [1 2 hole 4 5 3 7 8 6] [1 2 3 4 5 hole 7 8 6]
   [1 2 3 4 5 6 7 8 hole]]

** [[hole 1 2 4 5 3 7 8 6] [1 hole 2 4 5 3 7 8 6]
    [1 2 hole 4 5 3 7 8 6] [1 2 3 4 5 hole 7 8 6]
    [1 2 3 4 5 6 7 8 hole]]
```

Heuristic breadth-first search

Heuristic functions such as our **closeness_to_goal** function are particularly easy to use in the depth-first search scenario. This is because depth-first search always pursues paths in the search space to their very end making "decisions" about which way to go at each branch in the search tree. Breadth-first search expands all paths in parallel and normally takes no decisions about which particular path to pursue first. Thus, it is not quite so easy to arrange for the exploitation of a heuristic function. However, there are at least two possibilities.

One approach involves changing the breadth-first search function so that at any one state it always extends the most promising path, i.e. the path whose final node has the highest value of the **closeness_to_goal** function, no matter which layer of the search tree it is on. This variant is referred to as *best-first search* on the grounds that it always expands the "best" path first. To implement this strategy we need a function which is able to decide which of two paths is the most likely to lead to a goal node. This can be achieved by computing the closeness-to-goal of the final node on the path. The definition of the required function, (**better_path_h**), is shown in the upper part of Figure 4-8. Our agenda-using, breadth-first search function can now be made to implement best-first search simply by arranging for it to apply the **syssort** function to the complete agenda (i.e. old and new paths together). The modified function **extend_agenda2** is shown in the lower part of Figure 4-8. As before the definition of **agenda_search** remains unchanged.

Another approach is to change the breadth-first function so that at each level or layer in the search, it sorts its list of partial paths according to the **closeness_to_goal** function and then selects the N paths which seem most likely to lead to the goal — ignoring the remaining paths. This sort of breadth-first search always expands the N most promising paths at any one stage. It is said to execute *beam-search*. The value of N is said to be the *beam-width* of the search. Like hill-

```
/* better_path_h takes two paths and returns true if the final state of
   the first path is closer to or as close to the goal than the final state
   of the second path. */

define better_path_h(path1, path2);
   closeness_to_goal(hd(path1)) >= closeness_to_goal(hd(path2))
enddefine;

/* extend_agenda2 takes an agenda of paths, a path and a search method
   and returns a new agenda that incorporates the new extended paths. */

define extend_agenda2(agenda, path, search_type) -> new_agenda;
    vars extended_paths;
    new_paths(path) -> extended_paths;
    if search_type = "breadth"
    then [^^agenda ^^extended_paths] -> new_agenda
    elseif search_type = "depth"
    then [^^extended_paths ^^agenda] -> new_agenda
    elseif search_type = "hill_climbing"
    then syssort(extended_paths, better_path_h) -> extended_paths;
         if extended_paths = [] or
            better_path_h(path, hd(extended_paths))
         then [] -> new_agenda
         else [^(hd(extended_paths))] -> new_agenda
         endif
    elseif search_type = "best_first"
    then syssort([^^agenda ^^extended_paths], better_path_h)
         -> new_agenda
    endif
enddefine;
```

Figure 4-8 Breadth, depth, hill-climbing and best-first agenda search

climbing search, beam-search is an irrevocable strategy in that certain choices are completely ignored. This means that it does not systematically explore the whole search space.

If we want to obtain a beam-search strategy then we would need to modify the **extend_agenda** function radically so as to generate *all* the successors of a given *layer* in the tree and then truncate the resulting set down to the desired beam-width. These changes would make **extend_agenda** "inelegant", so we provide a self-contained special purpose variant of **agenda_search** in Figure 4-9. Here, if the new agenda has more paths than the beam-width it will be truncated down to that width, by the match process, to give a beam-width of two (chosen arbitrarily). This function also makes use of a depth bound. If any path in a layer is longer than the depth bound the search is terminated (since all paths in a layer are the same length). But as beam-search throws away some of the paths on each layer it can mean that it will *never* find a solution in some cases.

Running the **beam_search** function, with **chatty** set to <true> so that the agenda is output on each major cycle and a beam-width of "2", on the 8-puzzle problem shows the way in which the number of partial paths on the agenda which it outputs is always restricted to two. Remember that the internal representation of paths on the agenda is from finish to start:

```
true -> chatty;

extend_agenda2 -> extend_agenda;
```

```
/* beam_search takes an initial state, a goal, a maximum depth and a
   beam-width and returns a solution path or false.  With chatty on
   it displays its agenda (not the current path) at each outer cycle. */

define beam_search(initial, goal, depth, beam_width) -> path;
    vars agenda layer state new_paths i;
    [ [^initial] ] -> agenda;
    until agenda = [] do
        if chatty then agenda ==> endif;
        agenda -> layer;
        [] -> agenda;
        until layer = [] do
            layer --> [?path ??layer];
            if is_goal(hd(path), goal) then rev(path) -> path; return
            elseif length(path) > depth then false -> path; return
            else
                extend_agenda(agenda, path, "best_first") -> agenda;
            endif;
        enduntil;
        if length(agenda) > beam_width
        then [^( for i from 1 to beam_width do agenda(i) endfor )]
            -> agenda
        endif;
    enduntil;
    false -> path;
enddefine;
```

Figure 4-9 Beam-width search

```
beam_search([hole 1 2 4 5 3 7 8 6], [1 2 3 4 5 6 7 8 hole], 10, 2)
==>

** [[[hole 1 2 4 5 3 7 8 6]]]
** [[[1 hole 2 4 5 3 7 8 6] [hole 1 2 4 5 3 7 8 6]]
   [[4 1 2 hole 5 3 7 8 6] [hole 1 2 4 5 3 7 8 6]]]
** [[[1 2 hole 4 5 3 7 8 6]
    [1 hole 2 4 5 3 7 8 6]
    [hole 1 2 4 5 3 7 8 6]]
   [[1 5 2 4 hole 3 7 8 6]
    [1 hole 2 4 5 3 7 8 6]
    [hole 1 2 4 5 3 7 8 6]]]
** [[[1 2 3 4 5 hole 7 8 6]
    [1 2 hole 4 5 3 7 8 6]
    [1 hole 2 4 5 3 7 8 6]
    [hole 1 2 4 5 3 7 8 6]]
   [[1 5 2 4 8 3 7 hole 6]
    [1 5 2 4 hole 3 7 8 6]
    [1 hole 2 4 5 3 7 8 6]
    [hole 1 2 4 5 3 7 8 6]]]
** [[[1 2 3 4 5 6 7 8 hole]
    [1 2 3 4 5 hole 7 8 6]
    [1 2 hole 4 5 3 7 8 6]
    [1 hole 2 4 5 3 7 8 6]
    [hole 1 2 4 5 3 7 8 6]]
   [[1 2 3 4 hole 5 7 8 6]
    [1 2 3 4 5 hole 7 8 6]
    [1 2 hole 4 5 3 7 8 6]
    [1 hole 2 4 5 3 7 8 6]
    [hole 1 2 4 5 3 7 8 6]]]

** [[hole 1 2 4 5 3 7 8 6]
   [1 hole 2 4 5 3 7 8 6]
   [1 2 hole 4 5 3 7 8 6]
   [1 2 3 4 5 hole 7 8 6]
   [1 2 3 4 5 6 7 8 hole]]
```

Ordered search and the A* Algorithm

In some search problems it is important to find the *best* or *shortest* solution rather than just any solution, no matter how much effort is expended. Of course, as a bonus, we would like to expand as few nodes as possible in undertaking this search. Best-first

```
/* This is extend agenda as before, but able to deal with A* search. */

define extend_agenda3(agenda, path, search_type) -> new_agenda;
    vars extended_paths;
    new_paths(path) -> extended_paths;
    if search_type = "breadth"
    then [^^agenda ^^extended_paths] -> new_agenda
    elseif search_type = "depth"
    then [^^extended_paths ^^agenda] -> new_agenda
    elseif search_type = "hill_climbing"
    then syssort(extended_paths, better_path_h) -> extended_paths;
         if extended_paths = [] or
            better_path_h(path, hd(extended_paths))
         then [] -> new_agenda
         else [^(hd(extended_paths))] -> new_agenda
         endif
    elseif search_type = "best_first"
    then syssort([^^agenda ^^extended_paths], better_path_h)
         -> new_agenda
    elseif search_type = "a_star"
    then prune(extended_paths) -> extended_paths;   /* side-effects! */
         syssort([^^agenda ^^extended_paths], better_path_g_h)
         -> new_agenda
    endif
enddefine;
```

Figure 4-11 Agenda mechanism extended to include A*

3. Take the first node from the list *open*, if it is a goal node exit with success.

4. Place the chosen node in the list *closed*. Expand the chosen node (ignoring any children that already occur in the direct path back to the start) and for each of the selected children:

   (i) compute the "f" value by adding any extra "g" component to the value of the chosen node and computing the new "h" component.

   (ii) if the child is neither in *closed* or *open*, add it to *open*. If the child is already in *open*, keep in *open* whichever version has the better "f" value. If the child is already in *closed*, compare the "f" value of the new child with it. If the new value is worse, ignore the new child. If the new value is better, remove the old child from *closed* and place the new child in *open*.

The POP-11 code to adapt **extend_agenda3** for this algorithm is given in Figure 4-11.

The new version of **extend-agenda** requires two subsidiary functions, given in Figure 4-12. **prune** takes the list of children, i.e. **expanded_paths** and checks them against the open and closed lists as described in the algorithm above, step 4 (ii). Note that this function can have two side-effects on variables which are not local to it. It may change either the variable, **visited**, local to **agenda_search**, or the variable **paths**, local to **extend-agenda3**.

Function **path_member** is used to check whether or not a path, ending with a particular node, already exists on either open or closed.

Let us try A* search on an example:

```
extend_agenda3 -> extend_agenda;

false -> chatty;

agenda_search([2 hole 5 1 7 3 4 8 6], [1 2 3 4 5 6 7 8 hole],
              "a_star", 30) ==>

** [[2 hole 5 1 7 3 4 8 6]
    [2 5 hole 1 7 3 4 8 6]
    [2 5 3 1 7 hole 4 8 6]
    [2 5 3 1 7 6 4 8 hole]
    [2 5 3 1 7 6 4 hole 8]
    [2 5 3 1 hole 6 4 7 8]
    [2 hole 3 1 5 6 4 7 8]
    [hole 2 3 1 5 6 4 7 8]
    [1 2 3 hole 5 6 4 7 8]
    [1 2 3 4 5 6 hole 7 8]
    [1 2 3 4 5 6 7 hole 8]
    [1 2 3 4 5 6 7 8 hole]]
```

We can compare the efficiency of the different search methods offered by counting the number of nodes that each expands as it searches for the goal. This can be achieved by augmenting the function **successors** so that it keeps a global count of the number of times it is called (or less accurately by taking the length of **visited**). This measure is not the same as the maximum agenda size which is a measure of the space efficiency of the algorithm.

In general A* will do well in terms of the number of nodes expanded whereas all the other methods occasionally do much worse. Note that breadth-first and A* always give the same (minimum) length of solution path. Depth-first, best first, beam-search and hill-climbing each sometimes do very well but sometimes do badly either in solution path length or in number of nodes explored. In particular, hill-climbing and beam-search occasionally fail altogether because they discard possibilities that in fact lead to the solution. The relative weightings of the "g" and "h"

```
/* prune takes a list of extended paths and checks each one to see
   whether it has been encountered before. prune has side-effects
   on the variables agenda in extend-agenda3 and visited in agenda_search. */

define prune(extended_paths) -> pruned_paths;
    vars new_path expanded_path unexpanded_path;
    [] -> pruned_paths;
    for new_path in extended_paths do
        path_member(new_path, visited) -> expanded_path;
        path_member(new_path, agenda) -> unexpanded_path;
        if not(expanded_path) and not(unexpanded_path)
        then [^^pruned_paths ^new_path] -> pruned_paths;
        elseif expanded_path and
               better_path_g_h(new_path, expanded_path)
        then delete(expanded_path, visited) -> visited;  /* ! */
             [^^pruned_paths ^new_path] -> pruned_paths;
        elseif unexpanded_path and
               better_path_g_h(new_path, unexpanded_path)
        then delete(unexpanded_path, agenda) -> agenda;  /* ! */
             [^^pruned_paths ^new_path] -> pruned_paths;
        endif
    endfor
enddefine;

/* path_member takes a path and a list of paths. It returns in
   existing_path the first path it finds that has the same final
   node value as the given path. If no such path can be found it
   returns false. */

define path_member(path, path_list) -> existing_path;
    for existing_path in path_list do
        if hd(path) matches hd(existing_path)
        then return
        endif
    endfor;
    false -> existing_path
enddefine;
```

Figure 4-12 Dealing with duplicate paths

component in our heuristic function means that sometimes there is not much difference in efficiency (on this puzzle) between A*, best-first for short solutions. However, in the final block A* does much better than all other methods. Breadth-first search almost always expands a great many nodes and depth-first can produce absurdly long solutions.

The following table, Figure 4-13, was generated for a variety of starting states using the range of search methods described. In each case the "moves" is the length of the solution minus one, i.e. the number of tile movements in that solution. Different depth bounds are set for some blocks of searches. Where beam-search is applied, the beam-width is "10". The maximum agenda width for beam-search is greater than 10 in the table, as the tables shows the maximum agenda size before pruning down to 10 entries only. There is an arbitrary preset limit of 2500 on the maximum number of nodes that will be expanded by any search in order to work within reasonable time and memory constraints. The column headed "agenda" gives the maximum length that the agenda reaches during the search.

In the first block, where a single move solution is possible, depth-first search does not find it, though because of the imposed depth bound it does find a longer solution and explores a huge number of states so to do. Without the depth bound the search would have run out of memory. Something similar happens in the second block. In the third block, depth-first search is reasonably successful, by chance, but in the fifth block the system ran out of memory before depth-first could find any solution at all. In two blocks, beam-search and hill-climbing search failed to find a solution, having discarded paths that might lead to a solution. Note that the number of moves and the number of nodes explored is generally dependent on the imposed depth bound. In the fifth and sixth blocks, A* starts to show its superiority quite dramatically both in terms of the length of the solution path as well as the total number of nodes explored. Best-first does generally well but not as well as A*. Hill-climbing is alright sometimes, e.g. in the third and fourth blocks, but fails in the fifth and sixth blocks. Iterative deepening does just about as well as breadth-first throughout, at the cost of expanding more nodes but with much smaller agenda sizes.

We have applied heuristics only to help choose which path to expand next, and which paths to discard in hill-climbing and beam search. We always fully expand a node and compute all its successors. If the actual cost of expanding a node were high, it might be worthwhile to apply heuristics to choose the extent to which a node should be expanded. It would also be possible to use heuristics to prune the agenda of unpromising paths for search methods other than beam-search.

Heuristic Search in Prolog

All the necessary search concepts have been introduced in the earlier sections, so here we will confine ourselves to showing (i) how the agenda mechanism in Prolog, introduced in the previous chapter, can be adapted for heuristic search, and (ii) a method of representing the 8-puzzle.

We will represent the 8-puzzle board as a list as we did in POP-11 and compute successors of a state by the same kind of *exchange* manipulation that allows us to deal

initial_configuration	search_type	moves	nodes	depth_bound	agenda
[1 2 3 4 5 6 7 hole 8]	a_star	1	1	15	3
[1 2 3 4 5 6 7 hole 8]	best_first	1	1	15	3
[1 2 3 4 5 6 7 hole 8]	hill_climbing	1	1	15	1
[1 2 3 4 5 6 7 hole 8]	beam	1	1	15	3
[1 2 3 4 5 6 7 hole 8]	breadth	1	3	15	5
[1 2 3 4 5 6 7 hole 8]	i_deepening	1	1	15	3
[1 2 3 4 5 6 7 hole 8]	depth	15	556	15	16
[4 1 2 hole 5 3 7 8 6]	a_star	5	5	15	5
[4 1 2 hole 5 3 7 8 6]	best_first	5	5	15	5
[4 1 2 hole 5 3 7 8 6]	hill_climbing	5	5	15	1
[4 1 2 hole 5 3 7 8 6]	beam	5	33	15	28
[4 1 2 hole 5 3 7 8 6]	breadth	5	39	15	28
[4 1 2 hole 5 3 7 8 6]	i_deepening	5	42	15	7
[4 1 2 hole 5 3 7 8 6]	depth	13	1095	15	15
[1 hole 6 4 3 8 7 2 5]	a_star	9	13	15	13
[1 hole 6 4 3 8 7 2 5]	best_first	9	9	15	11
[1 hole 6 4 3 8 7 2 5]	hill_climbing	9	9	15	1
[1 hole 6 4 3 8 7 2 5]	beam	9	93	15	30
[1 hole 6 4 3 8 7 2 5]	breadth	9	342	15	270
[1 hole 6 4 3 8 7 2 5]	i_deepening	9	460	15	11
[1 hole 6 4 3 8 7 2 5]	depth	9	759	15	16
[8 1 3 hole 2 5 4 7 6]	a_star	9	13	15	13
[8 1 3 hole 2 5 4 7 6]	best_first	9	9	15	11
[8 1 3 hole 2 5 4 7 6]	hill_climbing	9	9	15	1
[8 1 3 hole 2 5 4 7 6]	beam	9	93	15	30
[8 1 3 hole 2 5 4 7 6]	breadth	9	350	15	262
[8 1 3 hole 2 5 4 7 6]	i_deepening	9	461	15	10
[8 1 3 hole 2 5 4 7 6]	depth	13	166	15	15
[2 hole 5 1 7 3 4 8 6]	a_star	11	31	30	26
[2 hole 5 1 7 3 4 8 6]	best_first	25	603	30	426
[2 hole 5 1 7 3 4 8 6]	hill_climbing	–1	4	30	1
[2 hole 5 1 7 3 4 8 6]	beam	–1	181	30	60
[2 hole 5 1 7 3 4 8 6]	breadth	11	1566	30	1049
[2 hole 5 1 7 3 4 8 6]	i_deepening	11	2060	30	12
[2 hole 5 1 7 3 4 8 6]	depth	–1	2500	30	28
[7 1 2 8 5 3 4 6 hole]	a_star	14	59	30	49
[7 1 2 8 5 3 4 6 hole]	best_first	28	93	30	72
[7 1 2 8 5 3 4 6 hole]	hill_climbing	–1	2	30	1
[7 1 2 8 5 3 4 6 hole]	beam	–1	171	30	60
[7 1 2 8 5 3 4 6 hole]	breadth	–1	2500	30	1619
[7 1 2 8 5 3 4 6 hole]	i_deepening	–1	2500	30	12
[7 1 2 8 5 3 4 6 hole]	depth	–1	2500	30	27

NOTE: –1 moves means that no solution was found
2500 in the nodes column is a preset limit

Figure 4-13 Comparison of search methods

essentially with only two fundamental tile movements. The difference here is that we can carry out the *exchange* transformation via Prolog unification (another case of using a built-in mechanism to save programming effort), see Figure 4-14. The following example shows how a tile movement is computed via gradual decomposition of the board, first into columns and then into down and up movements within those columns:

```
?- spy.

?- successor([1, 2, 3, 4, 5, 6, 7, 8, hole], Next).

** (1) Call : successor([1, 2, 3, 4, 5, 6, 7, 8, hole], _1)?
** (2) Call : slide([[1, 4, 7], [2, 5, 8], [3, 6, hole]],
                    [[_2, _3, _4], [_5, _6, _7], [_8, _9, _10]])?
** (3) Call : move_tile([1, 4, 7], [_2, _3, _4])?
** (4) Call : down([1, 4, 7], [_2, _3, _4])?
** (4) Fail : down([1, 4, 7], [_2, _3, _4])?
** (5) Call : up([1, 4, 7], [_2, _3, _4])?
** (5) Fail : up([1, 4, 7], [_2, _3, _4])?
** (3) Fail : move_tile([1, 4, 7], [_2, _3, _4])?
** (6) Call : move_tile([2, 5, 8], [_5, _6, _7])?
** (7) Call : down([2, 5, 8], [_5, _6, _7])?
** (7) Fail : down([2, 5, 8], [_5, _6, _7])?
** (8) Call : up([2, 5, 8], [_5, _6, _7])?
** (8) Fail : up([2, 5, 8], [_5, _6, _7])?
** (6) Fail : move_tile([2, 5, 8], [_5, _6, _7])?
** (9) Call : move_tile([3, 6, hole], [_8, _9, _10])?
** (10) Call : down([3, 6, hole], [_8, _9, _10])?
** (10) Exit : down([3, 6, hole], [3, hole, 6])?
** (9) Exit : move_tile([3, 6, hole], [3, hole, 6])?
** (2) Exit : slide([[1, 4, 7], [2, 5, 8], [3, 6, hole]],
                    [[1, 4, 7], [2, 5, 8], [3, hole, 6]])?
** (1) Exit : successor([1, 2, 3, 4, 5, 6, 7, 8, hole],
                        [1, 2, 3, 4, 5, hole, 7, 8, 6])?

Next = [1, 2, 3, 4, 5, hole, 7, 8, 6] ?
```

Computing whether one state is closer to the goal than another is almost a straight translation from POP-11. The only real differences are that POP-11 allowed us to index into a state directly, where here we define procedure **position/3** and we have also had to define **abs/2**, which is not built-in in our Prolog. Otherwise the decomposition of the tasks is exactly as in POP-11. Note that we have achieved the same result as the **for** loop in the POP-11 function **distance_to_goal** by defining a

```
/* successor(+Current_state, -Next_state)
   Given a Current_state, successor succeeds with the Next_state first by
   columns and then by rows. */

successor([A,B,C,D,E,F,G,H,I],[A1,B1,C1,D1,E1,F1,G1,H1,I1]) :-
  slide([[A,D,G],[B,E,H],[C,F,I]],[[A1,D1,G1],[B1,E1,H1],[C1,F1,I1]]).

successor([A,B,C,D,E,F,G,H,I],[A1,B1,C1,D1,E1,F1,G1,H1,I1]) :-
  slide([[A,B,C],[D,E,F],[G,H,I]],[[A1,B1,C1],[D1,E1,F1],[G1,H1,I1]]).

/* deal with each column or row. X, Y and Z are bound to either whole rows
   or whole columns. */

slide([X,Y,Z],[X1,Y,Z]) :- move_tile(X,X1).
slide([X,Y,Z],[X,Y1,Z]) :- move_tile(Y,Y1).
slide([X,Y,Z],[X,Y,Z1]) :- move_tile(Z,Z1).

/* deal with a column or row, downs and rights before ups and lefts.
   C1 and C2 are bound to either a whole row or a whole column. */

move_tile(C1,C2) :- down(C1,C2).
move_tile(C1,C2) :- up(C1,C2).

/* move tile down or to the right. X and Y are bound to individual tiles. */

down([X,Y,hole],[X,hole,Y]).
down([X,hole,Y],[hole,X,Y]).

/* move tile up or to the left. X and Y are bound to individual tiles. */

up([hole,X,Y],[X,hole,Y]).
up([X,hole,Y],[X,Y,hole]).
```

Figure 4-14 Moving tiles in the 8-puzzle in Prolog

subsidiary recursive procedure `count_tiles/3`. These definitions assume, as in the POP-11 versions, that the goal state is `[1,2,3,4,5,6,7,8,hole]` and even if a different goal state is offered to `agenda_search/5`, see Figure 4-15, the heuristics as defined will nevertheless use this implicit goal state.

Previous chapters gave Prolog definitions for `successors/2`, `last/2`, `new_paths/3`, `chatty_print/1` and for `is_goal/2`. These definitions can just be carried over. We need to augment the previous definitions of `agenda_search/5` and `extend_agenda/4`, see Figure 4-17 to allow for best-first, hill-climbing and A* search. This will require keeping a record of all nodes visited

```
/* position(+Tile, +State, -Position)
   position, given a Tile and a State, succeeds with the tile's position
   in that state. */

position(Tile, [Tile | _], 1) :- !.

position(Tile, [ _ | Rest], N) :-
    position(Tile, Rest, M),
    N is M + 1.

/* abs(+Number, -Absolute_value)
   Absolute_value is the absolute value of number. */

abs(D, D) :- D >= 0, !.

abs(D, NewD) :- NewD is -D.

/* columndist(+Tile, +State, -Distance)
   columndist computes the minimum number of moves to get a Tile to its
   home column in the given state. */

columndist(Tile, State, Dist) :-
    position(Tile, State, Pos),
    D is ((Tile - 1) mod 3) - ((Pos - 1) mod 3),
    abs(D, Dist).

/* rowdist(+Tile, +State, -Distance)
   rowdist computes the minimum number of moves to get a Tile to its
   home row in the given state. */

rowdist(Tile, State, Dist) :-
    position(Tile, State, Pos),
    D is ((Tile - 1) div 3) - ((Pos - 1) div 3),
    abs(D, Dist).

/* distance_to_goal(+State, -Distance)
   distance_to_goal computes the minimum manhattan cost of getting all the
   tiles in the given state to their correct positions. */

distance_to_goal(State, N) :-
    count_tiles(State, State, N).
```

Figure 4-15 Computing distance to goal in the 8-puzzle in Prolog

```
/* count_tiles(+State, +State, -Distance)
   count_tiles computes the total minimum number of moves to get all
   the tiles back to their correct locations in the given state. */

count_tiles([], _, 0).

count_tiles([hole | Rest], State, N) :-
     count_tiles(Rest, State, N).

count_tiles([Tile | Rest], State, N) :-
     rowdist(Tile, State, D1),
     columndist(Tile, State, D2),
     count_tiles(Rest, State, M),
     N is D1 + D2 + M.

/* closeness_to_goal(+State, -Value)
   closeness_to_goal computes the inverse value, 100 max, of
   getting the tiles in the given state to their goal positions. */

closeness_to_goal(State, Value) :-
     distance_to_goal(State, N), !, Value is 100 - N.

/* closer_to_goal(+State1, +State2)
   closer_to_goal succeeds if state1 is nearer the goal than state2. */

closer_to_goal(State1, State2) :-
   distance_to_goal(State1, M), distance_to_goal(State2, N), !,
   M =< N.

/* better_path_h(+Path1, +Path2)
   better_path_h succeeds if Path1 is nearer the goal than Path2. */

better_path_h(Path1, Path2) :-
   Path1 = [State1 | _], Path2 = [State2 | _], !,
   closer_to_goal(State1, State2).

/* better_path_g_h(+Path1, +Path2)
   better_path_g_h compares Path1 and Path2 taking into account
   both their lengths plus the closeness to the goal of their most
   recent states.  It succeeds if Path1 is closer or as close as
   Path2. */

better_path_g_h(Path1, Path2) :-
   length(Path1, G1), Path1 = [State1 | _],
   distance_to_goal(State1, H1),
   length(Path2, G2), Path2 = [State2 | _],
   distance_to_goal(State2, H2),
   F1 is G1 - 1 + H1,
   F2 is G2 - 1 + H2, !,
   F1 =< F2.
```

Figure 4-16 Evaluation functions for the 8-puzzle in Prolog

(the "closed" list) via extra arguments to **agenda_search/5** and **extend_agenda/4**.

Procedure **extend_agenda/7** now has five clauses, one for each search type. It also has two extra arguments to hold the gradually accumulating "global" list of nodes visited so far. Clause three deals with hill-climbing and succeeds only if a

```
/* agenda_search(+Agenda, +Goal, +Search_type, +Visited, +Depth, -Path)
   agenda_search takes an Agenda of paths, a Goal, a Search type, a list of nodes
   already Visited and a maximum Depth, and succeeds with a Solution path. */

agenda_search([Path | _], Goal, _, _, _, Solution) :-
    Path = [Current_location | _],
    is_goal(Current_location, Goal), !,
    chatty_print(Path),
    rev(Path, [], Solution).

agenda_search([Path | Paths], Goal, Search_type, Visited, Depth, Solution) :-
    length(Path, Length), Length > Depth, !,
    chatty_print(Path),
    agenda_search(Paths, Goal, Search_type, Visited, Depth, Solution).

agenda_search([Path | Paths], Goal, Search_type, Visited, Depth, Solution) :-
    chatty_print(Path),
    Path = [Current_location | _],
    successors(Current_location, Successors),
    new_paths(Path, Successors, Extended_paths),
    extend_agenda(Paths, Path, Extended_paths, Search_type, [Path | Visited],
                                               New_visited, New_agenda),
    agenda_search(New_agenda, Goal, Search_type, New_visited, Depth, Solution).

/* extend_agenda(+Paths, +Path, +Extended_paths, +Search_type, +Visited, -New_visited, -New_agend
   extend_agenda takes an Agenda, a Path, a list of Extended paths, a Search type
   and a list of nodes already Visited and succeeds with a New agenda containing
   the new paths and with a possibly augmented list of Visited nodes. */

extend_agenda(Agenda, _, Extended_paths, depth, _, _, New_agenda) :-
    append(Extended_paths, Agenda, New_agenda).

extend_agenda(Agenda, _, Extended_paths, breadth, _, _, New_agenda) :-
    append(Agenda, Extended_paths, New_agenda).

extend_agenda(Agenda, Path, Extended_paths, hill_climbing, _, _, New_agenda) :-
    sort(Extended_paths, [Best_new_path | _], better_path_h),
    better_path_h(Best_new_path, Path),
    append([Best_new_path], Agenda, New_agenda).

extend_agenda(Agenda, _, Extended_paths, best_first, _, _, New_agenda) :-
    append(Agenda, Extended_paths, Unsorted_agenda),
    sort(Unsorted_agenda, New_agenda, better_path_h).

extend_agenda(Agenda, _, Extended_paths, a_star, Visited, New_visited, New_agenda) :-
    prune(Extended_paths, New_extended_paths, Visited, New_visited, Agenda, New_paths),
    append(New_paths, New_extended_paths, Unsorted_agenda),
    sort(Unsorted_agenda, New_agenda, better_path_g_h).
```

Figure 4-17 Modified agenda mechanisms for A* and best-first in Prolog

child path better than the current path can be added to the agenda. Clause four deals with best-first search and sorts the new agenda, considering the existing agenda plus any new paths, using the criterion of **better_path_h/2**. This simply examines the final state of the two paths being compared to see which is nearer the goal state. The final clause of **extend_agenda/7** deals with the A* case and sorts the new agenda using the **better_path_g_h/2** criterion. This computes the length of the path so far plus an estimate of the distance yet remaining (i.e. f = g + h).

In the POP-11 version function **prune** worked by "side-effecting" the variables **visited** and **agenda**. This was included to ensure that the path with the best "f" value was always chosen. We also need to define a procedure **prune/6** which checks each of the extended paths to see if it is already on either the open or the closed list, see Figure 4-18. This procedure makes use of a subsidiary procedure **path_member/4** which combines the work of the POP-11 function **path_member** together with the built-in POP-11 function **delete**.

Procedure **prune/6** recurses on its first argument, the putative list of new paths to be added to the agenda. The second clause deals with the case where the final state of new path being considered has not been met before, in which case the new path is retained to be added to the new agenda. The third clause deals with the case where the final state of the new path being considered has already been visited. If the new path is better value, the old one on the visited list is deleted and the new path retained to be added to the new agenda. Clause four deals with the case where the new path being considered is already on the agenda (i.e. there is a path with an identical final state on the agenda). In this case the two are compared and if the new path is better value it is preferred over the existing agenda entry. The final clause of **prune/6** is the catchall and simply omits the new path being considered from the agenda.

One extra difficulty is that we cannot rely on an equivalent of the built-in POP-11 function **syssort** so in Figure 4-19 we provide a procedure **sort/3** which conducts an insertion sort making use of whichever path comparison method it is supplied as argument. The second clause of **insert/4** carries out the comparison by forming its fourth argument value (a predicate name) into a goal with **=..** and calling it.

The behaviour of the Prolog procedure **agenda_search/7** is the same as that of the POP-11 function **agenda_search**. Here is the same single example of the the program working in A* mode. The first argument is the initial agenda, the second is the goal state, the third is the search type required, the fourth the initial list of visited nodes and the fifth will hold the solution path:

```
?- retractall(chatty).
yes
?- agenda_search([[[2, hole, 5, 1, 7, 3, 4, 8, 6]]],
                  [1, 2, 3, 4, 5, 6, 7, 8, hole], a_star, [], 30, S).
```

```
/* prune(+Extended_paths, -New_extended_paths, +Visited, -New_visited, +Paths,
        -New_paths)
   prune takes a list of extended paths, a list of already visited nodes
   and an agenda (Paths), and succeeds with new versions of all of these
   according to the ordered state space search algorithm. */

prune([], [], Visited, Visited, Paths, Paths).

prune([New_path | Extended_paths], [New_path | New_extended_paths], Visited,
        New_visited, Paths, New_paths)
    :-
    not(path_member(New_path, _, Visited, _)),
    not(path_member(New_path, _, Paths, _)),
    prune(Extended_paths, New_extended_paths, Visited, New_visited, Paths,
          New_paths).

prune([New_path | Extended_paths], [New_path | New_extended_paths],
      Visited, New_new_visited, Paths, New_paths)
    :-
    path_member(New_path, Expanded_path, Visited, New_visited), !,
    better_path_g_h(New_path, Expanded_path),
    prune(Extended_paths, New_extended_paths, New_visited, New_new_visited,
          Paths, New_paths).

prune([New_path | Extended_paths], [New_path | New_extended_paths],
      Visited, New_visited, Paths, New_new_paths)
    :-
    path_member(New_path, Unexpanded_path, Paths, New_paths), !,
    better_path_g_h(New_path, Unexpanded_path),
    prune(Extended_paths, New_extended_paths, Visited, New_visited,
          New_paths, New_new_paths).

prune([New_path | Extended_paths], New_extended_paths, Visited, New_visited,
      Paths, New_paths)
    :-
    prune(Extended_paths, New_extended_paths, Visited, New_visited, Paths,
          New_paths).

/* path_member(+Path, -Found_path, +Path_list, -New_Path_list)
   path_member takes a path and a list of paths and succeeds with a Found_path
   which ends with the same node as the given Path and a New_Path_list
   which omits the Found_Path. */

path_member(Path, Found, [Found | Path_list], Path_list) :-
   Path = [Node | _],
   Found = [Node | _].

path_member(Path, Found, [Other | Path_list], [Other | New_path_list]) :-
   path_member(Path, Found, Path_list, New_path_list).
```

Figure 4-18 Dealing with duplicate paths in Prolog

```
/* sort(+Unsorted_list, -Sorted_list, +Comparison_method)
   sort sorts its first argument to give its second argument
   using the comparison method in its third argument. */

sort([], [], Pred).

sort([Item | Items], Sorted, Pred) :-
    sort(Items, New_Items, Pred),
    insert(Item, New_Items, Sorted, Pred).

/* insert(+Item, +List, -Extended_list, +Comparison_method)
   insert Item in List to give Extended_list as per the
   Comparison_method. */

insert(Item, [], [Item], _).

insert(Item, [First | Rest], [Item, First | Rest], Pred) :-
    Check =.. [Pred, Item, First],
    call(Check).

insert(Item, [First | Rest], [First | New_Rest], Pred) :-
    insert(Item, Rest, New_Rest, Pred).
```

Figure 4-19 Insertion sort in Prolog

```
S = [[2, hole, 5, 1, 7, 3, 4, 8, 6],
     [2, 5, hole, 1, 7, 3, 4, 8, 6],
     [2, 5, 3, 1, 7, hole, 4, 8, 6],
     [2, 5, 3, 1, 7, 6, 4, 8, hole],
     [2, 5, 3, 1, 7, 6, 4, hole, 8],
     [2, 5, 3, 1, hole, 6, 4, 7, 8],
     [2, hole, 3, 1, 5, 6, 4, 7, 8],
     [hole, 2, 3, 1, 5, 6, 4, 7, 8],
     [1, 2, 3, hole, 5, 6, 4, 7, 8],
     [1, 2, 3, 4, 5, 6, hole, 7, 8],
     [1, 2, 3, 4, 5, 6, 7, hole, 8],
     [1, 2, 3, 4, 5, 6, 7, 8, hole]] ?
yes
```

To test out the Prolog programs given above, we generate part of the table given in Figure 4-13. This new table, see Figure 4-20, gives the same values for path lengths and numbers of nodes expanded for the Prolog versions of the code.

initial state	search_type	moves	nodes
[1, 2, 3, 4, 5, 6, 7, hole, 8]	a_star	1	1
[1, 2, 3, 4, 5, 6, 7, hole, 8]	best_first	1	1
[1, 2, 3, 4, 5, 6, 7, hole, 8]	hill_climbing	1	1
[1, 2, 3, 4, 5, 6, 7, hole, 8]	breadth	1	3
[1, 2, 3, 4, 5, 6, 7, hole, 8]	i_deepening	1	1
[1, 2, 3, 4, 5, 6, 7, hole, 8]	depth	15	556
[4, 1, 2, hole, 5, 3, 7, 8, 6]	a_star	5	5
[4, 1, 2, hole, 5, 3, 7, 8, 6]	best_first	5	5
[4, 1, 2, hole, 5, 3, 7, 8, 6]	hill_climbing	5	5
[4, 1, 2, hole, 5, 3, 7, 8, 6]	breadth	5	39
[4, 1, 2, hole, 5, 3, 7, 8, 6]	i_deepening	5	42
[4, 1, 2, hole, 5, 3, 7, 8, 6]	depth	13	1095
[1, hole, 6, 4, 3, 8, 7, 2, 5]	a_star	9	13
[1, hole, 6, 4, 3, 8, 7, 2, 5]	best_first	9	9
[1, hole, 6, 4, 3, 8, 7, 2, 5]	hill_climbing	9	9
[1, hole, 6, 4, 3, 8, 7, 2, 5]	breadth	9	342
[1, hole, 6, 4, 3, 8, 7, 2, 5]	i_deepening	9	460
[1, hole, 6, 4, 3, 8, 7, 2, 5]	depth	9	759
[8, 1, 3, hole, 2, 5, 4, 7, 6]	a_star	9	13
[8, 1, 3, hole, 2, 5, 4, 7, 6]	best_first	9	9
[8, 1, 3, hole, 2, 5, 4, 7, 6]	hill_climbing	9	9
[8, 1, 3, hole, 2, 5, 4, 7, 6]	breadth	9	350
[8, 1, 3, hole, 2, 5, 4, 7, 6]	i_deepening	9	461
[8, 1, 3, hole, 2, 5, 4, 7, 6]	depth	13	166

Figure 4-20 Comparison of agenda-based search methods in Prolog

Various changes could be made to the programs to make them more efficient. One would be a reduction in the use of **append/3** on the agenda. Another would be to avoid re-sorting the complete agenda in best-first and A* search. At any stage we can assume that the agenda is already sorted, so all we need to do is *merge* the sorted new extended paths with the sorted agenda to give a sorted new agenda for the next cycle.

Reading

Almost all AI textbooks deal extensively with heuristic search and problem solving, for example the AI Handbook, Vol 1, Section II-C (Barr and Feigenbaum, 1981), provides an excellent introduction to all aspects of search. Aleksander and Burnett (1987, Chapters 3 and 4) provide a treatment of search issues which is notable for its excellent use of colour graphics. Stillings *et al.* (1987) look at search from the perspective of cognitive science. Burton and Shadbolt's discussion covers the central points and provides sample algorithms in POP-11 (Burton and Shadbolt, 1987). A* is described by Hart, Nilsson and Raphael (1968) and for further details see the article in the AI Handbook Vol. 1 (C3b) devoted to this algorithm.

Both Bratko (1990) and O'Keefe (1990) deal extensively with the material in this chapter (including the 8-puzzle). O'Keefe, in particular, shows how Prolog code can be defined for efficiency and how to choose appropriate data-structures. Both O'Keefe and Bratko point out the problems of the using **append/3**, especially in breadth-first search where the agenda gets very large.

Exercises

1. Write either a Prolog or a POP-11 program to produce a table of solution path lengths and number of nodes explored for breadth, depth etc. as shown in Figure 4-13. Examine the behaviour of the various search methods for other start states and for other problems, e.g. the jugs problem. See the effect of altering the depth bound and the beam-width on the table.

2. Adapt either the POP-11 or the Prolog code for the 8-puzzle to the 15-puzzle, possibly representing states as [1 2 3 4 5 6 7 8 9 10 11 12 13 14 hole].

3. Extend the Prolog to cope with beam-search.

4. Adapt the Prolog definitions so that any goal state can be supplied and *distance_to_goal* etc. work appropriately.

5. Write alternative versions of **better_path_g_h** to degrade the search performance with the search type set to "A* search" into breadth, depth, cheapest first.

6. Adapt the map of Brighton to include distances and search it to find minimum length routes.

7. Adapt the POP-11 function **heuristic_search** or **extend_agenda** so that when hill-climbing it allows children to be expanded that may have the same value of closeness to the goal and not just a better value.

8. Experiment with different versions of **`better_path_g_h`** to improve the performance of A* search over that given. Possibilities include varying the proportion of the g and h components in f, and also using a more informed h component.

9. Adapt the code given to cope with the 15-puzzle (i.e. a 4x4 matrix).

10. Remove as many of the calls to **`append/3`** as possible in the Prolog code for agenda based search, e.g. by using difference lists as described in either Bratko (1990) or O'Keefe (1990). Establish how much faster this makes the programs run. Also try to ensure that the minimum amount of sorting is carried out and that where two sorted lists are to be merged, they are *merged* rather than appended and resorted.

Notes

The following adjustments are needed to make **showtree** display trees containing 8-puzzle states.

```
define width(tree, name) -> w;
    5 -> w
enddefine;

define height(tree, name) -> h;
    5 -> h
enddefine;

define draw_node(node,val);
    vars r1 r2 c1 c2 name i;
    val --> [?r1 ?r2 ?c1 ?c2];
    hd(node_draw_data()(node)) -> name;
    box(c1, r1, c2-2, r2);
    c1 + 1 -> c1;
    r1 + 1 -> r1;
    for i from 1 by 3 to 7 do
        vedjumpto(r1, c1);
        vedinsertstring(substring(i,3,name));
        r1 + 1 -> r1;
    endfor
enddefine;

define root(tree) -> root_name;
   vars tile state subtrees;
   tree --> [?state ??subtrees];
   '' -> root_name;
   for tile in state do
       if tile = "hole"
       then root_name >< ' ' -> root_name
       else root_name >< tile -> root_name
       endif
   endfor
enddefine;
```

5
Heuristic Search of Game Trees

In some situations heuristic functions can be used relatively independently of a search process. For example, programs which take the role of a player in a two-person game (e.g. chess) just need to decide at any given stage which of the possible moves is the best one. If we have a heuristic function which says how close a given state is to a goal state then the best move can be identified as the one which has the highest value of the heuristic function. Unfortunately, the efficacy of this approach is greatly undermined by the foothills problem, i.e. the inability of the heuristic function to take account of states that lie "beyond" the immediate successors of the current state. This is known as the *horizon effect*.

One way we might try to improve the effectiveness of the heuristic is as follows. Instead of applying the heuristic function directly to the successors of the current node, we apply it to the successor of the successor (or the successor of the successor of the successor...). Then we "back-up" the values found to derive effective values for the successor, i.e. choose the child that produces the best great-great-grandchild! The value eventually computed (via back-up) for the child is called a *dynamic* value because it depends on the values of the grand-children, great grand children and so on. At the end of this chain we compute a *static* value using our heuristic function. Note, therefore, that the dynamic value of a child is computed from (and therefore *after*) the values of grandchildren and so on.

The idea behind this is that as we explore further and further ahead the situations we find there will usually be simplified and it will be easier to see which are winning positions and which are losing ones. In other words the heuristic function that we can apply will tend to be more accurate as the states get nearer to the goal.

If the problem is one in which we can always make any move we want then it makes sense to back-up the best value at any given layer of the search tree. The reasoning here is quite straightforward. If we can move to *any* successor-node we will always move to the best one, i.e. the one with the highest value of the heuristic function. Therefore, at the current node we can be sure of achieving the score belonging to the highest scoring successor node. This implies that we should back-up the maximum score to get the *effective* score for the current node.

Unfortunately, in a two-person game the situation is slightly different. We cannot always make any move we want. In fact every other move "belongs" to the opponent. If the opponent is rational and good at the game then the move made will probably be exactly the one we do *not* want, i.e. the one which moves the game to a state which has the lowest value of our heuristic function. In other words the opponent will be attempting to reach a different goal state and prevent you reaching your goal.

Typically each player chooses a move which increases his or her chances of winning and decreases the opponent's chances. If the heuristic function which measures the value of a state gives increasingly large positive values for states to your advantage, then you will tend to choose moves which increase its value while your

---

```
/* distance_to_goal takes a node and computes how far it is from
   either the goal of having 2 or 3 sticks to deal with. */

define distance_to_goal(node) -> distance;
   vars sticks;
   node --> [?sticks];
   if sticks = 2 or sticks = 3 then 0 -> distance /* PROGRAM WINS */
   elseif sticks = 1 then 9 -> distance          /* PROGRAM LOSES */
   else (sticks - 2) -> distance
   endif
enddefine;

/* static_value computes the heuristic worth of a node, scoring
   9 for the best and 0 for the worst, i.e. from MAX's viewpoint. */

define static_value(node) -> proximity;
   (9 - distance_to_goal(node)) -> proximity;
enddefine;

/* successors5 takes a node in nim and produces a list of successor nodes. */

define successors5(node) -> children;
   vars sticks;
   node --> [?sticks];
   if sticks = 1 then [] -> children
   elseif sticks = 2 then [[1]] -> children
   else [[^(sticks - 2)] [^(sticks - 1)]] -> children
   endif
enddefine;
```

Figure 5-1 Successors function for nim

opponent will attempt to choose moves with will decrease its value.

This means that from any node which corresponds to a move made by the opponent we can be virtually certain of achieving the score belonging to the *lowest-scoring* successor node. Therefore if we are backing-up values to get an effective value for a current node, it is prudent to always back-up the *lowest* score in any layer of the search space which corresponds to the opponent's go. This process of switching between backing-up maximum scores and backing-up minimum scores is called *minimaxing*.

Computing successors in the game of nim

A concrete example may help to make this a little clearer. Unfortunately, most two-person games have rather complex successor functions. However, there is a two-person game with an exceedingly simple implementation. This is the game of *nim*. A simplified version of nim is made up of two players and a single pile of sticks. More complex versions have more piles of sticks. Each player takes turns to remove one or two sticks from the pile. The player who is forced to take the last stick is the loser. One drawback of this simple example is that the use of the minimaxing technique looks a bit heavy-handed given the simplicity of the game and the paucity of possible moves at each point. Another point to note is that there is in fact a deterministic algorithm for choosing one's best move *without* search which we are ignoring here.

Now the only significant feature in the game of nim is the number of sticks in the current pile. Therefore we can represent a state in this game using a list containing a single integer value. We could just use an integer itself, but we have enclosed it in a list to make the representation similar to those for the jugs problem and the 8-puzzle. The successors of a node (i.e. a state) correspond to the states arising when one player removes either one or two sticks from the pile. Thus a function can compute the successors of a node just by subtracting one and two from the number of sticks in the corresponding state.

A goal node in nim is any state which will force another player to take the last stick. Thus a goal node can be specified as any state which features either two sticks or three sticks. Figure 5-1 gives a very simple closeness-to-goal *static value* heuristic which returns a value corresponding to the difference between the number of sticks in the current state and the number of sticks in a goal state. Actually this is a virtually useless heuristic. It does not discriminate properly between states which are close to one player winning and states which are close to the other player winning. Note that the implementation is customised so as to return single digit values in the examples which we will work through below.

The successor function shown simply constructs a list of sublists each containing an integer derived by subtracting one and two from the integer provided as input.

Given the defined functions we can construct a representation of the search space for a 9-stick nim game using **showtree** (see Note 1 at the end of this chapter) to display the output of our depth-bounded **limited_search_tree** function as depicted in Figure 5-2.

Minimax evaluation

Nim is a two-person game so a program which is going to take the part of a player in this game needs to be able to decide which move to make at any given stage. As was noted above, one way a program might make such a decision would be to apply the **static_value** function to all the successors of the current node and then make the move which corresponds to the node which has the highest value. In this usage the heuristic function is referred to as a *static evaluation* function and the values it computes are called *static values*.

To improve on this strategy a program can back-up static values for nodes which appear at a deeper level in the search space. But, as we noted above, in a two-person game it makes no sense to just back-up maximum values. A program should only do this in layers of the search space which correspond to *its* go. The program must back-up minimum values in any layer which corresponds to the opponent's go.

```
successors5 -> successors;
showtree(limited_search_tree([[9]], [0], 4));
```

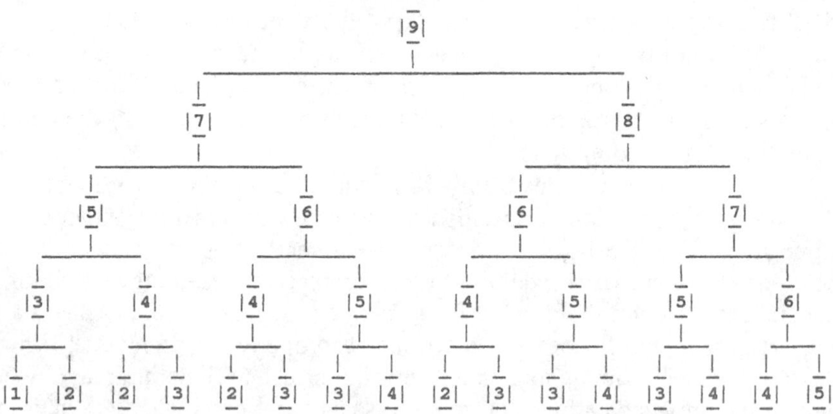

Figure 5-2 Search tree for nim

The minimax procedure, which is just the process of backing up maximum and minimum values alternately, is referred to as a *dynamic evaluation function* and the values it computes are called *dynamic values*. The depth of the layer of the search tree in which the procedures derives static values is referred to as its *lookahead*.

To simplify the discussion we will refer to the program which is going to play the game as "MAX" and to the opponent (i.e. typically the human) as "MIN". These names reflect the fact that the program is trying to reach states which have a *max*imum value of the heuristic function, while the opponent is trying to reach states which have a *min*imum value.

The implementation of the minimax procedure consists of two functions. The first one is called `MAXs_go`, see the upper portion of Figure 5-3. This just takes a number representing a given depth in the search space and returns a boolean value indicating whether or not a node at this layer corresponds to a move to be dealt with by MAX (i.e. the program). Note that the function works on the assumption that a node at layer 0 corresponds to the state left by a move just made by MIN. Therefore the next level must contain nodes which correspond to MAX's possible moves at that stage. The function tests whether the input is an even number by seeing what the remainder is when it is divided by 2. If the remainder is 0, then the original number must be even.

The main function is called `minimax_search`. The function takes three inputs which are put in the variables `node`, `depth` and `lookahead`. The node input is just a description of a node; the depth input is an integer representing the depth of the search space in which the node appears. Lookahead holds the maximum lookahead depth. The function returns the dynamic value of the node it is given. The function first compares the current depth of search with the maximum lookahead depth. If the depth is greater than or equal to the lookahead value then the function returns the static value of the node by calling the `static_value` function. Because the `static_value` function is defined in term's of the value to MAX, it is necessary to ensure that lookahead has an even value (i.e. refers to one of MAX's layers). If the depth is not greater than the lookahead value the function iterates over the successors of the input node, calling `minimax_search` on each one to find its value.

If the function is dealing with successor nodes which belong to a layer of the search space corresponding to MIN's moves it must make sure to choose the next node with the minimum value. If the function is dealing with successor nodes which belong to a layer corresponding to MAX's moves, the function chooses the successor node with the maximum value. The function uses the built-in functions `max` and `min` to gather the maximum or minimum values, using either -1000 or +1000 as arbitrary small and large starting points (in case there are no successors at all):

```
trace minimax_search;

successors5 -> successors;
```

```
/* MAXs_go returns true if depth is an even number. */

define MAXs_go(depth) -> boolean;
   (depth rem 2) = 0 -> boolean
enddefine;

/* minimax_search takes a node, a depth in the game tree and a
   lookahead value and returns its value. If it is MAXs_go, the best
   successor node is the one with the highest value, otherwise it's
   the one with the lowest value. */

define minimax_search(node, depth, lookahead) -> value;
    vars successor next_value;
    if depth >= lookahead
    then static_value(node) -> value;
    else if MAXs_go(depth)
        then -1000 -> value
        else 1000 -> value
        endif;
        for successor in successors(node) do
            minimax_search(successor, depth + 1, lookahead)
                -> next_value;
            if MAXs_go(depth)
            then max(next_value, value) -> value
            else min(next_value, value) -> value
            endif
        endfor
    endif
enddefine;
```

Figure 5-3 Computing the minimax value of a node

```
minimax_search([9], 0, 4) ==>

> minimax_search [9] 0 4
!> minimax_search [7] 1 4
!!> minimax_search [5] 2 4
!!!> minimax_search [3] 3 4
!!!!> minimax_search [1] 4 4
!!!!< minimax_search 0
!!!!> minimax_search [2] 4 4
!!!!< minimax_search 9
!!!< minimax_search 0
```

```
!!!> minimax_search [4] 3 4
!!!!> minimax_search [2] 4 4
!!!!< minimax_search 9
!!!!> minimax_search [3] 4 4
!!!!< minimax_search 9
!!!< minimax_search 9
!!< minimax_search 9
!!> minimax_search [6] 2 4
!!!> minimax_search [4] 3 4
!!!!> minimax_search [2] 4 4
!!!!< minimax_search 9
!!!!> minimax_search [3] 4 4
!!!!< minimax_search 9
!!!< minimax_search 9
!!!> minimax_search [5] 3 4
!!!!> minimax_search [3] 4 4
!!!!< minimax_search 9
!!!!> minimax_search [4] 4 4
!!!!< minimax_search 7
!!!< minimax_search 7
!!< minimax_search 9
!< minimax_search 9
!> minimax_search [8] 1 4
!!> minimax_search [6] 2 4
!!!> minimax_search [4] 3 4
!!!!> minimax_search [2] 4 4
!!!!< minimax_search 9
!!!!> minimax_search [3] 4 4
!!!!< minimax_search 9
!!!< minimax_search 9
!!!> minimax_search [5] 3 4
!!!!> minimax_search [3] 4 4
!!!!< minimax_search 9
!!!!> minimax_search [4] 4 4
!!!!< minimax_search 7
!!!< minimax_search 7
!!< minimax_search 9
!!> minimax_search [7] 2 4
!!!> minimax_search [5] 3 4
!!!!> minimax_search [3] 4 4
!!!!< minimax_search 9
!!!!> minimax_search [4] 4 4
!!!!< minimax_search 7
```

```
!!!< minimax_search 7
!!!> minimax_search [6] 3 4
!!!!> minimax_search [4] 4 4
!!!!< minimax_search 7
!!!!> minimax_search [5] 4 4
!!!!< minimax_search 6
!!!< minimax_search 6
!!< minimax_search 7
!< minimax_search 7
< minimax_search 9
** 9
```

The output means that the backed-up value of the 9-stick pile at level zero is "9", as is the value of the 7-stick pile at level 1 (because this *is* the value backed up in preference to the value "7" from the 8-stick pile).

We can adapt **limited_search_tree** into a new function **minimax_search_tree** which constructs the tree of possible moves together with the static and dynamic values which are computed for them, see Figure 5-4. This function searches the tree much like **minimax_search** but at each level it returns a tree for the node being considered (whose root is the node and value) rather than merely its value as did **minimax_search**.

Function **minimax_search_tree** builds a list of subtrees at each level. In order to extract the values in root nodes of each of these subtrees (to decide which value gets backed up) it extracts the appropriate component of the subtree, i.e. **subtree(1)(2)**; in other words, the second element of the first sublist:

```
minimax_search_tree([9],0,4) ==>
** [[9 9]
    [[7 9]
     [[5 9] [[3 0] [[1 0]] [[2 9]]] [[4 9] [[2 9]] [[3 9]]]]
     [[6 9] [[4 9] [[2 9]] [[3 9]]] [[5 7] [[3 9]] [[4 7]]]]]
    [[8 7]
     [[6 9] [[4 9] [[2 9]] [[3 9]]] [[5 7] [[3 9]] [[4 7]]]]
     [[7 7] [[5 7] [[3 9]] [[4 7]]] [[6 6] [[4 7]] [[5 6]]]]]]

vars subtree;
minimax_search_tree([5],2,4) -> subtree;
subtree ==>
** [[5 9] [[3 0] [[1 0]] [[2 9]]] [[4 9] [[2 9]] [[3 9]]]]
subtree(1)(2) ==>
** 9
```

The tree itself is shown in Figure 5-5 (see Note 2 at the end of this chapter).

```
/* minimax_search_tree takes a node, a depth value and a lookahead
   and returns the tree searched using minimaxing. Leaf nodes
   in the tree contain the number of sticks together with a static
   value. Other nodes contain the number of sticks together with
   the dynamic value. */

define minimax_search_tree(node, depth, lookahead) -> tree;
    vars successor value next_value subtree;
    if depth >= lookahead
    then [[^^node ^(static_value(node))]] -> tree
    else if MAXs_go(depth)
        then -1000 -> value
        else 1000 -> value
        endif;
        [] -> tree;
        for successor in successors(node) do
            minimax_search_tree(successor, depth + 1, lookahead)
                -> subtree;
            subtree(1)(2) -> next_value;
            if MAXs_go(depth)
            then max(next_value, value) -> value
            else min(next_value, value) -> value
            endif;
            [^^tree ^subtree] -> tree;
        endfor;
        [[^^node ^value] ^^tree] -> tree
    endif
enddefine;
```

Figure 5-4 Generating a minimax search tree

```
showtree(minimax_search_tree([9],0,4));
```

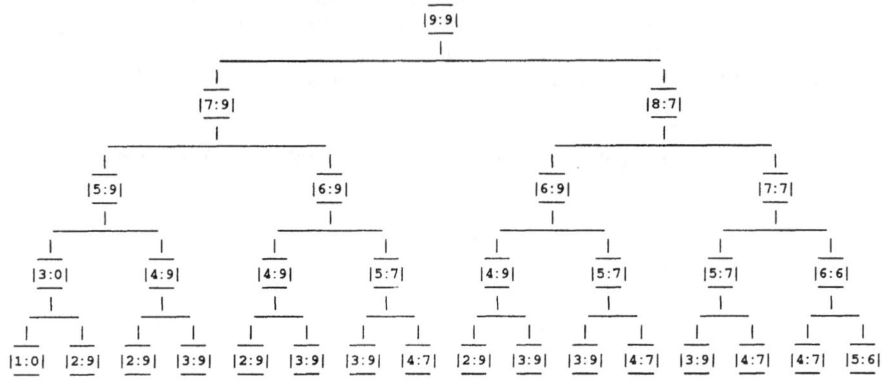

Figure 5-5 Example of a minimax search tree

Worked example

We can clarify the way in which the minimax procedure works by looking at a representation of the evaluation process for the 9-stick nim state shown in Figure 5-5. In this representation, nodes have labels consisting of two integers separated by a colon. The integer on the left represents the state, i.e. the number of sticks in the pile. The integer on the right represents the evaluation. Note that these evaluations are computed from the bottom of the diagram towards the top.

Imagine that MAX wants to evaluate what to do, being faced with nine sticks. Think of MAX as the program and MIN as yourself, so it is the program faced with nine sticks.

To compute a dynamic evaluation of this node MAX considers all the nodes in the search space to a depth of four layers (we have just assumed an arbitrary lookahead value of 4). We treat the root of the tree as layer 0. Fourth layer nodes correspond to nodes where it is again MAX's turn to move and so are evaluated using the heuristic function according to their value to MAX. Note that the nodes with three sticks and two sticks have high values (i.e. 9) because MAX can force a win from there. Note also that at the fourth layer the node with one stick has a very low value (i.e. 0) because MAX would lose by taking this (last) stick! MIN, of course, wants to prevent MAX winning and so the third layer nodes have evaluations which minimise the value. That is why MIN prefers the value 7 to 9 when it considers the five stick node on the third layer. In fact, the value 9 has been backed right up to the seven stick node which MAX should choose. This indicates that if MAX does take two sticks (i.e. moves to the seven stick node from the nine stick node), it can force a win, no matter what MIN (i.e. you) do. MAX is trying to get to the position of having to choose between either two sticks or three sticks because in either case it can make MIN take the last stick. If it can make MIN deal with four sticks, whatever MIN does, it will leave either two sticks or three sticks for MAX. By a similar chain of argument, if it can make MIN deal with 7 sticks, it can force a win. This is the basis of a non-search solution to this particular simple game.

Alpha-beta cutoffs

In games more complicated than nim, the size of the minimax search tree may be quite large, especially if there is a high branching factor or deep lookahead, so methods of reducing the amount of needless search will be valuable. If we use the `minimax_search` function to compute dynamic evaluations of nodes, there is an easy way of cutting down on the total number of nodes which need to be looked at. The basic idea is quite simple. Let us imagine that we are trying to find the maximum evaluation for the successors of a node. As soon as we have an evaluation for one successor, this value becomes a *lower bound* for the evaluation of the current node. If, during the evaluation of some other successor, it becomes apparent that its value will fall below this lower bound, then the evaluation can be terminated immediately. Moreover, if it turns out that a successor has an evaluation which exceeds the lower bound, then the lower bound is effectively increased to the appropriate value.

The complementary case occurs where we are trying to find the minimum evaluation for a set of successor nodes. As soon as we have an evaluation of one node, this becomes an *upper* bound on the ultimate evaluation of the current node. If during the evaluation of some other successor it becomes apparent that the evaluation will fall above this upper bound, the evaluation can be terminated immediately. Technically, the lower bound on the evaluation of a node is called an *alpha threshold* and the upper bound is called a *beta threshold*. The termination of an evaluation process in the case where the evaluation is already known to fall below the alpha threshold is called a *alpha cutoff*; and the termination of an evaluation in the case where the evaluation is already known to fall above the beta threshold is called a *beta cutoff*.

The two canonical cases are given in Figure 5-6. In both cases the nodes show *values* only and are given labels so that they can be referred to. As canonical cases they are not especially related to our nim example. Consider the upper diagram. In evaluating node "a", the program has explored the tree below "b" to be able to back up the value 9 to "b". It then starts exploring the tree at "c". To do this it first explores the tree at "f" and this backs up the value 13. The tree at "g" however gets the value 7, from below. It does not matter what value "h" has or *any* node to the right of it on that level. If "h" gets a value larger than 7, then "g"'s 7 will go up the tree to "c" (because it is a minimising layer). If it gets a value smaller then 7, then this smaller value will go up the tree to "c". But at the next level up, in *either* case, "b"'s existing value 9 will be preferred because this is a maximising level. Thus once we have the given relationship between "b" and "g" we can ignore (i.e. prune) all further siblings of "g" to the right.

A similar line of reasoning applies in the lower diagram, though here the value of "g" is greater than that of "b" (and maximising and minimising are interchanged).

The process of "ignoring" successor nodes during the derivation of dynamic values is referred to as *alpha-beta pruning* but its efficacy depends entirely on the order in which nodes happen to be encountered in the search tree. It has been shown that in the best case, the application of alpha-beta pruning can reduce the number of nodes which need to be evaluated from N to √N (Bratko, 1990). In the case we have

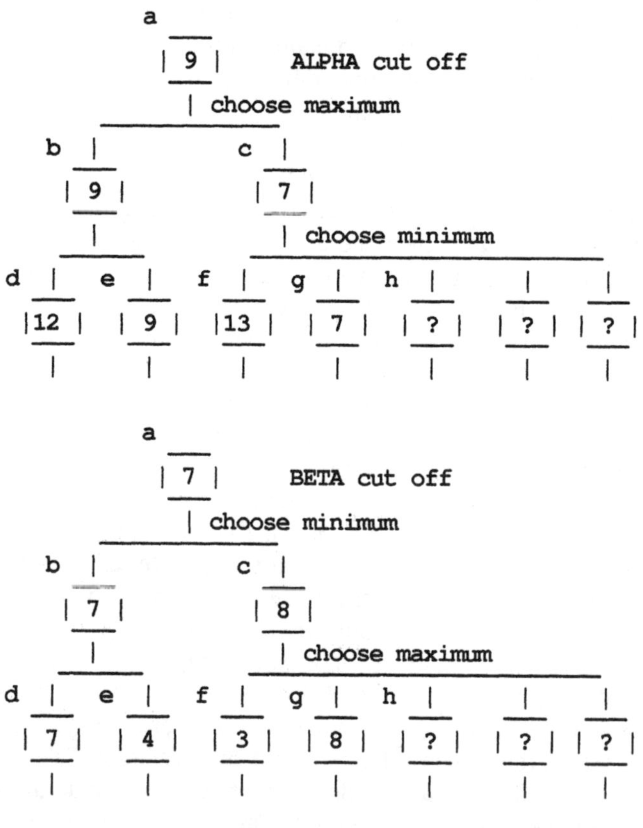

Figure 5-6 Alpha-beta pruning

```
/* alphabeta_search augments minimax_search by including lower
   and upper bounds as arguments.  The tree is pruned whenever
   the lower bound is equal or greater to the upper bound. It
   returns the value of the node it is given. */

define alphabeta_search(node, depth, lookahead, lower, upper)
                                                        -> value;

    vars successor;
    if depth >= lookahead
    then static_value(node) -> value;
    else if MAXs_go(depth)
        then lower -> value
        else upper -> value
        endif;
        for successor in successors(node) do
            alphabeta_search(successor, depth + 1, lookahead, lower,
                upper) -> value;
            if MAXs_go(depth)
            then max(value, lower) -> lower;
                lower -> value;
            else min(value, upper) -> upper;
                upper -> value;
            endif;
            if lower >= upper
            then if chatty then [pruning] ==> endif;
                quitloop
            endif
        endfor;
    endif
enddefine;
```

Figure 5-7 Computing the alpha-beta minimax value for a node

looked at, the implementation of alpha-beta pruning has barely any effect at all; it permits a grand total of twelve nodes to be ignored. However, in more realistic applications, the advantages of pruning would be much more apparent.

The modifications required to make the **minimax_search** function implement alpha-beta pruning are quite straightforward; see Figure 5-7. Instead of three inputs, the new version of the function **alphabeta_search** will take five inputs. The extra two inputs will simply be the current values of the alpha and beta thresholds. The alpha threshold input provides a lower bound for the value of successor nodes and the beta threshold input provides an upper bound. Thus, all the function has to do when maximising is raise the current alpha threshold whenever it turns out that a successor node evaluation exceeds its current value (and lower the beta threshold when minimising), and to terminate via **quitloop**, if ever it turns out that its alpha threshold exceeds or is equal to its beta threshold.

We can test the implementation using the inputs we used before but adding suitable initial values for the alpha and beta thresholds. The alpha threshold is initialised to a large negative value. The beta threshold is set to a large positive value. The trace output produced is shown below:

```
trace alphabeta_search;

true -> chatty;

alphabeta_search([9],0,4,-1000,1000) ==>

> alphabeta_search [9] 0 4 -1000 1000
!> alphabeta_search [7] 1 4 -1000 1000
!!> alphabeta_search [5] 2 4 -1000 1000
!!!> alphabeta_search [3] 3 4 -1000 1000
!!!!> alphabeta_search [1] 4 4 -1000 1000
!!!!< alphabeta_search 0
!!!!> alphabeta_search [2] 4 4 -1000 0
!!!!< alphabeta_search 9
!!!< alphabeta_search 0
!!!> alphabeta_search [4] 3 4 0 1000
!!!!> alphabeta_search [2] 4 4 0 1000
!!!!< alphabeta_search 9
!!!!> alphabeta_search [3] 4 4 0 9
!!!!< alphabeta_search 9
!!!< alphabeta_search 9
!!< alphabeta_search 9
!!> alphabeta_search [6] 2 4 -1000 9
!!!> alphabeta_search [4] 3 4 -1000 9
!!!!> alphabeta_search [2] 4 4 -1000 9
!!!!< alphabeta_search 9
!!!!> alphabeta_search [3] 4 4 -1000 9
!!!!< alphabeta_search 9
!!!< alphabeta_search 9
** [pruning]
!!< alphabeta_search 9
!< alphabeta_search 9
!> alphabeta_search [8] 1 4 9 1000
!!> alphabeta_search [6] 2 4 9 1000
!!!> alphabeta_search [4] 3 4 9 1000
```

```
!!!!> alphabeta_search [2] 4 4 9 1000
!!!!< alphabeta_search 9
** [pruning]
!!!< alphabeta_search 9
!!!> alphabeta_search [5] 3 4 9 1000
!!!!> alphabeta_search [3] 4 4 9 1000
!!!!< alphabeta_search 9
** [pruning]
!!!< alphabeta_search 9
!!< alphabeta_search 9
** [pruning]
!< alphabeta_search 9
< alphabeta_search 9
** 9
```

As expected the value of the node is "9". We can adapt **alphabeta_search** into **alphabeta_search_tree** to produce a search tree just as we did for **minimax_search**, see Figure 5-8.

Figure 5-5 showed the tree produced by **minimax_search_tree** and Figure 5-9 which shows the same tree after pruning by by **alphabeta_search_tree**. Certain of the intermediate nodes values are different because they are constrained by the thresholds compared to those of the unpruned tree.

We have used positive values for nodes throughout and alternatively maximised and minimised. There is an alternative representation, called *negmax*, which alternatively uses positive and negative values and then maximises only. This leads to slightly more compact code.

Implementing a nim-playing program

Given the functions which have now been defined, the implementation of a nim-playing program is perfectly straightforward. The program can consist of a function containing a single **repeat** loop. The initial number of sticks is first read in via **readline**. Inside the main loop the successors of the state are obtained and each one is evaluated using the dynamic evaluation function. The function then announces its move by simply printing out the successor with the highest score. At the end of the loop a new value is read in and checked.

The minimax and alpha-beta functions are designed to compute the dynamic value of a node at layer 0. MAX has to choose the best node at layer 1, so the search program is called with 1 as the value of depth in order to compute the best successor.

The definition is shown in Figure 5-10. The behaviour produced when this function is called is as follows:

```
/* alphabeta_search_tree takes a node, a depth and a lookahead value
   and returns the search tree with subtrees pruned from it. */

define alphabeta_search_tree(node, depth, lookahead, lower, upper)
                                                          -> tree;
    vars successor value subtree;
    if depth >= lookahead
    then [[^^node ^(static_value(node))]] -> tree
    else if MAXs_go(depth)
        then lower -> value
        else upper -> value
        endif;
        [] -> tree;
        for successor in successors(node) do
            alphabeta_search_tree(successor, depth + 1, lookahead,
                lower, upper) -> subtree;
            subtree(1)(2) -> value;
            if MAXs_go(depth)
            then max(value, lower) -> lower;
                lower -> value;
            else min(value, upper) -> upper;
                upper -> value;
            endif;
            [^^tree ^subtree] -> tree;
            if lower >= upper
            then if chatty then [pruning] ==> endif;
                quitloop
            endif;
        endfor;
        [[^^node ^value] ^^tree] -> tree
    endif
enddefine;
```

Figure 5-8 Generating the alpha-beta minimax search tree

```
showtree(alphabeta_search_tree([9], 0, 4, -1000, 1000));
```

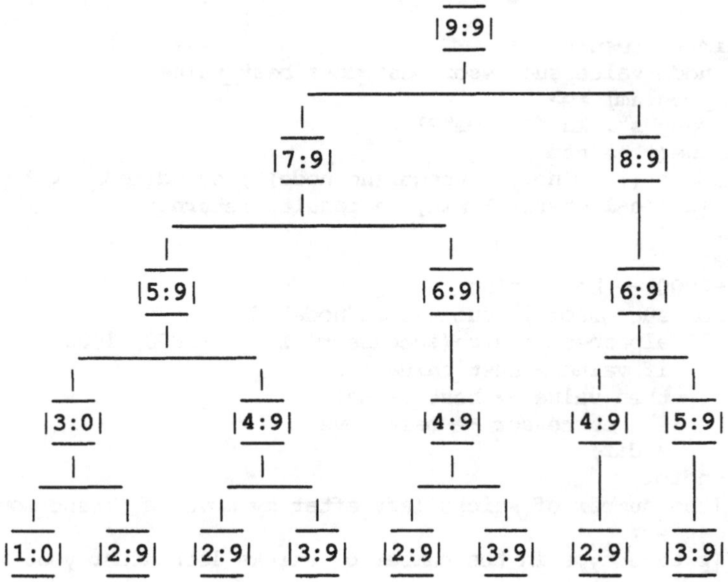

Figure 5-9 An example of an alpha-beta minimax tree

```
/* nim returns either [you win] or [I win] or a close variant */

define nim -> result;
    vars node value successor best_move best_value;
    [nim program] ==>
    [how many sticks do I get?] ==>
    readline() -> node;
    if node = [] or not(isinteger(hd(node))) or hd(node) < 2
    then [illegal start, I win] -> result; return
    endif;
    repeat
        -2000 -> best_value;
        for successor in successors(node) do
            alphabeta_search(successor, 1, 4, -1000, 1000) -> value;
            if value > best_value
            then value -> best_value;
                successor -> best_move
            endif;
        endfor;
        [the number of sticks left after my move is ^(best_move(1))]
            ==>
        [please type in the number of sticks left after your move]
            ==>
        readline() -> node;
        if node = [1] then [you win] -> result; return endif;
        if node = [0] then [I win] -> result; return endif;
        unless member(node, successors(best_move))
        then [illegal move, I win] -> result; return
        endunless
    endrepeat;
enddefine;
```

Figure 5-10 Program to play nim

```
false -> chatty;

untrace alphabeta_search;

nim() ==>

** [nim program]
** [how many sticks do I get ?]
? 9
** [the number of sticks left after my move is 7]
```

```
** [please type in the number of sticks left after your move]
? 6
** [the number of sticks left after my move is 4]
** [please type in the number of sticks left after your move]
? 3
** [the number of sticks left after my move is 1]
** [please type in the number of sticks left after your move]
? 0
** [I win]
```

Recall that the **static_value** function was organised to return fairly sensible values where the number of sticks is "9" or less. You can beat this program by starting with a large number of sticks (and playing sensibly).

Minimaxing in Prolog

Re-implementing the POP-11 functions and procedures in Prolog is straightforward and the procedures carry out identical tasks in largely similar ways. The **successor/2** procedure, **static_value/2**, **distance_to_goal/2** and **maxs_go/1** follow the POP-11 directly, see Figure 5-11.

The **for** loop in the POP-11 code is implemented via the calls to **find_best/4** and **find_best1/5**. These cycle through the successors of the given node and for each one compute the minimax value, selecting the best value overall as its result. At even levels the program finds the maximum via **compare/4**; at odd levels the minimum is found, see Figure 5-12.

Procedure **minimax_search/4** has two cases to consider. In clause 1, if the depth is greater than the lookahead value, the static value of the node is computed and returned. This means that the value of lookahead should be an even number (or the definition of **static_value/2** changed to take account of the value of depth. Clause 2 computes the successors and finds the one with the best minimax value. Procedure **find_best/4** has one clause to deal with even numbered layers and one for odd numbered layers. In the one case it sets a lower bound and in the other an upper bound and calls **find_best1/5** to work its way through the successors.

Procedure **find_best1/5** recursively works through the successors and calls **compare1/4** to update the best value so far if necessary. This procedure takes account of the depth at which the comparison is being made to see whether it should be maximising or minimising the "best" value.

Let us try out the Prolog version of minimaxing on the same example nine stick example as before:

```
?- minimax_search([9], 0, 4, Value).
Value = 9
```

```
/* distance_to_goal(+Node, -Distance)
   distance_to goal computes the distance of Node to the goal. */

distance_to_goal([1], 9) :- !.
distance_to_goal([2], 0) :- !.
distance_to_goal([3], 0) :- !.

distance_to_goal([Sticks],Dist) :-
   Dist is Sticks - 2.

/* static_value(+Node, -Proximity)
   static value computes the proximity to the goal with 9 the highest,
   i.e. from MAX's point of view. */

static_value(Sticks, Proximity) :-
   distance_to_goal(Sticks, Distance),
   Proximity is 9 - Distance.

/* successor(+Node, -Successor)
   successor computes the Successor of Node. */

successor([2],[1]) :- !.

successor([Sticks],[Next]) :-
    not(Sticks = 1),
    Next is Sticks - 2.

successor([Sticks],[Next]) :-
    not(Sticks = 1),
    Next is Sticks - 1.

/* maxs_go(+Depth)
   maxs_go succeeds if the depth is an even number. */

maxs_go(Depth) :-
    0 is Depth mod 2.
```

Figure 5-11 Successor function for nim in Prolog

```
/* minimax_search(+Node, +Depth, +Lookahead, -Value)
   minimax_search succeeds with the Value of a Node given its Depth and
   a Lookahead value. */

minimax_search(Node, Depth, Lookahead, Value) :-
     Depth >= Lookahead, !,
     static_value(Node, Value).

minimax_search(Node, Depth, Lookahead, Value) :-
     successors(Node, Successors),
     find_best(Successors, Depth, Lookahead, Value).

/* find_best(+Successors, +Depth, +Lookahead, -Value)
   find_best works through the list of successors and returns in
   value the best value produced by minimaxing on each one in turn. */

find_best(Successors, Depth, Lookahead, Value) :-
   maxs_go(Depth), !,
   find_best1(Successors, Depth, Lookahead, -1000, Value).

find_best(Successors, Depth, Lookahead, Value) :-
   find_best1(Successors, Depth, Lookahead, 1000, Value).

/* find_best1(+Successors, +Depth, +Lookahead, +So_far, +Value)
   find_best1 succeeds with the maximum Value from minimaxing on each of the
   successors. So_far holds the best value gained at any particular
   point in the cycle. */

find_best1([], _, _, So_far, So_far).

find_best1([Successor | Successors], Depth, Lookahead, So_far, Value) :-
   New_depth is Depth + 1,
   minimax_search(Successor, New_depth, Lookahead, This_value),
   compare1(Depth, This_value, So_far, Better),
   find_best1(Successors, Depth, Lookahead, Better, Value).

/* compare1(+Depth, +This_value, +Best_so_far, -Better_one)
   According to the depth Better_one will hold the better of the
   current value being considered and the best one found so far.
   compare1 maximises at MAX's depth and minimises otherwise. */

compare1(Depth, This_value, So_far, This_value) :-
   maxs_go(Depth),
   This_value > So_far, !.

compare1(Depth, This_value, So_far, This_value) :-
   not(maxs_go(Depth)),
   This_value < So_far, !.

compare1(_, This_value, So_far, So_far).
```

Figure 5-12 Computing the minimax value in Prolog

```
yes
?- minimax_search([5], 3, 4, Value).
Value = 7
yes
?- minimax_search([2], 4, 4, Value).
Value = 9
yes
```

If we offer an odd value for lookahead, the wrong values emerge since the static value is computed with respect to MAX's go:

```
?- minimax_search([9], 0, 3, Value).
Value = 7
yes
```

Procedure **minimax_search/4** can be modified to do alpha-beta pruning as follows, see Figure 5-13. **find_best2/6** and **compare2/6** are augmented versions of similarly named procedures in minimax_search. The main differences are that extra arguments are used throughout to keep track of lower and upper bounds dynamically. **find_best2/6** contains a clause (clause 3) which prunes away any further successors by reducing the list of successors (its first argument) to the empty list.

By running **alphabeta_search/6** with "spy" on, one can compare its output with the POP-11 version given earlier. It makes use of **chatty_print/1** defined in the previous chapter:

```
?- spy alphabeta_search.
?- assert(chatty).

?- alphabeta_search([9],0,4,-1000,1000,V).

** (1) Call : alphabeta_search([9], 0, 4, -1000, 1000, _1)
** (2) Call : alphabeta_search([7], 1, 4, -1000, 1000, _2)
** (3) Call : alphabeta_search([5], 2, 4, -1000, 1000, _3)
** (4) Call : alphabeta_search([3], 3, 4, -1000, 1000, _4)
** (5) Call : alphabeta_search([1], 4, 4, -1000, 1000, _5)
** (5) Exit : alphabeta_search([1], 4, 4, -1000, 1000, 0)
** (6) Call : alphabeta_search([2], 4, 4, -1000, 0, _6)
** (6) Exit : alphabeta_search([2], 4, 4, -1000, 0, 9)
** (4) Exit : alphabeta_search([3], 3, 4, -1000, 1000, 0)
** (7) Call : alphabeta_search([4], 3, 4, 0, 1000, _7)
** (8) Call : alphabeta_search([2], 4, 4, 0, 1000, _8)
** (8) Exit : alphabeta_search([2], 4, 4, 0, 1000, 9)
** (9) Call : alphabeta_search([3], 4, 4, 0, 9, _9)
```

```
/* alphabeta(Node,Depth,Alpha Value,Beta Value,Lookahead,Resultant Value) */

alphabeta_search(Node, Depth, Lookahead, Lower, Upper, Value) :-
    Depth >= Lookahead, !,
    static_value(Node, Value).

alphabeta_search(Node, Depth, Lookahead, Lower, Upper, Value) :-
    successors(Node, Successors),
    find_best2(Successors, Depth, Lookahead, Lower, Upper, Value).

/* find_best2(+Successors, +Depth, +Lookahead, +Lower, +Upper, -Value)
   find_best2 cycles through Successors checking the values of Lower and
   Upper.  If Lower exceeds Upper, pruning takes place. */

find_best2([], Depth, _, Lower, _, Lower) :-
   maxs_go(Depth).

find_best2([], Depth, _, _, Upper, Upper) :-
   not(maxs_go(Depth)).

find_best2( _, Depth, _, Lower, Upper, Value) :-
    Lower >= Upper, !,
    chatty_print([pruning]),
    find_best2([], Depth, _, Lower, Upper, Value).

find_best2([Succ | Succs], Depth, Lookahead, Lower, Upper, Value) :-
    New_Depth is Depth + 1,
    alphabeta_search(Succ, New_Depth, Lookahead, Lower, Upper, This_value),
    compare2(Depth, This_value, Lower, New_lower, Upper, New_upper),
    find_best2(Succs, Depth, Lookahead, New_lower, New_upper, Value).

/* compare2(+Depth, +This_value, +Lower, -New_lower, +Upper, -New_upper)
   compare uses the depth to compare This_value with either the existing
   lower or existing upper bound.  One bound is modified if appropriate. */

compare2(Depth, This_value, Lower, This_value, Upper, Upper) :-
    maxs_go(Depth),
    This_value > Lower, !.

compare2(Depth, This_value, Lower, Lower, Upper, This_value) :-
    not(maxs_go(Depth)),
    This_value < Upper, !.

compare2(_, _, Lower, Lower, Upper, Upper).
```

Figure 5-13 Computing the alpha-beta minimax value in Prolog

```
** (9) Exit : alphabeta_search([3], 4, 4, 0, 9, 9)
** (7) Exit : alphabeta_search([4], 3, 4, 0, 1000, 9)
** (3) Exit : alphabeta_search([5], 2, 4, -1000, 1000, 9)
```

```
** (10) Call : alphabeta_search([6], 2, 4, -1000, 9, _10)
** (11) Call : alphabeta_search([4], 3, 4, -1000, 9, _11)
** (12) Call : alphabeta_search([2], 4, 4, -1000, 9, _12)
** (12) Exit : alphabeta_search([2], 4, 4, -1000, 9, 9)
** (13) Call : alphabeta_search([3], 4, 4, -1000, 9, _13)
** (13) Exit : alphabeta_search([3], 4, 4, -1000, 9, 9)
** (11) Exit : alphabeta_search([4], 3, 4, -1000, 9, 9)
[pruning]
** (10) Exit : alphabeta_search([6], 2, 4, -1000, 9, 9)
** (2) Exit : alphabeta_search([7], 1, 4, -1000, 1000, 9)
** (14) Call : alphabeta_search([8], 1, 4, 9, 1000, _14)
** (15) Call : alphabeta_search([6], 2, 4, 9, 1000, _15)
** (16) Call : alphabeta_search([4], 3, 4, 9, 1000, _16)
** (17) Call : alphabeta_search([2], 4, 4, 9, 1000, _17)
** (17) Exit : alphabeta_search([2], 4, 4, 9, 1000, 9)
[pruning]
** (16) Exit : alphabeta_search([4], 3, 4, 9, 1000, 9)
** (18) Call : alphabeta_search([5], 3, 4, 9, 1000, _18)
** (19) Call : alphabeta_search([3], 4, 4, 9, 1000, _19)
** (19) Exit : alphabeta_search([3], 4, 4, 9, 1000, 9)
[pruning]
** (18) Exit : alphabeta_search([5], 3, 4, 9, 1000, 9)
** (15) Exit : alphabeta_search([6], 2, 4, 9, 1000, 9)
[pruning]
** (14) Exit : alphabeta_search([8], 1, 4, 9, 1000, 9)
** (1) Exit : alphabeta_search([9], 0, 4, -1000, 1000, 9)
V = 9 ?
yes
```

Reading

The AI Handbook, Vol 1, Section II-C (Barr and Feigenbaum, 1981), provides pseudo-code algorithms for an implementation of alpha-beta pruning using the neg-max formalism. Winston also provides good pseudo-code descriptions of the minimax and alpha-beta pruning strategies (Winston, 1984, Chapter 4) as does Nilsson (1980, Chapters 2 and 3). Rich (1983, Chapter 3) looks at these strategies from a slightly more elementary perspective. See also Chapter 5 of Charniak and McDermott (1985).

Bratko (1990) offers another view of minimaxing and alpha-beta pruning in Prolog and also discusses some of the limitations of these techniques. Sterling and Shapiro (1986) also deals with this issue in Prolog. A very detailed theoretical analysis of these techniques can be found in Pearl (1984).

Exercises

1. Write the Prolog equivalent of the POP-11 function `nim`.

2. Write Prolog programs to generate minimax search trees and alpha-beta search trees as given for POP-11.

3. Adjust the nim static value function so that it deals sensibly with large numbers of sticks and takes account of the depth at which it is called.

4. Extend the nim program to deal with more than one pile of sticks.

5. Implement a POP-11 successor function and a heuristic for the game of "noughts and crosses" ("tic-tac-toe"). Use the "nim" function defined above as a template for developing a function which will play a game of noughts and crosses with the user. You will need to think about how the user and the program will describe moves to each other and how these descriptions can be converted into the representation scheme used internally.

Notes

1. Displaying a nim state.

```
define root(tree) -> root_name;
    vars x subtrees;
    tree --> [[?x] ??subtrees];
    x >< '' -> root_name
enddefine;
```

2. Displaying a nim state including its value.

```
define root(tree) -> root_name;
    vars sticks value subtrees;
    tree --> [[?sticks ?value] ??subtrees];
    sticks >< ':' >< value -> root_name
enddefine;
```

6
Problem Reduction (AND/OR-tree search)

Introduction

In the previous chapters we have dealt exclusively with different kinds of state-space search. In that representation, there was a starting state, a goal state and intermediate states linked implicitly via a successor function. The general shape of all states was the same. They were distinguished by the values of their internal components.

In this chapter we look at *problem reduction*. The basic idea here is that a problem is represented as one or more goals to be solved and a step in the problem solving process is either the immediate solution of one of these goals or its division into a set of (one hopes) simpler subgoals.

The technique in question, construed in abstract terms, is basically just an exploitation of the idea that for any given goal there are a set of *subgoals*, such that satisfying the subgoals satisfies the goal. The process of decomposing a goal into its subgoals is referred to as *goal-reduction*. We will start by taking a very simple case where there is only one way of decomposing a goal into subgoals and therefore there is *no* search. To illustrate what this means we will look at the Tower of Hanoi problem.

Problem-reduction and the Tower of Hanoi

One of the most well-known uses of problem reduction is its application to the Tower of Hanoi problem. The problem is described as follows:

> "Given three graduated discs (large, medium and small) and three pegs (A, B, and C), where the three discs are arranged on peg A so that the largest is on the bottom and the smallest is on the top: Move the discs to peg C so that they end

up in the same order (largest on the bottom, smallest on the top). Only one disc may be moved at a time, and a larger disc may not be put on top of a smaller one." (Stillings *et al.*, p. 173)

In fact, we can have Tower of Hanoi problems featuring N discs rather than just three (the original version of the problem was said to involve the transfer of 64 discs). Whatever the value of N, the specification of the problem remains the same: transfer the N, size-ordered discs from peg A to peg C without ever putting a larger disc on a smaller disc. Viewed in these terms, the problem can be solved by decomposing it into the following three subtasks.

1. move the N-1 top discs on A (the "N-1 tower") to B
2. move the exposed, bottom disc from A to C
3. move the N-1 tower from B to C

Steps 1 and 3 have the same form as the original goal. Thus they too can be decomposed into three subgoals. Of course in decomposing step 1, we will need to substitute C for B and B for C to make things work out; in decomposing step 3 we must substitute B for A and A for B, and so on.

When we decompose step 1 into three subgoals the value of N in the first step of the subgoals will be 1 less than its value in the goal. Thus, the value of N decreases by 1 for each decomposition. This means that if we continue decomposing goals long enough we will eventually find that the "N-1 tower" has only one disc. The goal of transferring a single disk can be performed (i.e. satisfied) directly, by performing a single action. Since all goals will eventually decompose into subgoals which can be satisfied by single actions, a complete solution for the whole problem can be found by generating a list of all the single actions needed to satisfy the *final* subgoals. We can demonstrate this by writing a POP-11 function which does the required decomposition and generates the corresponding sequence of necessary actions; see Figure 6-1. Note that this function embodies a particular goal decomposition which is applied rigidly at every level. There is *no search* and no backtracking.

The function assumes that the current state of the discs is represented as a list of three sublists. Each sublist represents the state of one peg and the label of the peg (A, B or C) appears as the final element of the sublist. The initial elements of the sublist are just the sizes of the rings which are on that peg. Thus, the initial state is represented as:

```
[[small medium large A] [B] [C]]
```

Note the way in which the **hanoi** function detects whether the goal it has been called on is one which can be performed by a single action. The match expression discovers whether the first peg has only one disc on it. If it has then the task of moving the discs on peg A to peg C can be performed using a single action. Thus the function prints

```
/* hanoi takes a description of a Tower of Hanoi state
   and returns the final description. */

define hanoi(goal) -> result;
   vars disc bottom_disc A B C A_name tower;
   if goal matches [[?disc ?A_name] ?B ?C]
   then [move ^disc from ^A_name to ^C] ==>
        [[^A_name] ^B [^disc ^^C]] -> result
   else goal --> [[??tower ?bottom_disc ?A_name] ?B ?C];
        hanoi([[^^tower ^A_name] ^C ^B]) --> [?A ?C ?B];
        hanoi([[^bottom_disc ^A_name] ^B ^C]) --> [?A ?B ?C];
        hanoi([^B ^A ^C]) --> [?B ?A ?C];
        [^A ^B ^C] -> result;
   endif
enddefine;
```

Figure 6-1 Tower of Hanoi program

out a description of the action required and returns an appropriately modified state description. If peg A has more than 1 disc on it, then the problem is decomposed into three subgoals and these are achieved via recursive calls on "hanoi". The behaviour of the function is as follows:

```
trace hanoi;
hanoi([[small medium large A][B][C]]) ==>

> hanoi [[small medium large A] [B] [C]]
!> hanoi [[small medium A] [C] [B]]
!!> hanoi [[small A] [B] [C]]
** [move small from A to [C]]
!!< hanoi [[A] [B] [small C]]
!!> hanoi [[medium A] [small C] [B]]
** [move medium from A to [B]]
!!< hanoi [[A] [small C] [medium B]]
!!> hanoi [[small C] [A] [medium B]]
** [move small from C to [medium B]]
!!< hanoi [[C] [A] [small medium B]]
!< hanoi [[A] [C] [small medium B]]
!> hanoi [[large A] [small medium B] [C]]
** [move large from A to [C]]
!< hanoi [[A] [small medium B] [large C]]
```

```
!> hanoi [[small medium B] [A] [large C]]
!!> hanoi [[small B] [large C] [A]]
** [move small from B to [A]]
!!< hanoi [[B] [large C] [small A]]
!!> hanoi [[medium B] [small A] [large C]]
** [move medium from B to [large C]]
!!< hanoi [[B] [small A] [medium large C]]
!!> hanoi [[small A] [B] [medium large C]]
** [move small from A to [medium large C]]
!!< hanoi [[A] [B] [small medium large C]]
!< hanoi [[B] [A] [small medium large C]]
< hanoi [[A] [B] [small medium large C]]
** [[A] [B] [small medium large C]]
```

The complete solution for the problem can be shown more clearly as follows:

```
untrace hanoi;
hanoi([[small medium large A] [B] [C]]) ==>

** [move small from A to [C]]
** [move medium from A to [B]]
** [move small from C to [medium B]]
** [move large from A to [C]]
** [move small from B to [A]]
** [move medium from B to [large C]]
** [move small from A to [medium large C]]

** [[A] [B] [small medium large C]]
```

Implementing arbitrary AND/OR-trees

The `hanoi` function shows how goal-reduction can be pre-defined as part of a function. But in this case the way that any goal is decomposed is fixed and there is only one way of doing the decomposition. So to bring out the true generality of the idea, we need to show how it can work inside a search process where there may be more than one method available to decompose each goal and the system has to search through these to find the one that works (best). To do this we need to rework the implementation of the search function so as to allow for the use of subgoals.

The existing implementation of search is organised around a successor function. This just takes a predecessor node as input and returns the corresponding successors. A goal always corresponds to some successor node (or, at least, we hope it does) and a successor node can always be achieved provided that its predecessor can be achieved. This shows that a predecessor is just a kind of single subgoal.

It will be recalled from Chapter 2 that the simplest way of implementing an ordinary successor function involves setting up a database of lists, with each list specifying a unique predecessor/successor link. The successor function is then defined in terms of a **foreach** loop which iterates over the database picking out any items which feature the predecessor in question. In the envisaged scenario, goals can have N subgoals rather than just one and this means, in effect, that successor nodes can have N predecessors. So if we want to use the simple, database approach for the implementation of the successor function, we will have to arrange things such that lists in the database can link a successor node with N predecessors. One approach might be to use lists of the form:

[<predecessor1> <predecessor2> ... <predecessorN> <SUCCESSOR>]

However, since, in the current context the emphasis is on goal-reduction, it makes more sense to use lists of the form:

[<SUCCESSOR> <predecessor1> <predecessor2> ... <predecessorN>]

In this format, the goal appears as the first element and the subgoals come after. This arrangement is more convenient since it enables the list to be more easily read as a goal-reduction "rule" (see below).

A search space which contains nodes corresponding to goals and their subgoals forms an AND/OR-tree. For any node corresponding to a goal, the successors are just those rules which have the effect of satisfying the goal. Any one rule will do; thus, where there are several rules for the same goal or <SUCCESSOR>, they constitute alternatives and the node is an OR-node. For any node corresponding to a rule, the successors are the predecessors of the rule. To apply the rule, *all* the predecessors (or subgoals) must be dealt with; thus, the node is an AND-node.

The point to note is that the conventions we have just introduced for creating a database of successor/predecessor links allow us to construct explicit AND/OR-trees. If **foo** is the name of an OR-node then the database will contain a set of lists of the form:

[foo <predecessor1>....]
[foo <predecessor2>....]
...
[foo <predecessorN>....]

If **foo** is an AND-node then the database will contain a list of the form:

[foo <predecessor1> <predecessor2> ... <predecessorN>]

Thus, OR-branches in the search space are indicated by including multiple entries with the same first element. AND-branches are indicated by including entries which have more than two elements. A complete AND/OR-tree is constructed just by implementing a certain configuration of AND- and OR-nodes. So as to make life slightly more convenient we will, from here on, refer to successor/predecessor associations of the type described above as *search rules*. Search rules which have no subgoals will be called *facts*. Finally, a list containing search rules will be called a *rulebase*.

Implementing the AND/OR-tree search function

Given the conventions introduced for setting up the AND/OR-tree forming a given search space, we can implement a backward search function as shown in Figure 6-2. Note that, for the sake of simplicity, we have embedded the **foreach** loop which would form the basis for the successor function inside the search function. This assumes that the rules are held in a variable called **rulebase**. We call this *backwards* search because we are working backward from complex to easier goals.

The function **backwards_search1** undertakes a depth first search in that it deals with the goals in order, starting with the first goal, calls itself recursively on the first of subgoals and then on the first of the subsubgoals and so on. If the first

```
/* backwards_search1 takes a list of goals as input and returns true
   if they can all be solved, and false otherwise. */

define backwards_search1(goals) -> boolean;
   vars goal subgoals other_goals;
   if goals = [] then true -> boolean
   else goals --> [?goal ??other_goals];
        foreach [^goal ??subgoals] in rulebase do
             backwards_search1(subgoals) -> boolean;
             if boolean
             then backwards_search1(other_goals) -> boolean;
                  if boolean then return endif
             endif
        endforeach;
        false -> boolean;
   endif;
enddefine;
```

Figure 6-2 Backwards search of an AND/OR tree

recursive call to **backwards-search1** should fail, then the **foreach** loop will cycle round to a further (if any exists) successor rule (without yet making the second call to **backwards_search1**). If the first call succeeds but the second fails, again further rules are tried if they exist. If both calls succeed, the function terminates with true. It thus uses depth first search and exits as soon as the first solution is found. The function will systematically explore the whole space if no solution can be found (if there are no loops) before returning **<false>**. We have used recursion to deal with the **other_goals**. It would have been just as easy to have used a loop instead which looped through each of the goals input to the search function and merely called itself recursively in dealing with each of their subgoals.

Implementing planning as AND/OR-tree search

To implement a simple form of planning behaviour using our generic, AND/OR-tree search function, we first need to set up the appropriate AND/OR search space (i.e. rulebase). Below is a set rules which define an *implicit* AND/OR tree for a "book" problem. This is a variant on the "cake" problem of Burton and Shadbolt, 1987). These rules are in the form [<SUCCESSOR> <predecessor(s)>]:

```
[/* FACTS */
 [[have paper]]
 [[have cash]]
 [[in house]]
 [[have phone]]
 /* RULES */
 [[have book] [have cash] [in store]]
 [[have book] [have creditcard] [have phone]]
 [[have book] [have paper] [have pen] [have time]]
 [[have creditcard] [have bankaccount]]
] -> rulebase1;
```

We have placed facts earlier in the rulebase than rules. This is to ensure that in searching, the system checks facts first before continuing the search via the rules. All the entries are lists of elements; in each case the first element corresponds to a goal and the remaining elements form the corresponding subgoals or "preconditions". Calling the new search function on the input corresponding to a goal of the planning task considered produces the following behaviour:

```
trace backwards_search1;
rulebase1 -> rulebase;

backwards_search1([[have book]]) ==>

> backwards_search1 [[have book]]
!> backwards_search1 [[have cash] [in store]]
!!> backwards_search1 []
!!< backwards_search1 <true>
!!> backwards_search1 [[in store]]
!!< backwards_search1 <false>
!< backwards_search1 <false>
!> backwards_search1 [[have creditcard] [have phone]]
!!> backwards_search1 [[have bankaccount]]
!!< backwards_search1 <false>
!< backwards_search1 <false>
!> backwards_search1 [[have paper] [have pen] [have time]]
!!> backwards_search1 []
!!< backwards_search1 <true>
!!> backwards_search1 [[have pen] [have time]]
!!< backwards_search1 <false>
!< backwards_search1 <false>
< backwards_search1 <false>
** <false>
```

We can vary the behaviour simply by changing the rulebase. Thus by adding a fact as follows:

```
[/* FACTS */
 [[have paper]]
 [[have cash]]
 [[in house]]
 [[have phone]]
 [[have creditcard]] /* NEW FACT ADDED */
 /* RULES */
 [[have book] [have cash] [in store]]
 [[have book] [have creditcard] [have phone]]
 [[have book] [have paper] [have pen] [have time]]
 [[have creditcard] [have bankaccount]]
] -> rulebase2;
```

ensures that the behaviour produced is as shown below. Note that the new rules and facts are added onto the front of the rulebase so that these new rules are tried *earlier* by the **foreach** than the original entries:

```
rulebase2 -> rulebase;

backwards_search1([[have book]]) ==>

> backwards_search1 [[have book]]
!> backwards_search1 [[have cash] [in store]]
!!> backwards_search1 []
!!< backwards_search1 <true>
!!> backwards_search1 [[in store]]
!!< backwards_search1 <false>
!< backwards_search1 <false>    /* BACKTRACKING */
!> backwards_search1 [[have creditcard] [have phone]]
!!> backwards_search1 []
!!< backwards_search1 <true>
!!> backwards_search1 [[have phone]]
!!!> backwards_search1 []
!!!< backwards_search1 <true>
!!!> backwards_search1 []
!!!< backwards_search1 <true>
!!< backwards_search1 <true>
!< backwards_search1 <true>
!> backwards_search1 []
!< backwards_search1 <true>
< backwards_search1 <true>
** <true>
```

Where the choice of a rule eventually leads to a **<false>**, the **foreach** ensures that the program backtracks to consider remaining applicable rules at that choice point.

One of the shortcomings of the above approach to "planning" is that our program only returns true or false and not a plan; another issue is that the rules as we have set them out cannot express changes in the world as a result of achieving some goal. These issues are dealt with properly in the next chapter.

Implementing reasoning as AND/OR-tree search

The AND/OR-tree search function is not only applicable in the case where we wish to solve a simplified planning problem. It can also be applied in many other cases. Any problem whose solution we can think of in terms of goal-reduction can be solved by the application of AND/OR-tree search. To obtain a specific implementation we only need to set up the appropriate rulebase.

For example, AND/OR-tree search can be used to solve simple reasoning problems. In this application goals correspond roughly to "conclusions" and subgoals correspond roughly to bits of "evidence". Search rules state that certain collections of evidence (subgoals) allow the drawing (achievement) of a given conclusion (goal).

They therefore constitute simple *inference rules*. An example may help to make this clear. Let us set up a rulebase as follows:

```
[/* FACTS */
 [[weak battery]]
 [[damp weather]]
 [[old car]]
 /* RULES */
 [[low current][damp weather][weak battery]]
 [[old starter][old car]]
 [[car wont start][low current][old starter]]
 [[write off][car wont start][not AA member]]
 [[not AA member][irresponsible]]
] -> rulebase3;
```

The general context for this rulebase involves car problems. The first rule states, in effect, that a weak battery and damp weather are, together, evidence supporting the conclusion that the current is low. The **[[car wont start][low current][old starter]]** rule states that low current and an old starter are evidence supporting the conclusion that the car wont start, and so on. If we run the **backwards_search1** function on the goal list **[[car wont start]]** the behaviour produced corresponds to a simple reasoning process in which the appropriate bits of evidence are sought out and then combined together so as to justify the original conclusion (or "hypothesis"). Thus:

```
rulebase3 -> rulebase;

backwards_search1([[car wont start]]) ==>

> backwards_search1 [[car wont start]]
!> backwards_search1 [[low current] [old starter]]
!!> backwards_search1 [[damp weather] [weak battery]]
!!!> backwards_search1 []
!!!< backwards_search1 <true>
!!!> backwards_search1 [[weak battery]]
!!!!> backwards_search1 []
!!!!< backwards_search1 <true>
!!!!> backwards_search1 []
!!!!< backwards_search1 <true>
!!!< backwards_search1 <true>
!!< backwards_search1 <true>
!!> backwards_search1 [[old starter]]
!!!> backwards_search1 [[old car]]
!!!!> backwards_search1 []
```

```
!!!!< backwards_search1 <true>
!!!!> backwards_search1 []
!!!!< backwards_search1 <true>
!!!< backwards_search1 <true>
!!!> backwards_search1 []
!!!< backwards_search1 <true>
!!< backwards_search1 <true>
!< backwards_search1 <true>
!> backwards_search1 []
!< backwards_search1 <true>
< backwards_search1 <true>
** <true>
```

Given the fact that we are construing goals as conclusions and subgoals as bits of evidence it might make sense to rename the search function "show". If we did this the tracing would look like this:

```
show([[car wont start]]) ==>

> show [[car wont start]]
!> show [[low current] [old starter]]
!!> show [[damp weather] [weak battery]]
!!!> show []
!!!< show <true>
!!!> show [[weak battery]]
!!!!> show []
!!!!< show <true>
!!!!> show []
!!!!< show <true>
!!!< show <true>
!!< show <true>
!!> show [[old starter]]
!!!> show [[old car]]
!!!!> show []
!!!!< show <true>
!!!!> show []
!!!!< show <true>
!!!< show <true>
!!!> show []
!!!< show <true>
!!< show <true>
!< show <true>
!> show []
```

```
!< show <true>
< show <true>
** <true>
```

In a relatively liberal reading this trace output says that to show that the car won't start it needs to be shown that the current is low and the starter is old. To show that the current is low it needs to be shown that the weather is damp and the battery is weak. Both of these things can be shown trivially because, in the current rulebase they are just facts. Finally, to show that the starter is old it needs to be shown that the car is old. Again this is just a fact. Thus it can be shown that the car won't start. Q.E.D.:

```
show([[write off]]) ==>

> show [[write off]]
!> show [[car wont start] [not AA member]]
!!> show [[low current] [old starter]]
!!!> show [[damp weather] [weak battery]]
!!!!> show []
!!!!< show <true>
!!!!> show [[weak battery]]
!!!!!> show []
!!!!!< show <true>
!!!!!> show []
!!!!!< show <true>
!!!!< show <true>
!!!< show <true>
!!!> show [[old starter]]
!!!!> show [[old car]]
!!!!!> show []
!!!!!< show <true>
!!!!!> show []
!!!!!< show <true>
!!!!< show <true>
!!!!> show []
!!!!< show <true>
!!!< show <true>
!!< show <true>
!!> show [[not AA member]]
!!!> show [[irresponsible]]
!!!< show <false>
!!< show <false>
!< show <false>
```

```
< show <false>
** <false>
```

If we try to "show" that the car is a write-off the trace output is as shown above. Because it cannot be shown that the owner is irresponsible it cannot be shown that the owner is not a member of the AA. This means that it cannot be shown that the car is a write-off.

Loops in the search space

Loops can occur in problem reduction searches if the rules either directly or indirectly involve recursive definitions without an appropriate fact to stop the recursion, as in the definitions of **[happy]**, **[loved]** and **[desirable]** below:

```
[ /* FACTS */
  [[rich]]
  [[good job]]
  /* RULES */
  [[happy] [rich] [successful] [loved]]
  [[successful] [respected] [rich]]
  [[loved] [desirable]]
  [[desirable] [successful] [happy]]
  [[respected] [good job]]
] -> rulebase4;

rulebase4 -> rulebase;

backwards_search1([[successful]]) ==>

> backwards_search1 [[successful]]
!> backwards_search1 [[respected] [rich]]
!!> backwards_search1 [[good job]]
!!!> backwards_search1 []
!!!< backwards_search1 <true>
!!!> backwards_search1 []
!!!< backwards_search1 <true>
!!< backwards_search1 <true>
!!> backwards_search1 [[rich]]
!!!> backwards_search1 []
!!!< backwards_search1 <true>
!!!> backwards_search1 []
!!!< backwards_search1 <true>
```

```
!!< backwards_search1 <true>
!< backwards_search1 <true>
!> backwards_search1 []
!< backwards_search1 <true>
< backwards_search1 <true>
** <true>

backwards_search1([[happy]]) ==>

> backwards_search1 [[happy]]
!> backwards_search1 [[rich] [successful] [loved]]
!!> backwards_search1 []
!!< backwards_search1 <true>
!!> backwards_search1 [[successful] [loved]]
!!!> backwards_search1 [[respected] [rich]]
!!!!> backwards_search1 [[good job]]
!!!!!> backwards_search1 []
!!!!!< backwards_search1 <true>
!!!!!> backwards_search1 []
!!!!!< backwards_search1 <true>
!!!!< backwards_search1 <true>
!!!!> backwards_search1 [[rich]]
!!!!!> backwards_search1 []
!!!!!< backwards_search1 <true>
!!!!!> backwards_search1 []
!!!!!< backwards_search1 <true>
!!!!< backwards_search1 <true>
!!!< backwards_search1 <true>
!!!> backwards_search1 [[loved]]
!!!!> backwards_search1 [[desirable]] /* RULE LEADS TO LOOP */
!!!!!> backwards_search1 [[successful] [happy]]
!!!!!!> backwards_search1 [[respected] [rich]]
!!!!!!!> backwards_search1 [[good job]]
!!!!!!!!> backwards_search1 []
!!!!!!!!< backwards_search1 <true>
!!!!!!!!> backwards_search1 []
!!!!!!!!< backwards_search1 <true>
!!!!!!!< backwards_search1 <true>
!!!!!!!> backwards_search1 [[rich]]
!!!!!!!!> backwards_search1 []
!!!!!!!!< backwards_search1 <true>
!!!!!!!!> backwards_search1 []
!!!!!!!!< backwards_search1 <true>
```

```
!!!!!!!< backwards_search1 <true>
!!!!!!< backwards_search1 <true>
!!!!!!> backwards_search1 [[happy]] /* STARTS TO LOOP HERE */
!!!!!!!> backwards_search1 [[rich] [successful] [loved]]
!!!!!!!!> backwards_search1 []
!!!!!!!!< backwards_search1 <true>
!!!!!!!!> backwards_search1 [[successful] [loved]]
!!!!!!!!!> backwards_search1 [[respected] [rich]]
!!!!!!!!!!> backwards_search1 [[good job]]

/* INTERRUPTED */
```

'he problem is that in trying to show **[happy]** the program tries to show **[loved]** .nd in trying to show **[loved]** it needs to show **[desirable]** and thence to show **happy]**. We will solve this presently, but first deal with a different issue.

The program proves **[successful]** twice over in the above trace. This latter is ıot because of a loop but is an inefficiency. This could be avoided as follows. Once omething has been proved the system could record that fact so that it does not have o be proved again and it could just be looked up as a new fact. This can be achieved y adding any successfully proved goals to the database as part of **ackwards_search1**. We have provided a new procedure **prove** which has **data-ase** as a local variable. This ensures that any changes that the new **ackwards_search** make to the database are not permanent, see Figure 6-3.

There are several ways of dealing with loops. The simplest, which we have dopted, is to set a limit on the depth of the search and backtrack if the limit is eached (as in depth-limited state space search). A second method would be to keep record of the direct ancestors of each goal and ensure that search for a particular oal fails if that goal is already an ancestor.

Trying **backward_search** with these improvements now gives the following output. The database does not contain the rule **[[happy] [poor] [free] [lov-ng]]**:

```
trace add backwards_search;

prove([[successful]], rulebase4, 5) ==>

> backwards_search [[successful]] 5
!> backwards_search [[respected] [rich]] 4
!!> backwards_search [[good job]] 3
!!!> backwards_search [] 2
!!!< backwards_search <true>
!!!> backwards_search [] 3
!!!< backwards_search <true>
```

```
/* backwards_search takes a list of goals as input and returns
   true if they can all be solved, and otherwise returns false. It
   checks for loops by ensuring that the search remains within a
   depth limit. */

define backwards_search(goals, depth) -> boolean;
   vars goal goal_list subgoals other_goals;
   if goals = [] then true -> boolean
   elseif depth <= 0 then  false -> boolean
   else goals --> [?goal ??other_goals];
        foreach [^goal ??subgoals] do
            backwards_search(subgoals, depth-1) -> boolean;
            if boolean
            then unless present([^goal]) then add([^goal]) endunless;
                 backwards_search(other_goals, depth) -> boolean;
                 if boolean then return endif
            endif
        endforeach;
        false -> boolean
   endif
enddefine;

/* prove takes a list of goals and rulebase and returns true if
   all the goals can be solved, and false otherwise.  It passes on
   a depth limit to backwards_search to avoid loops. */

define prove(goals, rulebase, depth) -> boolean;
   vars database;
   rulebase -> database;
   backwards_search(goals,depth) -> boolean
enddefine;
```

Figure 6-3 Avoiding loops in AND/OR search by setting a depth limit

```
!!< backwards_search <true>
!!> add [[respected]]
!!< add
!!> backwards_search [[rich]] 4
!!!> backwards_search [] 3
!!!< backwards_search <true>
!!!> backwards_search [] 4
!!!< backwards_search <true>
!!< backwards_search <true>
```

```
!< backwards_search <true>
!> add [[successful]]
!< add
!> backwards_search [] 5
!< backwards_search <true>
< backwards_search <true>
** <true>

prove([[happy]], rulebase4, 4) ==>

> backwards_search [[happy]] 4
!> backwards_search [[rich] [successful] [loved]] 3
!!> backwards_search [] 2
!!< backwards_search <true>
!!> backwards_search [[successful] [loved]] 3
!!!> backwards_search [[respected] [rich]] 2
!!!!> backwards_search [[good job]] 1
!!!!!> backwards_search [] 0
!!!!!< backwards_search <true>
!!!!!> backwards_search [] 1
!!!!!< backwards_search <true>
!!!!< backwards_search <true>
!!!!> add [[respected]]
!!!!< add
!!!!> backwards_search [[rich]] 2
!!!!!> backwards_search [] 1
!!!!!< backwards_search <true>
!!!!!> backwards_search [] 2
!!!!!< backwards_search <true>
!!!!< backwards_search <true>
!!!< backwards_search <true>
!!!> add [[successful]]
!!!< add
!!!> backwards_search [[loved]] 3
!!!!> backwards_search [[desirable]] 2
!!!!!> backwards_search [[successful] [happy]] 1
!!!!!!> backwards_search [] 0
!!!!!!< backwards_search <true>
!!!!!!> backwards_search [[happy]] 1
!!!!!!!> backwards_search [[rich] [successful] [loved]] 0
!!!!!!!< backwards_search <false>
!!!!!!< backwards_search <false>
!!!!!!> backwards_search [[respected] [rich]] 0
```

```
!!!!!!< backwards_search <false>
!!!!!< backwards_search <false>
!!!!< backwards_search <false>
!!!< backwards_search <false>
!!< backwards_search <false>
!< backwards_search <false>
< backwards_search <false>
** <false>
```

In the first case above `[[successful]]` could be proved (with no loop problems) within a preset depth limit of 5. In the second case `[[happy]]` could not be proved and the (arbitrary) depth limit of four prevented the search looping.

It is slightly unrealistic having to decide ahead of time how deep to set the depth limit, but we could get round this using *iterative deepening* as we did in state-space search (see later in this chapter).

Solution tree

In the earlier chapters, where the search tree for a search problem was an OR-tree, a solution for the problem consisted of a *path* connecting the root node with a goal node. This path was just a sequence of nodes.

In the case where the search tree for a search problem is an AND/OR-tree, a solution has a quite different form. It is an *AND-tree* rather than a path. In both cases the search tree contains alternatives, i.e. the OR branches, whereas a *particular solution* necessarily contains no OR branches, thus giving a path in one case and an AND-tree in the other.

The reason for this is quite straightforward. A given solution involves achieving a sequence of goals. But achieving any one goal may involve achieving N subgoals. To write out a solution we must therefore specify the subgoals which need to be achieved in order to achieve any given goal. If we do this for a given solution we end up with a tree structure. The root of the AND-tree is the original goal. Its children are the subgoals of the initial goal (i.e. the subgoals which when satisfied, enabled the initial goal to be satisfied). The children of a child node are just *its* subgoals, and so on. AND-trees of this form are called *solution trees*.

In the case where we are construing search rules as inference rules, the solution-tree produced by a search function is called a *proof tree*. The idea here is that the original goal corresponds to a "theorem" and the process of searching for a solution corresponds to an attempt to prove the theorem given the formal system of rules making up the rulebase.[1]

---

[1] In this context, facts correspond to the axioms of the formal system.

```
/* backwards_search_tree takes a list of goals as input and returns
   the solution AND tree for them if it exists, and otherwise returns
   false. */

define backwards_search_tree(goals, depth) -> tree;
    vars goal first_tree other_trees goal subgoals other_goals;
    if goals = [] then [] -> tree
    elseif depth <= 0 then false -> tree
    else goals --> [?goal ??other_goals];
        foreach [^goal ??subgoals] do
            backwards_search_tree(subgoals, depth-1) -> first_tree;
            if islist(first_tree)
            then unless present([^goal]) then add([^goal]) endunless;
                backwards_search_tree(other_goals, depth)
                    -> other_trees;
                if islist(other_trees)
                then [[^goal ^^first_tree] ^^other_trees] -> tree;
                    return
                endif
            endif
        endforeach;
        false -> tree;
    endif
enddefine;

/* proof_tree takes a single goal as input and returns its proof tree
   or false if there is none. */

define proof_tree(goal, rulebase, depth) -> tree;
   vars database;
   rulebase -> database;
   backwards_search_tree([^goal], depth) -> tree;
   if islist(tree) then hd(tree) -> tree endif
enddefine;
```

Figure 6-4 Constructing a solution AND tree

We can easily construct a version of the new search function which returns a representation of the solution AND-tree for a given problem, or **<false>** if a solution cannot be found. The function is shown in Figure 6-4. Note that if it is provided with an empty list of goals as input, it simply returns an empty list (i.e. an empty tree). Otherwise it constructs a solution tree for the goals presented by building a list which has as its first element a sublist consisting of the first goal followed by its solution-tree (obtained via a recursive call) followed by solution-trees for all the other goals.

```
showtree(proof_tree([write off], rulebase5, 10));
```

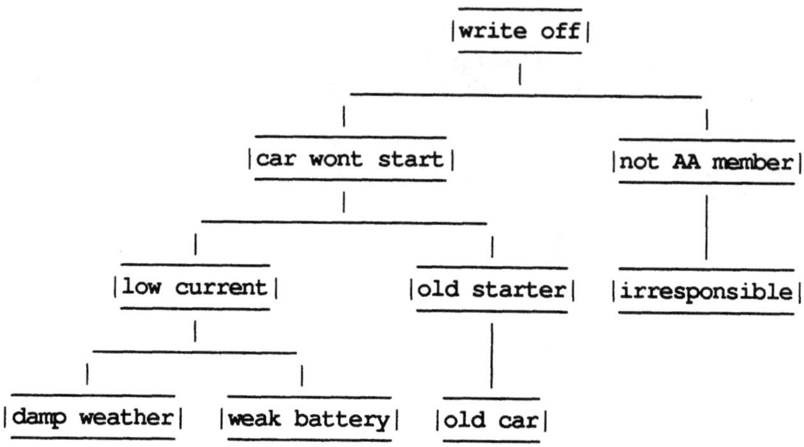

Figure 6-5 An example AND solution tree

We can demonstrate the behaviour of this function by getting it to construct a solution tree for the goal list `[write off]`. As we saw above, given the earlier rulebase about cars, this goal cannot be achieved. However, if we add a new fact `[[irresponsible]]` as follows:

```
untrace add;

[[[irresponsible]]
 [[weak battery]]
 [[damp weather]]
 [[old car]]
 [[low current] [damp weather] [weak battery]]
 [[low current] [headlights on] [cold weather]]
 [[old starter] [old car]]
 [[car wont start] [low current] [old starter]]
 [[write off] [car wont start] [not AA member]]
 [[not AA member] [irresponsible]]
] -> rulebase5;
```

```
proof_tree([write off], rulebase5, 10) ==>
** [[write off]
    [[car wont start]
     [[low current] [[damp weather]] [[weak battery]]]
     [[old starter] [[old car]]]]
    [[not AA member] [[irresponsible]]]]
```

We can, of course, use the **showtree** command to obtain a representation of this tree, see Figure 6-5. However, due to the fact that the search function assumes that its input will be a *list* of goals, it always returns a list of solution trees. This means that the solution tree for a single goal actually forms the first element of the result of the search function. Thus, to get the representation we want we need to specify the first element of the result in the showtree command; see the definition of **proof_tree** (also see Note 1 at end of chapter).

Note that **showtree** does not distinguish between different kinds of tree. In earlier chapters we have chosen to view the output of **showtree** as an OR-tree, here we choose to view it as an AND-tree.

The AND/OR search tree

It is possible to adapt **backwards_search_tree** so that it outputs the whole AND/OR-tree rather than simply the first solution AND-tree that it finds, see Figure 6-6. We have replaced one of the recursive calls by a **for** loop and arranged that the tree contains the nodes **[AND]** and **[OR]**. The tips of the tree are either **[KNOWN]** or **[UNKNOWN]** depending on whether or not the subgoal in question is a fact or cannot be further decomposed. The function makes the same check for loops as before. Where a node has only a *single* successor, be it an "and" or an "or" successor, the redundant extra **[AND]** or **[OR]** node is omitted:

```
/* AO_search_tree takes a list of goals as input and returns
   the search AND/OR tree as output. */

define AO_search_tree(goals, depth) -> and_tree;
    vars goal sub_tree  subgoals and_tree or_tree item;
    if goals = [] then [[KNOWN]] -> and_tree
    elseif depth <= 0 then [[DEPTH LIMITED]] -> and_tree
    else [[AND]] -> and_tree;
        for goal in goals do
            if present([^goal ==])
            then [[OR]] -> or_tree;
                foreach [^goal ??subgoals] do
                    AO_search_tree(subgoals, depth-1) -> sub_tree;
                    [^^or_tree ^sub_tree] -> or_tree
                endforeach;
                if or_tree matches [[OR] ?item]
                then item -> or_tree
                endif;
            else [[UNKNOWN]] -> or_tree
            endif;
            [^^and_tree [^goal ^or_tree]] -> and_tree
        endfor;
        if and_tree matches [[AND] ?item] then item -> and_tree endif
    endif
enddefine;
```

Figure 6-6 Constructing the AND/OR search tree

```
rulebase5 -> database;

AO_search_tree([[write off]], 10) ==>
** [[write off]
   [[AND]
    [[car wont start]
     [[AND]
      [[low current]
       [[OR]
        [[AND] [[damp weather] [[KNOWN]]]
               [[weak battery] [[KNOWN]]]]
        [[AND]
         [[headlights on] [[UNKNOWN]]]
         [[cold weather] [[UNKNOWN]]]]]]
      [[old starter] [[old car] [[KNOWN]]]]]]
    [[not AA member] [[irresponsible] [[KNOWN]]]]]]
```

The output from **showtree** is shown in Figure 6-7. Notice that the node `[low current]` could, in principle, be proven via two rules.

State space search and problem reduction

Although we have emphasised the distinction between state space search and problem reduction the choice of method depends on the way that one represents the problem rather than being an inherent property of the problem itself. It is possible to recast the problems explored in this chapter as state space problems. We may think of a state as made up of a list of goals. The initial state is the initial list of goals and the final goal state is a list just containing the null state, `[[]]`. Intermediate states are

```
showtree(AO_search_tree([[write off]], 10));
```

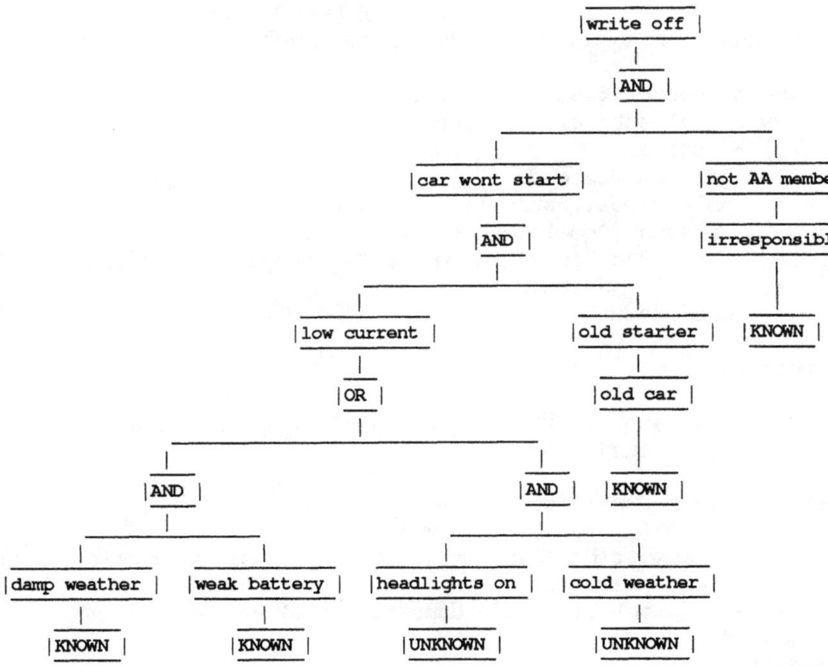

Figure 6-7 An example AND/OR search tree

generated via the rules as already represented in **rulebase2**. For example *one* successor state to `[[have book]]` is `[[have cash][in store]]`. The successor state to `[[have paper]]` is `[[]]`, whereas `[[have pen]]` has *no* successor state.

By redefining **successors6** to model a state space interpretation we can (partially) solve the above problems using state space methods. In earlier chapters states in state space search always had the same number of components. Here we have a situation where a state may have an arbitrary number of components. This does not matter except that it makes checking for loops a little trickier. We cannot just see if a new state is exactly equal to a previously visited state. A loop exists in this formulation if a new state contains all the goals that some previous state contained (plus possibly some others as well). Figure 6-8 shows a state space version of successors which does *not* check for loops:

```
/* successors6 takes a state consisting of a list of goals as input and
   returns a list of new states consisting of lists of subgoals
   derivable from the original goals with any duplications removed. */

define successors6(state) -> states;
    vars goal subgoals remainder;
    [] -> states;
    for goal in state do
        delete(goal, state) -> remainder;
        foreach [^goal ??subgoals] in rulebase do
            [^^states ^(remove_dups([^^subgoals ^^remainder]))]
                -> states
        endforeach
    endfor
enddefine;

/* remove_dups takes a list as input and returns a list with any
   duplicated elements removed. */

define remove_dups(list) -> newlist;
    if list = [] then [] -> newlist
    elseif member(hd(list), tl(list)) then remove_dups(tl(list))
           -> newlist
    else hd(list) :: remove_dups(tl(list)) -> newlist
    endif
enddefine;
```

Figure 6-8 Successor function for rules in state space search

```
rulebase2 -> rulebase;

successors6([[have creditcard]]) ==>
** [[] [[have bankaccount]]]

successors6([[have paper] [have cash] [have phone]]) ==>
** [[[have cash] [have phone]]
    [[have paper] [have phone]]
    [[have paper] [have cash]]]

successors6([[have phone]]) ==>
** [[]]

successors6([[pink icing]]) ==>
** []

successors6([[have book]]) ==>
** [[[have cash] [in store]]
    [[have creditcard] [have phone]]
    [[have paper] [have pen] [have time]]]
```

In the first case, there is a single rule for **`[have creditcard]`** but it is also a fact in the rulebase, so there are two possible states generated, one consist of the terminating state and the other consists of the rule's subgoal. In the second case, each of the inputs is a fact, so we get three new states, each of which omits *one* of these facts. In the third case the single component of the the state is a fact, so we get the final empty goal state as output. In the last case, nothing is known about the input so we get no successors as output. The above definition of successors can result in successor states that contain duplicated goals. In the final case **`[have book]`** has three rules associated with it, so we get three new states.

We can show the search space OR-tree via the function **`limited_search_tree`** given as Figure 3-3 in Chapter 3. This function, takes a *path* containing an initial state, a goal state and a maximum tree depth and returns the corresponding search tree. Note that although this function checks for loops along each path of states, the check will not work properly in this case because of the more complex nature of these states consisting of sets of goals:

```
successors6 -> successors;

limited_search_tree([[[have book]]], [[]], 10) ==>
** [[[have book]]
    [[[have cash] [in store]] [[[in store]]]]
    [[[have creditcard] [have phone]]
     [[[have phone]] [[]]]
     [[[have bankaccount] [have phone]] [[[have bankaccount]]]]
     [[[have creditcard]] [[]] [[[have bankaccount]]]]]
    [[[have paper] [have pen] [have time]]
     [[[have pen] [have time]]]]]
```

The tree can be displayed via **showtree** as usual, see Figure 6-9. We have had to make some adjustments in order to draw the nodes as shown (see Note 2 at end of this chapter).
In this tree, two paths only lead to success, i.e. to the empty nodes. These two paths are equivalent and differ only in the order in which the goals are dealt with. **[have phone]** on the far right which is not a fact.

We demonstrate the way that successors are generated by adding a couple of impossible goals into a new initial state, see Figure 6-10. In this figure all paths lead to dead-ends with states still containing goals to be proved - there are no solutions in this search tree.

```
showtree(limited_search_tree([[[have book]]], [[]], 10));
```

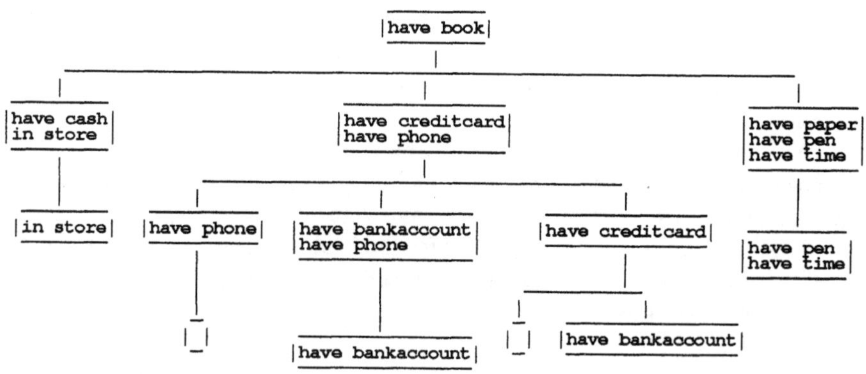

Figure 6-9 Search tree with two solutions using rulebase2

```
limited_search_tree([[[rich][have book][happy]]], [[]], 10)
-> tree;
showtree(tree);
```

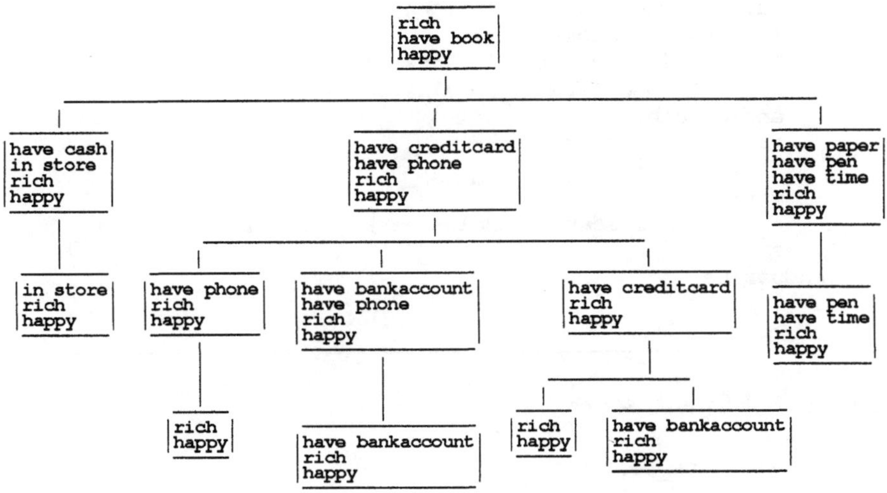

Figure 6-10 Search tree with no solution

Forward AND/OR-tree search

We have seen that a backward AND/OR-tree search provided with a rulebase containing inference rules can "show" certain conclusions by determining whether the bits of evidence which support them (i.e. their subgoals) can also be shown. But what about forward search? In a reasoning context, we might expect that this process would start out from a set of facts and try to see what conclusions can be derived. But any conclusion constitutes a bit of evidence which might enable the drawing of a further conclusion. So the question arises, at what point should this sort of forward AND/OR-tree search stop? One approach is to say that the process should come to a halt at the point where *no* further conclusions can be derived, i.e. the search is exhaustive. The definition of a function which implements this approach is shown in Figure 6-11.

We can test the behaviour of this function by seeing what conclusions it draws given the input `[[damp_weather] [weak_battery]]`:

```
/* forwards_search takes a list of facts as input and returns a
   list of all the facts that can be derived, including the originals. */

define forwards_search(facts) -> result;
   vars conclusion, conclusions;
   [] -> conclusions;
   foreach [?conclusion ^^facts] do
        [^^conclusions ^conclusion] -> conclusions
   endforeach;
   if conclusions = [] then
      facts -> result
   else
      forwards_search(conclusions) -> result
   endif
enddefine;
```

Figure 6-11 Forwards search

```
trace forwards_search;

rulebase5 -> database;

forwards_search([[damp weather] [weak battery]]) ==>

>forwards_search [[damp weather] [weak_battery]]
!>forwards_search [[low_current]]
!<forwards_search [[low_current]]
<forwards_search [[low_current]]

** [[low current]]
```

Unfortunately, although this forward function appears to work, it is clear that it will not work in general. There are a number of problems. First of all, consider what would have happened if we had called the function giving it `[[weak_battery] [damp_weather]]` instead of `[[damp_weather] [weak_battery]]`. In this case, because of the mis-match between the ordering of the facts in the two lists, the foreach loop would not have picked up the search rule:

```
[[low current] [damp weather] [weak battery]]
```

and therefore the conclusion `[low current]` would not have been derived. We might be able to get around this problem by making sure that facts are always arranged into some type of deterministic sequence (e.g. by sorting them). However, there are further problems which we cannot solve so easily. For example, given the two rules:

```
[[low current] [damp weather] [weak battery]]
[[car wont start] [low current] [old starter]]
```

we would like to be able to conclude `[car wont start]` given the facts `[[damp weather] [weak battery] [old starter]]`. But the function as configured would not do this. It does not add in new conclusions to its list of `facts` while it is scanning the database (using `foreach`). Thus, it would never construct the list of facts `[[low current] [old starter]]`; thus it would never pick out the rule `[[car wont start] [low current] [old starter]]` and derive the conclusion `[car wont start]`.

In general, the difficulty with forward AND/OR-tree search is the fact that there is no sensible way of deciding which subset of the subgoals which have already been satisfied (or provided) should be used in the attempt to pick-out search rules from the rulebase. Our function just assumes that all the given subgoals should be used in the order they are presented. In some cases this assumption may work out. In others, search rules which could profitably be applied will be missed.

Terminology

We have tried to use a consistent terminology in talking about AND/OR-tree search. However, it is important to realise that the process we have been discussing is extremely general and has found applications in a wide variety of tasks (some of which we will look at in ensuing chapters). It also provides an effective metaphor for fundamental processes in logical inference. What this means is that the process we have been calling AND/OR-tree search goes under a variety of different names. Moreover, the things that we have been calling search rules, facts etc. are also liable to be referred to in different ways.

In the case where search rules are effectively inference rules, the search process implemented by a backward function is often called *top-down reasoning* and the process implemented by the forward function is often called *bottom-up reasoning*. These terms reflect the fact that if we think of search as the process of constructing a solution-tree, then the forward variant constructs the tree from the bottom up (i.e. tip-nodes first), while the backward variant constructs the tree from the top down.

Production systems

Another terminological issue revolves around the order in which we express goal/subgoal relationships, i.e. search rules. We have adopted the convention that search rules are written as follows:

[<GOAL> <subgoal1> <subgoal2> ... <subgoalN>]

However, it would be quite permissible to write rules some other way, e.g. to put the subgoals before the goal. Of course, if we do this we must ensure that the search function makes the right assumption about which bits of the structure are the subgoals and which bit is the goal.

Quite often, where search rules are written back-to-front (i.e. subgoals first) they are called *productions*:

[<subgoal1> <subgoal2> ... <subgoalN> <GOAL>]

In some cases productions may express the fact that the satisfying of a given set of subgoals effectively achieves a *set* of goals. In this case some kind of separator will normally be inserted to show where the subgoals end and the goals begin, e.g.

[<subgoal1> <subgoal2> ... <subgoalN> => <goal-1> <goal-2> ...]

Collections of productions are usually called *production systems* and these have played quite an important role in AI. Production systems tend to range between two different extremes. They may correspond almost perfectly to a set of inference rules (i.e. a rulebase) and in this case the so-called *production system interpreter* implements either a forwards- or backwards-chaining search in the implicit AND/OR-tree. But there are other forms of production system where the productions feature goals which correspond to "actions". These have the form:

[<condition-1> <condition-2> ... <condition-N> <action>]

These rules are said to "fire" whenever it is observed that all the conditions specified on the left-hand side hold simultaneously. The action will typically involve adding or deleting some data to a database. This sort of production system is not quite so easily construed as a form of search function.

AND/OR Search in Prolog

AND/OR-tree search is the basis for the implementation of Prolog. Prolog programs consist of collections of structures which correspond roughly to what we have called

```
/* rule(+[<SUCCESSOR>,<predecessor(s)>]) */

rule([[have,smarties]]).   /* FACTS */
rule([[have,eggs]]).
rule([[have,flour]]).
rule([[have,money]]).
rule([[have,car]]).
rule([[in,kitchen]]).

rule([[decorate,cake],[have,cake],[have,icing]]).    /* RULES */
rule([[decorate,cake],[have,cake],[have,smarties]]).
rule([[have,money],[in,bank]]).
rule([[have,cake],[have,money],[in,store]]).
rule([[have,cake],[in,kitchen],[have,phone]]).
rule([[in,store],[have,car]]).
rule([[in,bank],[have,car]]).

/* backwards_search(+List_of_goals_to_be_satisfied)
   backwards_search succeeds if the list of goals can be proved. */

backwards_search([]).

backwards_search([Goal | Goals]) :-
    rule([Goal | Subgoals]),
    backwards_search(Subgoals),
    backwards_search(Goals).

/* backwards_search_tree(+List_of_goals_to_be_satisfied, -Resultant_AND-tree)
   backwards_search_tree takes a list of goals and returns the proof tree
   without checking for loops */

backwards_search_tree([], []).

backwards_search_tree([Goal | Goals], [[Goal | Tree] | Trees]) :-
    rule([Goal | Subgoals]),
    backwards_search_tree(Subgoals, Tree),
    backwards_search_tree(Goals, Trees).
```

Figure 6-12 Backwards search in Prolog

search rules. Running a Prolog program is achieved by executing the underlying search function on a given set of goals. But Prolog is more powerful than the search function we have implemented mainly due to the fact that it allows the programmer to include variables in rules.

Given the above, it is not surprising that implementing **backwards_search** and **backwards_search_tree** in Prolog is straightforward as they rely on the built-in mechanisms of Prolog in a very direct way, see Figure 6-12. **backwards_search/1** has two cases to consider. In the first the list of goals to be satisfied is empty so it succeeds immediately. In the second it divides the list goals into the first and the remainder and finds a rule to use on the first goal. This rule will normally involve further subgoals, so **backwards_search/1** calls itself to deal with these subgoals and then calls itself again to deal with remainder of the original goals. **backwards_search_tree/2** has much the same division of labour except that it constructs the solution tree in its second argument.

Running the Prolog program on the "decorate cake" example, a variant on the POP-11 example on p. 136 of Burton and Shadbolt (1987), gives the AND-tree in Figure 6-13 (using the Prolog library **showtree** together with an appropriate definition of **root**, see note 1 at end of this chapter).

This Prolog program will loop with certain rulesets for just the same reasons as the POP-11 function given at the start of this chapter. One simple method of dealing with loops is to limit the depth of the search tree by an extra argument to **backwards_search/1** and **backwards_search_tree/2**. This argument holds the inverse of the depth of the search tree which is not allowed to reduce below zero.

```
?- backwards_search_tree([[decorate,cake]], [T]), showtree(T).
T = [[decorate, cake],
          [[have, cake], [[have, money]],
                         [[in, store], [[have, car]]]],
          [[have, smarties]]] ?
yes
```

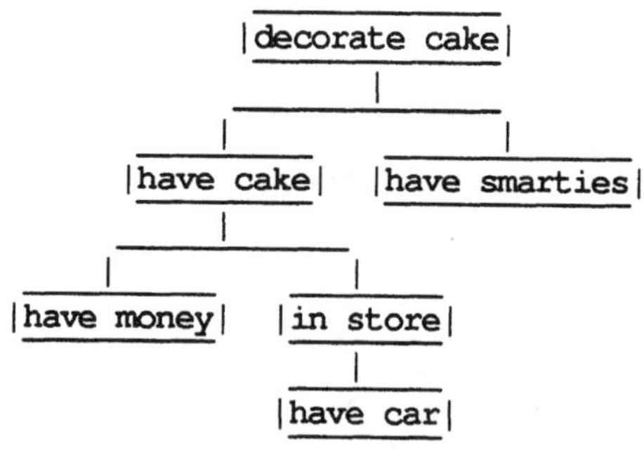

Figure 6-13 Solution tree for decorating the cake, in Prolog

Figure 6-14 gives the definition of **backwards_search/2**. Again there are two clauses, but the second clause now checks the value of the depth. In the first recursive call to **backwards_search_tree/3** which searches the subgoals for the current goal, the value of depth is incremented. In the second recursive call the value of depth is not incremented, since these goals are siblings of the current goal.

The following interaction compares **backwards_search_tree/2** with **backwards_search_tree/3** using the rules given in Figure 6-14. We set the third argument of **backwards_search_tree/3** to 5 as the maximum depth:

```
?- backwards_search_tree([[stop1]], Tree).
Tree = [[[stop1]]]
?
yes
?- backwards_search_tree([[go]], Tree).

;;; PROLOG ERROR - MEMORY LIMIT (pop_prolog_lim) EXCEEDED
```

```
/* backwards_search_tree(+List_of_goals_to_be_satisfied, +Depth, -Tree)
   backwards_search succeeds with Tree if the list of goals can
   be proved without exceeding the Depth-limit */

backwards_search_tree([], _, []).

backwards_search_tree([Goal | Goals], Depth, [[Goal | Tree] | Trees])
    :-
    Depth > 0,
    rule([Goal | Subgoals]),
    New_depth is Depth - 1,
    backwards_search_tree(Subgoals, New_depth, Tree),
    backwards_search_tree(Goals, Depth, Trees).

/* SOME RULES FOR TESTING LOOP CHECKING */

rule([[stop1]]).
rule([[stop2]]).
rule([[go],[next]]).          /* MUTUALLY RECURSIVE */
rule([[next],[stop1],[go]]).          /* RULES */
rule([[next],[stop1],[stop2]]).
```

Figure 6-14 Limited depth AND/OR tree search

```
?- backwards_search_tree([[stop1]], 5, Tree).
Tree = [[[stop1]]]
?
yes
?- backwards_search_tree([[go]], 5, Tree).
Tree = [[[go], [[next], [[stop1]], [[go], [[next], [[stop1]],
        [[stop2]]]]]]] ? ;
Tree = [[[go], [[next], [[stop1]], [[stop2]]]]] ? ;
no
```

Trying to prove `[[go]]` without a depth check leads to an "infinite" loop whereas with a depth check, the query succeeds. Note that it does not find the shallowest tree first. Figure 6-15 shows the tree graphically.

It is possible to avoid the problem of having to choose the depth-limit ahead of time (e.g. "4") by applying *iterative-deepening* to AND/OR tree search in much the same way as we did to state-space search. The idea is that one starts with a small depth limit (e.g. "1") and if the search is unsuccessful, try again with a larger limit, see Figure 6-16. We still impose a depth-limit, but here it is an overall limit beyond

---

```
?- backwards_search_tree([[go]], 5, [Tree]), showtree(Tree).

              ____
             |go  |
              ‾‾‾‾
               |
           ________
          |next    |
           ‾‾‾‾‾‾‾‾
               |
        _______________
        |             |
     ________       ____
    |stop1   |     |go  |
     ‾‾‾‾‾‾‾‾       ‾‾‾‾
                      |
                  ________
                 |next    |
                  ‾‾‾‾‾‾‾‾
                      |
               _______________
               |             |
            ________      ________
           |stop1   |    |stop2   |
            ‾‾‾‾‾‾‾‾      ‾‾‾‾‾‾‾‾
```

Figure 6-15 Solution AND tree with depth limit of 4

which no iteration should venture. As in the state-space version, the same search is repeated at ever increasing depths, and so there is repeated work, and if we force backtracking, also repeated solutions.

In the following example, iterative deepening increases the search tree depth from 0 to 1 to 2 before finding the first solution:

```
?- spy iterative_deepening_backwards_search.
Spypoint placed on iterative_deepening_backwards_search/4
yes
?- iterative_deepening_backwards_search([[go]], 0, 20, Tree).
** (1) Call : iterative_deepening_backwards_search([[go]], 0, 20, _1)?
** (2) Call : iterative_deepening_backwards_search([[go]], 1, 20, _1)?
** (3) Call : iterative_deepening_backwards_search([[go]], 2, 20, _1)?
** (3) Exit : iterative_deepening_backwards_search([[go]], 2, 20,
                                   [[[go], [[next], [[stop1]], [[stop2]]]]])?
** (2) Exit : iterative_deepening_backwards_search([[go]], 1, 20,
                                   [[[go], [[next], [[stop1]], [[stop2]]]]])?
** (1) Exit : iterative_deepening_backwards_search([[go]], 0, 20,
                                   [[[go], [[next], [[stop1]], [[stop2]]]]])?
Tree = [[[go], [[next], [[stop1]], [[stop2]]]]] ?
yes
```

```
/* iterative_deepening_backwards_search(+Goals, +Depth, +Depth_limit, -Tree)
   iterative deepening succeeds with the search Tree for the given Goals,
   if backwards_search_tree succeeds within the overall Depth_limit. */

iterative_deepening_backwards_search(Goals, Depth, Depth_limit, Tree) :-
    backwards_search_tree(Goals, Depth, Tree).

iterative_deepening_backwards_search(Goals, Depth, Depth_limit, Tree) :-
    Depth < Depth_limit,
    New_depth is Depth + 1,
    iterative_deepening_backwards_search(Goals, New_depth, Depth_limit, Tree).
```

Figure 6-16 Iterative deepening AND/OR tree search in Prolog

Reading

Some helpful readings for the topics covered in this chapter are Rich (1983, Chapter 8) and Feigenbaum and McCorduck (1984, Part 3). Charniak and McDermott (1985, Chapter 8) provide a broad coverage of the reasoning as does Volume 2 of the AI handbook (Barr and Feigenbaum 1982, pp. 77-222). Bratko (1990), Chapter 13, deals with AND/OR tree search in Prolog, and Burton and Shadbolt (1987) deal with this topic in POP-11. Sterling and Shapiro (1986) deal much more extensively with AND/OR tree search in Prolog under the heading of meta-interpreters, as does O'Keefe (1990).

Exercises

1. Implement a set of rules which capture stereotypic relationships between occupations and personal characteristics, e.g.

```
[doctor white_coat stethoscope superiority_complex]
[stock_broker bloodshot_eyes gin_and_tonic_in_hand]
[hgv_driver yorkie_in_hand]
[social_worker guardian_under_arm no_shoes]
```

Write programs in POP-11 and in Prolog which take as input a list of basic characteristics and return a list of all the occupations that someone with those characteristics might hold.

2. Extend the Prolog definition of **backwards_search/1** which checks for loops so that it also records facts that have been proved thus saving them being reproved a second time.

3. Write a Prolog version of **AO_search_tree**.

4 Write a Prolog state-space version of **successors** and use it to generate OR search trees.

5. Write a POP-11 version of iterative deepening AND/OR search.

6. Adjust the loop checking mechanism in the POP-11 state space version so that it works correctly. Also make **successors** remove identical duplicated goals in a state.

7. In either POP-11 or Prolog write an AND/OR search procedure that checks for loops by recording and checking the ancestors of each goal.

Notes

1. To make **showtree** work properly for AND/OR trees we make the following adjustments:

```
define root(tree) -> root_name;
   vars word goal subtrees;
   tree --> [?goal ??subtrees];
   '' -> root_name;
   for word in goal do
       root_name >< word >< ' ' -> root_name
   endfor
enddefine;
```

2. To make **showtree** work properly for nodes of arbitrary width or height we make the following adjustments:

```
define root(tree) -> root_name;
    vars i word this_name state;
    tree --> [?state ==];
    initv(length(state)) -> root_name;
    for i to length(state) do '' -> this_name;
        for word in state(i) do
             this_name >< word >< ' ' -> this_name;
        endfor;
        allbutlast(1, this_name) -> root_name(i)
    endfor
enddefine;

define width(tree,name) -> w;
    vars i, l = length(name), w = 0;
    if name = {} then 3 -> w
    else for i from 1 to l do
             max(length(name(i)), w) -> w
         endfor;
         w + 2 -> w
    endif
enddefine;

define height(tree, name) -> h;
    if name = {} then 3 -> h else length(name) + 2 -> h endif
enddefine;
```

```
define draw_node(node,val);
    vars r1 r2 c1 c2 i name;
    val --> [?r1 ?r2 ?c1 ?c2];
    hd(node_draw_data()(node)) -> name;
    box(c1, r1, c2-2, r2);
    c1 + 1 -> c1; r1 + 1 -> r1;
    for i from 1 to length(name) do
        vedjumpto(r1, c1);
        vedinsertstring(name(i));
        r1 + 1 -> r1;
    endfor
enddefine;

define name_&_subtrees(tree) -> name -> subtrees;
    root(tree) -> name;
    tl(tree) -> subtrees
enddefine;
```

7
Planning (microworld search)

Introduction

Descriptions corresponding to nodes in a search space can vary in complexity. In the case of simple, path-finding search, the descriptions we used were **atomic**; that is to say they were just single words labeling a given location, e.g. "old_steine". In the case of the search space for the water jugs problem, the descriptions we used were list structures with two components, each component identifying the amount of liquid in one of the two jugs. In the case of the search space for the 8-puzzle, the descriptions used were list structures with nine components, e.g. `[1 2 3 4 5 6 7 8 hole]`. When considering sets of goals as a states in the previous chapter, each state could be made up of some arbitrary number of such goals. In principle, descriptions (i.e. nodes) can be as complex as we like. Provided the successor function can be computed, the search process can be applied in the usual way.

In the previous chapter we introduced the idea of searching AND-OR trees though the nodes in the resultant trees were still atomic, corresponding to particular goals or subgoals.

We can apply our search functions to search spaces in which nodes correspond to very *complex* descriptions. But in what cases might we want to do this? There are a variety of possibilities. But one case which has been extensively studied in AI involves the use of descriptions which describe the current state of a physical environment. We can illustrate what this means using an example. Consider the following list expression:

```
[ [ontable b1]
  [ontable b3]
  [b1 on b2]
  [cleartop b2] ]
```

Given the assumption that the words "b1", "b2" etc. are labels of blocks, this expression constitutes a description of a physical environment consisting of a table and three blocks; cf. Figure 7-1. The first and second sublists express the fact that the blocks "b1" and "b3" are both on the table. The third sublist expresses the fact that the block "b1" is on top of "b2 and the fourth sublists state that "b2" has nothing on top of it. The artificial environment represented by this sort of description is referred to as a **microworld**. Microworlds consisting of blocks and table tops are often used as testbeds in AI and called **blocksworlds**.

There are a number of points to note about blocksworld descriptions. First of all, the sublists are not in any particular order. Each one just describes some feature of the environment which is being represented. Secondly, only some features of the microworld are explicitly represented. Typically, represented features include things like shape, size, position and colour of blocks. Features which are not usually represented include things such as state-of-repair, aesthetic value, country of manufacture, weight, smell, etc. Note that, in some sense, microworld descriptions provide an abstract perspective on the environment which they represent.

We can obtain some quite sophisticated behaviour by applying our search function to search spaces consisting of microworld states. If we implement a successor function which returns the set of microworld states which arise as the result of performing a single **action** in the microworld (e.g. the picking up of a block), then a solution path connecting some starting state to some goal state will constitute a sequence of actions which achieves the goal state. This is interesting because a sequence of actions for performing a given goal can be construed as a **plan** for achieving that goal. Therefore the application of search to search spaces consisting of microworld descriptions can be construed as a form of **planning**. We saw a very simple application of this idea in the previous chapter, but here we develop it further to include the effects of actions.

One problem with this idea is the fact that the successor function looks as if it is going to be very hard to implement. To find the successors of a given microworld

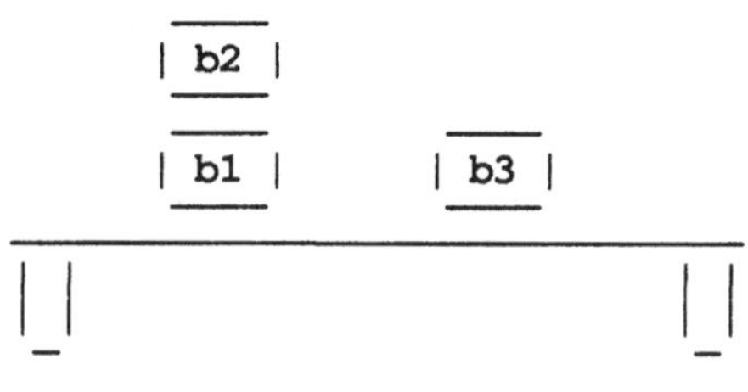

Figure 7-1 A simple blocksworld

state which are produced as a result of the application of a given action seems to necessitate taking account of every possible configuration of the microworld in which the action would be feasible. If the microworld description is quite complex (e.g. if it refers to a large number of blocks and possible relationships) then there may be a astronomical number of possible configurations to take account of. Does this mean that, in practice, the successor function will be impossible to implement?

In fact the successor function can be implemented; and the way in which we go about it involves using the same "trick" we used to implement the successor function for the water jugs problem. Recall that in the water jugs problem, a given action (e.g. filling one jug from the other jug) can be performed in a wide variety of different situations: 3 pints in one jug and 2 pints in the other, 1 pint in one jug and 3 pints in the other, and so on. Instead of making our successor function consider every single possibility explicitly, we just wrote rules which ensured that a given action would only be performed (i.e. a given successor would only be generated) if the features of the input state satisfied certain criteria (e.g. contents of jug X greater than contents of jug Y).

We can use exactly the same approach to implement a successor function for microworld descriptions. We just construct rules which ensure that a given successor is only produced if the features of the input state description satisfy certain criteria. Using this approach, our successor function will only need one rule for every possible action rather than one rule for every possible combination of action and microworld state.

Operators

Typically, the successor function for microworld descriptions is made up from rules of a rather specific form. These rules state, in effect, that a given successor node exists provided that the description of the current node includes certain features, e.g. `[ontable b1]`. Moreover, they specify the *form* of the successor node in terms of additions and deletions to be applied to the current node. That is to say, they specify the successor node as that variant of the current node which is derived either by adding some features to it, or by deleting some features from it, or both.

In the literature, a rule of this type is normally referred to as an **`operator`** on the grounds that it provides all the information about what happens in the microworld when a given operation (i.e. action) is applied. The best known form of operator in AI is the *STRIPS* operator described by Fikes and Nilsson (1971).

STRIPS operators are linear data structures with four fields. The first field provides a description of (i.e. a label or title for) the action implemented. The second provides a list of *preconditions* for the action; these are just the set of features which the current node must have in order for the successor in question to exist. The third and fourth fields provide lists of *additions* and *deletions*. Figure 7-2 shows a typical STRIPS operator represented as a list of four sublists.

```
[[place b1 on table]                 ACTION—IMPLEMENTED
[[holding b1]]                       PRECONDITIONS
[[ontable b1] [emptyhand]]]          ADDITIONS
[[holding b1]]                       DELETIONS
```

Figure 7-2 A STRIPS-like operator

Strategies for microworld search

Let us consider some arbitrary state S. In general, it will be possible to apply many actions to S; so S is likely to have a large number of successor states. Conversely, there may be only a small number of ways of producing S using a single action; so S is likely to have a relatively small number of predecessors. What this means is that the branching factor of the space for forwards search will be much higher than the branching factor of the space for backwards search. Thus, backwards search is likely to do less work in discovering a path connecting two arbitrary states.

This seems to suggest that backwards search is the best strategy in the case where nodes correspond to microworld states. But there is a problem. If the successor function is implemented using operators then predecessor states are not defined! An operator just says that a state which has certain features can be transformed into a successor state by adding and deleting components. It does not say exactly what the original state *is*.

In fact, the problem is even worse than this. In general, where microworld descriptions are used, a goal node will just be any state which has certain features. But in the case where goal nodes are not fully defined, the search space for a backwards function has no root. This means that backwards search cannot be applied directly due to the fact that it has no well-defined starting position.[1]

Fortunately, there is quite a simple way of getting around this problem. We implement a form of backwards search which starts out with the set of features (preconditions) which are required in a goal state. The first thing the function does is check whether the current microworld representation has all the desired features. If it does, then the search is terminated. If it does not then the function finds out which operators would serve to *achievel* the desired preconditions. The process then begins again only this time these newly desired preconditions are the preconditions of the operators rather than the preconditions of the original goal state.

[1] For the same reason, ordinary backwards-chaining search cannot be applied to the water jugs problem.

In a sense, this strategy is a cheat. In the absence of fully defined predecessor states, sets of preconditions are forced to play the role of "partial state descriptions". However, it turns out to work rather well, as we will see.

A very important point to note is the fact that, in the new strategy, the structure of the search tree is an AND/OR tree. Given some set of N preconditions which the search function wants to achieve, there will, in the simplest case, be a set of N operators each one of which will achieve one of the preconditions. Each of these operators will itself have some preconditions which will need achieving.

If we visualise the search tree which is explored by the function, we see that some nodes correspond to specific preconditions. It will be possible to satisfy an arbitrary precondition in a number of alternative ways (corresponding to the operators which have the effect of adding the desired feature) and these alternatives constitute the successors of the node in the usual fashion. In effect, the precondition node can be achieved provided that any of the successor nodes can be achieved.

But each of these successor nodes corresponds to an operator; and any operator has a set of preconditions all of which must be satisfied before the corresponding action can be applied. The preconditions constitute the successors of the operator node, but whereas in the usual case, they are disjoint (i.e. they represent alternatives) here they are conjoint. Thus, the operator node can only be achieved if *all* the successor nodes can be achieved.

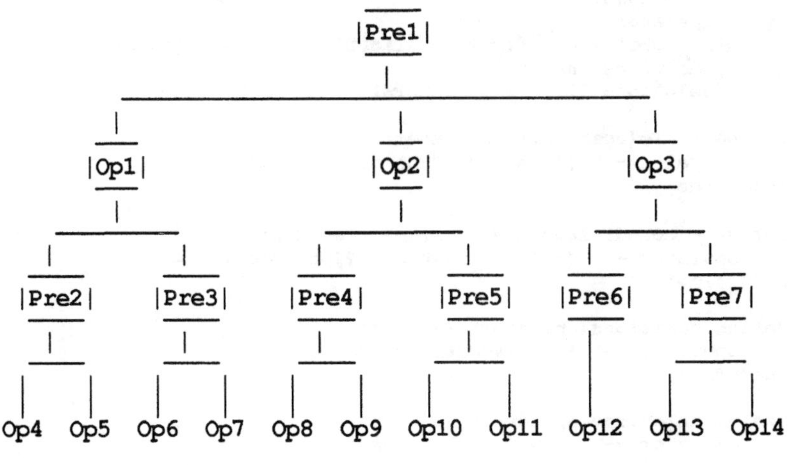

Figure 7-3 An AND/OR tree of operators

```
[[   [operator stand_back]
     [preconditions [near box]]
     [additions [safe]]
     [deletions [near box]]]
 [   [operator go_forward]
     [preconditions [safe]]
     [additions [near box]]
     [deletions [safe]]]
 [   [operator light_firework_safely]
     [preconditions [near box][box open][have fire][firework out]]
     [additions [firework alight]]
     [deletions [firework out]]]
 [   [operator open_box]
     [preconditions [near box][box closed]]
     [additions [box open]]
     [deletions [box closed]]]
 [   [operator close_box]
     [preconditions [near box][box open]]
     [additions [box closed]]
     [deletions [box open]]]
 [   [operator use_lighter]
     [preconditions [have lighter]]
     [additions [have fire]]
     [deletions]]
 [   [operator strike_match]
     [preconditions [have matches]]
     [additions [have fire]]
     [deletions]]
 [   [operator enjoy_firework]
     [preconditions [firework alight][box closed][safe]]
     [additions [happy]]
     [deletions ]] ] -> operators1;

define title(operator) -> header;
    operator --> [[operator ??header] = = =]
enddefine;

define preconditions(operator) -> preconds;
    operator --> [= [preconditions ??preconds] = =]
enddefine;

define additions(operator) -> adds;
    operator --> [= = [additions ??adds] =]
enddefine;

define deletions(operator) -> dels;
    operator --> [= = = [deletions ??dels]]
enddefine;
```

Figure 7-4 Firework operators

Search spaces consisting of nodes which can have either conjoint or disjoint successors are called *AND/OR-trees* as we saw in the previous chapter. Nodes which have conjoint successors are the *AND-nodes* or *AND-branches*. Nodes which have disjoint successors are the *OR-nodes* or *OR-branches*. In the simplest case, an AND/OR-tree consists of alternate layers of AND-nodes and OR-nodes. A very simple example of this organisation occurs when nodes correspond to microworld operators and preconditions, provided that any operator has a set of preconditions each of which can be satisfied by a unique operator. This situation is depicted in Figure 7-3, where nodes corresponding to preconditions have labels prefixed with "Pre" and nodes corresponding to operators have nodes prefixed with "Op".

Implementing the new search function

To clarify the way in which the new search strategy works we will look at the way it can be used to solve a specific microworld search problem. The problem we will focus on is a simple planning problem about lighting fireworks. This involves discovering a sequence of actions which will enable the the firework lighter to be happy and safe.

The most convenient approach involves creating a rulebase of STRIPS-like operators. The list shown in Figure 7-4 contains eight operators together with functions to extract the various components of an operator. Given this list of operators we can implement the backwards-chaining search process in terms of two functions: an **achieve1** function which attempts to achieve an arbitrary set of preconditions (given a microworld) and returns the list of operators used, together with the final version of the microworld; and a **find_plan** function which calls **achieve1** giving it the initial state of the world, an arbitrary depth limit and the features making up the goal description. **achieve1** is yet another variant of **backwards_search**. We have adapted the loop checking version of **backwards_search** from the previous chapter which maintains a depth limit. These two functions are shown in Figure 7-5, as well as a function for printing comments on what achieve is doing at different stages. Note that here we are using the database to store the microworld representation rather than the operator lists which implement the successor function.

Function **achieve1** is an adaptation of the version of **backwards_search** from the previous chapter which checked for loops. Points of difference include:

(i) **backwards_search** merely added successfully proved goals to the database, whereas **achieve1** both adds the "additions" and removes the "deletions".

(ii) **achieve1** has **initial_state** as an argument and **database** as a local output variable. These two variables hold the initial and final states of world. Given that an operator may delete some part of the state and yet later find it not to be needed for the eventual plan, we need to be able to reset the world state to its

```
/* achieve1 takes a list of goals, a database and a depth limit and returns
   a plan consisting of a list of operator titles and the resultant database. */

define achieve1(goals, initial_state, depth) -> plan -> database;
    vars goal operator other_goals sub_plan rest_plan;
    initial_state -> database;
    if goals = [] then [] -> plan;
    elseif depth <= 0 then false -> plan;
    else chatty_print([attempting ^goals]);
        goals --> [?goal ??other_goals];
        if present(goal)
        then chatty_print([^goal is already true]);
            achieve1(other_goals, initial_state, depth)
                -> plan -> database;
        else
            for operator in operators do
                if member(goal, additions(operator))
                then chatty_print([trying ^(title(operator))]);
                    achieve1(preconditions(operator), initial_state,
                        depth-1) -> sub_plan -> database;
                    if islist(sub_plan)
                    then allremove(deletions(operator));
                        alladd(additions(operator));
                        chatty_print([state now is ^^database]);
                        achieve1(other_goals, database, depth)
                            -> rest_plan -> database;
                        if islist(rest_plan)
                        then
                          [^^sub_plan ^(title(operator)) ^^rest_plan]
                                -> plan; quitloop
                        else chatty_print([backtracking]);
                        endif
                    else chatty_print([backtracking]);
                    endif;
                endif
            endfor
        endif;
        unless allpresent(goals) then
            false -> plan; initial_state -> database
        endunless
    endif
enddefine;

/* find_plan takes an initial state and a list of goals and returns a plan
   or false.  It sets an arbitrary depth limit of 10 on achieve1. */

define find_plan(initial_state, goals) -> plan;
    vars final_state;
    achieve(goals, initial_state, 10) -> plan -> final_state;
enddefine;
```

Figure 7-5 Planning as backwards search with operators

value before that operator was tried, hence the use of these two variables.

(iii) **achieve1** cycles through all the applicable operators, rather than through the subgoal lists, though the subgoal list of a rule from the previous chapter is roughly equivalent to the add list of an operator.

iv) Given the possibility that achieving later goals may undo goals already achieved (because of deletions), **achieve1** checks that *all* goals are present in the database and returns **false** as the value of the plan and resets the original database if *any* are not present.

v) We have added several calls to **chatty_print**, see Figure 7-6. These are used to print out what **achieve1** is doing at various points, so long as the global variable **chatty** is set to **true**.

vi) The main output of **achieve1** is a flat list representing a plan rather than either a boolean value as in **backwards_search** or an AND tree as in **backwards_search_tree**.

We have set an arbitrary depth limit of 10 inside **find_plan**; as in the previous chapter, this arbitrary limit could be avoided by applying iterative deepening. This limit does not affect the number of goals we try to achieve, but limits the number of operators that can be linked through their preconditions to achieve any single one of these goals.

The behaviour of **achieve1** can be summarised as follows. The function looks at the first goal in its list. If it is already present in the initial world state, the function calls itself recursively to deal with the remaining goals. If the goal is not present, the function scans the list of operators looking for one which has the desired feature in its list of "additions". A recursive call on **achieve1** is then made with the input being the preconditions of the operator. The result of this call is just the list of operators (i.e. a sub-plan) which was used to achieve the preconditions so this is simply merged into the main plan list. Next, the "additions" of the operator are added to the current state description and its "deletions" are deleted. The function then continues scanning the list of original goals (via a second recursive call as in **backwards_search**).

```
/* chatty_print prints its argument if chatty is true */

define chatty_print(comment);
    if chatty then comment ==> endif
enddefine;
```

Figure 7-6 Chatty print

We can get this search function to discover a sequence of actions which achieve [firework alight] and [box closed] given the initial microworld description [[have lighter] [safe] [firework out] [box closed]] as follows:

```
true -> chatty;
operators1 -> operators;
achieve1 -> achieve;

find_plan([[have lighter] [safe] [firework out] [box closed]],
        [[firework alight][box closed]]) ==>

** [attempting [[firework alight] [box closed]]]
** [trying [light_firework_safely]]
** [attempting [[near box] [box open] [have fire] [firework out]]]
** [trying [go_forward]]
** [attempting [[safe]]]
** [[safe] is already true]
** [state now is [near box] [have lighter] [firework out]
                                                        [box closed]]
** [attempting [[box open] [have fire] [firework out]]]
** [trying [open_box]]
** [attempting [[near box] [box closed]]]
** [[near box] is already true]
** [attempting [[box closed]]]
** [[box closed] is already true]
** [state now is [box open] [near box] [have lighter]
                                                    [firework out]]
** [attempting [[have fire] [firework out]]]
** [trying [use_lighter]]
** [attempting [[have lighter]]]
** [[have lighter] is already true]
** [state now is
        [have fire]
        [box open]
        [near box]
        [have lighter]
        [firework out]]
** [attempting [[firework out]]]
** [[firework out] is already true]
** [state now is
        [firework alight]
        [have fire]
        [box open]
```

```
            [near box]
            [have lighter]]
** [attempting [[box closed]]]
** [trying [close_box]]
** [attempting [[near box] [box open]]]
** [[near box] is already true]
** [attempting [[box open]]]
** [[box open] is already true]
** [state now is
            [box closed]
            [firework alight]
            [have fire]
            [near box]
            [have lighter]]

** [[go_forward]
    [open_box]
    [use_lighter]
    [light_firework_safely]
    [close_box]]
```

The above plan was found without any backtracking, as every operator first tried turned out to be the correct one to use. This will not always be the case:

```
find_plan([[have matches] [safe] [firework out] [box closed]],
                  [[firework alight][box closed]]) ==>

** [attempting [[firework alight] [box closed]]]
** [trying [light_firework_safely]]
** [attempting [[near box] [box open] [have fire] [firework out]]]
** [trying [go_forward]]
** [attempting [[safe]]]
** [[safe] is already true]
** [state now is [near box] [have matches] [firework out]
                                                   [box closed]]
** [attempting [[box open] [have fire] [firework out]]]
** [trying [open_box]]
** [attempting [[near box] [box closed]]]
** [[near box] is already true]
** [attempting [[box closed]]]
** [[box closed] is already true]
** [state now is [box open] [near box] [have matches]
                                                [firework out]]
```

```
** [attempting [[have fire] [firework out]]]
** [trying [use_lighter]]
** [attempting [[have lighter]]] /* BACKTRACKING HERE */
** [backtracking]                /* AS NO LIGHTER */
** [trying [strike_match]]
** [attempting [[have matches]]]
** [[have matches] is already true]
** [state now is
        [have fire]
        [box open]
        [near box]
        [have matches]
        [firework out]]
** [attempting [[firework out]]]
** [[firework out] is already true]
** [state now is
        [firework alight]
        [have fire]
        [box open]
        [near box]
        [have matches]]
** [attempting [[box closed]]]
** [trying [close_box]]
** [attempting [[near box] [box open]]]
** [[near box] is already true]
** [attempting [[box open]]]
** [[box open] is already true]
** [state now is
        [box closed]
        [firework alight]
        [have fire]
        [near box]
        [have matches]]

** [[go_forward]
   [open_box]
   [strike_match]
   [light_firework_safely]
   [close_box]]
```

Difference tables

The search strategy introduced above forms the main component in a process known as **Means-Ends Analysis** (MEA). This process was used in the **General Problem Solver** program of Newell and Simon (1963). However, our implementation does not do "proper" means-ends analysis; it just does an approximation of it. In real means-ends analysis the process of achieving a set of preconditions P does not necessarily involve finding operators which collectively achieve each element of P. It involves finding operators which reduce the "difference" between the current state and the state which exhibits all of P.

In many circumstances, reducing the difference between an existing state and a desired state may simply involve the process which we have implemented, i.e. finding some set of operators which achieve all the missing preconditions (and then achieving their preconditions, etc.). However, in general, a **difference table** may be used which shows the extent to which any operator reduces the difference between the existing state and the desired state. Obviously, the process we have implemented is just a special case of means-ends analysis; namely, the case where operators reduce the difference between a state subsuming P and a state not subsuming P by just adding all of P (cf. Rich, 1983, pp. 99-102.)

Goal interactions

The variant of backward search which we have introduced above detects whether later actions in a plan undo earlier goals but cannot repair the plan. At any one stage, the search process we have implemented tries to find out how to achieve certain effects in the microworld. If it finds an operator which has the desired effects it just "applies" it (i.e. performs the specified deletions and additions). But it may well be that the application of the operator has an affect on *another* goal we are trying to achieve.

We can demonstrate one aspect of this effect in our firework example as follows:

```
find_plan([[safe][box closed]],[[safe][box open]]) ==>

** [attempting [[safe] [box open]]]
** [[safe] is already true]
** [attempting [[box open]]]
** [trying [open_box]]
** [attempting [[near box] [box closed]]]
** [trying [go_forward]]
** [attempting [[safe]]]
** [[safe] is already true]
```

```
** [state now is [near box] [box closed]]
** [attempting [[box closed]]]
** [[box closed] is already true]
** [state now is [box open] [near box]]

** <false>
```

Getting the box open interfered with being safe so no plan could be found. Just to show the fragility of these kinds of planner, the following *does* work:

```
find_plan([[safe][box closed]],[[box open][safe]]) ==>

** [attempting [[box open] [safe]]]
** [trying [open_box]]
** [attempting [[near box] [box closed]]]
** [trying [go_forward]]
** [attempting [[safe]]]
** [[safe] is already true]
** [state now is [near box] [box closed]]
** [attempting [[box closed]]]
** [[box closed] is already true]
** [state now is [box open] [near box]]
** [attempting [[safe]]]
** [trying [stand_back]]
** [attempting [[near box]]]
** [[near box] is already true]
** [state now is [safe] [box open]]

** [[go_forward] [open_box] [stand_back]]
```

The classic case of interference between goals occurs where we have a blocksworld planning mechanism whose operators show that to construct a tower out of two blocks it has to put one on top of the other. If we give it a microworld state in which there are three blocks b1, b2 and b3, and ask it to achieve the state [[b1 on b2][b2 on b3]] it is quite likely to fail. The typical behaviour is as follows.

First of all the search mechanism tries to achieve [b1 on b2]. It checks that b1 has a "cleartop" and then applies a "put" operator to put b1 on b2. It then turns to the second feature which needs to be achieved: [b2 on b3]. To achieve this it first checks that b2 has a cleartop. It discovers that b2 does *not* have a cleartop so sets about achieving this. This involves taking b1 off b2 which effectively undoes the achievement of the first feature in the goal description.

This is a rather contrived scenario but the problem that it characterises is very pervasive. It is simply the fact that, in general, the achieving of any given feature via the application of an operator may have side-effects either on features which have already been achieved, or on features which will need to be achieved in the future. The problem is called the *frame problem* and at the present time it has no totally effective solution in its general form.

We can partially get round the problem of goal interactions as follows. When the existing version of **achieve1** detects that not all the original goals are achieved it simply returns false. In the new version of the function, see Figure 7-7, **achieve2** calls itself recursively at the point where it finds that not all goals have been achieved. At this point many of the goals will have been achieved and it may be possible simply to *extend* the otherwise unacceptable plan with a few extra actions that *repair* the plan. This is similar to STRIPS placing individual goals as well as conjunctions of goals on its stack.

Let us try this on the earlier example which failed:

```
achieve2 -> achieve;

find_plan([[safe][box closed]],[[safe][box open]]) ==>

** [attempting [[safe] [box open]]]
** [[safe] is already true]
** [attempting [[box open]]]
** [trying [open_box]]
** [attempting [[near box] [box closed]]]
** [trying [go_forward]]
** [attempting [[safe]]]
** [[safe] is already true]
** [state now is [near box] [box closed]]
** [attempting [[box closed]]]
** [[box closed] is already true]
** [state now is [box open] [near box]]    /* FAILURE STATE */
** [repair plan [[go_forward] [open_box]]
   for goals [[safe] [box open]]]
** [attempting [[safe] [box open]]]
** [trying [stand_back]]
** [attempting [[near box]]]
** [[near box] is already true]
** [state now is [safe] [box open]]
** [attempting [[box open]]]
** [[box open] is already true]
** [[go_forward] [open_box] [stand_back]]
```

The one that succeeded, still succeeds, without need of repair:

```
/* achieve2 takes a list of goals as input and returns a plan consisting of
   a list of operator titles. If the initial plan does not achieve all the
   goals, because of an interaction, a repair is added onto the end of the plan. */

define achieve2(goals, initial_state, depth) -> plan -> database;
    vars goal operator other_goals sub_plan rest_plan repair;
    initial_state -> database;
    if goals = [] then [] -> plan;
    elseif depth <= 0 then false -> plan;
    else chatty_print([attempting ^goals]);
        goals --> [?goal ??other_goals];
        if present(goal)
        then chatty_print([^goal is already true]);
            achieve2(other_goals, initial_state, depth)
                -> plan -> database;
        else
            for operator in operators do
                if member(goal, additions(operator))
                then chatty_print([trying ^(title(operator))]);
                    achieve2(preconditions(operator), initial_state,
                        depth-1) -> sub_plan -> database;
                    if islist(sub_plan)
                    then allremove(deletions(operator));
                        alladd(additions(operator));
                        chatty_print([state now is ^^database]);
                        achieve2(other_goals, database, depth)
                            -> rest_plan -> database;
                        if islist(rest_plan)
                        then
                          [^^sub_plan ^(title(operator)) ^^rest_plan]
                                -> plan;
                            quitloop
                        else chatty_print([backtracking]);
                        endif
                    else chatty_print([backtracking]);
                    endif;
                endif
            endfor
        endif;
        unless allpresent(goals) then
            chatty_print([repair plan ^plan for goals ^goals]);
            achieve2(goals, database, depth-1) -> repair -> database;
            if allpresent(goals)
            then plan <> repair -> plan
            else false -> plan;
                initial_state -> database;
            endif
        endunless
    endif
enddefine;
```

Figure 7-7 Constructing a plan involving goal interactions

```
find_plan([[safe] [box closed]],[[box open] [safe]]) ==>

** [attempting [[box open] [safe]]]
```

```
** [trying [open_box]]
** [attempting [[near box] [box closed]]]
** [trying [go_forward]]
** [attempting [[safe]]]
** [[safe] is already true]
** [state now is [near box] [box closed]]
** [attempting [[box closed]]]
** [[box closed] is already true]
** [state now is [box open] [near box]]
** [attempting [[safe]]]
** [trying [stand_back]]
** [attempting [[near box]]]
** [[near box] is already true]
** [state now is [safe] [box open]]
** [[go_forward] [open_box] [stand_back]]
```

Operators containing variables

One of the shortcomings of the approach we have outlined so far is that the operators do not contain variables. If we wanted to plan in a blocksworld it would be much better to have an operator for stacking (say) *any* block, rather than having identical operators for stacking block A, block B and so on. One possible set of such operators might be a follows, see Figure 7-8. We can read the last operator as saying that to unstack a block from another, the block must be on the other, the block must be clear and the robot hand must be empty.

However if we try to run our existing plan generating program we get nowhere because selecting a possible operator via a call to **member** will not work. The reason is that the various parts of the operator now contain variables and so the matching is more complex. Also when working backward through the preconditions, adding the additions and deleting the deletions we will have to ensure that we work with "instantiated" versions of these operator parts (i.e. ?x should be "b1" or whatever). The starting state in the following interaction is intended as a representation of the situation in Figure 7-3:

```
operators2 -> operators;
false -> chatty;
untrace achieve;

find_plan([[clear b2][clear b3][on b2 b1][on_table b1]
           [on_table b3][empty hand]], [[on_table b2]]) ==>

** <false>
```

```
[
 [   [operator pick up ?x]
     [preconditions [on_table ?x][clear ?x][empty hand]]
     [additions [holding ?x]]
     [deletions [on_table ?x][clear ?x][empty hand]]]

 [   [operator put down ?x]
     [preconditions [holding ?x]]
     [additions [on_table ?x][clear ?x][empty hand]]
     [deletions [holding ?x]]]

 [   [operator stack ?x on ?y]
     [preconditions [holding ?x][clear ?y]]
     [additions [on ?x ?y][clear ?x][empty hand]]
     [deletions [holding ?x][clear ?y]]]

 [   [operator unstack ?x from ?y]
     [preconditions [on ?x ?y][clear ?x][empty hand]]
     [additions [holding ?x][clear ?y]]
     [deletions [on ?x ?y][clear ?x][empty hand]]]

] -> operators2;
```

Figure 7-8 Blocksworld operators

The depth limit prevents **achieve2** recursing indefinitely in its attempt to repair the failed plan. Ideally we should now *match* the goal against the patterns in each operator's addition list and then set about trying to achieve the preconditions, having first substituted appropriate values for variables in the preconditions. This is straightforward for any variables that get their values via matching the goal, but more problematic for variables occurring in other parts of the additions list. For example, consider matching the goal `[clear b2]` againts the additions list of the operator `[stack ?x on ?y]`. What should be the value of `?y`?

Realistic planning systems undertake reasoning about variable values as part of the search process, via a mechanism called *goal regression*. We can get round this problem in a slightly unprincipled way by arranging to expand the list of operators containing variables into a list of operators mentioning specific block names. In other words we will sidestep the issue by expanding the list of operators containing variables into the much longer list of all possible operators for every variable value. Where the number of values is not too great, this is feasible at some cost in search effort in making the plan. The advantage is that we can use **find_plan** without any change.

There is a built-in function in POP-11 named **instance** which takes a pattern and returns a list with every match variable replaced by its current value:

```
vars x y;
23 -> x;
"fred" -> y;
instance([is ?y really only ?x years old]) ==>
** [is fred really only 23 years old]
```

Figure 7-9 gives a definition of **instantiate** which takes a list of operators containing variables and a list of block names and returns a complete list of operators mentioning specific block names. It calls **remove_dups** in order to remove any duplicated operators generated in the process:

```
/* instantiate takes a list of operators and a list of block names
   and returns a complete list of specific operators. It assumes that
   the variables used in the operators are x and y. */

define instantiate(operators, blocks) -> new_operators;
    vars x y;
    [^( for operator in operators do
            for x in blocks do
                for y in blocks do
                    unless x = y then instance(operator) endunless
                endfor
            endfor
        endfor)] -> new_operators;
    remove_dups(new_operators) -> new_operators;
enddefine;

/* remove_dups takes a list and returns a copy of the list omitting
   duplications. */

define remove_dups(inlist) -> outlist;
    if inlist = [] then [] -> outlist
    elseif member(hd(inlist), tl(inlist))
    then remove_dups(tl(inlist)) -> outlist
    else hd(inlist) :: remove_dups(tl(inlist)) -> outlist
    endif
enddefine;
```

Figure 7-9 Instantiating operators

```
[[put ?x on ?y][take ?x off ?y][burn ?x]] -> operators3;

instantiate(operators3, [small medium large]) ==>

** [[put small on medium]
    [put small on large]
    [put medium on small]
    [put medium on large]
    [put large on small]
    [put large on medium]
    [take small off medium]
    [take small off large]
    [take medium off small]
    [take medium off large]
    [take large off small]
    [take large off medium]
    [burn small]
    [burn medium]
    [burn large]]
```

We can try out the existing version of **find_plan** having first instantiated the block operators using the names **b1**, **b2** and **b3**. The initial state corresponds to the picture of blocks on a table at the start of this chapter. The goal is simply to get b2 on the table when it is initially stacked on top of b1 which is on the table:

```
false -> chatty;

instantiate(operators2, [b1 b2 b3]) -> operators;

find_plan([[clear b2][clear b3][on b2 b1][on_table b1]
           [on_table b3][empty hand]], [[on_table b2]]) ==>

** [[unstack b2 from b1]
    [put down b2]
    [pick up b2]
    [put down b2]
    [pick up b2]
    [put down b2]
    [pick up b2]
    [put down b2]]

find_plan([[clear b2][clear b3][on b2 b1][on_table b1]
           [on_table b3][empty hand]], [[on b1 b3][on b2 b1]]) ==>
```

```
** [[unstack b2 from b1]
    [put down b2]
    [pick up b1]
    [put down b1]
    [pick up b1]
    [put down b1]
    [pick up b1]
    [put down b1]
    [pick up b1]
    [stack b1 on b3]
    [pick up b2]
    [stack b2 on b1]]
```

Both these plans work but are non-optimal. The reason is that our loop checking mechanism is crude; it merely limits how deep any single chain of operators may be. Because it is searching depth-first, we get the first solution found (not the shortest) and this will tend to be a solution just within the depth bound, as we saw in the previous chapter when recursive rules were searched by **backwards_search**.

Inverting the order of the goals, the first of which is already true in the initial state, causes no problem though does not improve the quality of the solution:

```
find_plan([[clear b2][clear b3][on b2 b1][on_table b1]
          [on_table b3][empty hand]],[[on b2 b1][on b1 b3]]) ==>

** [[unstack b2 from b1]
    [put down b2]
    [pick up b1]
    [put down b1]
    [pick up b1]
    [put down b1]
    [pick up b1]
    [put down b1]
    [pick up b1]
    [stack b1 on b3]
    [pick up b2]
    [stack b2 on b1]]
```

By reducing the depth bound in `find_plan`, better solutions can be found. Thus if we reduce it to 4 we get the following:

```
find_plan([[clear b2][clear b3][on b2 b1][on_table b1]
          [on_table b3][empty hand]],[[on b2 b1][on b1 b3]]) ==>
```

```
/* operator(-[[operator, Operator_Name]
              [preconditions, Preconditions]
              [additions, Additions]
              [deletions, Deletions]]).    */

operator([[operator, stand_back],
          [preconditions, near_box],
          [additions, safe],
          [deletions, near_box]]).

operator([[operator, go_forward],
          [preconditions, safe],
          [additions, near_box],
          [deletions, safe]]).

operator([[operator, light_firework_safely],
          [preconditions, near_box, box_open, have_fire, firework_out],
          [additions, firework_alight],
          [deletions, firework_out]]).

operator([[operator, open_box],
          [preconditions, near_box, box_closed],
          [additions, box_open],
          [deletions, box_closed]]).

operator([[operator, close_box],
          [preconditions, near_box, box_open],
          [additions, box_closed],
          [deletions, box_open]]).

operator([[operator, use_lighter],
          [preconditions, have_lighter],
          [additions, have_fire],
          [deletions]]).

operator([[operator, strike_match],
          [preconditions, have_matches],
          [additions, have_fire],
          [deletions]]).

operator([[operator, enjoy_firework],
          [preconditions, firework_alight, box_closed, safe],
          [additions, happy],
          [deletions]]).
```

Figure 7-10 Firework operators in Prolog

```
/* achieve1(+Goals, +Initial_state, +Depth, -Plan, -Final_state)
   achieve1 takes a list of Goals and an Initial state of the world and a
   Depth and succeeds with a Plan and a Final state of the world. */

achieve1([], Initial, _, [], Final) :-
    Initial = Final.

achieve1([Goal | Goals], Initial, Depth, Plan, Final) :-
    Depth > 0,
    member(Goal, Initial), !,
    achieve1(Goals, Initial, Depth, Plan, Final),
    allpresent([Goal | Goals], Final).

achieve1([Goal | Goals], Initial, Depth, Plan, Final) :-
    Depth > 0,
    operator([[operator | Operator],
              [preconditions | Preconds],
              [additions | Adds],
              [deletions | Dels]]),
    member(Goal, Adds),
    New_depth is Depth - 1,
    achieve1(Preconds, Initial, New_depth, Pre_plan, Intermediate1),
    append(Pre_plan, Operator, Sub_plan),
    allremove(Dels, Intermediate1, Intermediate2),
    append(Adds, Intermediate2, Intermediate3),
    achieve1(Goals, Intermediate3, Depth, Plans, Final),
    allpresent([Goal | Goals], Final),
    append(Sub_plan, Plans, Plan).

/* find_plan(+Starting State, +Goal State, -Resultant Plan) */
   find_plan succeeds if achieve1 succeeds with a depth limit of 10 */

find_plan(Start_state, Goals, Plan) :-
    achieve1(Goals, Start_state, 10, Plan, _).
```

Figure 7-11 Simple planning in Prolog

```
** [[unstack b2 from b1]
    [put down b2]
    [pick up b1]
    [stack b1 on b3]
    [pick up b2]
    [stack b2 on b1]]
```

There are several solutions to the above issue. One is to employ iterative deepening.

Another is to keep track of goals that have already been achieved and not make use of an operator that would remove any of them via its deletions list.

Simple plan finding in Prolog

The Prolog equivalents of **achieve1** and **find_plan** are given below. The role of the POP-11 Database is played by two variables in the predicate **achieve1**. One holds the initial state of the world before the attempt to achieve some goals, the other holds the (usually changed) final state of the world after those goals have been achieved. We shall adapt the depth-bounded **backwards_search_tree/3** procedure from the previous chapter.

The "firework" operators are stored as individual clauses with the same meanings as the POP-11 versions, see Figure 7-10.

We have implemented a version of **achieve1/5** that checks for loops in just the same way as the POP-11 version, i.e. by making sure that the value of depth is always positive, see Figure 7-11. The main predicate is **achieve1/5** which deals with three cases. In the first, there are no goals to be achieved so it terminates with an empty plan and with whatever world it was given handed on unchanged. The second clause deals with the case where the goal to be achieved is already true in the given world. In that case **achieve1/5** calls itself recursively to deal with any remaining goals and hands on the resultant plan and resultant world that arise from them.

The final case does the real work. An operator is selected which has the first goal of **achieve1/5** amongst its additions list. **achieve** calls itself recursively to deal with the preconditions of this selected operator. The additions and deletions are added and removed from the given world to produce a resultant world. Finally the remaining goals are dealt with recursively and the resultant plan put together. A check is made to ensure that all the original goals are true in the resultant world. Note that we can make use of the built-in Prolog backtracking to ensure that operators are tried in sequence until one is found that is successful. Figure 7-12 shows definitions for Prolog equivalents of the built in procedures **allremove** and **allpresent**.

Here are two examples, the first is the same as the POP-11 example given earlier:

```
?- find_plan([have_matches, safe, firework_out, box_closed],
             [firework_alight, box_closed], Plan).
Plan = [go_forward, open_box, strike_match,
        light_firework_safely, close_box] ?
yes

?- find_plan([have_matches, safe, firework_out, box_closed],
             [happy, safe], Plan).
```

```
/* allremove(+Items to be Removed, +From this List, -Resultant List)
   allremove removes each item in its first list from its second list
   to give its third list. */

allremove([], World, World).
allremove([Item | Items], World, Result_World) :-
   remove(Item, World, New_World),
   allremove(Items, New_World, Result_World).

/* remove(+an Item, +From this List, -Resultant List)
   remove removes only the first instance of the Item,
   and fails if there is no instance to remove. */

remove(Item, [Item | Rest], Rest).
remove(Item, [First | Rest], [First | New_Rest]) :-
   remove(Item, Rest, New_Rest).

/* allpresent(+Given Items, +List which should contain given Items)
   allpresent succeeds if it can remove each one of the given items. */

allpresent(Items, List) :-
   allremove(Items, List, _).
```

Figure 7-12 State manipulating procedures for the planner

```
Plan = [go_forward, open_box, strike_match,
        light_firework_safely, close_box, stand_back,
        enjoy_firework] ?
yes
```

The blocks world was altogether more demanding of the POP-11 planner, so we shall try this out as well. As before, we face the issue of correctly instantiating the variables mentioned in the operators, see Figure 7-13.

We can rely on Prolog unification to ensure that the variables in these operators with the following problems get bound to sensible values without having to instantiate the operators themselves as we did in POP-11.

Running **find_plan** on the same problems as before gives, in the first case, a non-optimal solution. Remember that the basic search method is depth first with a depth limit of 10, so long solutions will often be derived first:

```
?- find_plan([[clear, b2],[clear, b3],[on, b2, b1],
              [on_table, b1], [on_table, b3],[empty_hand]],
```

```
                [[on, b1, b3],[on, b2, b1]], Plan).

Plan = [[unstack, b2, from, b1], [put_down, b2], [pick_up, b1],
        [put_down, b1], [pick_up, b1], [put_down, b1],
        [pick_up, b1], [put_down, b1], [pick_up, b1],
        [stack, b1, on, b3], [pick_up, b2],
        [stack, b2, on, b1]] ?
yes
```

Reducing the depth limit to 5 (e.g. via a new definition of **find_plan/3**) gives the optimal solution:

```
Plan = [[unstack, b2, from, b1], [put_down, b2], [pick_up, b1],
        [stack, b1, on, b3], [pick_up, b2], [stack, b2, on, b1]]
```

```
/* operator(-[[operator, Operator_Name]
           [preconditions, Preconditions]
           [additions, Additions]
           [deletions, Deletions]]).   */

operator([[operator, [pick_up, X]],
          [preconditions, [on_table, X],[clear, X],[empty_hand]],
          [additions, [holding, X]],
          [deletions, [on_table, X],[clear, X],[empty_hand]]]).

operator([[operator, [put_down, X]],
          [preconditions, [holding, X]],
          [additions, [on_table, X],[clear, X],[empty_hand]],
          [deletions, [holding, X]]]).

operator([[operator, [stack, X, on, Y]],
          [preconditions, [holding, X],[clear, Y]],
          [additions, [on, X, Y],[clear, X],[empty_hand]],
          [deletions, [holding, X],[clear, Y]]]).

operator([[operator, [unstack, X, from, Y]],
          [preconditions, [on, X, Y],[clear, X],[empty_hand]],
          [additions, [holding, X],[clear, Y]],
          [deletions, [on, X, Y],[clear, X],[empty_hand]]]).
```

Figure 7-13 Blocksworld operators in Prolog

However, inverting the order of the goals, causes *no* plan to be found because of the goal interactions. **achieve1/5** is able to detect that not all the goals have been achieved but cannot repair the interaction. Even with a depth limit of 10 the answer is **no**:

```
?- find_plan([[clear, b2],[clear, b3],[on, b2, b1],
              [on_table, b1], [on_table, b3],[empty_hand]],
             [[on, b2, b1],[on, b1, b3]], Plan).

no
```

We adopt the same partial solution to goal interactions as we did in POP-11. Once a plan has been found it is checked to ensure that all the goals are still true in the final state of the world. If so, the plan is adopted as the final plan. If not, **achieve2/5** calls itself recursively to attempt to repair the failed plan by adding new actions onto its end which will re-achieve the goals that have been knocked out by the interaction, see Figure 7-14.

To improve the quality of the solutions, we have reduced the depth limit to 5. The earlier problem without goal interactions works as before:

```
?- find_plan2([[clear, b2],[clear, b3],[on, b2, b1],
               [on_table, b1], [on_table, b3],[empty_hand]],
              [[on, b1, b3],[on, b2, b1]], Plan).

Plan = [[unstack, b2, from, b1], [put_down, b2], [pick_up, b1],
        [stack, b1, on, b3], [pick_up, b2], [stack, b2, on, b1]]
       ?
yes
```

But the problem with goal interactions now also succeeds:

```
?- find_plan2([[clear, b2],[clear, b3],[on, b2, b1],
               [on_table, b1], [on_table, b3],[empty_hand]],
              [[on, b2, b1],[on, b1, b3]], Plan).

Plan = [[unstack, b2, from, b1], [put_down, b2], [pick_up, b1],
        [stack, b1, on, b3], [pick_up, b2], [stack, b2, on, b1]]
       ?
yes
```

```
/* achieve2(+Goals, +Initial_state, +Depth, -Plan, -Final_state)
   achieve2 takes a list of Goals and an Initial state of the world
   and a Depth and succeeds with a Plan and a Final state of the world. */

achieve2([], Initial, _, [], Final) :-
    Initial = Final.

achieve2([Goal | Goals], Initial, Depth, Plan, Final) :-
    Depth > 0,
    member(Goal, Initial), !,
    achieve2(Goals, Initial, Depth, Plan1, Final1),
  ( allpresent([Goal | Goals], Final1), !,
    Final = Final1,
    Plan = Plan1
  ; New_depth is Depth -1,
    achieve2([Goal | Goals], Final1, New_depth, Plan2, Final2),
    append(Plan1, Plan2, Plan),
    Final = Final2 ).

achieve2([Goal | Goals], Initial, Depth, Plan, Final) :-
    Depth > 0,
    operator([[operator | Operator],
              [preconditions | Preconds],
              [additions | Adds],
              [deletions | Dels]]),
    member(Goal, Adds),
    New_depth is Depth - 1,
    achieve2(Preconds, Initial, New_depth, Pre_plan, Intermediate1),
    append(Pre_plan, Operator, Sub_plan),
    allremove(Dels, Intermediate1, Intermediate2),
    append(Adds, Intermediate2, Intermediate3),
    achieve2(Goals, Intermediate3, Depth, Plans, Final1),
    append(Sub_plan, Plans, Plan1),
  ( allpresent([Goal | Goals], Final1), !,
    Final = Final1,
    Plan = Plan1
  ; New_depth is Depth -1,
    achieve2([Goal | Goals], Final1, New_depth, Plan2, Final2),
    append(Plan1, Plan2, Plan),
    Final = Final2 ).

/* find_plan2(+Starting State, +Goal State, -Resultant Plan)
   find_plan2 succeeds if achieve2 succeeds with a depth limit of 5 */

find_plan2(Start_state, Goals, Plan) :-
    achieve2(Goals, Start_state, 5, Plan, _).
```

Figure 7-14 A planner that partially deals with goal interactions

Reading

Planning is one of the major topics in artificial intelligence and is covered in most good AI textbooks. The very simple implementation of planning which we have discussed in this chapter is dealt with by Burton and Shadbolt (1987, Chapter 9), Rich, (1983, pp. 247-266) and Winston (Winston, 1984, pp. 146-157). Chapter 7 of (Winston, 1984) looks at the frame problem in some depth. Aleksander and Burnett (1987) provide an accessible discussion of means-ends analysis complete with colour illustrations.

More advanced treatment of approaches to planning are provided by Charniak and McDermott (1985, Chapter 9), Nilsson (1980) and by Kowalski (1979). Chapter 1 of Ramsay and Barrett (1987) presents an introduction to the subject which includes the implementation of a large planning system in POP-11. Volume III of the AI Handbook contains a review of important material (Cohen and Feigenbaum, 1982, Section XV). The volume of general readings in artificial intelligence edited by Webber and Nilsson (Webber and Nilsson 1981) contains a classic paper on the frame problem by Hayes (Hayes, 1981) and also one on "learning and executing generalised robot plans" by Fikes, Hart and Nilsson (Fikes, Hart and Nilsson, 1981).

Chapter 16 of Bratko (1990) offers Prolog code for various planners, including one able to deal with goal regression (i.e. where operators involve variables).

Exercises

1. Implement a simple planning system in POP-11. Ideally, the system should use means-ends analysis and be able to cope intelligently in the case where it generates an "unintelligent" plan. But an easier approach would be to implement a system which uses simple forwards or backwards search in a state-space and which is able to stop itself from going into a loop.

The system should be able to construct plans for transporting objects between locations in one town to locations in another. A goal might be something like

```
[at_brighton hi_fi]
```

whose achievement would entail constructing a plan whose effect is to transport a hi-fi from its current location to the location labelled "at_brighton". Transporting different objects will entail using different forms of transportation. For instance

```
[at_brighton record]
```

might involve a plan which uses a "bus trip" operator, whereas

[at_brighton mattress]

might not.

2. Write an iterative deepening version of either the POP-11 or Prolog planner.

3. Improve either the POP-11 or the Prolog version of the planner by arranging that it keeps a record of goals already achieved and does not apply an operator that would remove such a goal.

4. Write a more principled POP-11 version of `achieve` that copes with operators containing variables by more sophisticated two-way matching.

5. Formulate a problem using operators with variables in Prolog where difficulties arise through failure to instantiate variables correctly — and fix them.

8
Parsing (search as analysis)

Introduction

When we are talking about search processes, the word "goal" has a very flexible meaning. In Chapter 6 we saw that one option is to construe goals in terms of conclusions or hypotheses. This means that search rules are, in effect, rules which show *what* conclusions can be drawn from *what* bits of evidence. The conclusion corresponds to the goal and the bits of evidence are just the subgoals. When we implement search rules in this way, the backward AND/OR-tree search function effectively tests whether it can draw certain conclusions from the available evidence; that is to say, it implements a form of primitive reasoning.

In the current chapter we will look at another way of implementing search rules and see that it enables us to extract a completely different sort of functionality from the AND/OR-tree search mechanism. The basic idea is that we will construe goals as entities or objects, and consider search rules to be descriptions showing the internal structure of an object. That is to say, a given search rule will be assumed to state that a given object is made up of a set of N components. Facts will be assumed to simply name components which are assumed to exist.

Solution trees as analyses

The application of backward search given a rulebase containing rules which describe the *structure* of objects will determine whether or not some high-level object exists given the known existence of N low-level objects. More importantly, the solution AND-tree for a backwards search will show the way in which the high-level object decomposes into lower-level objects, which themselves decompose into lower-level objects, etc. An example may help to clarify this idea. First of all let us set up a rulebase showing the way in which a "teaching institution" object is made up from components. The rulebase might look like this:

```
[ [[university] [university admin] [university buildings]]
  [[school] [school admin] [school buildings]]
  [[school buildings] [classrooms] [offices]]
  [[university buildings] [labs] [offices] [library]]
  [[school admin] [headmaster] [bursar]]
  [[university admin] [VC] [senate]]
] -> rulebase6;
```

Let us say that we now add the following facts into the database:

```
[ [[labs]]
  [[offices]]
  [[library]]
  [[VC]]
  [[senate]]
] -> facts6;
```

If we run **proof_tree** from Chapter 6 on these facts and this rulebase giving it the initial goal of **[school]**, the behaviour produced is as follows:

```
trace backwards_search_tree;

proof_tree([school], facts6 <> rulebase6, 10) ==>

> backwards_search_tree [[school]] 10
!> backwards_search_tree [[school admin] [school buildings]] 9
!!> backwards_search_tree [[headmaster] [bursar]] 8
!!< backwards_search_tree <false>
!< backwards_search_tree <false>
< backwards_search_tree <false>

** <false>
```

The search function cannot satisfy the goals **[[headmaster] [bursar]]** because these correspond to components[1] which, given our rulebase, do not exist. The behaviour is rather different if we give the search function the goal **[university]**:

```
proof_tree([university], facts6 <> rulebase6, 10) ==>

> backwards_search_tree [[university]] 10
!> backwards_search_tree [[university admin]
```

[1] We use the word "component" interchangeably with "object".

```
                          [university buildings]] 9
!!> backwards_search_tree [[VC] [senate]] 8
!!!> backwards_search_tree [] 7
!!!< backwards_search_tree []
!!!> backwards_search_tree [[senate]] 8
!!!!> backwards_search_tree [] 7
!!!!< backwards_search_tree []
!!!!> backwards_search_tree [] 8
!!!!< backwards_search_tree []
!!!< backwards_search_tree [[[senate]]]
!!< backwards_search_tree [[[VC]] [[senate]]]
!!> backwards_search_tree [[university buildings]] 9
!!!> backwards_search_tree [[labs] [offices] [library]] 8
!!!!> backwards_search_tree [] 7
!!!!< backwards_search_tree []
!!!!> backwards_search_tree [[offices] [library]] 8
!!!!!> backwards_search_tree [] 7
!!!!!< backwards_search_tree []
!!!!!> backwards_search_tree [[library]] 8
!!!!!!> backwards_search_tree [] 7
!!!!!!< backwards_search_tree []
!!!!!!> backwards_search_tree [] 8
!!!!!!< backwards_search_tree []
!!!!!< backwards_search_tree [[[library]]]
!!!!< backwards_search_tree [[[offices]] [[library]]]
!!!< backwards_search_tree [[[labs]] [[offices]] [[library]]]
!!!> backwards_search_tree [] 9
!!!< backwards_search_tree []
!!< backwards_search_tree [[[university buildings] [[labs]]
                           [[offices]] [[library]]]]
!< backwards_search_tree [[[university admin] [[VC]] [[senate]]]
   [[university buildings] [[labs]] [[offices]] [[library]]]]
!> backwards_search_tree [] 10
!< backwards_search_tree []
< backwards_search_tree [[[university] [[university admin]
  [[VC]] [[senate]]] [[university buildings] [[labs]]
  [[offices]] [[library]]]]]

** [[university]
    [[university admin] [[VC]] [[senate]]]
    [[university buildings] [[labs]] [[offices]]
     [[library]]]]
```

Not only does the search succeed in satisfying the original goal, it also returns a solution AND-tree which shows the internal structure of the "university" object given the rules in the rulebase. We can display this representation using **showtree** in the usual way (see Chapter 6, footnote 3), as in Figure 8-1.

Parsing

There is a special case of this particular usage of the search function which is of major importance in AI. This occurs when the bottom-level entities (the "facts") are arranged into a *sequence*, and form a linguistic entity such as a sentence. The solution AND-tree of a search in the case where search rules describe the internal structure of objects constitutes a description of the structure of the high-level object forming the goal of the search. If the object in question is a sentence, then the structural description can tell us about the *syntactic* structure of the sentence. Descriptions of syntactic structure, which are very important in natural language processing (and in compiler theory), are usually called *parse trees*.

How can we modify the search function such that it is able to cope appropriately with facts (i.e. objects) which are arranged into a sequence? We need to modify the behaviour of the function in two ways. Firstly, we must ensure that it will only satisfy a goal by invoking some facts if the facts are arranged in the right sequence. Secondly, we must ensure that it will not use a sequence of facts to satisfy a goal if those facts have already been used to satisfy some other goal.

A convenient way to obtain this new behaviour involves adding a second argument to the function and also arranging that it outputs two values rather than one.

```
untrace backwards_search_tree;
showtree(proof_tree([university], facts6 <> rulebase6, 10));
```

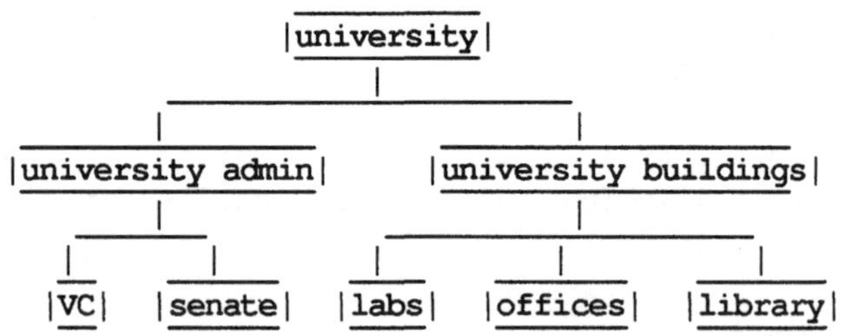

Figure 8-1 Deconstructing a university

The second argument will receive the sequence and the second output will pass on whatever is left over from the sequence once the goals have been satisfied. The function, renamed **backwards_parse_tree** is just a modified version of the *loop checking* **backwards_search_tree** introduced in Chapter 6. The only other change (apart from the extra argument and output) is a check to see if the first of the goals matches the first of the given sequence. This happens when the function has followed the chain of rules right down to the "bottom" and is trying to match the right-hand side of "lexical rule" (i.e. a word against the words in the sequence.

Let us see what all this means in the case where we want to discover the structure of a sequence of objects (i.e. words) forming a sentence. First of all we need to set up a rulebase in which the rules show how sentences are made up (according to the rules of grammar) out of lower-level linguistic objects such as noun-phrases and verb phrases. To keep the rulebase simple, we will use a system of abbreviations. "s" will stand for "sentence"; "np" will stand for "noun phrase"; "pp" will stand for "prepositional phrase", and so on. The final seven rules which relate lexical categories such as "det" to actual words such as "the" are the lexical rules. The earlier rules which relate grammatical categories together are the syntactic rules:

```
[ [s np vp]
  [np snp] [np snp pp]
  [snp det noun]
  [pp prep snp]
  [vp verb np]
  [noun man] [noun flies] [noun girl] [noun plane] [noun computer]
  [verb hated] [verb kissed] [verb flies]
  [det the] [det a]
] -> grammar1;
```

Let us start with a trivial case of parsing the sequence [the girl] as an "np":

```
trace backwards_parse_tree;
grammar1 -> database;

backwards_parse_tree([np], [the girl], 10) ==> ==>

> backwards_parse_tree [np] [the girl] 10
!> backwards_parse_tree [snp] [the girl] 9
!!> backwards_parse_tree [det noun] [the girl] 8
!!!> backwards_parse_tree [the] [the girl] 7
!!!!> backwards_parse_tree [] [girl] 6
!!!!< backwards_parse_tree [girl] []
!!!< backwards_parse_tree [girl] [the]
!!!> backwards_parse_tree [noun] [girl] 8
```

```
/* backwards_parse_tree takes a list of goals, e.g. categories and a
   list containing a sequence of words and a depth limit. It returns a list
   containing the parse tree and a list of any unused words.  If the parse
   fails it returns false plus the original list of words. */

define backwards_parse_tree(goals, sequence, depth)
                                            -> trees -> remainder;
    vars goal rest subgoals other_goals first_tree other_trees;
    if goals = []
    then [] -> trees; sequence -> remainder
    elseif depth <= 0 then false -> trees; sequence -> remainder
    else goals --> [?goal ??other_goals];
        if sequence matches [^goal ??rest]
        then backwards_parse_tree(other_goals, rest, depth-1)
                -> other_trees -> remainder;
            [^goal ^^other_trees] -> trees;
            return
        else foreach [^goal ??subgoals] do
                backwards_parse_tree(subgoals, sequence, depth-1)
                    -> first_tree -> rest;
                if islist(first_tree)
                then backwards_parse_tree(other_goals, rest, depth)
                        -> other_trees -> remainder;
                    if islist(other_trees)
                    then
                     [[^goal ^^first_tree] ^^other_trees] -> trees;
                        return
                    endif
                endif
            endforeach
        endif;
        false -> trees; sequence -> remainder;
    endif;
enddefine;
```

Figure 8-2 Parsing as backwards search

```
!!!!> backwards_parse_tree [man] [girl] 7
!!!!< backwards_parse_tree [girl] <false>
!!!!> backwards_parse_tree [flies] [girl] 7
!!!!< backwards_parse_tree [girl] <false>
!!!!> backwards_parse_tree [girl] [girl] 7
!!!!!> backwards_parse_tree [] [] 6
!!!!!< backwards_parse_tree [] []
```

```
!!!!< backwards_parse_tree [] [girl]
!!!!> backwards_parse_tree [] [] 8
!!!!< backwards_parse_tree [] []
!!!< backwards_parse_tree [] [[noun girl]]
!!< backwards_parse_tree [] [[det the] [noun girl]]
!!> backwards_parse_tree [] [] 9
!!< backwards_parse_tree [] []
!< backwards_parse_tree [] [[snp [det the] [noun girl]]]
!> backwards_parse_tree [] [] 10
!< backwards_parse_tree [] []
< backwards_parse_tree [] [[np [snp [det the] [noun girl]]]]

** [[np [snp [det the] [noun girl]]]]
** []
```

Notice how the system works its way down through the rules from "np" to "snp" to "det" and to "noun" and tries to match "noun" against "man" before it tries "girl". Notice also that **backwards_parse_tree** returns two values, the tree and the unused words, in this case, **[]**, because all the words were used. This would be an extremely costly strategy if there were a realistic number of words in the lexicon part of **grammar1**:

```
untrace backwards_parse_tree;

backwards_parse_tree([np], [the girl from ipanema], 10) ==> ==>
** [[np [snp [det the] [noun girl]]]]
** [from ipanema]

backwards_parse_tree([s], [the man hated the computer], 10) ==>
                                                              ==>
** [[s [np [snp [det the] [noun man]]]
       [vp [verb hated] [np [snp [det the] [noun computer]]]]]]
** []

backwards_parse_tree([s], [the girl flies the plane], 10) ==>
                                                            ==>
** [[s [np [snp [det the] [noun girl]]]
       [vp [verb flies] [np [snp [det the] [noun plane]]]]]]
** []
```

We can use **showtree** to display the structure of the solution tree as shown in Figure

```
backwards_parse_tree([s], [the man hated the computer], 10)
-> trees -> r;
showtree(hd(trees));
```

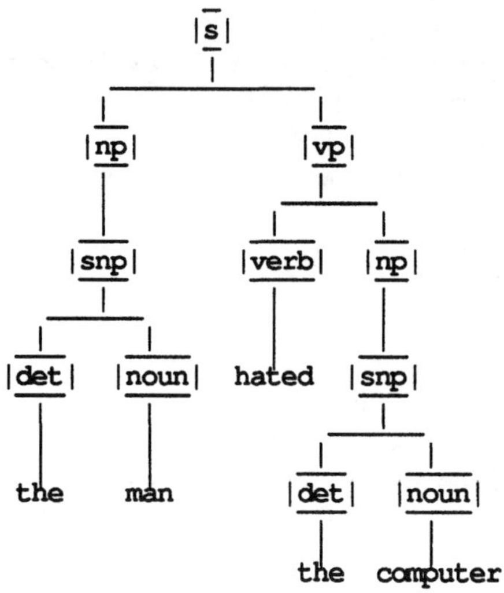

Figure 8-3 A parse tree

8-3[2]:

```
backwards_parse_tree([s], [the man], 10) ==> ==>
** <false>
** [the man]

backwards_parse_tree([s], [the girl kissed the computer], 10) ==>
                                                              ==>
** [[s [np [snp [det the] [noun girl]]]
       [vp [verb kissed] [np [snp [det the] [noun computer]]]]]]
** []
```

So far in these examples there have been no particular search problems. The rules in the database were ordered in such a way that what turned out to be the right rules were usually tried first (e.g. the rules for "np"). More importantly the rules did not

[2] We employ the default version of **root** defined in library showtree.

cause the search process to loop. However this looping behaviour is easy enough to produce. Let us add extra rules of the form:

```
[ [snp det ap noun]
  [ap ap adj] [ap adj]
  [adj big] [adj red] [adj hot]
] -> grammar2;
```

The intention of these "ap" (adjectival phrase) rules is to allow noun phrases of the form "the big computer", "the red hot computer", "the big big man" etc, i.e. a determiner, an arbitrary number of adjectives and a noun. For sentences (or other structures) not containing adjectives, everything goes well, but here is part of a trace involving an adjective:

```
grammar1 <> grammar2 -> database;

backwards_parse_tree([np], [the big man], 10) ==> ==>

** [[np [snp [det the] [ap [adj big]] [noun man]]]]
** []
```

Because of the depth limit, the parse works. But if we examine the centre part of the overall trace we see that the function recurses fruitlessly until it hits this limit:

```
/* EARLIER PARTS OF TRACE OMITTED */

!!!> backwards_parse_tree [ap noun] [big man] 8
!!!!> backwards_parse_tree [ap adj] [big man] 7
!!!!!> backwards_parse_tree [ap adj] [big man] 6
!!!!!!> backwards_parse_tree [ap adj] [big man] 5
!!!!!!!> backwards_parse_tree [ap adj] [big man] 4
!!!!!!!!> backwards_parse_tree [ap adj] [big man] 3
!!!!!!!!!> backwards_parse_tree [ap adj] [big man] 2
!!!!!!!!!!> backwards_parse_tree [ap adj] [big man] 1
!!!!!!!!!!!> backwards_parse_tree [ap adj] [big man] 0
!!!!!!!!!!!< backwards_parse_tree [big man] <false>

/* LATER PARTS OF TRACE OMITTED */
```

The problem is that the "ap" rule we have given is "left_recursive", that is ap contains itself as its first sub-structure. In general there will be recursive rules in our grammars but unless special care is taken, these rules can lead to loops.

Data-driven (bottom-up) parsing

We have implemented the **backwards_parse_tree** function using backward search. Could we implement it using forward search? In Chapter 6 we noted that, in general, forward AND/OR-tree search was not a particularly practical proposition. The reason being that given some collection of satisfied subgoals, it is not at all clear how they should be arranged so as to enable the picking-out of an appropriate search rule. But of course in the special case we are currently considering there is no difficulty. Given some collection of satisfied subgoals, we know that the only goals we can consider to be solved are the ones which have the subgoals in the right *sequence*. This makes the whole process much more tractable.

It turns out that implementing a forward search function which constructs solution trees (i.e. parse trees) is a little bit more tricky. However, there is no difficulty in implementing a forward function **forwards_parse_goals** which simply returns its goals if they cover the sequence or **<false>**. The function takes, as inputs, a list of goals and a sequence of words or structures. If goals match the sequence, the process is deemed to be finished and it terminates. Otherwise it tries the rules in turn seeing whether it can find the *right-hand side* of any rule somewhere in the sequence. If it can, it replaces the right-hand side by the left-hand side and recursively continues parsing. If no rule can be found the function returns false. A depth limit is applied to catch loops.

```
/* forwards_parse_goals takes a list of goals and of words and returns the
   list of goals if the sequence conforms to them, or false. */

define forwards_parse_goals(goals, sequence, depth) -> outgoals;
    vars goal subgoals before after;
    if sequence matches goals then goals -> outgoals
    elseif depth <= 0 then false -> outgoals
    else foreach [?goal ??subgoals] do
            if sequence matches [??before ^^subgoals ??after] then
                forwards_parse_goals(goals, [^^before ^goal ^^after],
                    depth-1) -> outgoals;
                if islist(outgoals) then return endif
            endif
        endforeach;
        false -> outgoals
    endif
enddefine;
```

Figure 8-4 Bottom-up parsing

Typically we set the goals to be `[s]`. If the sentence is in the language which is covered by the grammar, then this process of substituting syntactic categories will continue up to the point where the sequence is itself reduced to `[s]`:

```
trace forwards_parse_goals;
grammarl -> database;

forwards_parse_goals([s], [the man hated the computer], 20) ==>

> forwards_parse_goals [s] [the man hated the computer] 20
!> forwards_parse_goals [s] [the noun hated the computer] 19
!!> forwards_parse_goals [s] [the noun hated the noun] 18
!!!> forwards_parse_goals [s] [the noun verb the noun] 17
!!!!> forwards_parse_goals [s] [det noun verb the noun] 16
!!!!!> forwards_parse_goals [s] [snp verb the noun] 15
!!!!!!> forwards_parse_goals [s] [np verb the noun] 14
!!!!!!!> forwards_parse_goals [s] [np verb det noun] 13
!!!!!!!!> forwards_parse_goals [s] [np verb snp] 12
!!!!!!!!!> forwards_parse_goals [s] [np verb np] 11
!!!!!!!!!!> forwards_parse_goals [s] [np vp] 10
!!!!!!!!!!!> forwards_parse_goals [s] [s] 9
!!!!!!!!!!!< forwards_parse_goals [s]
!!!!!!!!!!< forwards_parse_goals [s]
!!!!!!!!!< forwards_parse_goals [s]
!!!!!!!!< forwards_parse_goals [s]
!!!!!!!< forwards_parse_goals [s]
!!!!!!< forwards_parse_goals [s]
!!!!!< forwards_parse_goals [s]
!!!!< forwards_parse_goals [s]
!!!< forwards_parse_goals [s]
!!< forwards_parse_goals [s]
!< forwards_parse_goals [s]
< forwards_parse_goals [s]

** [s]

forwards_parse_goals([s], [the holy man], 20) ==>

> forwards_parse_goals [s] [the holy man] 20
!> forwards_parse_goals [s] [the holy noun] 19
!!> forwards_parse_goals [s] [det holy noun] 18
!!< forwards_parse_goals <false>
!< forwards_parse_goals <false>
```

```
!> forwards_parse_goals [s] [det holy man] 19
!!> forwards_parse_goals [s] [det holy noun] 18
!!< forwards_parse_goals <false>
!< forwards_parse_goals <false>
< forwards_parse_goals <false>

** <false>

untrace forwards_parse_goals;

forwards_parse_goals([det holy noun], [the holy man], 20) ==>

** [det holy noun]

forwards_parse_goals([s], [the man flies the flies], 20) ==>

** [s]
```

The behaviour of the function is shown above. It should be noted that our forward search function **forwards_parse_goals** does not do a lot of redundant work on *these* examples, partly because of the grammar and partly because of the given sentences. In the second example, the system identifies the "det" and the "noun" but can get no further because "holy" is not recognised. If we supply the three goals **[det holy noun]** and the same sequence the search succeeds. However the trace output of **forwards_parse_goals([s], [the man flies the flies], 20) ==>** is nearly 300 lines long, caused partly by the ambiguity of the word **flies** which can be either a noun or a verb.

Building trees bottom-up

It is possible to extend the definition of **forwards_parse_goals** so that it returns the parse trees rather than simply the category(s) such as **[s]**. Recall that in bottom-up parsing we replaced a sequence of subgoals by the corresponding goal. To produce a tree, we simply replace a sequence of subtrees by the corresponding piece of tree, i.e. **[^goal ^^trees]**. These pieces of tree gradually accumulate and coalesce on the way up until finally the tree for the whole sentence is produced.

There is, however, a complication in that we now need to match our grammar rules not just against sequences such as **[the man]** or **[snp vp]** but also against sequences that contain bits of tree inter-mixed from the earlier stages of the parse. We have two choices. Either we can change the grammar rules in the database to allow this kind of match or we can change the matching in **forwards_parse_goals**. We will choose the latter and re-use the existing grammars.

```
/* forwards_parse_trees takes a list of goals and a sequence of words
   and returns a list containing the parse-trees, or false if no parse
   trees can be built */

define forwards_parse_trees(goals, sequence, depth) -> trees;
    vars goal subgoals before after tree;
    if topcats(sequence, goals) then sequence -> trees
    elseif depth <= 0 then false -> trees
    else
        foreach [?goal ??subgoals] do
            if sequence matches
                [??before ??tree: ^(topcats(%subgoals%)) ??after]
            then
                forwards_parse_trees(goals,
                    [^^before [^goal ^^tree] ^^after], depth-1)
                    -> trees;
                if islist(trees) then return endif
            endif
        endforeach;
        false -> trees
    endif
enddefine;

/* topcats takes a tree (or a list of words) and a list categories
   (or a list of words) as input, and returns true if the major
   categories in the tree match the list of categories. If
   both inputs are lists of words, it returns true if they match. */

define topcats(tree, cats) -> boolean;
    if tree = [] and cats = [] then true -> boolean
    elseif tree = [] or cats = [] then false -> boolean
    elseif atom(hd(tree))
    then hd(tree) = hd(cats) and topcats(tl(tree), tl(cats))
            -> boolean
    else hd(hd(tree)) = hd(cats) and topcats(tl(tree), tl(cats))
            -> boolean
    endif
enddefine;
```

Figure 8-5 Building parse trees bottom-up

The more complex matching occurs in two places: one is to detect when parsing is complete, the other is during the process of seeing whether a candidate grammar rule can be used. In both cases we make use of the function **topcats** in Figure 8-5. This function behaves as follows. In each case it picks each top-level item from the first argument and sees if it matches against the corresponding item in its second argument:

```
topcats([the old man], [the old man]) ==>
** <true>

topcats([fred  [np [snp [det the] [noun man]]]], [fred np]) ==>
** <true>

topcats([[s [np [snp [det the] [noun man]]]
            [vp [verb flies] [np [snp [det the]
                                      [noun flies]]]]]],
        [s]) ==>
** <true>
```

The complexity of **forwards_parse_trees** comes in the use of **topcats** to restrict the matching on **??tree**. We have used a technique called *partial application* to create dynamically a special version of **topcats** (each time this match is tried) which fixes its second argument to the value of the subgoals of the rule being considered. Tracing the behaviour of this function gives:

```
trace forwards_parse_trees;

forwards_parse_trees([s], [the man hated the computer], 20) ==>

> forwards_parse_trees [s]
  [the man hated the computer] 20
!> forwards_parse_trees [s]
   [the [noun man] hated the computer] 19
!!> forwards_parse_trees [s]
    [the [noun man] hated the [noun computer]] 18
!!!> forwards_parse_trees [s]
     [the [noun man] [verb hated] the [noun computer]] 17
!!!!> forwards_parse_trees [s]
      [[det the] [noun man] [verb hated] the [noun computer]] 16
!!!!!> forwards_parse_trees [s]
       [[snp [det the] [noun man]] [verb hated] the [noun computer]] 15
!!!!!!> forwards_parse_trees [s]
        [[np [snp [det the] [noun man]]] [verb hated] the [noun computer]] 14
!!!!!!!> forwards_parse_trees [s]
         [[np [snp [det the] [noun man]]] [verb hated] [det the] [noun computer]] 13
!!!!!!!!> forwards_parse_trees [s]
          [[np [snp [det the] [noun man]]]
           [verb hated] [snp [det the] [noun computer]]] 12
!!!!!!!!!> forwards_parse_trees [s]
           [[np [snp [det the] [noun man]]]
            [verb hated] [np [snp [det the] [noun computer]]]] 11
!!!!!!!!!!> forwards_parse_trees [s]
            [[np [snp [det the] [noun man]]]
```

```
            [vp [verb hated] [np [snp [det the] [noun computer]]]]] 10
!!!!!!!!!!!> forwards_parse_trees [s]
            [[s [np [snp [det the] [noun man]]]
                [vp [verb hated] [np [snp [det the] [noun computer]]]]]] 9
!!!!!!!!!!!< forwards_parse_trees
            [[s [np [snp [det the] [noun man]]]
                [vp [verb hated] [np [snp [det the] [noun computer]]]]]]
!!!!!!!!!!< forwards_parse_trees
           [[s [np [snp [det the] [noun man]]]
               [vp [verb hated] [np [snp [det the] [noun computer]]]]]]
!!!!!!!!!< forwards_parse_trees
          [[s [np [snp [det the] [noun man]]]
              [vp [verb hated] [np [snp [det the] [noun computer]]]]]]
!!!!!!!!< forwards_parse_trees
         [[s [np [snp [det the] [noun man]]]
             [vp [verb hated] [np [snp [det the] [noun computer]]]]]]
!!!!!!!< forwards_parse_trees
        [[s [np [snp [det the] [noun man]]]
            [vp [verb hated] [np [snp [det the] [noun computer]]]]]]
!!!!!!< forwards_parse_trees
       [[s [np [snp [det the] [noun man]]]
           [vp [verb hated] [np [snp [det the] [noun computer]]]]]]
!!!!!< forwards_parse_trees
      [[s [np [snp [det the] [noun man]]]
          [vp [verb hated] [np [snp [det the] [noun computer]]]]]]
!!!!< forwards_parse_trees
     [[s [np [snp [det the] [noun man]]]
         [vp [verb hated] [np [snp [det the] [noun computer]]]]]]
!!!< forwards_parse_trees
    [[s [np [snp [det the] [noun man]]]
        [vp [verb hated] [np [snp [det the] [noun computer]]]]]]
!!< forwards_parse_trees
   [[s [np [snp [det the] [noun man]]]
       [vp [verb hated] [np [snp [det the] [noun computer]]]]]]
!< forwards_parse_trees
  [[s [np [snp [det the] [noun man]]]
      [vp [verb hated] [np [snp [det the] [noun computer]]]]]]
< forwards_parse_trees
 [[s [np [snp [det the] [noun man]]]
     [vp [verb hated] [np [snp [det the] [noun computer]]]]]]

** [[s [np [snp [det the] [noun man]]]
       [vp [verb hated] [np [snp [det the] [noun computer]]]]]]
```

The behaviour is largely the same as **forwards_parse_goals** given earlier, except that bits of tree are included in the input and output at each level rather than merely category names.

Advantages of bottom-up search

Forward search applied to a rulebase consisting of linguistic rules is often referred to as *bottom-up parsing*. Backward search is called *top-down parsing*. As was noted in the previous chapter, the terms *top-down* and *bottom-up* reflect that fact that the backward process constructs the solution-tree working from the top-down. The forward process works in the opposite way. Note that bottom-up search is likely to be more efficient than top-down whenever the branching factor in the search tree is particularly high, i.e. whenever we have several competing rules at any given level.

Backwards and forwards parsing in Prolog

Top-down parsing in Prolog to produce a parse tree is a simple extension of code from earlier chapters and follows much the same method as for the POP-11 version. As before, we will adapt the loop checking version of our backwards search procedure.

Procedure **backwards_parse_tree/5** has three cases to consider, see Figure 8-6. The first case is where there are no further goals in which case it returns an empty parse-tree and whatever sequence it was given as the remainder. The second case is where the first word in the sequence matches the first goal in the goal list. In this case it parses the remaining goals and the remaining sequence and adds the given word onto the front of the parse-tree. The final case takes the first goal from the goal list, finds a rule which has that goal on its left-hand side. It then continues parsing the sequence first with the subgoals from the right-hand side of the rule thus found and then with whatever further goals it originally had. It constructs an appropriate tree out of the parts of trees so produced.

The behaviour of **backwards_parse_tree** is similar to its POP-11 version:

```
?- spy backwards_parse_tree.
Spypoint placed on backwards_parse_tree/5
yes

?- backwards_parse_tree([np], [the, girl], 10, Rem, Tree).

** (1) Call : backwards_parse_tree([np], [the, girl], 10, _1, _2)?
** (2) Call : backwards_parse_tree([snp], [the, girl], 9, _3, _4)?
** (3) Call : backwards_parse_tree([det, noun], [the, girl], 8, _5, _6)?
** (4) Call : backwards_parse_tree([the], [the, girl], 7, _7, _8)?
** (5) Call : backwards_parse_tree([], [girl], 7, _7, _9)?
** (5) Exit : backwards_parse_tree([], [girl], 7, [girl], [])?
** (4) Exit : backwards_parse_tree([the], [the, girl], 7, [girl], [the])?
** (6) Call : backwards_parse_tree([noun], [girl], 8, _5, _10)?
** (7) Call : backwards_parse_tree([man], [girl], 7, _11, _12)?
** (7) Fail : backwards_parse_tree([man], [girl], 7, _11, _12)?
```

```
/* rule(-grammar_rule)
   each rule predicate has as its argument a list containing either a syntactic
   or lexical rule */

rule([s, np, vp]).
rule([np, snp]).
rule([np, snp, pp]).
rule([snp, det, noun]).
rule([pp, prep, snp]).
rule([vp, verb, np]).
rule([noun, man]).
rule([noun, flies]).
rule([noun, girl]).
rule([noun, plane]).
rule([noun, computer]).
rule([verb, hated]).
rule([verb, kissed]).
rule([verb, flies]).
rule([det, the]).
rule([det, a]).
rule([prep, with]).

/* backwards_parse_tree(+Goals, +Sequence, +Depth, -Remainder, -Trees)
   backwards_parse_tree takes a list of Goals and a sequence of words
   and returns the corresponding parse-trees and any words left unused at
   the end of the sequence */

backwards_parse_tree([], Rem, _, Rem, []).

backwards_parse_tree([Word | Goals], [Word | Words], Depth, Remainder,
                                                        [Word | Trees]) :-
   backwards_parse_tree(Goals, Words, Depth, Remainder, Trees), !.

backwards_parse_tree([Goal | Goals], Sequence, Depth, Remainder,
                                             [[Goal | Tree] | Trees]) :-
   Depth > 0,
   rule([Goal|Subgoals]),
   New_depth is Depth - 1,
   backwards_parse_tree(Subgoals, Sequence, New_depth, Intermediate, Tree),
   backwards_parse_tree(Goals, Intermediate, Depth, Remainder, Trees).
```

Figure 8-6 Top-down parsing in Prolog

```
** (8) Call : backwards_parse_tree([girl], [girl], 7, _11, _12)?
** (9) Call : backwards_parse_tree([], [], 7, _11, _13)?
** (9) Exit : backwards_parse_tree([], [], 7, [], [])?
** (8) Exit : backwards_parse_tree([girl], [girl], 7, [], [girl])?
** (10) Call : backwards_parse_tree([], [], 8, _5, _14)?
** (10) Exit : backwards_parse_tree([], [], 8, [], [])?
```

```
** (6) Exit : backwards_parse_tree([noun], [girl], 8, [], [[noun, girl]])?
** (3) Exit : backwards_parse_tree([det, noun], [the, girl], 8, [],
              [[det, the], [noun, girl]])?
** (11) Call : backwards_parse_tree([], [], 9, _3, _15)?
** (11) Exit : backwards_parse_tree([], [], 9, [], [])?
** (2) Exit : backwards_parse_tree([snp], [the, girl], 9, [],
              [[snp, [det, the], [noun, girl]]])?
** (12) Call : backwards_parse_tree([], [], 10, _1, _16)?
** (12) Exit : backwards_parse_tree([], [], 10, [], [])?
** (1) Exit : backwards_parse_tree([np], [the, girl], 10, [],
              [[np, [snp, [det, the], [noun, girl]]]])?

Rem = []
Tree = [[np, [snp, [det, the], [noun, girl]]]] ?

yes

?- nospy.
?- backwards_parse_tree([s], [the, girl, flies, the, plane, expertly],
                        10, Rem, T).

Rem = [expertly]
T = [[s, [np, [snp, [det, the], [noun, girl]]],
         [vp, [verb, flies],
              [np, [snp, [det, the], [noun, plane]]]]]] ?

yes
```

In the final example above, the sentence is parsed with the exception of the trailing "expertly" which is treated as a remainder. Note that extra words can only be accepted at the end of the sequence on not within it. In the next example a more complex sentence is parsed. Note that the first solution found treats the whole trailing phrase "with the man expertly" as remainder. This is because the grammar rules are ordered such that the rule for an "np" without a trailing "pp" is prior to the rule which includes the "pp". By forcing backtracking, this other "np" rule is used, see Figure 8-7 for the output of `showtree/1` in this case (using the standard definition of `root`):

```
?- backwards_parse_tree([s],
                        [the, girl, with, a, computer, flies,
                         the, plane, with, the, man, expertly],
                        10, Rem, [T]),
   showtree(T).

Rem = [with, the, man, expertly]
T = [s, [np, [snp, [det, the], [noun, girl]], [pp, [prep, with],
```

```
        [snp, [det, a], [noun, computer]]]], [vp, [verb, flies],
        [np, [snp, [det, the], [noun, plane]]]]] ? ;

Rem = [expertly]
T = [s, [np, [snp, [det, the], [noun, girl]], [pp, [prep, with],
        [snp, [det, a], [noun, computer]]]], [vp, [verb, flies],
        [np, [snp, [det, the], [noun, plane]], [pp, [prep, with],
        [snp, [det, the], [noun, man]]]]]] ? ;

no
```

The Prolog grammar rule formalism

The Prolog version of **backwards_parse_tree** above was designed to be a close match to the POP-11 version provided earlier. In fact Prolog has built in top-down parsing capabilities based around a special notation for grammar rules using the operator "-->". Below is a very brief example. References to more extended use of this notation are given at the end of the chapter. All we need do is express the grammar rules themselves and then treat each category as a predicate which succeeds if it is given a list of words which starts with the category in question (and returns the remaining words). These predicates are built automatically when compiling the grammar rules by adding extra arguments:

```
s --> np, vp.
np --> snp.
np --> snp, pp.
snp --> det, noun.
pp --> prep, snp.
vp --> verb, np.
noun --> [man].
noun --> [girl].
noun --> [computer].
verb --> [hated].
verb --> [kissed].
det --> [the].
det --> [a].
```

In the example below we first show the predicate that is automatically generated for **np** and then trace it with the same argument as in the **backwards_parse_tree** example earlier:

```
?- listing(np).
```

```
?- backwards_parse_tree([s],
                        [the, girl, with, a, computer, flies,
                        the, plane, with, the, man, expertly],
                        10, Rem, [T]),
   showtree(T).
```

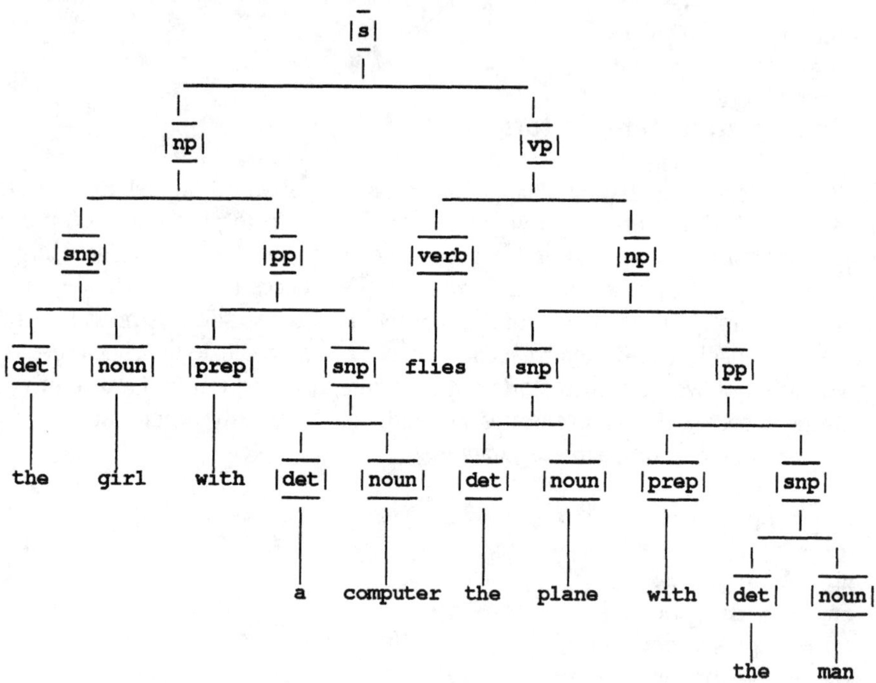

Figure 8-7 Second parse-tree

```
np(_1, _2) :-
    snp(_1, _2).
np(_1, _2) :-
    snp(_1, _3),
    pp(_3, _2).

?- spy.
Spypoint placed on np/2
Spypoint placed on s/2
```

```
Spypoint placed on noun/2
Spypoint placed on vp/2
Spypoint placed on det/2
Spypoint placed on pp/2
Spypoint placed on verb/2
Spypoint placed on snp/2
yes
?- np([the, girl], []).
** (1) Call : np([the, girl], [])?
** (2) Call : snp([the, girl], [])?
** (3) Call : det([the, girl], _1)?
** (3) Exit : det([the, girl], [girl])?
** (4) Call : noun([girl], [])?
** (4) Exit : noun([girl], [])?
** (2) Exit : snp([the, girl], [])?
** (1) Exit : np([the, girl], [])?
yes
```

Grammar rules using --> can also be used in a very straightforward way to generate parse trees, by adding further arguments by hand.

Bottom-up parsing in Prolog

Although Prolog provides only a top-down (i.e. backwards) search mechanism and a built-in operator for making grammars, it is easy to write a Prolog version of the bottom-up (i.e. forwards) parsing procedure given earlier in POP-11.

Procedure **forwards_parse_goals/3** has only two cases to consider, see Figure 8-8. If it is given a sequence which matches its goals it succeeds. In the second case it searches the grammar rules for one which has a right-hand side that is a subsequence of the sequence it has been given. If successful, it replaces that subsequence by the left-hand side of the rule and calls itself recursively with shortened sequence:

```
?- forwards_parse_goals([the, green, frog], [the, green, frog],
                        10).
yes
?- forwards_parse_goals([snp], [the, green, frog], 10).
no
?- forwards_parse_goals([snp], [the, man], 10).
yes
?- forwards_parse_goals([snp, snp], [the, man, a, girl], 10).
yes
?- forwards_parse_goals([s],
```

/* forwards_parse_goals(+Goals, +Sequence, +Depth)
forwards_parse_goals takes a sequence of words and succeeds if it can reduce this sequence to the given Goals by repeatedly replacing subsequences using the grammar rules */

```
forwards_parse_goals(Goals, Goals, _) :- !.

forwards_parse_goals(Goals, Sequence, Depth) :-
   Depth > 0,
   rule([Cat | Subcats]),
   sublist(Start, Subcats, Rest, Sequence),
   replace(Start, [Cat], Rest, Intermediate),
   New_depth is Depth - 1,
   forwards_parse_goals(Goals, Intermediate, New_depth).
```

/* sublist(-Start, +Subcats, -Rest, +Description)
sublist isolates Subcats within Description and returns the words preceding and following it */

```
sublist(Start, Subcats, Rest, Description) :-
   append(L2, Rest, Description),
   append(Start, Subcats, L2).
```

/* replace(+Start, +Replacement, +Rest, -Description)
replace links Start, Replacement and Rest into a single list which it returns in Description */

```
replace(Start, Replacement, Rest, Description) :-
   append(Start, Replacement, L2),
   append(L2, Rest, Description).
```

Figure 8-8 Bottom-up recognising in Prolog

```
                                  [the, girl, hated, the, plane, with, a,
                                   man], 20).
yes
```

Our solution is not very efficient because of the way it uses the double call to **append/3** in **sublist/4** to generate all possible subsequences of the given sequence which it then tests against each of the rules. If you spy **forwards_parse_goals** you will see that the second argument (the given sequence) is gradually transformed to become equal to the first argument. This contrasts with backwards search where the first argument (the goals) is gradually transformed to becoming equal to the sequence.

Procedure **forwards_parse_goals** can be adapted to return a parse-tree by employing a similar method as in POP-11 earlier. As before, see Figure 8-9 the appropriate bits of tree are inserted in the sequence rather than simply the left-hand side of the matching rule. We show only a single example, in Figure 8-10.

Both the forwards (goal driven, top-down, downwards) and the backwards (data driven, bottom-up, upwards) parsing methods given in POP-11 and in Prolog work *depth-first*. That is, where there is a choice of possible things to do (either replacing a goal by its subgoals in different ways or collapsing a subsequence of the input in different ways), these systems make a choice and then move on to deal with

---

```
/* forwards_parse_trees(+Goals, +Sequence, +Depth, Trees)
   forwards_parse_goals takes a sequence of words and succeeds with Trees
   if it can reduce this sequence to the given Goals by repeatedly replacing
   subsequences by pieces of tree using the grammar rules */

forwards_parse_trees(Goals, Sequence, _, Trees) :-
    topcats(Sequence, Goals), !,
    Sequence = Trees.

forwards_parse_trees(Goals, Sequence, Depth, Trees) :-
    Depth > 0,
    rule([Cat | Subcats]),
    sublist(Start, Subtrees, Rest, Sequence),
    topcats(Subtrees, Subcats),
    replace(Start, [[Cat | Subtrees]], Rest, Intermediate),
    New_depth is Depth - 1,
    forwards_parse_trees(Goals, Intermediate, New_depth, Trees).

/* topcats(+Trees, +Cats)
   topcats succeeds if Trees and Cats are both flat lists equal.
   It also succeeds if Trees is a list of trees and Cats is a list
   of the major categories of these trees. */

topcats([], []).

topcats([Word | Trees], [Word | Cats]) :-
    topcats(Trees, Cats).

topcats([[Cat | _] | Trees], [Cat | Cats]) :-
    topcats(Trees, Cats).
```

Figure 8-10 Bottom-up production of a parse tree in Prolog

the repercussions of that choice. Only if the system reaches a dead end or runs out of depth, does it move back to the previous choice point and try a different choice. One of the problems of this is that the parsers we offer here are very susceptible to the order of the rules in the grammar. For example, we have deliberately put the rules for "np"s in a non-optimal order so that the systems first attempt to parse on the basis of there being no "pp" before backtracking (if needed) to try to incorporate a "pp".

One could get around this partially by working *breadth first* (either forwards or backwards) via some variant on the agenda mechanism described for state-space search. There would be a cost in the amount of storage required by the program to keep partial parses.

More realistic parsers decouple the process of parsing almost entirely from the expression of the grammar rules, e.g. by employing a chart parser (see, e.g. Gazdar and Mellish, 1989b).

```
?- forwards_parse_trees([s], [the, girl, kissed, a, man], 20, [Tree]),
   showtree(Tree).
Tree = [s, [np, [snp, [det, the], [noun, girl]]],
           [vp, [verb, kissed],
                [np, [snp, [det, a], [noun, man]]]]] ?
yes
```

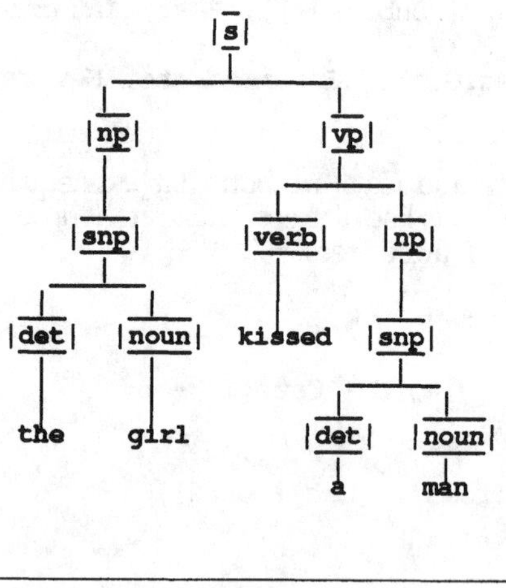

Figure 8-10 Building a parse tree by forwards search in Prolog

Why is parsing useful

If we are interested in constructing programs which are capable of dealing, to some degree, with natural language then we need to be able to have some way of extracting the meaning of an arbitrary sentence. It turns out that knowing what the syntactic structure of a sentence is can be very helpful here. The basic idea that syntactic structure tells us something about meaning (i.e. semantics) is called the principle of *compositional semantics*. The principle is attributed to the philosopher Frege. Frege hypothesised that the meaning of any complete linguistic entity could be derived from the meanings of its syntactic components. Their meanings could, in turn, be derived from the meanings of *their* syntactic components. Ultimately, syntactic components will just be words whose meanings can be assumed to be given.

We can attempt to put Frege's idea into practice as follows. Imagine that we want to write a program which is able to converse about the contents of a blocksworld[3], i.e. is able to answer questions about where certain blocks are and what blocks are on top of which other blocks.

A possible approach would be as follows. First of all we set up a representation for the blocksworld model. We can do this in the usual way (see Chapter 4), using a list of lists:

```
[ [isa block objR] [colour red objR]   [size large objR]
  [isa block objr] [colour red objr]   [size small objr]
  [isa block objG] [colour green objG] [size large objG]
  [isa block objg] [colour green objg] [size small objg]
  [isa block objB] [colour blue objB]  [size large objB]
  [isa block objb] [colour blue objb]  [size small objb]
  [objb ison objG]
  [objG ison objR]
  [objR ison table]
  [objg ison table]
  [objr ison objB]
  [objB ison table] ] -> database;
```

Note that we have given blocks names which indicate what their "size" and "colour" are. An upper case final letter indicates a large block. A small letter indicates a small block. The letter itself indicates the colour. Thus the large red block is called "objR". The small red block is called "objr". Obviously this convention is for our convenience only. The program that we will write will not take any notice of it. Notice also that the table has no properties other than that of supporting some of the blocks.

[3] This section is based on the POPLOG Teach File and Library program "msblocks" by David Hogg and Aaron Sloman.

Let us imagine that we want our program to be able to respond effectively to a question such as "where is the big blue block?" To respond sensibly to this, the program needs to find out which block is being referred to. Technically, it needs to find out what the *referent* of the noun phrase "big blue block" is. How can it do this?

To explain the implementation we first of all need to introduce the built-in POP-11 function called **which**. This function takes a list of match-patterns and a list of variables which are used as query-variables in the match-patterns. It then tries to find a way of matching the lists against the database such that all the query variables are consistently instantiated. If it can do this it just returns the values of the query variables. For example, if we do:

```
which("x",[ [size large ?x] [colour blue ?x] [isa block ?x] ]) ==>
```

the function returns the list:

```
** [objB]
```

This is because, the input lists will only match against the database *all at once* in the case where **?x** is matched against the word **objB**. If it turns out that there is more than one way to match the lists, **which** returns all the candidate instantiations. Thus:

```
which("x", [ [size small ?x] [isa block ?x] ]) ==>
** [objr objg objb]
```

Using the "which" function we can always find out which object(s) is being referred to provided that we are given an appropriate list of match patterns. So one way to work out what object is referred to by a question like "where is the big blue block?" is to try to derive some match patterns which will enable us to derive the object using the **which** function.

Let us note that if the input question contains a subsequence whose parse tree looks like:

```
[[det ...][adj ...][n...]]
```

then the subsequence must be a *noun phrase*, i.e. it must be a reference to an object. This implies that a set of match-patterns which will pick-out the appropriate object from the microworld representation will look like this:

```
[[isa block ?x] [= ... ?x]]
```

where the "..." is just the adjective in the subsequence. Thus the subsequence "the big block" has a parse tree:

```
/* meaning takes a parse-tree and returns the meaning built out of match
   patterns. If the meaning cannot be found it returns [] */

define meaning(parse_tree) -> result;
   vars snp result adj pp ap np noun word aps;
   if parse_tree matches [noun ?word] then
      [[isa ^word ?x]] -> result
   elseif parse_tree matches [adj ?word] then
      [[= ^word ?x]] -> result
   elseif parse_tree matches [snp ?noun] then
      meaning(noun) -> result
   elseif parse_tree matches [ap ?adj] then
      meaning(adj) -> result
   elseif parse_tree matches [ap ?adj ?ap] then
      [^^(meaning(adj)) ^^(meaning(ap))] -> result;
   elseif parse_tree matches [snp ?ap ?noun] then
      [^^(meaning(ap)) ^^(meaning(noun))] -> result;
   elseif parse_tree matches [np [det =] ?snp] then
      meaning(snp) -> result
   elseif parse_tree matches [pp [prep =] ?np] then
      meaning(np) -> result
   elseif parse_tree matches [s [wh1 where][vbe is] ?np] then
      [where ^(meaning(np))] -> result
   elseif parse_tree matches [s [wh2 what][vbe is] ?pp] then
      [what ^(meaning(pp))] -> result
   else
      [] -> result
   endif;
enddefine;
```

Figure 8-11 Extracting the meaning from a parse tree

```
[[det the][adj big][n block]]
```

and the appropriate match-patterns which will enable us to pick out the block being referred to are:

```
[[isa block ?x][= big ?x]]
```

Now, we can always just set up a mapping between specific sequences of words and specific match-patterns. But how should our implementation respond where there is more than one subsequence and hence, more than one set of match-patterns? This is where the compositional semantics comes in. We arrange for the implementation to

```
vars grammar3;

[ [s v np pp]
  [s wh1 vbe np]
  [s wh2 vbe pp]
  [np pn]
  [np det snp]
  [np det snp pp]
  [snp noun]
  [snp ap noun]
  [ap adj]
  [ap adj ap]
  [pp prep np]
  [noun block]
  [noun box]
  [noun table]
  [noun one]
  [wh1 where]
  [wh2 what]
  [pn it]
  [v put]
  [v move]
  [v pickup]
  [v putdown]
  [vbe is]
  [adj white]
  [adj red]
  [adj blue]
  [adj green]
  [adj big]
  [adj small]
  [adj large]
  [adj little]
  [prep on]
  [prep onto]
  [prep to]
  [prep over]
  [prep in]
  [prep at]
  [prep under]
  [prep above]
  [prep by]
  [det each]
  [det every]
  [det the]
  [det a]
  [det some]
] -> grammar3;
```

Figure 8-12 Blocksworld grammar

respond to this situation by "composing" a new list of match-patterns which is formed by bringing together match-patterns produced for the syntactic components of the subsequence.

We can express this in the form of a function as is shown in Figure 8-13. Note that the function implements what is basically just a mapping between specific parse-trees and specific match patterns. But in the case where a complex parse-tree is input, the function combines together the meanings (i.e. match-patterns) of the *components* of the parse-tree. Note that we have arranged things such that in the case where the parse-tree indicates an original sentence beginning with either the word "what" or "where", the word is tagged onto the front of the result. This will enable the "conversation" program which we will implement below to deal with these two different types of question more appropriately. The function therefore associates a piece of meaning with each of the syntactic rules in the grammar. However sometimes it overlooks important distinctions. Thus for example the meaning of a noun phrase "np" is the same whatever the determiner (e.g. "the", "a" or "some") and prepositional phrases "pp" effectively ignore their prepositions!.

Given the reasonably large grammar (rulebase) defined in Figure 8-12, we can obtain quite complex parse trees from our **parse** function. Since we are now using the database for a different purpose, we need to define a new function which will locally reset the **database** to the grammar list. This will enable the "parse" function can work in the intended manner. This function can be defined very easily; see Figure 8-13.

We can now obtain the following behaviour:

```
parse_with([where is the big green block], grammar3) ==>
** [[s [wh1 where]
    [vbe is]
    [np [det the]
      [snp [ap [adj big]
         [ap [adj green]]] [noun block]]]]]
```

If we call the **meaning** function on this parse tree, the result is as follows:

```
meaning(parse_with([where is the big green block], grammar3)) ==>
** [where [[= big ? x] [= green ? x] [isa block ? x]]]
```

Tracing the **meaning** function shows us more clearly what is going on here:

```
/* parse_with takes a list of words and a grammar and returns a parse-tree
   for a sentence. If the parse fails it returns false. If there are extra
   words on the end of the sentence it prints a message */

define parse_with(sentence, grammar) -> tree;
   vars database remainder;
   grammar -> database;
   backwards_parse_tree([s], sentence, 30) -> tree -> remainder;
   unless remainder = []
   then [^^remainder has been ignored] =>
   endunless;
   if islist(tree) then hd(tree) -> tree endif
enddefine;
```

Figure 8-13 Parsing with a particular grammar

```
trace meaning;

meaning(parse_with([where is the big green block], grammar3)) ==>

>meaning [s [whl where] [vbe is] [np [det the] [snp [ap [adj big]
                                     [ap [adj green]]] [noun block]]]]
!>meaning [np [det the] [snp [ap [adj big] [ap [adj green]]]
                                                [noun block]]]
!!>meaning [snp [ap [adj big] [ap [adj green]]] [noun block]]
!!!>meaning [ap [adj big] [ap [adj green]]]
!!!!>meaning [adj big]
!!!!<meaning [[= big ? x]]
!!!!>meaning [ap [adj green]]
!!!!!>meaning [adj green]
!!!!!<meaning [[= green ? x]]
!!!!<meaning [[= green ? x]]
!!!<meaning [[= big ? x] [= green ? x]]
!!!>meaning [noun block]
!!!<meaning [[isa block ? x]]
!!<meaning [[= big ? x] [= green ? x] [isa block ? x]]
!<meaning [[= big ? x] [= green ? x] [isa block ? x]]
<meaning [where [[= big ? x] [= green ? x] [isa block ? x]]]

** [where [[= big ? x] [= green ? x] [isa block ? x]]]
```

Note that the result returned by the call:

```
!!!>meaning [ap [adj big] [ap [adj green]]]
```

is the following list of match-patterns:

```
[[= big ? x] [= green ? x]]
```

This list is a composition of the results returned by the calls:

```
!!!!>meaning [adj big]
```

and

```
!!!!!>meaning [adj green]
```

```
/* analyse takes a sentence as input and passes it to subsidiary functions
   for parsing and response */

define analyse(sentence);
   vars trees tree match_patterns;
   if sentence = [bye] then return endif;
   parse_with(sentence, grammar3) -> tree;
   if tree = false then
      [cannot parse sentence] =>
   else
      meaning(tree) -> match_patterns;
      if match_patterns = [] then
         [that does not make sense] =>
      elseif hd(match_patterns) = "where" then
         process_where_question(match_patterns)
      elseif hd(match_patterns) = "what" then
         process_what_question(match_patterns)
      endif;
   endif;
enddefine;
```

Figure 8-14 Distinguishing different kinds of sentence

Building a top-level interpreter

Now that we have a function which computes the meaning of "where" and "what" type input questions in terms of match-patterns, we can write the top-level of the program, i.e. the functions which will interact with the user. First of all we need a function which can take an input question and decide whether it is a "where" question or a "what" question and respond appropriately. Given the way "meaning" treats questions, this is very easy to write. The definition is shown in Figure 8-14.

Next, we need to write the functions which are going to actually deal with the two different types of question. To respond to a "where" question, we need to compute the meaning of the question in terms of match-patterns, match the patterns against the database (using "which") so as to find out which specific objects fit the given description, and finally, output some text which indicates either (1) the fact that there is no single block matching the description or (2) that the block is on a specific thing in the model. The definition of a function which carries out these tasks is shown in the upper part of Figure 8-15. The definition of a function which processes "what" questions using roughly the same strategy is shown in the lower part of the figure.

Finally, we need a function which will interact with the user, i.e. repeatedly read in questions and get them processed. This definition of this function, which is

```
/* process_where_question takes the meaning of a [where is the....] question
   and searches the database of block facts for an appropriate answer */

define process_where_question(question);
   vars patterns objects x y;
   question --> [where ?patterns];
   which("x",patterns) -> objects;
   if objects = [] then
      [no block matches that description] =>
   elseif objects matches [?x] then
      if [^x ison ?y] isin database
      then [on top of ^y] =>
      else [^x is not on top of anything] =>
      endif
   else
      [more than one block matches that description] =>
   endif;
enddefine;

/* process_what_question takes the meaning of a [what is on the....] question
   and searches the database of block facts for an appropriate answer */

define process_what_question(question);
   vars patterns objects x y;
   question --> [what ?patterns];
   which("x",patterns) -> objects;
   if objects = [] then
      [no block matches that description] =>
   elseif objects matches [?x] then
      if [?y ison ^x] isin database
      then [^y is on top of ^x] =>
      else [nothing is on top of ^x] =>
      endif
   else
      [more than one block matches that description] =>
   endif;
enddefine;
```

Figure 8-15 Dealing with two kinds of questions

called **converse**, is shown in Figure 8-16. An interaction with the program we have implemented is as follows:

```
converse();
```

```
** [hello]
? where is the large red block
** [on top of table]
? what is on the large red block
** [objG is on top of objR]
? where is the large red block darling
** [darling has been ignored]
** [on top of table]
? where is the green block
** [more than one block matches that description]
? where is the small green block
** [on top of table]
? where is the white block
** [no block matches that description]
? where is the table
** [no block matches that description]
? where is the large green block
** [on top of objR]
? where are my socks
** [cannot parse sentence]
? bye
** [bye]
```

Obviously, the program we have implemented only allows the most primitive sort of "natural language" interaction. Nevertheless it does illustrate the reason why parse-

---

```
/* converse repeatedly takes input from the user and passes it to analyse
   for response, until the user types bye */

define converse;
   vars input;
   [hello] =>
   until input = [bye] do
      readline() -> input;
      analyse(input);
   enduntil;
   [bye] =>
enddefine;
```

Figure 8-16 Handling interaction with the user

trees are useful in natural language processing. The most important point to note is the fact that parsing is essentially just an implementation of the search mechanism for AND/OR-trees in the special case where rules describe the internal structure of linguistic entities (such as sentences) and "facts" are arranged into a given sequence that will normally correspond to the sequence of words in a sentence.

Meaning in Prolog

We can extract meanings in Prolog in much the same manner as in POP-11. First we express the same facts about the same world of blocks, see Figure 8-17.

The individual predicates of **meaning/3** correspond exactly to the **elseif** branches of the POP-11 function. It has one clause to deal with each part of a possible parse-tree:

```
?- meaning([noun, box], Meaning, Variable).
Meaning = fact(isa, box, _1)
Variable = _1 ?

yes

?- meaning([adj, red], Meaning, Variable).
Meaning = fact(_1, red, _2)
Variable = _2 ?

yes
?- meaning([ap, [adj, big], [ap, [adj, red]]], Meaning,
           Variable).
Meaning = fact(_1, big, _2), fact(_3, red, _2)
Variable = _2 ?

yes
?- meaning([snp, [ap, [adj, big], [ap, [adj, red]]],
           [noun, box]], Meaning, Variable).
Meaning = (fact(_1, big, _2), fact(_3, red, _2)),
          fact(isa, box, _2)
Variable = _2 ?

yes
?- meaning([noun, elephant], Meaning, Variable).
Meaning = fact(isa, elephant, _1)
Variable = _1 ?
```

```
/* fact(Relation, Value, Object_name) */

fact(isa, block, objR).
fact(size, large, objR).
fact(colour, red, objr).
fact(isa, block, objG).
fact(size, large, objG).
fact(colour, green, objg).
fact(isa, block, objB).
fact(size, large, objB).
fact(colour, blue, objb).
fact(objb, ison, objG).
fact(objR, ison, table).
fact(objr, ison, objB).
fact(colour, red, objR).
fact(isa, block, objr).
fact(size, small, objr).
fact(colour, green, objG).
fact(isa, block, objg).
fact(size, small, objg).
fact(colour, blue, objB).
fact(isa, block, objb).
fact(size, small, objb).
fact(objG, ison, objR).
fact(objg, ison, table).
fact(objB, ison, table).

/* meaning(+Tree, -Meaning, -Variable)
   meaning takes a parse-tree and succeeds with a meaning containing match
   patterns and the variable used in the match patterns.  The meaning
   consists of either where(f1, f2...fn) or what(f1, f2...fn) where f1...fn
   are match patterns based on fact(<relation>, <value>, X) and X is the
   match variable. */

meaning([noun, Word], fact(isa, Word, X), X).
meaning([adj, Word], fact(_, Word, X), X).
meaning([snp, Noun], Meaning, X) :-
   meaning(Noun, Meaning, X).
meaning([ap, Adj], Meaning, X) :-
   meaning(Adj, Meaning, X).
meaning([ap, Adj, Ap], (M1, M2), X) :-
   meaning(Adj, M1, X),
   meaning(Ap, M2, X).
meaning([snp, Ap, Noun], (M1, M2), X) :-
   meaning(Ap, M1, X),
   meaning(Noun, M2, X).
meaning([np, [det, _], Snp], Meaning, X) :-
   meaning(Snp, Meaning, X).
meaning([pp, [prep, _], Np], Meaning, X) :-
   meaning(Np, Meaning, X).
meaning([s, [wh1, where], [vbe, is], Np], where(Meaning), X) :-
   meaning(Np, Meaning, X).
meaning([s, [wh2, what], [vbe, is], Pp], what(Meaning), X) :-
   meaning(Pp, Meaning, X).
meaning(_, [], _).
```

Figure 8-17 Extracting the meaning from a parse-tree in Prolog

```
/* rule(+grammar_rule) */

rule([s, v, np, pp]).
rule([s, wh2, vbe, pp]).
rule([np, det, snp]).
rule([snp, noun]).
rule([ap, adj]).
rule([pp, prep, np]).
rule([noun, box]).
rule([noun, one]).
rule([wh2, what]).
rule([v, put]).
rule([v, pickup]).
rule([vbe, is]).
rule([adj, red]).
rule([adj, green]).
rule([adj, small]).
rule([adj, little]).
rule([prep, to]).
rule([prep, onto]).
rule([prep, at]).
rule([prep, above]).
rule([det, each]).
rule([det, the]).
rule([det, some]).
rule([s, wh1, vbe, np]).
rule([np, pn]).
rule([np, det, snp, pp]).
rule([snp, ap, noun]).
rule([ap, adj, ap]).
rule([noun, block]).
rule([noun, table]).
rule([wh1, where]).
rule([pn, it]).
rule([v, move]).
rule([v, putdown]).
rule([adj, white]).
rule([adj, blue]).
rule([adj, big]).
rule([adj, large]).
rule([prep, over]).
rule([prep, on]).
rule([prep, in]).
rule([prep, under]).
rule([prep, by]).
rule([det, every]).
rule([det, a]).
```

Figure 8-18 The blocksworld grammar in Prolog

```
yes
```

Note that meaning/3 makes no direct reference itself to the grammar. If the parse-tree indicates that "elephant" is a noun, then **meaning/3** builds a meaning for it.

The predicates to conduct the conversation and process the two kinds of sentences which can be dealt with follow the same organisation as in POP-11. We have used a built-in library to provide a Prolog version of the POP-11 function **readline/0**.

The work done by **which** in POP-11 is here done in Prolog by **bagof/3** in **process_meaning/2**. The following examples demonstrate the behaviour of some of the components of the conversational system:

```
?- where_is([objb]).
on top of objG
yes
```

```
:- library(readline).

/* converse drives the program. */

converse :-
   write('Hello'), nl,
   one_line(Input),
   possibly_more(Input).

/* one_line(-Input)
   one_line reads in and deals with a line from the user. */

one_line(Input) :-
   readline(Input),
   analyse(Input).

/* possibly_more(+Input)
   possibly_more enables further input to be collected. */

possibly_more([bye]) :-
   write('Bye'), nl.

possibly_more(_) :-
   one_line(Input),
   possibly_more(Input).

/* analyse(+Input)
   analyse parses, extracts the meaning from and responds to
   the user's input. */

analyse([bye]).

analyse(Sentence) :-
   backwards_parse_tree([s], Sentence, 30, Extra, [Tree]),
   maybe_write(Extra),
   meaning(Tree, Meaning, X),
   process_meaning(Meaning, X), !.

analyse(Sentence) :-
   write('cannot parse sentence'), nl.

/* maybe_write(+Input)
   maybe_write writes any extra words of input. */

maybe_write([]).

maybe_write(Extra) :-
   write(Extra),
   write(' has been ignored'), nl.
```

Figure 8-19 Blocksworld conversation in Prolog

```
?- what_is_on([objG]).
objb is on top of objG
yes

?- meaning([noun, box], Meaning, Variable).
Meaning = fact(isa, box, _1)
Variable = _1 ?

yes
?- meaning([noun, box], Meaning, Variable),
   process_meaning(where(Meaning), Variable).
no block matches that description
Meaning = fact(isa, box, _1)
Variable = _1 ?

yes
?- meaning([noun, block], Meaning, Variable),
   process_meaning(where(Meaning), Variable).
more than one block matches that description
Meaning = fact(isa, block, _1)
Variable = _1 ?

yes
```

Finally, we try out the whole system:

```
?- converse.
Hello
? where is the small block
more than one block matches that description
? where is the small green block
on top of table
? what is on the large red block
objG is on top of objR
? where is the green block darling
[darling] has been ignored
more than one block matches that description
? where is the tiny little cube
cannot parse sentence
? bye
Bye
yes
```

```
/* process_meaning(+Meaning, +Pattern variable))
   process_meaning takes a meaning structure containing patterns
   and a pattern variable and deals with it. */

process_meaning([], _) :-
    write('that does not make sense'), nl.

process_meaning(where(Patterns), X) :-
    bagof(X, Patterns, Objects), !,
    where_is(Objects).

process_meaning(what(Patterns), X) :-
    bagof(X, Patterns, Objects), !,
    what_is_on(Objects).

process_meaning(_, _) :-
    write('no block matches that description'), nl.

/* where_is(+Object)
   where_is takes an object and answers the where question. */

where_is([Object]) :-
    fact(Object, ison, Site), !,
    write('on top of '),
    write(Site), nl.

where_is([Object]) :-
    write(Object),
    write(' is not on top of anything'), nl.

where_is([_ | _]) :-
    write('more than one block matches that description'), nl.

/* what_is_on(+Object)
   what_is_on takes an object and answers the what is on question. */

what_is_on([Object]) :-
    (fact(Cover, ison, Object) ; Cover = nothing),
    write(Cover),
    write(' is on top of '),
    write(Object), nl.

what_is_on([_ | _]) :-
    write('more than one block matches that description'), nl.
```

Figure 8-20 Dealing with different question types in Prolog

Reading

Burton and Shadbolt (1987) cover simple natural language processing using POP-11 but their treatment exploits the transition net formalism rather than the phrase structure grammar formalism used here. Noble's book *Natural Language Processin* (Noble, 1988) looks at the problem of natural language in more depth with algo-rithms presented in POP-11. This book forms an ideal next stop for anyone intereste in the NLP subfield. Chapter 5 of Ramsay and Barrett (1987) present a large languag processing program in POP-11; however, this is a state of the art implementatio rather than a toy system. Inevitably, it is quite complex. A more detailed treatmen is to be found in either Natural Language Processing in POP-11 or Natural Languag Processing in Prolog by Gazdar and Mellish (1989a,b).

Volume 1 of the AI handbook (Barr and Feigenbaum 1981, Section IV) intro-duces a wide variety of NLP strategies and programs. Winston (1984, Chapter 9) an Charniak and McDermott (1985, Chapter 4) both provide a comprehensive coverag of sentence parsing and the use of *augmented transition nets*. Chapter 10 of Charnia and McDermott deals with the processing of larger linguistic entities such as stories Aleksander and Burnett's discussion (1987) makes extensive use of colour illustra-tions to clarify the linguistic background for elementary NLP strategies. Bundy *et a* (1980) begin their discussion of language processing by looking at the problem o sentence generation. Examples in this text are in LOGO and LISP. Ramsay's genera overview of the field (Ramsay, 1986) includes a very useful annotated bibliograph A major introductory text in this area is (Winograd, 1983).

Bratko (1990) and Sterling and Shapiro (1986) both have chapters on parsin using the grammar rule notation.

Exercises

1. Extend either of the **converse** programs given above so that it is able to handl questions of the form

where is <block> ?

which block is on <block> ?

which is the small green block?

which is objb?

and

is <block> on <block or table> ?

To do this you will need to implement mechanisms which deal with each type of question ("analyse_where_question" etc.) and modify the "meaning" function very slightly so that it tacks on the appropriate labels to lists of match patterns.

2. Extend either of the **converse** programs given above so that they accept factual statements about the blocks (as well as questions) and make appropriate changes to the representation of the blocksworld: for example,

objz is a small white box.

3. Extend either of the **converse** programs given above so that they they accept commands, such as

put the small green block on the table.

4. Extend your answer to no. 3 to incorporate the planning program from Chapter 7 so that commands can be given which rely on the system being able to plan how to carry out the command.

5. Compare forwards and backwards parsing methods across a range of sentences and grammars, e.g. in terms of the size of the search space, efficiency and possibly kind of solution first found.

9 Expert Systems (probabilistic search)

Introduction

We saw in Chapter 6 that in the case where search rules associate given conclusions with bits of evidence the behaviour produced by the search function simulates a simple form of reasoning. Backwards search corresponds to a process in which a high-level hypothesis is "proved" by invoking lower-level hypotheses and, ultimately, basic facts. Forwards-search corresponds to a process in which an attempt is made to see what conclusions can be drawn by combining basic facts together in different ways.

The complexity and sophistication of the reasoning process produced by the search function is limited only by the sophistication of the rulebase. So far we have only looked at very trivial cases but the basic approach will handle arbitrarily complex domains. Provided that knowledge about a given domain can be expressed in the form of inference rules (search rules), then, we can always build a program which will reason about that domain by applying the ordinary search mechanism.

This opens up the possibility of constructing computer programs which will provide the user with the kind of expert reasoning which can usually only be obtained from a real human expert. For example, we might set up a rulebase which captures the reasoning processes involved in diagnosing some kind of disease. Or alternatively, a rulebase which captures the reasoning processes involved in diagnosing faults in some complex piece of machinery. Once we have the rulebase set up, we can, in principle, obtain "expert" diagnoses simply by running the search function.

Unfortunately, there are at least two problems. Firstly, we have to find some way of making sure that, in any given case, the rulebase contains the correct *facts*. Setting up a rulebase whose rules enable the diagnosis of complex diseases is all very well. But if we want to use the rulebase to obtain a diagnosis of a disease in a given case we need to make sure that we first put in the appropriate facts (e.g. symptoms).

A second problem relates to the nature of the rules themselves. So far we have always assumed that any kind of reasoning process can be implemented in terms of ordinary inference rules. As currently described, these show what conclusions can be drawn from what sort of evidence. But, of course, in many cases, reasoning processes do not involve the application of hard-and-fast inference rules. They involve the application of rules in which bits of evidence provide *support* for a given conclusion without justifying it completely. A medical diagnosis will typically be constructed on the basis of this sort of rule. A given symptom will not completely justify a given diagnosis, it will just provide evidence in favour of it.

Both these problems can be solved quite neatly using a technique which was originally applied in a famous AI program called MYCIN. This program used search-like processes and a rulebase of inference rules to provide diagnoses of blood disorders. The important thing about MYCIN from our point of view is the way in which it solved the two problems noted above. It solved the problem concerning the provision of basic facts by arranging things so that the search function could ask the user questions. It solved the problem concerning non-hard-and-fast inference rules by allowing search rules to be associated with *certainty factors*.

Probabilistic rules

We will deal with the implementation of certainty factors first. The basic idea is quite straightforward. Normally, search rules construed as inference rules have been of the form:

[<conclusion> <bit-of-evidence-1> <bit-of-evidence-2> ...]

A rule of this type states that the <conclusion> is justified if we can show the existence of <bit-of-evidence-1>, <bit-of-evidence-2> etc. As far as the search function is concerned, the rule is just a search rule: the <conclusion> goal can be satisfied provided that all the <bit-of-evidence> subgoals can be satisfied.

An obvious way to implement inference processes which are not hard-and-fast is to provide some means of associating certainty factors with inference rules. A certainty factor might just be a probability value, i.e. a real number between 0 and 1. In this case, an inference rule associated with a given certainty factor C has a different reading to the ordinary inference rule. We say that the probability of the <conclusion> being justified given the existence of all the bits of evidence is C.

Unfortunately, this does not quite solve the problem. Recall that the process of showing that the bits of evidence exist will involve satisfying all the <bit-of-evidence> subgoals. These subgoals may correspond to facts and in this case they are just satisfied automatically. On the other hand they may only be satisfiable by invoking other inference rules. This raises the question of what should happen if the other inference rules are *also* probabilistic. In this case, the <bit-of-evidence> subgoals can only be satisfied with a given level of certainty.

The problem is actually a very general one. It can be stated as follows. Given a set of assumptions, all of which are associated with a given level of certainty, and which, in combination, justify the drawing of a given conclusion, how can we combine together the certainties of the assumptions so as to assign a certainty to the conclusion?

Basic probability theory

Basic probability theory seems to provide an answer. It states that if two arbitrary events[1] A and B are associated with given levels of probability P(A) and P(B), the probability of A and B occurring together is just $P(A) \times P(B)$.

Let us put this in the context of concrete example. Imagine that we have an inference rule of the form:

```
[[wind none] 0.3 [pressure high][clouds alto_stratus]]
```

This states that the probability of the conclusion [wind none] (i.e. "no wind") given the fact that there are alto-stratus clouds and the pressure is high is exactly 0.3. Note that the rule is of the usual search-rule form except for the presence of the certainty factor which appears between the goal and the subgoals, and the fact that goals are list objects rather than word objects.

Let us imagine that we have found that the [pressure high] subgoal can be satisfied with a certainty of 0.6 and that the [clouds alto_stratus] subgoal can be satisfied with a certainty of 0.5. Seemingly, probability theory dictates that the probability of the [wind none] conclusion being justified is:

$$0.5 \times 0.6 \times 0.3$$

since the probability of both subgoals together is just the product of the corresponding certainties.

What is rather unfortunate is the fact that we are left drawing the conclusion [wind none] with an extremely low level of certainty, namely 0.09. This seems *extremely* low given the fact that we are fairly certain that there is high pressure and fairly certain that the clouds are alto-stratus.

In fact, this way of combining together certainty factors is quite inappropriate. The whole point of the given inference rule is that the combination of high pressure and alto-stratus is a *special case* which should lead to the conclusion [no wind]. Thus, straightforward application of the product rule from probability theory is

[1] In probability theory an "event" can be anything with which we can associate a given probability. Thus, events can correspond to bits of evidence.

inappropriate. The product rule works on the basis that there is *nothing* special about the conjunction of the pieces of evidence.[2]

Fuzzy set theory

A strand of probability theory attributable to Zadeh, called Fuzzy Set theory (Zadeh 1965), provides a solution.[3] Fuzzy set theory states that, for ordinary conjunctive inference rules (i.e. the sort of rule we have considered so far), the certainty of a given conclusion is just the *minimum* of the certainties of the premises (i.e. the <bit-of-evidence subgoals). This seems to make reasonably good intuitive sense. If our certainty that the pressure is high is 0.6, and our certainty that the clouds are alto-stratus is 0.5, then it seems acceptable to say that our certainty that the pressure is high *and* that the clouds are alto-stratus is the lesser of the two figures, namely 0.5.

Fuzzy set theory also provides a way of combining together a set of certainties for the *same* conclusion. This is essential if we want to find out what the overall certainty of a conclusion is. Recall, that in the usual search scenario, there will be a range of ways of deriving a certain conclusion. In a simple case, these will just correspond to the search rules which feature the given conclusion, e.g.

```
[[westerly wind] [low pressure] [unstable weather]]
[[westerly wind] [warm front]]
```

If we are only interested in testing to see whether the conclusion *can* be proved, then any way of deriving it is sufficient. But where our rules are probabilistic then we can never prove a conclusion completely. We can only show that it has a certain degree of certainty (probability of being true). So, if there are N ways of deriving a conclusion deriving it one way gives it a certain degree of certainty, deriving it another way gives it an extra degree of certainty, and so on. The question is, how can we add up all these probabilities to work out what the overall certainty of the conclusion is?

Shortliffe, in his work on the MYCIN system (Shortliffe, 1976), proposed the following method. If H is a conclusion which has previously been shown to have certainty C1, then, if we find a way of showing that it also has a certainty C2 (using a different proof tree), then the overall certainty of H is:

$C1 + C2 - (C1 \times C2)$ *if C1 and C2 are both positive*

$C1 + C2 + (C1 \times C2)$ *if C1 and C2 are both negative*

$(C1 + C2) / (1 - \min(\mathrm{abs}(C1), \mathrm{abs}(C2)))$ *if C1 and C2 have different signs*

---

[2] Technically, it assumes that they are statistically independent.
[3] Fuzzy Set theory is a generalisation of Boolean logic.

These rules seem to provide the sort of effect we are looking for. For example in the case where we have derived two different levels of (positive) certainty for a given conclusion we would like to somehow add them together so as to get an increased level overall. But we cannot just add them together. In general this will give us a probability that exceeds 1. Shortliffe's first rule above allows them to be added together in a way which will increase the level of certainty but not cause it to exceed 1. The other rules take care of the other cases in a similar way.

MYCIN-like search

How can we implement these ideas about certainty factors in the search function? As usual there are a number of possibilities; we will look at a very simple approach. First of all, let us set up a rulebase which captures reasoning processes related to the domain of weather-prediction.[4] The rules will all be probabilistic; that is to say all rules will be associated with a given certainty factor. The certainty factor will indicate the probability of the conclusion given the premises (i.e. bits of evidence):

```
[ [[season winter] 1 [month december]]
  [[season winter] 1 [month january]]
  [[season winter] 0.9 [month february]]
  [[season spring] 0.7 [month march]]
  [[season spring] 0.9 [month april]]
  [[season spring] 0.6 [month may]]
  [[season summer] 0.8 [month june]]
  [[season summer] 1 [month july]]
  [[season summer] 1 [month august]]
  [[season autumn] 0.8 [month september]]
  [[season autumn] 0.7 [month october]]
  [[season autumn] 0.6 [month november]]
  [[pressure high] 0.6 [weather_yesterday good]
                       [stability_of_the_weather stable]]
  [[pressure high] 0.9 [clouds high]]
  [[pressure high] 0.9 [clouds none]]
  [[temp cold] 0.9 [season winter] [pressure high]]
  [[temp cold] 0.6 [season summer] [pressure low]]
  [[wind none] 0.3 [pressure high]]
  [[wind east] 0.3 [pressure high]]
  [[wind west] 0.6 [pressure low]]
  [[temp warm] 0.8 [wind south]]
```

[4] The rulebase is a slightly modified version of the one provided in Chapter 3 of Ramsay and Barrett (1987).

```
    [[temp cold] 0.9 [wind east] [clouds none] [season winter]]
    [[temp warm] 0.9 [wind none] [pressure high]
                                 [season summer]]
    [[rain yes] 0.4 [whereabouts west]]
    [[temp cold] 0.4 [whereabouts north]]
    [[rain no] 0.7 [whereabouts east]]
    [[rain yes] 0.3 [season spring] [clouds low]]
    [[rain yes] 0.3 [season spring] [clouds high]]
    [[temp warm] 0.7 [season summer]]
    [[rain yes] 0.2 [season summer] [temp warm]]
    [[rain yes] 0.6 [pressure low]]
    [[rain yes] 0.6 [wind west]]
    [[rain yes] 0.8 [clouds low]]
    [[temp cold] 0.8 [season autumn] [clouds none]]
    [[temp cold] 0.7 [season winter]]
 ] -> rulebase7;
```

If you examine this rulebase carefully, you will find that the rules seem to make sense. The second-to-last rule, for example, captures the proposition that the probability of it being cold, given the fact that it is autumn and the fact that there are no clouds, is quite high (0.8). Many other propositions are captured by this rulebase, e.g. the fact that it rains more in the west, the fact that it is colder in the north and the fact that high pressure and no wind are usually associated with warm weather.

In setting up this rulebase we have departed from the format followed in previous chapters. Rules are of the form:

[<goal> <certainty> <subgoal1> <subgoal2> ...]

rather than of the form:

[<goal> <subgoal1> <subgoal2> ...]

To take account of this we need to update our backwards search function and, of course, the way in which we change the function must reflect the certainty-combination rules provided by Fuzzy set theory. If we want the function to implement a search process similar to that implemented by the MYCIN program, we also need to arrange things such that in the case where it is unable to find a fact it is looking for, it asks the user a question. It will be easier if we address the latter task first.

We need to change the function so that, given any particular goal, it checks the rulebase to see if there are any rules (or facts) which might satisfy that goal, and if not, asks the user whether the goal can be assumed to be "given by assumption". This involves calling the database function "present" to check whether the desired entry is present and then, if it is not, calling the interactive function "yesno". The new version of the function is as shown in Figure 9-1.

However the function terminates (like previous versions of backwards search) when it finds its *first* solution. It does *not* seek out all solutions and join them together as multiple evidence for the goal.

Note also that in the case where the rulebase contains no rule which will enable the satisfaction of the given goal, the function **yesno** is called. In effect, the function asks the user whether the goal can be assumed to be satisfied. If the user responds with a "yes", the **yesno** function returns **<true>** and the overall result is a list with the word **USER_RESPONSE** substituted in for the solution tree.

Testing the search function on the goal `[rain yes]` produces the following behaviour (note that words typed after the **?** prompt are input from the user):

```
/* backwards_search_tree1 takes a list of goals and produces a list of
   solution trees or false if no solution can be found */

define backwards_search_tree1(goals) -> tree;
   vars goal subgoals other_goals first_tree other_trees;
   if goals = [] then [] -> tree; return
   else goals --> [?goal ??other_goals];
        if present([^goal ==]) then
           foreach [^goal = ??subgoals] do
                backwards_search_tree1(subgoals) -> first_tree;
                if islist(first_tree)
                then backwards_search_tree1(other_goals)
                     -> other_trees;
                     if islist(other_trees)
                     then [[^goal ^^first_tree] ^^other_trees]
                          -> tree; return
                     endif
                endif
           endforeach;
        elseif yesno([is ^(goal(2)) the value of ^(goal(1))]) then
               backwards_search_tree1(other_goals) -> other_trees;
               if islist(other_trees)
               then [[^goal [[USER RESPONSE]]] ^^other_trees] -> tree;
                    return
               endif
        endif;
   endif;
   false -> tree
enddefine;
```

Figure 9-1 Building solution trees with input from the user

```
vars tree;
rulebase7 -> database;
trace backwards_search_tree1;

backwards_search_tree1([[rain yes]]) -> tree;

> backwards_search_tree1 [[rain yes]]
!> backwards_search_tree1 [[whereabouts west]]
** [is west the value of whereabouts]
? no
!< backwards_search_tree1 <false>
!> backwards_search_tree1 [[season spring] [clouds low]]
!!> backwards_search_tree1 [[month march]]
** [is march the value of month]
? no
!!< backwards_search_tree1 <false>
!!> backwards_search_tree1 [[month april]]
** [is april the value of month]
? yes
!!!> backwards_search_tree1 []
!!!< backwards_search_tree1 []
!!< backwards_search_tree1 [[[month april] [[USER RESPONSE]]]]
!!> backwards_search_tree1 [[clouds low]]
** [is low the value of clouds]
? yes
!!!> backwards_search_tree1 []
!!!< backwards_search_tree1 []
!!< backwards_search_tree1 [[[clouds low] [[USER RESPONSE]]]]
!< backwards_search_tree1 [[[season spring] [[month april]
   [[USER RESPONSE]]]] [[clouds low] [[USER RESPONSE]]]]
!> backwards_search_tree1 []
!< backwards_search_tree1 []
< backwards_search_tree1 [[[rain yes] [[season spring]
  [[month april] [[USER RESPONSE]]]] [[clouds low]
  [[USER RESPONSE]]]]]
```

We assigned the result of this call into the global variable **tree**. Thus we can get the tree printed out using the **showtree** command, see Figure 9-2.

In a liberal reading of this solution tree we might say that the search function showed that it is raining by showing that it is springtime and the clouds are low. It showed that it is springtime by showing that it is April; and it showed that it is April

```
showtree(hd(tree));

            ____________
            |rain yes|
            ____________
                 |
       ____________________
       |                  |
 _______________    _____________
 |season spring|    |clouds low|
 _______________    _____________
       |                  |
 _____________      _______________
 |month april|      |USER RESPONSE|
 _____________      _______________
       |
 _______________
 |USER_RESPONSE|
 _______________
```

Figure 9-2 A solution tree

and the clouds are low by asking the user[5].

Implementing certainty-factors

We have now shown that the backwards search function can be adapted so as to handle the case where facts can be extracted either directly from the rulebase itself or indirectly from the user. Attention can now turn to the second modification required. This involves arranging things such that the function can combine certainty values together in a manner which reflects the dictates of Fuzzy set theory (and the implementation of the MYCIN program).

The approach here involves changing the function such that instead of returning a solution tree (proof tree) for the input goals (conclusions), it returns a certainty value for them. In the case where the function obtains one certainty value **c1** for the subgoals of the current goal, and another **c2** for all the remaining goals, it should simply multiply **c1** by the certainty factor for the search rule in question and then

[5] We define root to make showtree work nicely

```
define root(tree) -> root_name;
    vars property value subtrees;
    tree --> [[?property ?value] ??subtrees];
    property >< ' ' >< value -> root_name
enddefine;
```

return the minimum of the result and **c2**. This will lead to a correct application of the Fuzzy set theory formulae.

Obviously, in the case where a goal is satisfied by querying the user, the goal can be assumed to have been satisfied with perfect certainty, i.e. with a certainty value of 1. The overall certainty value to be returned is therefore just the **c2** value, i.e. the certainty for the remaining goals. The new definition is shown in Figure 9-3.

Testing this function on the same goal leads to the following behaviour. Note that the user responses are identical:

```
trace backwards_search_value;
```

```
/* backward_search_value takes a list of goals and returns the certainty
   factor derived from the first successful solution which it finds for each
   goal */

define backwards_search_value(goals) -> certainty;
   vars goal subgoals other_goals c c1 c2;
   if goals = [] then 1 -> certainty; return
   else goals --> [?goal ??other_goals];
         if present([^goal ==]) then
            foreach [^goal ?c ??subgoals] do
                  backwards_search_value(subgoals) -> c1;
                  if isnumber(c1)
                  then backwards_search_value(other_goals) -> c2;
                        if isnumber(c2)
                        then min(c * c1, c2) -> certainty;
                              return
                        endif
                  endif
            endforeach;
         elseif yesno([is ^(goal(2)) the value of ^(goal(1))]) then
                  backwards_search_value(other_goals) -> c2;
                  if isnumber(c2)
                  then c2 -> certainty;
                        return
                  endif
         endif;
   endif;
   false -> certainty
enddefine;
```

Figure 9-3 Computing the certainty value of a solution tree

```
backwards_search_value([[rain yes]]) ==>
> backwards_search_value [[rain yes]]
!> backwards_search_value [[whereabouts west]]
** [is west the value of whereabouts]
? no
!< backwards_search_value <false>
!> backwards_search_value [[season spring] [clouds low]]
!!> backwards_search_value [[month march]]
** [is march the value of month]
? no
!!< backwards_search_value <false>
!!> backwards_search_value [[month april]]
** [is april the value of month]
? yes
!!!> backwards_search_value []
!!!< backwards_search_value 1
!!< backwards_search_value 1
!!> backwards_search_value [[clouds low]]
** [is low the value of clouds]
? yes
!!!> backwards_search_value []
!!!< backwards_search_value 1
!!< backwards_search_value 1
!< backwards_search_value 0.9
!> backwards_search_value []
!< backwards_search_value 1
< backwards_search_value 0.27
** 0.27
```

Thus, the `[rain yes]` conclusion is derived in this solution with a certainty of 0.27, i.e. with a fairly low degree of certainty given the evidence provided.

But the above changes still return the certainty factor for the *first* solution found. Further modification is required to ensure that *all* solutions are found and their certainty factors combined as described earlier. In this case we have to make some decision about negative evidence and we have arranged that the value -1 is returned as the certainty factor if the user answers "no" when asked a factual question. An implication of this is that each time we fail to prove a goal, this failure in itself reduces our certainty of the goal. We could make failure more neutral by returning the value 0 if the user answers "no" to a question. Another implication is that if we can prove the goal by a variety of routes, this increases our certainty of the goal. A second change that has to be made is to store the user's answer to each question because the same question should not be asked more than once (where it is required by more than one solution tree). This is achieved by using the built-in procedure **add** to add the goal asked about to the database together with 1 if the answer was "yes" or -1 if the answer was "no", e.g. `[[month april] 1]`. This has the same form as the other rules in the database except that there are no subgoals, i.e. it is a fact.

Running **backwards_search_values** gives the following behaviour:

```
rulebase7 -> database;

backwards_search_values([[rain yes]]) ==>
** [is west the value of whereabouts]
? yes
** [is march the value of month]
? no
** [is low the value of clouds]
? yes
** [is april the value of month]
? yes
** [is may the value of month]
? no
** [is high the value of clouds]
? no
** [is june the value of month]
? no
** [is south the value of wind]
? yes
** [is good the value of weather_yesterday]
? yes
** [is stable the value of stability_of_the_weather]
? yes
** [is none the value of clouds]
? no
** [is july the value of month]
? no
** [is august the value of month]
? no
** [is low the value of pressure]
? no
** 0.204799

database ==>
** [[[pressure low] -1]                        /* STORED ANSWERS TO */
    [[month august] -1]                        /* QUESTIONS         */
    [[month july] -1]
```

```
/* backwards_search_values takes a list of goals and returns the overall
   certainty that they are all true by exploring the whole search space.
   Negative answers score -1. */

define backwards_search_values(goals) -> certainty;
    vars goal subgoals other_goals boolean c c1 c2;
    if goals = [] then 1 -> certainty
    else goals --> [?goal ??other_goals];
        if present([^goal ==]) then
            0 -> certainty;
            foreach [^goal ?c ??subgoals] do
                backwards_search_values(subgoals) -> c1;
                backwards_search_values(other_goals) -> c2;
                combine(min(c * c1, c2),certainty) -> certainty;
            endforeach;
        else yesno([is ^(goal(2)) the value of ^(goal(1))])
                -> boolean;
            if boolean then 1 -> c1 else -1 -> c1 endif;
            add([^goal ^c1]);
            backwards_search_values(other_goals) -> c2;
            min(c1, c2) -> certainty;
        endif;
    endif;
enddefine;

/* combine takes two certainty values each of which refers to the same goal
   and computes their combined effect as per the rules given in the text. */

define combine(c1,c2) -> certainty;
   if c1 >= 0 and c2 >= 0
   then c1 + c2 - (c1 * c2) -> certainty
   elseif c1 < 0 and c2 < 0
   then c1 + c2 + (c1 * c2) -> certainty
   else (1 - min(abs(c1),abs(c2))) -> certainty;
       unless certainty = 0
       then (c1 + c2)/certainty -> certainty
       endunless
   endif
enddefine;
```

Figure 9-4 Computing the the certainty value from the whole search tree

```
[[clouds none] -1]
[[stability_of_the_weather stable] 1]
[[weather_yesterday good] 1]
```

```
[[wind south] 1]
[[month june] -1]
[[clouds high] -1]
[[month may] -1]
[[month april] 1]
[[clouds low] 1]
[[month march] -1]
[[whereabouts west] 1]
[[season winter] 1 [month december]]
[[season winter] 1 [month january]]

/* AND SO ON, AS IN THE ORIGINAL RULEBASE */
```

Notice that the system explores all ways of establishing [rain yes]. Notice also that it has no way (in the system as given) of inferring that if the month is April then the month is not August! See, e.g. Ramsay and Barrett (1987) on how to deal with this.

Forwards or backwards

The version of the search function developed in this chapter is similar, in its behaviour, to the AI system called MYCIN. MYCIN is usually referred to as an *expert system* on the grounds that the way in which it carries out the search process roughly approximates the way in which a real human expert might go about constructing a medical diagnosis. The inference rules employed are probabilistic and in the case where some piece of evidence is required but not given as a fact, the program just the asks the user whether it can be assumed to exist.

The search strategy employed by MYCIN (and the function constructed above) employs backwards search, i.e. reasoning backwards from goals to known facts. This is inevitable given the assumption that all facts are provided directly by the user in query responses. If there are no facts in the rulebase, there is no basis on which a forwards search can be initiated. However, although the interactive behaviour of MYCIN is incompatible with forwards search, the probabilistic aspect of its behaviour is not. It is quite possible for a forwards search function to implement the Fuzzy set rules in exactly the same way as the backwards function.

An interesting intermediate strategy involves search which alternates between forwards behaviour and backwards behaviour. This sort of system might initially accept some basic facts (e.g. symptoms). It would then work bottom-up until some hypotheses have been developed. From these hypotheses it could work top-down so as to generate a new set of primitive goals which can be presented as queries to the patient. The patient's answers constitute satisfaction of the primitive goals; thus another phase of bottom-up search can begin. Eventually, this *bi-directional* strategy will tend to isolate a single high-level conclusion representing a diagnosis (if a single

```
/* rule(+Rule)
   rule([<Successor>, <Certainty>, <Predecessor(s)>]) */

rule([[season, winter], 1, [month, december]]).
rule([[season, winter], 1, [month, january]]).
rule([[season, winter], 0.9, [month, february]]).
rule([[season, spring], 0.7, [month, march]]).
rule([[season, spring], 0.9, [month, april]]).
rule([[season, spring], 0.6, [month, may]]).
rule([[season, summer], 0.8, [month, june]]).
rule([[season, summer], 1, [month, july]]).
rule([[season, summer], 1, [month, august]]).
rule([[season, autumn], 0.8, [month, september]]).
rule([[season, autumn], 0.7, [month, october]]).
rule([[season, autumn], 0.6, [month, november]]).
rule([[pressure, high], 0.6,
     [weather_yesterday, good], [stability_of_the_weather, stable]]).
rule([[pressure, high], 0.9, [clouds, high]]).
rule([[pressure, high], 0.9, [clouds, none]]).
rule([[temp, cold], 0.9, [season, winter], [pressure, high]]).
rule([[temp, cold], 0.6, [season, summer], [pressure, low]]).
rule([[wind, none], 0.3, [pressure, high]]).
rule([[wind, east], 0.3, [pressure, high]]).
rule([[wind, west], 0.6, [pressure, low]]).
rule([[temp, warm], 0.8, [wind, south]]).
rule([[temp, cold], 0.9,
     [wind, east], [clouds, none], [season, winter]]).
rule([[temp, warm], 0.9,
     [wind, none], [pressure, high], [season, summer]]).
rule([[rain, yes], 0.4, [whereabouts, west]]).
rule([[temp, cold], 0.4, [whereabouts, north]]).
rule([[rain, no], 0.7, [whereabouts, east]]).
rule([[rain, yes], 0.3, [season, spring], [clouds, low]]).
rule([[rain, yes], 0.3, [season, spring], [clouds, high]]).
rule([[temp, warm], 0.7, [season, summer]]).
rule([[rain, yes], 0.2, [season, summer], [temp, warm]]).
rule([[rain, yes], 0.6, [pressure, low]]).
rule([[rain, yes], 0.6, [wind, west]]).
rule([[rain, yes], 0.8, [clouds, low]]).
rule([[temp, cold], 0.8, [season, autumn], [clouds, none]]).
rule([[temp, cold], 0.7, [season, winter]]).
```

Figure 9-5 The weather rules in Prolog

diagnosis only is wanted).

This strategy seems to combine the good-features of backwards search with the good features of forwards search and in fact, there is a well-known expert system called "Internist" which exploits it. The system diagnoses diseases of the internal organs like heart, lungs, and liver.

Probabilistic search in Prolog

Only a small change is needed to the predicate **backwards_search_tree/2** introduced in Chapter 6 to take account of the new rule format which includes a certainty value. The rules themselves are very similar to those in Chapter 6 except for the inclusion of the certainty value, see Figure 9-5.

Augmenting **backwards_search_tree/2** to return a certainty value rather than a tree is also straightforward except that some of the arithmetic functions available in POP-11 have to be defined by hand in POPLOG Prolog, see Figure 9-6. This time **backwards_search_tree/2** has three cases to deal with. The first clause represents the stopping condition that when there is an empty list of goals there is an empty tree. The second clause is similar to the previous definitions and deals with the case where there is a rule for the first of the goals. The third clause deals with the case where there is no rule for the goal and the user should be asked directly. Function **yesno/2** prints its first argument and returns in its second argument a list of whatever the user types in response:

```
?- yesno([month, april], Answer).
is april the value of month
? yes
Answer = [yes] ? ;
no

?- yesno([jack, sprat], [no]).
is sprat the value of jack
? no
yes
```

Running **backwards_search_tree/2** produces the same behaviour as in POP-11:

```
?- backwards_search_tree([[rain, yes]], Tree).
is west the value of whereabouts
? no
is march the value of month
? no
is april the value of month
```

```
/* backwards_search_tree(+Goals, -Trees).
   backwards_search_tree takes a list of goals and constructs a list of
   search trees. Where no rule can be found the user is asked about the goal.
   The first solution found for each goal is returned. */

backwards_search_tree([], []).

backwards_search_tree([Goal | Goals], [[Goal | Tree] | Trees]) :-
    rule([Goal, Certainty | Subgoals]),
    backwards_search_tree(Subgoals, Tree),
    backwards_search_tree(Goals, Trees).

backwards_search_tree([Goal | Goals],
                      [[Goal, 'USER_RESPONSE'] | Trees]) :-
    yesno(Goal, [yes]),
    backwards_search_tree(Goals, Trees).

/* yesno(+Goal, ?Answer)
   yesno prints a question constructed from the Goal and returns the user's
   answer or matches it against the desired answer. */

:- library(readline).

yesno([Property, Value], Answer) :-
    write('is '),
    write(Value),
    write(' the value of '),
    write(Property), nl,
    readline(Answer).
```

Figure 9-6 Finding a solution tree in Prolog

```
/* backwards_search_value(+Goals, -Certainty).
   backwards_search_value takes a list of goals and returns the certainty
   of them all being true based on taking the minimum of the certainties
   of a set of goals as the certainty of the set. */

backwards_search_value([], 1).

backwards_search_value([Goal | Goals], Certainty) :-
    rule([Goal, C | Subgoals]),
    backwards_search_value(Subgoals, C1),
    backwards_search_value(Goals, C2),
    C_here is C * C1,
    min(C_here, C2, Certainty).

backwards_search_value([Goal | Goals], C2) :-
    yesno(Goal, [yes]),
    backwards_search_value(Goals, C2).

/* min(+X, +Y, -Z).
   min returns in Z the minimum of X and Y */

min(X, Y, X) :-
    X =< Y, !.
min(X, Y, Y).
```

Figure 9-7 Computing the certainty value of a solution tree in Prolog

```
? yes
is low the value of clouds
? yes
Tree = [[[rain, yes], [[season, spring],
        [[month, april], USER_RESPONSE]],
        [[clouds, low], USER_RESPONSE]]] ?
yes

?- backwards_search_value([[rain, yes]], Value).
is west the value of whereabouts
? no
is march the value of month
? no
is april the value of month
? yes
is low the value of clouds
```

```
? yes
Value = 0.27 ?
yes
```

Extending the procedure to compute the combined certainty of all solutions requires the same extra facilities as in POP-11, namely a method of working through all the applicable rules and combining their certainties as well as storing user's answers so that the same question does not get asked twice over. In POP-11 we used a **foreach** to loop through the rules. Here we use **bagof** to generate the list of rules to be considered and a new predicate **backwards_search_or** to consider them all, see Figure 9-8.

In many respects this is the same kind of search that was discussed in Chapter 5, namely searching a game tree using minimaxing. As there, the whole tree is searched below a given point (or at least down to a given depth) and values from the leaf nodes are fed upwards to combine to give the overall score of the root node.

Let us demonstrate **combine/3**. Note that **abs/2** was defined in Chapter 4 in connection with the 8-puzzle:

```
?- combine(0.5, 0.5, K).
K = 0.75 ? ;
no

?- combine(0, 1, K).
K = 0 ? ;
no
```

In each case **combine/3** returns only a single solution because of the cuts.

The predicate **backwards_search_value/2** considers the whole solution space, and so searches an AND/OR tree. The rule for combining certainties at the AND nodes is to take the minimum of the contributing values. The rule for combining certainties at the OR nodes is via the predicate **combine/3** called within **backwards_search_or/2**. Running **backwards_search_values/2** gives largely the same behaviour as the POP-11 version, though some of the questions are asked in a slightly different order.

We use **augment/3** to add to the database of rules once a question has been asked. This means that if you rerun the program it may make use of rules asserted as part of the previous run unless the original ruleset is recompiled before restarting. Unlike the POP-11 procedure of the same name, **yesno/2** does not loop until the user either types "yes", "no", "y" or "n". This means that mistyping exactly either "yes" or "no" will produce unexpected certainty values and questions:

```
?- backwards_search_values([[rain, yes]], V).
is west the value of whereabouts
```

```
/* backwards_search_values(+Goals, -Certainty).
   backwards_search_values takes a list of goals and computes the overall
   certainty that the goals are all true via all possible paths.  paths which
   fail reduce the overall certainty. */

backwards_search_values([], 1).

backwards_search_values([Goal | Goals], Certainty) :-
    bagof([C | Subgoals], rule([Goal, C | Subgoals]), List),
    backwards_search_or(List, C1),
    backwards_search_values(Goals, C2),
    min(C1, C2, Certainty).

backwards_search_values([Goal | Goals], Certainty) :-
    yesno(Goal, Answer),
    augment(Goal, Answer, C1),
    backwards_search_values(Goals, C2),
    min(C1, C2, Certainty).

/* backwards_search_or(+Bag_of_subgoals, -Certainty)
   backwards_search_or takes a bag of alternative subgoals each associated
   with a certainty and computes the combined certainty of the set. */

backwards_search_or([], 0).

backwards_search_or([[C | Subgoals] | Others], Certainty) :-
    backwards_search_values(Subgoals, C1),
    backwards_search_or(Others, C2),
    C_here is C * C1,
    combine(C_here, C2, Certainty).
```

Figure 9-8 Computing the certainty value of the search space

```
/* combine(+C1, +C2, -Certainty)
   combine computes certainty from C1 and C2 as for an OR node. */

combine(C1, C2, Certainty) :-
    C1 >= 0, C2 >= 0, !,
    Certainty is C1 + C2 - (C1 * C2).

combine(C1, C2, Certainty) :-
    C1 < 0, C2 < 0, !,
    Certainty is C1 + C2 + (C1 * C2).

combine(C1, C2, 0) :-
    abs(C1, C11),  abs(C2, C22),
    min(C11, C22, 1), !.

combine(C1, C2, Certainty) :-
    abs(C1, C11),  abs(C2, C22),
    min(C11, C22, C3),
    Certainty is (C1 + C2)/(1 - C3).

/* augment(+Goal, +Answer, -Value)
   augment returns the numerical value of answer and also adds the goal
   with its numerical value to the database. The new database entries
   are similar in form to existing rules, except that they have no
   subgoals. */

augment(Goal, [yes], 1) :-
    asserta(rule([Goal, 1])).

augment(Goal, [no], -1) :-
    asserta(rule([Goal, -1])).
```

Figure 9-9 Computing certainty values in Prolog

```
? yes
is march the value of month
? no
is april the value of month
? yes
is may the value of month
? no
is low the value of clouds
? yes
is high the value of clouds
```

```
? no
is june the value of month
? no
is july the value of month
? no
is august the value of month
? no
is south the value of wind
? yes
is good the value of weather_yesterday
? yes
is stable the value of stability_of_the_weather
? yes
is none the value of clouds
? no
is low the value of pressure
? no
V = 0.204799 ?
yes

?- listing(rule).
rule([[pressure, low], -1]). /* HERE ARE THE FACTS   */
rule([[clouds, none], -1]).  /* THAT HAVE BEEN ADDED */
rule([[stability_of_the_weather, stable], 1]). /* AS A RESULT */
rule([[weather_yesterday, good], 1]). /* OF THE USER'S ANSWERS */
rule([[wind, south], 1]).
rule([[month, august], -1]).
rule([[month, july], -1]).
rule([[month, june], -1]).
rule([[clouds, high], -1]).
rule([[clouds, low], 1]).
rule([[month, may], -1]).
rule([[month, april], 1]).
rule([[month, march], -1]).
rule([[whereabouts, west], 1]).
rule([[season, winter], 1, [month, december]]).
rule([[season, winter], 1, [month, january]]).

/* AND SO ON, AS IN THE ORIGINAL RULES */
```

Reading

The main reference for MYCIN is (Shortliffe, 1976). Chapter 3 or Ramsay and Barrett (1987) provides a discussion of, and a POP-11 implementation for a MYCIN-like system. Charniak and McDermott (1985, Chapter 8) provide an excellent discussion of ways of dealing with uncertainty in expert systems. Volume 2 of the AI handbook (Barr and Feigenbaum, 1981) covers most of the more important expert systems. Forsyth (1984, pp. 51-62) discusses the processing of certainty factors.

Bratko (1990) describes a more complex expert system mechanism in Prolog including the possibility of answering "why" and "how" questions.

Exercises

1. Write a set of probabilistic rules which would enable the "backwards_search" function provided above to diagnose bicycle faults. The rules will need to be set up so as to capture relationships between faults and symptoms, e.g.

[[fault chain-off] 0.8 [pedals spinning][back-wheel jammed]]

Define a function called "diagnose_fault" which will take a list of symptoms and produce a list of possible diagnoses with their associated certainties.

2. Change the value of an answer "no" from -1 to 0 in `backwards_search_values` and see what effect it has.

3. Augment `backwards_search_values` and/or the rulebase so that answering yes to one question about which month it is automatically excludes the other possibilities (and, e.g. agreeing that the clouds are "high" excludes them being "low").

4. Compare the programs to compute the minimax value of a node with the programs given in this chapter to compute the certainty value of a node.

5. Write a program to draw the AND/OR search tree defined by the weather rules.

10
Concept learning (description search)

Introduction

We have seen that, in general, search is a process which tries to link up goals with facts. In forwards search, the search function works forwards from the set of facts looking for the set of goals. In backwards search, the search function works backwards from the goals looking for the supporting facts. Although, normally, both the goals and the facts are *given* we have seen in the previous chapter that in the case where we construe goals as conclusions and facts as premises it is sometimes advantageous to make the search function generate the goals and/or the facts. Forwards search can be used to discover which high-level conclusions can be drawn from the given set of facts and backwards search can be used to see which sets of facts might enable the drawing of given conclusions.

The latter process (generating facts by searching backwards from goals) has a very useful application outside the domain of expert reasoning. To understand this application we need to come to terms with yet another way of construing the goals and facts which make up search rules. We have to construe goals and facts as names of *properties* or *features*. In this construal, goals always correspond to higher-level (i.e. more abstract) features while facts will correspond to lower-level (i.e. more concrete) features. Search rules will simply state that a given higher-level feature subsumes some given lower-level features.[1]

Consider the following rulebase:

```
[ [polygon rectangle]
  [polygon triangle]
```

---

[1] Note that from here on we will use the word "feature" interchangeably with "property".

```
[triangle equilateral_triangle]
[triangle right_angled_triangle] ]
```

In the normal construal we would read the first search rule as stating that the goal "polygon" can be satisfied if the subgoal "rectangle" can be satisfied. However, in the new construal we say that the first search rule states that the "polygon" feature subsumes the "rectangle" feature. We read the last search rule as stating that the "triangle" feature subsumes the "right_angled_triangle" feature. Moreover, since there are no rules in this rulebase which have "right_angled_triangle" appearing as the first element we assume that this feature is a concrete feature which does not subsume any lower-level feature.

Let us imagine that we have a version of the backwards search function which takes in a list of goals and generates the sets of facts which would enable the goals to be satisfied. If the rulebase contains rules relating higher-level features to lower-level features then our new search function will, effectively, take in a list of higher-level features and return all the different sets of concrete features which are compatible with (i.e. subsumed by) the set of higher-level features. In the case of the rulebase above, if we give the search function the input:

```
[polygon]
```

we would expect the output:

```
[ [equilateral_triangle]
  [right_angled_triangle]
  [rectangle] ]
```

Let us make the assumption that a set of concrete features is a *description* of a specific object, namely the object which has the given concrete features. In this case a single set of concrete features identifies a specific object and N sets of concrete features collectively identify a *set* of objects. Given our new search function, we can generate sets of concrete features from a set of higher-level features. This means that any set of high-level features constitutes, in effect, a *description* which deterministically identifies a set of objects. For clarity, we will use the term *primitive description* to refer to a description which identifies a single object.

All this is interesting for two reasons. Firstly, descriptions which identify sets of objects are known in logic as *intensional descriptions*. The set of objects identified by an intensional description is sometimes called the *extension* of the description. In the framework we are envisaging, the ordinary backwards search function provides an explicit computational link between intensional descriptions and their corresponding extensions.

But the real reason to be interested in this new way of construing the rulebase is that it provides a way of making a link between search processes and one of the main mechanisms which has been developed in AI for *concept learning*. This mechanism performs a task known as *learning from examples*. This involves learning a given concept from a sequence of primitive descriptions some of which describe things which are examples of the concept and some of which describe things which are *not* examples of the concept.

The mechanism is said to "learn" a concept but what it actually does is try to construct a definition of the concept in the form of an intensional description. Initially, the mechanism just constructs an "empty" description and then, every time it receives a new example (positive or negative), it finds the most specific (and most general) description whose extension excludes all the negative examples but includes all the positive ones. Its internal functioning is, in fact, quite complex. However, we can get a very good understanding of it without going very far beyond the simple backwards search function envisaged in earlier chapters.

Generalisation hierarchies

Below, we have a rulebase in which the goals and facts are easily construed as features. The first rule in the rulebase says that the "object" feature subsumes the "colour" feature and the "shape" feature (i.e. if something is an object then it has a colour and a shape). The second rule states that the "colour" feature subsumes the "striped" feature, and so on:

```
[ [object colour shape]
  [colour striped]
  [colour uniform]
  [uniform primary]
  [uniform pastel]
  [primary red]
  [primary blue]
  [primary yellow]
  [pastel pink]
  [pastel green]
  [pastel grey]
  [shape block]
  [shape sphere]
  [block brick]
  [block wedge]
  [brick cube]
  [brick cuboid] ] -> blocks;
```

Clearly a rule which states that some higher-level feature subsumes some lower-level feature is effectively saying that the higher-level feature is a *generalisation* of the lower-level feature. Thus, the AND/OR tree which is expressed in this rulebase is effectively a generalisation hierarchy in which ancestor nodes are generalisations of descendant nodes.

Generalisation hierarchies have played a very important role in many different aspects of AI. They come in a variety of forms. Apart from hierarchies which describe generality relationships between features, we can also have hierarchies which describe generality relationships between types of object. These are normally called ISA hierarchies on the grounds that links from child to parent nodes show that the child is an example of the class represented by the parent.

So as to make this point a little clearer (and also so as to be able to show exactly what the generalisation hierarchies represented by the above rulebase actually are) let us write a version of the **backwards_search_tree** function which will construct what is, in effect, a list of the solution trees for a given set of goals. The "solution tree" for a goal which corresponds to the highest level feature, is just the generalisation hierarchy for that feature. Thus we can construct representations of generalisation hierarchies just by constructing representations of solution trees. This new function is called **backwards_search_trees**; its definition is shown in Figure 10-1. This program is a variant on **AO_search_tree** defined in Chapter 6.

This function takes a list as input and iterates over it checking whether each element is a valid goal (using the familiar call on **present**). If an item turns out to be a valid goal then a list is returned which features the goal itself followed by the tree

```
/* backwards_search_trees takes a list of descriptions and returns the
   ISA trees below them. */

define backwards_search_trees(descriptions) -> tree;
   vars goal subgoals;
   [] -> tree;
   for goal in descriptions do
      if present([^goal ==]) then
         [^^tree [^goal
          ^(foreach [^goal ??subgoals] do
               explode(backwards_search_trees(subgoals))
            endforeach)]] -> tree;
      else
         [^^tree ^goal] -> tree;
      endif
   endfor;
enddefine;
```

Figure 10-1 Generating a generalisation hierarchy

```
blocks -> database;
showtree(hd(backwards_search_trees([object])));
```

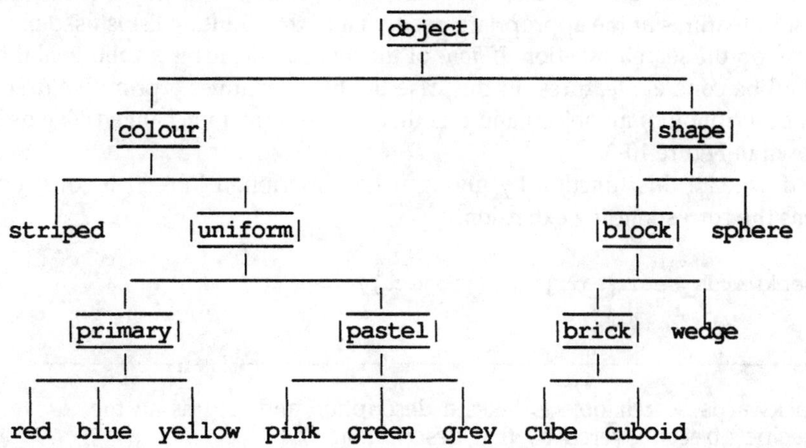

Figure 10-2 Generalisation hierarchy

representations of all the different sets of subgoals (obtained via recursive calls on **backwards_search_trees**). If the item turns out not to be a goal then it is just included in the result list explicitly.

We can use **showtree** to construct a graphical representation of the AND/OR tree defined above. This representation is shown in Figure 10-2. It allows one to see the exact form of the implicit generalisation hierarchies embedded in the rulebase.

Deriving extensions

A function which generates the extension of an intensional description can also be derived by modifying the backwards-search mechanism. The function should take, as input, a list of goals (i.e. high-level features) and return the sets of facts (i.e. concrete features) each of which would suffice to enable the goals to be satisfied. The construction of this new search function is made a lot easier if we define a function which simply tests whether a given item corresponds to an abstract feature. The task is identical to testing whether an item is a goal or not. Thus the function can be defined as in Figure 10-2.

Given this definition it is quite easy to write the new version of the backwards search function. The function uses the matcher (with **`is_abstract_feature`** as a restriction procedure) to find the first item in the list of goals which constitutes an abstract rather than a concrete feature. It then iterates over the rulebase finding all the rules for the given "goal". Each set of subfeatures found in this way is substituted into the list of features at the appropriate position and the resulting list is used in a recursive call on the search function. If *none* of the items in the list is a valid goal then they must all be concrete features. In this case the list constitutes a primitive description (i.e. a description of an object) and it is therefore returned unchanged. The definition is shown in Figure 10-3.

If we call this function by giving it the description [object] it constructs and returns the corresponding extension:

```
backwards_search_objects([object]) =>
```

```
/* backwards_search_objects takes a description and returns all the
   specific objects covered by that description. */

define backwards_search_objects(description) -> extension;
    vars before after subgoals goal;
    [] -> extension;
    if description matches
       [??before ?goal:is_abstract_feature ??after] then
       foreach [^goal ??subgoals] do
         [^^extension
          ^^(backwards_search_objects([^^before ^^subgoals ^^after])
         ] -> extension;
       endforeach
    else  /* ALL PARTS OF THE DESCRIPTION ARE CONCRETE */
        [^description] -> extension
    endif;
enddefine;

/* is_abstract_feature returns true if its input is an abstract feature,
   and false otherwise. */

define is_abstract_feature(feature) -> boolean;
   present([^feature ==]) -> boolean
enddefine;
```

Figure 10-3 Computing the extension of description

```
** [[striped cube] [striped cuboid] [striped wedge]
    [striped sphere] [red cube] [red cuboid] [red wedge]
    [red sphere] [blue cube] [blue cuboid] [blue wedge]
    [blue sphere] [yellow cube] [yellow cuboid] [yellow wedge]
    [yellow sphere] [pink cube] [pink cuboid] [pink wedge]
    [pink sphere] [green cube] [green cuboid] [green wedge]
    [green sphere] [grey cube] [grey cuboid] [grey wedge]
    [grey sphere]]
```

So we see that, given the **backwards_search_objects** function and the rulebase, the description **[object]** effectively identifies the complete set of possible objects in this scenario. The extension of the description **[pastel brick]** is much smaller:

```
backwards_search_objects([pastel brick]) ==>

** [[pink cube]
    [pink cuboid]
    [green cube]
    [green cuboid]
    [grey cube]
    [grey cuboid]]
```

If we want to compute the extensions of descriptions in some other scenario we need to set up a new rulebase. For example, we might set up a rulebase in which the rules specify the way in which lower-level linguistic objects are examples of higher-level linguistic objects. This rulebase is just the familiar phrase-structure grammar discussed in Chapter 6:

```
[ [s np vp]
  [np snp]
  [snp det noun]
  [vp verb np]
  [noun girl]
  [noun man]
  [verb hated]
  [verb moved]
  [det the]
  [det a] ] -> grammar4;
```

The extension of the description [s] is quite large. It includes all possible sentences in the language described by this grammar:

```
grammar4 -> database;
```

```
/* backwards_search_descriptions takes a list of descriptions and returns
   all the descriptions that they cover. */

define backwards_search_descriptions(goals) -> descriptions;
    vars before after subgoals goal;
    [] -> descriptions;
    if goals matches [== ?goal:is_abstract_feature ==]
    then for goal in goals do
            goals --> [??before ^goal ??after];
            foreach [^goal ??subgoals] do
                [^^descriptions
                    ^^(backwards_search_descriptions
                            ([^^before ^^subgoals ^^after])
                    )
                ] -> descriptions;
            endforeach;
        endfor;
        [^goals ^^descriptions] -> descriptions;
    endif;
enddefine;
```

Figure 10-4 Generating descriptions by backwards search

```
backwards_search_objects([s]) ==>

** [[the girl hated the girl]
    [the girl hated the man]
    [the girl hated a girl]
    [the girl hated a man]
    [the girl moved the girl]
    [the girl moved the man]
    [the girl moved a girl]
    [the girl moved a man]
    [the man hated the girl]
    [the man hated the man]
    [the man hated a girl]
    [the man hated a man]
    [the man moved the girl]
    [the man moved the man]
    [the man moved a girl]
    [the man moved a man]
    [a girl hated the girl]
```

```
    [a girl hated the man]
    [a girl hated a girl]
    [a girl hated a man]
    [a girl moved the girl]
    [a girl moved the man]
    [a girl moved a girl]
    [a girl moved a man]
    [a man hated the girl]
    [a man hated the man]
    [a man hated a girl]
    [a man hated a man]
    [a man moved the girl]
    [a man moved the man]
    [a man moved a girl]
    [a man moved a man]]
```

Compare the extension of "s" with the more limited extension below:

```
backwards_search_objects([det noun verb]) ==>

** [[the girl hated]
    [the girl moved]
    [the man hated]
    [the man moved]
    [a girl hated]
    [a girl moved]
    [a man hated]
    [a man moved]]
```

Quantifying generality

Recall that, in the current scenario, goals are being construed as components of descriptions and facts are being construed as components of *primitive* descriptions. All descriptions have well-defined extensions which are computed by the **backwards_search_objects** function.

Descriptions can vary in their degree of generality. The description [striped shape] is more general than the description [striped brick] but less general than the description [object]. Clearly, the degree of generality in a description is affected by the height at which the component terms appear in the generalisation hierarchies represented by the rulebase. This suggests that we might measure generality in terms of "height of component terms".

But this approach is not particularly convenient. In the case where a description includes terms which appear at different heights in the generalisation hierarchies, it is not clear what overall "height" we should assign to the description as a whole. A far simpler approach involves quantifying generality in terms of "size of extension".

Any description in the envisaged scenario has a well-defined extension and the size of this extension can be easily derived. More general descriptions will tend to have component terms which are higher in the corresponding generalisation hierarchies and therefore they will tend to have larger extensions. Thus we can measure degree of generality simply in terms of size of extension. Of course, in some sense, this is the obvious approach. The *generality* of a description is the degree to which it covers multiple cases. But the degree to which it covers multiple cases is just the number of multiple cases covered, i.e. the size of the corresponding extension.

Let us imagine that we have some way of working out all the descriptions that can be derived from some given rulebase. Each one of these descriptions has a well-defined extension and we can compute this using the **backwards_search_objects** function. We can compute the generality of the description just by measuring the length of the extension; so if we wanted, we could arrange all the descriptions into a sequence of increasing generality.

```
/* make description table constructs a table made up of lists of
   descriptions each paired with the specific objects that they
   cover. The lists of paired descriptions and specific objects is
   sorted by length. */

define make_description_table() -> description_table;
    vars description;
    [^(for description in backwards_search_descriptions([object]) do
        [^description ^^(backwards_search_objects(description))]
      endfor)
    ] -> description_table;
    syssort(description_table, shorter) -> description_table;
enddefine;

/* shorter returns true if the first list is shorter than the second,
   and otherwise false. */

define shorter(list1, list2) -> boolean;
   length(list1) < length(list2) -> boolean
enddefine;
```

Figure 10-5 Computing an ordered description table

Having done this it would be very easy to work out what is the most general description whose extension includes a given set of objects. Or perhaps, what is the most general description whose extension *excludes* one set of objects but *includes* all of another set. These tasks are exactly the tasks which are performed by the simple concept learning mechanism described above. Thus, it seems, that if we implement all the envisaged machinery, it is going to be quite easy for us to implement that particular type of learning:

```
blocks -> database;

backwards_search_descriptions([primary block]) ==>

** [[primary block] /* DESCRIPTIONS BUT NOT SPECIFIC OBJECTS */
    [red block]
    [red brick]
    [blue block]
    [blue brick]
    [yellow block]
    [yellow brick]
    [primary brick]
    [red brick]
    [blue brick]
    [yellow brick]
    [primary cube]
    [primary cuboid]
    [primary wedge]]

backwards_search_objects([primary block]) ==>

** [[red cube]  /* SPECIFIC OBJECTS BUT NOT DESCRIPTIONS */
    [red cuboid]
    [red wedge]
    [blue cube]
    [blue cuboid]
    [blue wedge]
    [yellow cube]
    [yellow cuboid]
    [yellow wedge]]
```

Concept learning

First of all, let us clarify the mechanism that we want to implement. It will attempt to learn a "concept" from some sequence of positive and negative examples of that concept. It will do so by constructing a definition of it, and this definition will take the form of an intensional description whose extension includes all the presented positive examples but excludes all the presented negative examples. The extension of any given description will be computed using the **`backwards_search_objects`** function and a rulebase which is assumed to be given.

The mechanism will work as follows. Initially it will construct the set of all possible descriptions and, for each one, derive its extension. These will be arranged into a sequence such that descriptions with smaller extensions (less generality) always precede descriptions with larger extensions (more generality). The mechanism will then enter a loop in each iteration of which it will request a new example from the user. The user will also be asked to specify if the example is a positive example of the desired concept or a negative example. The most general description whose extension includes all the positive examples but none of the negative ones will then be identified. If such a description does not exist the mechanism will terminate and output the most recent description.

At each stage in this iteration, the identified description constitutes a definition of the desired concept. After every new input, the mechanism updates its current concept definition so as to make sure that it is still compatible with all the presented information.

Implementing the generalisation mechanism

To implement the envisaged concept learning mechanism there are a number of functions which we need to construct. First and foremost, we need to construct the function which will compute the complete set of possible descriptions. In fact this function can be written as a variant of the **`backwards_search_objects`** function. To derive this variant we need to modify the original function so that instead of outputting primitive descriptions and recursing on ordinary descriptions it outputs ordinary descriptions and *ignores* primitive descriptions. The definition is shown in Figure 10-4.

We can now turn attention to the function which will take the complete set of descriptions and order them according to their level of generality. To do this the function will use the **`backwards_search_objects`** function to compute extensions. It can be constructed as shown in Figure 10-6. Note that this function cheats a little. The function which is specified in the call on **`syssort`** compares the lengths of complete entries in the "description_table". Complete entries include the description itself followed by the extension. To compute generality we should really just look at the length of the extension. But since the length of an entry will always be the length of

```
/* is_negative_example returns true if its input is a member
   of the non-local variable (negative_examples) and false otherwise. */

define is_negative_example(primitive_description) -> boolean;
   member(primitive_description, negative_examples) -> boolean
enddefine;

/* subset_of returns true if list1 is a subset of list2, and false
   otherwise. */

define subset_of(list1, list2) -> boolean;
   vars item;
   true -> boolean;
   for item in list1 do
      unless member(item, list2) then false -> boolean; return
      endunless
   endfor;
enddefine;

/* covers takes a description and a set of examples. It scans
   the non-local variable, description_table, to find the description
   entry and returns true if the examples input turn out to be a subset
   of the extension of the given description in the table. */

define covers(description, examples) -> boolean;
   vars extension;
   if [^description ??extension] isin description_table
   then subset_of(examples, extension) -> boolean
   else false -> boolean
   endif;
enddefine;
```

Figure 10-6 Determining whether a description covers a list of examples

the extension + 1, we can just look at the overall length.

Having implemented the **make_description_table** function and assigned its result to the variable **description_table**, we can begin to work on the main part of the implementation. This will be a function which will take a list of positive examples and a list of negative examples and find the most specific (i.e. least general) description whose extension includes all the positive examples but none of the negative examples. We will assume that the list of positive examples is contained in the global variable **positive_examples** and the list of negative examples is contained in the global variable **negative_examples**.

Next we need a function which will test whether some arbitrary primitive description is a description of an object which has already been presented as a negative example of the concept to be learned. This function is very simple to implement. Its definition is shown in the upper portion of Figure 10-6.

Finally we need to define a function which will test whether some given set of primitive descriptions is subsumed in a given extension. This function will be called **covers** since it will compute whether or not some given description *covers* a given range of objects. The implementation of **covers** is made easier if we initially implement a function which tests whether one set is a subset of another. Both definitions are shown in Figure 10-6. Note that the **covers** mechanism works by (a) getting the extension of the given description by looking up the appropriate entry in the description table and by (b) checking whether the given examples constitute a subset of this extension.

The implementation of the function which computes a satisfactory description given a list of positive examples and a list of negative examples is now straightforward. It must search through the description table (which is ordered according to generality of descriptions) looking for the first (i.e. most specific) description whose extension includes all the positive examples but none of the negative examples. It can be defined as shown in the upper part of Figure 10-7.

We can implement the part of the program which is going to interact with the user (the provider of positive and negative examples) in terms of a function to process new examples and a function to actually carry out the interaction; see the lower portion of Figure 10-7.

If in an interaction with the **learn** function we provide:

```
[red cube]
[blue cuboid]
[yellow wedge]
```

as positive examples and:

```
[blue sphere]
```

as a negative example, the description:

```
[primary block]
```

is derived. We can regard this description as a definition of the concept which covers the given list of positive examples but not the negative example. The interaction is as follows:

```
learn();
** [type in a primitive description]
```

```
/* best_description takes a list of negative examples and positive examples
   and via the description table returns that description which excludes all
   the negative examples and covers all the positive examples. */

define best_description(negative_examples, positive_examples) -> description;
    vars entry primitive_description;
    for entry in description_table do
        if not(entry matches [?description ==
                             ?primitive_description:is_negative_example ==])
        and covers(description, positive_examples) then return
        endif
    endfor;
    false -> description
enddefine;

/* process_example takes a primitive description and a boolean denoting whether
   the example is positive or not and returns a new description. */

define process_example(primitive_description, positive) -> description;
    if positive then
        [^primitive_description ^^positive_examples] -> positive_examples;
    else
        [^primitive_description ^^negative_examples] -> negative_examples;
    endif;
    best_description(negative_examples, positive_examples) -> description;
enddefine;

/* learn sets up the initial list of positive and negative examples together
   with the description table and then loops asking the user for a new example.
   The loop terminates when a positive example cannot be processed. */

define learn;
    vars input positive description_table positive_examples
        negative_examples;
    make_description_table() -> description_table;
    [] -> positive_examples; [] -> negative_examples;
    repeat forever
        [type in a primitive description] ==>
        readline() -> input; if input = [bye] then return endif;
        yesno([is it positive?]) -> positive;
        process_example(input, positive) -> description;
        if description then [concept definition is ^description] ==>
        else quitloop
        endif;
    endrepeat;
enddefine;
```

Figure 10-7 Learning a concept description from examples

```
? red cube
** [is it positive ?]
? yes
** [concept definition is [red brick]]
** [type in a primitive description]
? blue cuboid
** [is it positive ?]
? yes
** [concept definition is [primary brick]]
** [type in a primitive description]
? blue sphere
** [is it positive ?]
? no
** [concept definition is [primary brick]]
** [type in a primitive description]
? yellow wedge
** [is it positive ?]
? yes
** [concept definition is [primary block]]
** [type in a primitive description]
? bye
```

The focussing algorithm

The concept learning mechanism which we have implemented above works in roughly the same way as the main AI mechanism for this task, namely the *version space* or *focussing* algorithm. However, it has at least one major flaw which that algorithm does not have. Note that given the way we have implemented the mechanism it has no way of knowing when it has fully learned the desired concept. If it cannot find a description whose extension includes all the given positive examples and none of the given negative examples, it simply exits. However, ideally we would like the function to be able to detect the point at which it has a definition of the concept which cannot be improved on any further.

To achieve this effect, the focussing and version space algorithms adopt a slightly different approach to the task. Instead of always looking for a single best description they actually maintain at all times a set of *two* best descriptions. One of these is the most general description which is compatible with all the positive and negative examples presented so far. The other is the most specific description compatible with all the presented examples.

The great advantage of keeping both a most-general and a most-specific description is that it is possible to detect the point at which the descriptions cannot be improved on any further. This point arises when the descriptions are *identical*.

Clearly, if the most-general description is identical to the most-specific description, then it is the case that the most-general description cannot be made any more specific without making it more specific than the *most* specific description which is compatible with all the examples presented so far. Thus we know that it cannot be made any more specific. Similarly, we know that the most-specific description cannot be made any more general without making it more general than the *most*-general description.

If the most-specific description cannot be made any more general and the most-general description cannot be made any more specific the algorithm cannot improve its descriptions any further. Thus the current descriptions are the best that can be achieved. Since they are identical either one provides a definition of the desired concept.

Focussing in Prolog

We now give a simple Prolog version of the focussing algorithm that maintains both a *most general* and a *most specific* solution and exits should these become the same. The Prolog code does not implement a description table as in the earlier part of the chapter but searches the isa hierarchies repeatedly. The relative simplicity of the code hides a great deal of backtracking search behaviour, in that generalisation and specialisation are defined at base in terms of chaining along these hierarchies.

Our database, Figure 10-8, is largely as drawn in Figure 10-2, with the predicate `isa` representing both the relationship between classes (such as `uniform` and `primary`) as well as between a class and an instance (such as `brick` and `cube`).

We will represent a description of an object as a two element Prolog list, with the first element taken from the colour hierarchy and the second from the shape hierarchy, such as:

```
[striped, block]
```

or

```
[uniform, brick]
```

As before, we need ways of generalising and specialising such descriptions in this space. The predicate `covers/2` defines the relation between a pair of descriptions, where the first is a generalisation of the second, see Figure 10-8. `covers/2` is itself defined in terms of `ancestor/2` which relates a pair of descriptors from one of the hierarchies. `ancestor/2` is defined so that it searches either up the hierarchy (if the child is known and an ancestor sought) or down the hierarchy (if the ancestor is known and a child sought), for instance:

```
/* isa(?Colour, ?Shape) */

isa(colour, uniform).
isa(colour, striped).
isa(uniform, primary).
isa(uniform, pastel).
isa(primary, red).
isa(primary, blue).
isa(primary, yellow).
isa(pastel, pink).
isa(pastel, green).
isa(pastel, grey).

isa(shape, block).
isa(shape, sphere).
isa(block, brick).
isa(block, wedge).
isa(brick, cube).
isa(brick, cuboid).
```

Figure 10-8 Isa hierarchy in Prolog

```
?- covers(D, [uniform, sphere]).
D = [uniform, sphere] ? ;
D = [uniform, shape] ? ;
D = [colour, sphere] ? ;
D = [colour, shape] ? ;
no

?- covers([red, brick], D).
D = [red, brick] ? ;
D = [red, cube] ? ;
D = [red, cuboid] ? ;
no
```

Repeatedly calling for solutions to the query **covers([colour, shape], D)** would provide all possible descriptions D, and restricting these to be at the tips of the hierarchies gives the extension of this concept. Repeating an earlier POP-11 example of the use **backwards_search_objects** gives:

```
?- bagof([C, S],
        (covers([pastel, brick], [C, S]), tip(C), tip(S)),
        Extension).
C = _1
S = _2
Extension = [[pink, cube], [pink, cuboid], [green, cube],
             [green, cuboid], [grey, cube], [grey, cuboid]] ?
```

Procedure **generalise/3** takes a general description and a positive primitive description and constructs, using **covers/2**, a more general description that covers both of them. **specialise/3** takes a general description and a negative primitive description and constructs, also using **covers/2**, a less general description that excludes the negative example, see Figure 10-8.

The main part of the algorithm is provided by **dealwith/4** and by **learn1/2**. These predicates maintain the current most general description (that excludes all the negative examples so far) and the current most specific description (that covers all the positive examples so far). The initial value of the most general description is `[colour, shape]` and the initial value of the most specific description is the empty list `[]`. The four clauses of **dealwith/4** are for (i) negative examples (ii) the first positive example (iii) further positive examples, and (iv) a "catch all" for cases where the example cannot be incorporated.

When a positive example is entered, **generalise/3** builds a new most specific description. When a new negative example is entered, **specialise/3** builds a new most general description. Below is a similar interaction as that given in POP-11 earlier:

```
?- learn.
Most general concept is [colour, shape]
Most special concept is []

Type in a primitive description e.g. red cube? red cube
Is it positive? yes./no. ? yes
Most general concept is [colour, shape]
Most special concept is [red, cube]

Type in a primitive description e.g. red cube? blue cuboid
Is it positive? yes./no. ? yes
Most general concept is [colour, shape]
Most special concept is [primary, brick]

Type in a primitive description e.g. red cube? blue sphere
Is it positive? yes./no. ? no
Most general concept is [colour, block]
Most special concept is [primary, brick]
```

```
/* generalise(+Description, +Positive example, -New higher description)
   generalise succeeds if the higher description covers both the
   original description and the positive example. */

generalise(Description, Pos_example, Higher_description) :-
    covers(Higher_description, Description),
    covers(Higher_description, Pos_example).

/* specialise(+Description, +Negative example, -New lower description)
   specialise succeeds if the lower description is covered by the
   original description but excludes the negative example. */

specialise(Description, Neg_example, Lower_description) :-
    covers(Description, Lower_description),
    not(covers(Lower_description, Neg_example)).

/* covers(?Description1, ?Description2)
   covers succeeds if Description1 covers Description2. */

covers([Colour_high, Shape_high], [Colour_low, Shape_low]) :-
    ancestor(Colour_high, Colour_low),
    ancestor(Shape_high, Shape_low).

/* ancestor(?Ancestor, ?Child)
   ancestor succeeds if Ancestor is above Child in the isa hierarchy. */

ancestor(Ancestor, Ancestor).
ancestor(Ancestor, Child) :-
    nonvar(Child), !,
    isa(Intermediate, Child),          /* SEARCH UP THE HIERARCHY */
    ancestor(Ancestor, Intermediate).
ancestor(Ancestor, Child) :-
    nonvar(Ancestor),
    isa(Ancestor, Intermediate),       /* SEARCH DOWN THE HIERARCHY */
    ancestor(Intermediate, Child).

/* tip(?Word)
   tip succeeds if Word is at the tip of the isa hierarchy. */

tip(X) :- isa(_, X), not(isa(X, _)).
```

Figure 10-9 Generalising and specialising in Prolog

```
/* dealwith(+Value, +Description, +General, +Special)
   dealwith takes a description plus its value plus the current most
   general and most special lists and processes them. */

dealwith(neg, Description, General, Special) :-
   specialise(General, Description, NewGeneral),
   above(NewGeneral, Special),
   learn1(NewGeneral, Special).

dealwith(pos, Description, General, []) :-
   learn1(General, Description).

dealwith(pos, Description, General, Special) :-
   generalise(Special, Description, NewSpecial),
   above(General, NewSpecial),
   learn1(General, NewSpecial).

dealwith(_, Description, General, Special) :-
   write(Description),
   write(' is inconsistent and ignored.'), nl,
   learn1(General, Special).

/* learn1(+General, +Special)
   learn1 takes the most general and most specific descriptions so
   far and exits if they are the same, otherwise it recursively gets
   a new example for the next cycle. */

learn1(C, C) :-
    write('The concept is '),
    write(C), nl.

learn1(General, Special) :-
    write('Most general concept is '),
    write(General), nl,
    write('Most special concept is '),
    write(Special), nl, nl,
    getexample(Value, Description),
    dealwith(Value, Description, General, Special).
```

Figure 10-10 Learning mechanism in Prolog

```
Type in a primitive description e.g. red cube? yellow wedge
Is it positive? yes./no. ? yes
Most general concept is [colour, block]
Most special concept is [primary, block]
```

```
Type in a primitive description e.g. red cube? striped wedge
Is it positive? yes./no. ? yes
The concept is [colour, block]
yes
```

The interaction is the same as for that given earlier except that one more example is offered which causes the algorithm to exit.

The predicate **above/2** makes sure that the most specific description remains covered by the most general description. The remaining part of the program is devoted to collecting and checking input from the user and other odds and ends. It checks that primitive descriptions only are entered.

The program is very simple-minded and gets into a muddle if inconsistent data are entered (e.g. if the same description is offered as both a positive and a negative example). Also it avoids all the hard problems of specialisation by always specialising down the *shape* hierarchy if it can, before trying the *colour* hierarchy. In either case it specialises down left branches of the tree before right branches (and cannot backtrack). So the order of the examples from the user is important in determining the outcome. Because of this, the one difference between the factbase in Figure 10-10 and the tree drawn in Figure 10-2 is to put **striped** to the right of **uniform**, in order to force more sensible specialising behaviour.

Generalisation as search

In the present chapter we have tried to show that in the case where goals play the role of description-components, a slight variant of the backwards search function can be used to relate descriptions with extensions. We have seen that it is quite easy to exploit this property of the search function to implement a very simple version of a "learning-from-examples" mechanism and thereby to make a link between search processes and concept learning processes.

This is not the only way to make a link between search and learning. It has been shown by Mitchell (1982) that we can think about the process of *generalisation* as a search process.[2] In order to understand what is being proposed here, we need to make some adjustments in the way in which we are thinking about the learning mechanism. First of all, instead of assuming that the most-general and most-specific descriptions are re-derived from scratch by scanning through the complete description table, we should assume that these descriptions are actually explicitly updated so as to bring about the required increase/decrease in generality.

The mechanism via which this is achieved can be safely ignored here. The point to note is simply that, in general, it will be possible to prevent the extension of the

[2] In fact, Mitchell showed that both generalisation and specialisation can be understood in terms of search.

```
/* learn drives the learning program. */

learn :- learn1([colour, shape], []).

/* above(+Description1, +Description2)
   above succeeds if Description1 covers Description2 as well as if
   Description2 is the empty list. */

above(_, []).

above(High, Low) :-
    covers(High, Low).

/* getexample(-Value, -Description)
   getexample gets a Description and a Value from the user. */

getexample(Value, Description) :-
   repeat,                              /* TO ALLOW FOR INPUT ERRORS */
   askfor(Value, Description).

/* askfor(-Value, -Description)
   askfor gets a Description and a Value from the user. */

askfor(Value, [Colour, Shape]) :-
   write('Type in a primitive description e.g. red cube'),
   readline([Colour, Shape]),
   tip(Colour),
   tip(Shape),
   yesno(Value).

/* yesno(-Value)
   yesno provides the Value. */

:- library(readline).

yesno(pos) :-
   write('Is it positive? yes./no. '),
   readline([yes]), !.

yesno(neg).
```

Figure 10-11 User interaction with the learning program in Prolog

current most-general description from including some new negative example in more than one way.[3] Thus, each time we specialise a most-general description we face a range of choices. These choices form a search-tree and our decisions at each point constitute a path through that tree.

This way of looking at things may or may not be helpful with respect to the overall task at hand. However, it is worth bearing in mind that construing the specialisation operation in terms of a search process has been quite useful from the point of view of reasoning about the difficulties inherent in the process of concept learning using generalisation and specialisation. To cut a long story short, it has been shown that, in general, there is no heuristic which will enable a correct path to be found in the tree. Thus, in principle, the learning process will always face the possibility of needing to *backtrack* (Bundy, Silver and Plummer 1985).

Reading

A clear formulation of the original version of what is now called the focussing algorithm is provided in Chapters 11 and 12 of (Winston, 1984). The latter chapter also looks at links between learning, matching and analogy. Charniak and McDermott (1985) deal with the focussing strategy (which they call the *empiricist algorithm*) with sample algorithms presented in LISP. Volume 3 of the AI Handbook (Cohen and Feigenbaum, 1982, pp. 385-401) looks at a very well-known formulation of the algorithm called the *version space* algorithm and introduces a variety of other programs and techniques in the general area of learning (Section XIV). Rich, deals with the original Winstonian formulation of the focussing algorithm (pp. 368-374). Stillings *et al.* (1987) look at learning from a "cognitive science" point of view. Chapters 10 and 11 of Gilhooly (1989) provides a comparison of human and machine learning.

Bratko (1990) offers Prolog code for a number of learning programs including one similar to the above.

Exercises

1. Re-implement the program, provided above in Prolog, in POP-11 such that it maintains at all times a most-general description and a most-specific description. The most-general description should be the most general description which covers none of the presented negative examples. The most-specific description should be the most specific description which covers all of the positive examples. The main `learn` function should return an appropriate output at the point where the most-specific and the most-general descriptions become identical.

---

[3] Technically, this situation is known as a *far miss*.

2. Change the Prolog program so that it can backtrack if it makes the wrong speciali-sation choice.

3. Augment either the POP-11 or the Prolog program to work with more than two hierarchies.

11
Prolog (search as computation)

Introduction

The earlier chapters of this book have tried to show that the search mechanism has a surprisingly high degree of generality. It has been shown how OR-tree search can be used for route-finding, problem-solving and heuristic problem-solving, and how AND/OR-tree search can be used for planning, reasoning, parsing, expert diagnosis and concept learning. Most of these applications involve the use of some additional computational machinery and/or the construing of goals and facts in a particular way. But in all cases the search mechanism provides the basic driving force.

In some sense the generality of the search process is unlimited, since it turns out that a variant of the AND/OR-tree mechanism can actually be used to implement arbitrary forms of computation, i.e. it can function as a general purpose programming language. In this chapter we will look at an implementation of the AND/OR-tree search mechanism which can play this role. The mechanism will amount to a description in POP-11 of the basic mechanisms of Prolog. Unfortunately, the implementation necessarily involves using POP-11 in a slightly more complex way than we have been using it throughout this book. There are several places where much more compact code could be included by introducing data structures and built-in POP-11 functions that have not been used elsewhere. We have tried to keep this to a minimum, and indicated via footnotes alternative possibilities.

Search rules as predicates

There are a number of ideas which we need to come to terms with in order to understand the way in which the search mechanism can implement arbitrary forms of computation. First and foremost, we need to recognise that in some cases search rules can be conveniently interpreted as defining *predicates*, a predicate being a function which returns a truth value (i.e. <true> or <false>). Consider the rulebase which we used in

Chapter 6:

```
[ /* FACTS */
  [[weak battery]]
  [[damp weather]]
  [[old car]]
  /* RULES */
  [[low current][damp weather][weak battery]]
  [[old starter][old car]]
  [[car wont start][low current][old starter]]
  [[write off][car wont start][not AA member]]
  [[not AA member][irresponsible]]
] -> rulebase3;
```

The rules making up this rulebase were construed as relationships between conclusions and bits of evidence. For example, the rule:

```
[[car wont start][low current][old starter]]
```

was read as stating that the conclusion `[car wont start]` could be justified provided that the conclusions `[low current]` and `[old starter]` could be justified. An alternative is to construe all goals as predicates. On this view the rule above is effectively a definition of the predicate `[car wont start]`. It states that `[car wont start]` is true if `[low current]` is true and `[old starter]` is true.

If there was another rule in the rulebase whose first item is `[car wont start]`, e.g.

```
[[car wont start] [ignition broken]]
```

then we would say that the definition of the predicate `[car wont start]` is provided by the *combination* of the two rules.

It might be argued that the "predicate" construal has no real advantage over the "inference rule" construal. But in fact it provides us with a useful stepping-stone on the way to understanding how search can implement arbitrary forms of computation. Once we are comfortable with the idea that rules can provide definitions of predicates it becomes much easier to make the next step -- which involves assimilating the idea that rules can provide definitions of procedures and functions.

The use of variables in search rules

Of course, it is perfectly obvious that computation involves more than just the derivation of truth values. This is certainly one form of computation; but, in general, computation involves the construction and manipulation of arbitrary types of data. This seems to suggest that any system which only allows for the application of predicates cannot possibly be used to implement arbitrary forms of computation. And this is certainly the case.

What is rather remarkable, however, is the fact that by the very simple expedient of allowing search rules to contain *variables* it is possible to obtain general computational behaviour out of the search function. Consider the following rulebase:

```
[ [[friends X Y] [likes X Y] [likes Y X]]
  [[likes fred albert]]
  [[likes fred john]]
  [[likes albert fred]]
  [[likes john jane]] ] -> rulebase8;
```

The rules are of the normal form, except for the fact that rule components are list objects rather than word objects. There are four facts `[likes fred albert]`, `[likes fred john]` etc. and just one rule. Adopting the predicate construal, we should read the rule as stating that `[friends X Y]` is true if both `[likes X Y]` and `[likes Y X]` are true.[1] We know that application of the normal backwards search function to the goal `[friends X Y]` will fail because there is no way for the function to satisfy the subgoals `[likes X Y]` and `[likes Y X]`.

But what happens if we assume that `X` and `Y` are variables? In other words, what happens if we assume that these two items are objects which can take on arbitrary values? The rule should now be read as stating that `[friends X Y]` is true if `[likes X Y]` and `[likes Y X]` are true -- given that `X` and `Y` take on some particular values. This changes the picture somewhat. If X takes on the value `fred` and `Y` takes on the value `albert` then both the subgoals can be satisfied. Why? Because `[likes fred albert]` and `[likes albert fred]` are both facts in the rulebase.

But why should `X` and `Y` take on (i.e. be instantiated to) these values? One possibility might be that the search mechanism is modified so that in the case where it is trying to satisfy goals which contain variables, it scans the database to see which instantiations might be fruitful. The presence of the fact `[likes fred albert]` would, in this case, inform the search function that instantiating `X` to `fred` and `Y` to `albert` will allow the goal to be satisfied by invoking this fact.

Obviously, there are a lot of questions which need to be answered with respect to the mechanism we are envisaging. But even at this early stage, we can see that it

---

[1] Goals are assumed to define two-place predicates here. The first item of a goal is the predicate term and the second two items are the arguments.

would provide very real advantages. For one thing having rules with variables would seem to enable us to cut down on the total number of rules which we need to specify a given set of goal-reductions. The rulebase:

```
[ [friends fred albert]
  [friends albert fred]
  [friends fred john]
  [friends john fred]
  [friends fred jane]
  [friends jane fred]
  [friends albert john]
  [friends john albert]
  [friends albert jane]
  [friends jane albert]
  [friends john jane]
  [friends jane john] ]
```

rewritten using rules containing variables becomes:

```
[ [friends fred albert]
  [friends albert john]
  [friends john jane]
  [friends jane fred] ]
  [[friends X Y] [friends X Z] [friends Z Y]]
```

The single rule in this rulebase (i.e. the last element) allows us, in effect, to show that some unidentified person **X** is a friend of some other unidentified person **Y** if we can show that **X** is a friend of a person **Z** and **Z** is a friend of **Y**. We are therefore able to show all the missing facts simply by invoking (perhaps repeatedly invoking) the single rule.[2]

Apart from the fact that using variables allows us to reduce the size of rulebases, it also allows us to obtain a more general type of data manipulation than is possible with ordinary rules. For example, let us say that we attempt to ask the new search mechanism to satisfy the goal:

```
[likes fred Y]
```

Given our assumptions about the way the way the mechanism works, it will show us that it can satisfy this goal in a number of different ways by instantiating **Y** to a number of different values, namely, **albert**, **john** and **jane**. This is much more like what we think of as computation. The mechanism we are envisaging would take in

[2] As a Prolog program, this would derive that fred was friends with fred and would loop.

the "input" `[likes fred Y]` and produce an "output" corresponding to the set of instantiations for `Y` which enable the goal to be satisfied.

We have glossed over most of the complications; but this is, in a nutshell, the way in which the search mechanism can be used to implement arbitrary forms of computation. There are three main ideas underlying the search-as-computation construal: (1) the carrying out of the computation involves satisfying predicates, and rules describe the way in which given predicates can be satisfied; (2) the input to the computation takes the form of a set of goals; (3) the output takes the form of a truth value and (in the case of success) a set of variable instantiations. Below we will look at the way in which this new variant of the search function can be written in POP-11. First, however, we will consider the way in which the manipulation of *data structures* can be achieved in the current scenario.

Data structures

Some forms of computation involve the creation of data made up of structures rather than atomic elements such as **fred** and **albert**. This process sounds as if it is likely to involve a further modification of the search mechanism; but in fact, this is not the case. We have already seen that goals can be *atomic* entities (i.e. words) or *non-atomic* entities (i.e. lists). As far as the ordinary search mechanism is concerned it does not make any difference what the goals are; it treats all goals as atomic entities anyway. But the search function we are envisaging *is* concerned with the internal structure of goals. In the case where a goal contains variable terms then the internal structure of the goal can vary depending on which instantiations the mechanism is currently considering.

The point about this is that the instantiation of variables as carried out by the search function effectively involves *inserting* values into specific places in goals (i.e. lists). We can very easily exploit this process to obtain the construction of complex data objects. The basic idea is that we arrange things so that the instantiation mechanism causes a value which is itself a data-structure to be inserted into a goal structure, thereby forming a structured object. Arbitrarily complex objects can be constructed by simply getting data structures inserted into data structures, which are then inserted in further data structures, and so on.

The following rulebase may clarify this idea a little:

```
[ [tree leaf]
  [tree [branch X Y]] [tree X] [tree Y]] ]
```

Imagine that we ask the new search function to try to satisfy the goal:

```
  [tree Z]
```

where `Z` is assumed to be a variable. The search function is going to be able to satisfy this simply by invoking the first entry in the rulebase, i.e.:

```
[tree leaf]
```

The `Z` variable will be instantiated to `leaf`.

Notice that the search function will also be able to satisfy the original goal by invoking the rule:

```
[tree [branch X Y]] [tree X] [tree Y]]
```

Of course, this will involve it satisfying the subgoals:

```
[tree X] and [tree Y]
```

but it can satisfy both of these by invoking the fact `[tree leaf]`. In this case (if you think about it) `Z` will be instantiated to the list structure:

```
[branch X Y]
```

but of course this has variables in it and these have both been instantiated to `leaf`. Thus `X` is instantiated to:

```
[branch leaf leaf]
```

The search mechanism can always choose between satisfying a `tree` goal (or subgoal) by using either the fact or the rule. But if it uses the rule then it will have to go on and satisfy two `tree` subgoals. This means, in effect, that the structure which it ultimately constructs will have one more level to it. For instance, if the search function had satisfied the two `tree` subgoals by invoking the rule, this would have involved it in satisfying two more subgoals (in each case) and the ultimate instantiation for our `Z` variable would have been:

```
[branch [branch leaf leaf] [branch leaf leaf]]
```

The next possible instantiation for `Z` would be:

```
[branch
    [branch [branch leaf leaf][branch leaf leaf]]
    [branch [branch leaf leaf][branch leaf leaf]] ]
```

and so on.

There is probably no great advantage in labouring this point. Suffice it to say that given the implementation of a variable mechanism and the assumption that goals can have components which are themselves structures, the search mechanism has the potential to "build" arbitrarily complex data objects and therefore to implement forms of computation which involve the construction and manipulation of complex data structures.

Unification

The point has been reached where we can begin to think about the ways in which the various modifications which we have envisaged might be implemented. Firstly we need to specify the mechanism via which the search function arrives at instantiations for given variables (this was glossed over above). Secondly, given all that has been said about variables being instantiated to arbitrarily complex data structures, we need to think about what should happen in the case where the search function has to decide whether two variables which are instantiated to complex data structures are "equal". After all, if the search function cannot do this, it cannot decide whether a goal corresponds to a given fact. And if it cannot do this then it cannot do search.

Let us take the first problem first. We need a modification of the search function which will enable it to come up with sensible instantiations for variables. This is, in fact, quite easily arranged. Recall that, given a goal, the search function attempts to satisfy that goal by searching through the rulebase from beginning to end looking for an entry which has the goal as its first element. If the entry has no other elements (i.e. if it is a fact) then the goal is just automatically satisfied. If the entry does have other elements (i.e. if it is a rule) then the goal is satisfied provided that the subgoals can be satisfied.

A sensible instantiation for a variable in a goal will be anything which allows it to match (i.e. be regarded as the same as) the first item in an entry in the rulebase. This leads us towards a very simple solution. We simply modify the search function so that, at the point where it considers whether the first item of an entry in the rulebase is the same as the current goal, it simply instantiates any variables in the goal to the values of corresponding elements in the first item.

In fact, the solution is not *quite* this simple. In the case we have discussed the variables appear in the goal but not in the first item of the entry. But there are, of course, several other possibilities. There may be variables in the first item of the entry but *none* in the goal. Or there may be variables in both the goal and the first item of the entry. This leads us to specify our requirements in more general terms.

We would like a mechanism which tries to see if the goal can be made to match the first item of the entry; and we want it to instantiate variables in the goal using corresponding values from the first item -- and vice versa -- as necessary. The mechanism should check each component in the goal to see whether it matches the corresponding component in the first item. It gives a "yes" answer indicating an overall match only if all the components match.

But how should it check whether two components match? The rules can be formulated as follows. If neither component is an uninstantiated variable then they only match if they have identical values. If one component is an uninstantiated variable and the other is a constant (or an instantiated variable) then they match with the side-effect that the uninstantiated variable is instantiated to the value in question. If both components are uninstantiated variables then they match with the side-effect that they become *shared*. This means that if ever one of the pair becomes instantiated the other one does too -- and to the same value.

This mechanism goes quite a long way towards providing us with an implementation of the search function we have envisaged above. However, certain problems remain. For example, as was noted in the previous section, variables can become instantiated to arbitrarily complex data structures. What should the matching mechanism do in the case where it is trying to check the identity of two variables both of which are instantiated to data structures?

Reflection on the arguments put forward in the previous section will reveal that the data structures which can form the values of variables are always *tree-like* structures. This is because they are constructed via a process in which simple structures are inserted into other simple structures to make complex structures. Thus, to compare two data structures the matching mechanism should just check whether they match *as trees*. But of course it must take account of the fact that the trees may contain variables. Thus in the case where it is checking whether some subtree in one structure matches the corresponding subtree in the other structure and it discovers that instead of a subtree the second structure has an uninstantiated variable, the components should match but with the side-effect that the uninstantiated variable becomes instantiated to the subtree.

The matching mechanism which we are envisaging here is usually called *unification*. More technically, it is known as *graph unification*. It constitutes a general matching function which tests whether two arbitrary components match. Imagine that we have two components called A and B; we will say that A and B can be *unified* in either of the following two cases.

- One of the two components is either an instantiated variable or a constant and the other is an uninstantiated variable. In this case they match with the side-effect that the uninstantiated variable becomes instantiated to the value of the corresponding item.

- Neither component is an uninstantiated variable. In this case they match in two cases: (1) where both have atomic values and the values are identical and (2) where their values are both structures and all corresponding components of the structures can be unified.

Note that the second case here has a recursive definition. This allows for the possibility of having nested structures.

```
/* value_of takes a term and returns its value.  If the term is
   a "Prolog" variable, value_of calls itself recursively on its
   contents, otherwise it returns the term itself. */

define value_of(term) -> value;
   if is_var(term)
   then value_of(contents(term)) -> value
   else term -> value
   endif
enddefine;

/* the updater of value_of, assigns value to term.  If term
   contains a "Prolog" variable, the updater calls itself recursively
   on the contents, otherwise it assigns the value to the
   directly contents of the variable. */

define updaterof value_of(value, term);
   if is_var(contents(term))
   then value -> value_of(contents(term))
   else value -> contents(term)
   endif
enddefine;
```

Figure 11-1 Accessing Prolog terms

Implementing the unification matcher

The unification matcher, which is the major element in the new version of the search mechanism, has now been defined quite precisely. Still to be considered are those bits of machinery which will enable the search function to be used as a general-purpose programming language. In developing these bits of machinery, we will, as far as is possible, follow the approach taken in the Prolog. That is to say, we will provide a Prolog-like computational facility based on the new variant of the search function. We will also follow the Prolog conventions with respect to terminology; thus, we will refer to components of goals as *terms* and to search rules as *clauses*.

The first task is to implement the unification mechanism; but before we can do this we need to decide how we are going to implement the "variable" mechanism. There are a number of things which this must do for us. Obviously, it must provide some way of representing instantiated and uninstantiated variables; it must also provide some way of uninstantiated variables becoming instantiated, and it must provide a mechanism by which uninstantiated variables can become shared. Recall that this occurs whenever two uninstantiated variables are matched. And since an uninstantiated variable may wind up being matched against more than one other uninstantiated variable, it is quite possible for arbitrarily many uninstantiated variables to become shared. The implementation must allow for this possibility.

A convenient approach here is to represent variables as quasi single-field data objects, which we will call *REF* objects as if they really were POP-11 REF objects. It would be better to use built-in POP-11 REF objects or define a new class via **recordclass**, but either method would introduce a POP-11 data-structure which is not used elsewhere in the book. These quasi REF objects will be lists starting and finishing with **$** and the actual value (**foo**, say) in between, e.g.

```
[$ foo $]
```

There is nothing special about the dollar symbol or the fact that there are two of them. Its just our way of making an object that is unlikely to occur anywhere "by accident". As far as POP-11 is concerned this is just an ordinary list with three things in it.

Uninstantiated variables are represented as REF objects which contain some special object denoting "no instantiation". Instantiated variables are represented as REF objects which contain the item to which they are instantiated. Thus the value of an instantiated variable is just the contents of the corresponding REF object, e.g.

```
[$ [$ foo $] $]
```

So what are the advantages of this approach? Basically, it allows variable sharing to be handled in a very simple fashion. In the case where two variables **X** and **Y** are shared the REF object corresponding to **X** will contain the REF object corresponding to **Y** (or vice versa). If **Y** becomes shared with another variable, then that variable's REF object will become the new contents of **Y**'s REF. Thus, to find the ultimate value of a variable it is necessary to get the contents of the corresponding REF object. If this is another REF object, then it must represent a variable which is shared with the initial variable. Thus to find the ultimate value of the initial variable, it is necessary to get the contents of the new REF object, and so on and so forth. Eventually at the end of such a chain, the function either finds a particular value or the special object denoting "no instantiation".

This process can be implemented using a simple recursive function; see the first function in Figure 11-1. The function first checks whether the contents of the REF are another REF object. If so, it calls itself recursively on the contents. Otherwise, it just returns the contents. Note that the *contents* of a REF object are accessed using the function **contents**.

Note that an evaluation function is defined as well as its *updater*. A function which has an updater can be assigned to in the same way that the built-in function "hd" can be assigned to. We need this in order to be able to update the value of a term as well as access it.

```
/* is_uninstantiated_var takes a term and returns true if it is a "Prolog"
   variable and its value is a word starting with the underscore character. */

define is_uninstantiated_var(term) -> boolean;
   vars w;
   value_of(term) -> w;
   is_var(term) and isword(w) and w(1) = `_` -> boolean;
enddefine;

/* is_var returns true if its argument is a "Prolog" variable. */

define is_var(term) -> boolean;
   term matches [$ = $] -> boolean
enddefine;

/* cons_var takes a value and constructs a new "Prolog" variable. */

define cons_var(value) -> new_variable;
    [$ ^value $] -> new_variable
enddefine;

/* contents takes a "Prolog" variable and returns its immediate value. */

define contents(variable) -> value;
    variable --> [$ ?value $]
enddefine;

/* the updater of contents */

define updaterof contents(value, term);
    value -> hd(tl(term))
enddefine;

/* prterm prints a term without the extra $'s and [] around "Prolog" variables. */

define prterm(term);
    vars x;
    if is_var(term) then prterm(value_of(term))
    elseif islist(term)
    then pr("["); for x in term do prterm(x); sp(1) endfor; pr("]")
    else pr(term)
    endif
enddefine;
```

Figure 11-2 Procedures associated with Prolog variables

```
/* unify takes two terms and returns true if they unify, and otherwise
   false. It may have the side effect of making variables share, whether
   the unification is successful or not. */

define unify(term1, term2) -> boolean;
    vars i;
    true -> boolean;
    if is_uninstantiated_var(term1)
    then term2 -> value_of(term1)                     /* SIDE-EFFECT */
    elseif is_uninstantiated_var(term2)
    then term1 -> value_of(term2)
    else value_of(term1) -> term1;
        value_of(term2) -> term2;                     /* SIDE-EFFECT */
        if islist(term1) and islist(term2)
           and length(term1) = length(term2)
        then for i from 1 to length(term1) do
                unless unify(term1(i), term2(i))
                then false -> boolean; return
                endunless
            endfor
        else term1 = term2 -> boolean
        endif
    endif
enddefine;
```

Figure 11-3 The unification matcher

In order to be able to represent the fact that a variable is uninstantiated we need to have some special symbol which we can put in the variable's REF to indicate that it is not yet instantiated. But ideally we would like to use different symbols for different REFs so as to be able to distinguish between them (e.g. when we print them out -- see below). A convenient compromise is to say that a variable will be assumed to be uninstantiated if its REF contains an arbitrary word beginning with an underscore character. This convention allows us to achieve both our aims and to write a function to test a given term to see if it is an uninstantiated variable; see Figure 11-3. The other functions in Figure 11-3 are for accessing, creating and printing REF objects.

Given the availability of the functions defined, we can now get down to the main task, i.e. the implementation of the unification matcher. This follows the specification introduced above. The function accepts as input two terms and attempts to see if they can be unified.

First, it tests the status of the two terms. If one of them turns out to be an uninstantiated variable, the immediate value of the other one (which will be a constant or a REF object) is assigned to be its new value. In the case where the second term is an

```
/* top_level_instantiations_ok prints out the top level instantiations,
   if any, and reads whether the user types ";" in response.  If so,
   false is returned so that the search continues, otherwise true is
   returned. */

define top_level_instantiations_ok(insts) -> boolean;
   vars input pop_readline_prompt inst;
   '? ' -> pop_readline_prompt;
   if insts = []              /* THERE WERE NO TOP-LEVEL VARIABLES */
   then pr('yes'); nl(2);     /* INDICATE THAT THE SEARCH SUCCEEDED */
        true -> boolean       /* AND RETURN <TRUE> */
   else for inst in insts do         /* PRINT INSTANTIATIONS */
            pr(inst(1)); pr(' = ');
            prterm(inst(2)); nl(1)
        endfor;
        readline() -> input;
        if input = [;]
        then false -> boolean        /* CAUSE SEARCH TO CONTINUE */
        else pr('yes'); nl(2);       /* THE USER TYPED <RETURN> */
             true -> boolean
        endif
   endif
enddefine;
```

Figure 11-4 Checking the instantiations at the top level

uninstantiated variable this causes the two variables to become "shared".

If the second variable is instantiated (or is a constant), the first variable becomes instantiated to the value of the second variable. If the two terms turn out to be structures, the procedure tries to unify the components of the structures recursively. The definition of the function is shown in Figure 11-4. Note the way the built-in function **islist** is used to test whether the terms are atomic or non-atomic. **unify** may have side-effects even if the unification fails (via the calls to the updater of **value_of**). However this is taken care of later via a procedure which restores variables to their previous values when either unification or search fails.

Note that in the case where **term1** turns out to be a variable (i.e. when the call **is_uninstantiated_var(term1)** returns **<true>**), then **term2** is assigned to be the new **value_of** term1. If **term1** is a variable this will cause the REF for **term2** to become the contents of the REF for **term1**. If **term1** is uninstantiated, the effect is to cause **term1** and **term2** to become shared. If **term1** is instantiated the effect is to instantiate **term2** to the value of **term1**. If **term1** is *not* a variable then the assignment will just have the effect of instantiating **term2** directly. (Obviously, this all applies vice versa.)

Machinery to deliver output

We have said above that the search function together with the unification mechanism can be used to implement general computational behaviour. In order to clarify this point we intend to implement a Prolog-like programming *environment*. This will allow "programs" to be written and executed, and for output to be obtained. The execution of the programs will involve applications of the search function which will make use of the unification function; the writing of programs will involve setting up a rulebase in the normal way.

The first part of this task involves providing some machinery which will enable the "programmer" to obtain output. As we suggested, the general strategy here will be to allow the inputing of goals containing variable terms. In the case where the search mechanism is able to satisfy the goals, the instantiations of the variables appearing in the original goals will be printed out for the programmer's inspection. This printing-out of variable instantiations will constitute the production of output.

Let us assume that the variables which appear in the goals input by the programmer are held in a list of pairs together with their corresponding REF object. For efficiency it would be better to use a POP-11 association table but, again, this would introduce a data-structure not used elsewhere in the book. Each entry pair in this list of pairs will map a given variable name onto the corresponding REF object.

We now define a function `top_level_instantiations_ok` to be called at the point where the search function has found a way of satisfying all the goals presented as input; see the lower part of Figure 11-4. This function just prints out the instantiations used and then enters into a simple interaction with the user. This interaction is modelled on the sort of interaction which Prolog implements. In it, the user can either ask for an alternative set of instantiations (i.e. a continuation of the search) by typing ; or bring the execution to an end by pressing <RETURN>.

The search function

We now have the unification function and the machinery with which we can arrange for output to be presented to the user. Attention can therefore turn to the central task which is the implementation of the new search function. There are a number of subsidiary mechanisms to be constructed. For example, we need a function which can construct representations for the variables in a given goal (i.e. structure). This can be defined as in Figure 11-5. The function `set_vars` takes a POP-11 list representing a structure and recursively converts all the user variables into internal variables, i.e. REF objects. The function works its way through whatever structure it is given. Every time it comes across an item that it should treat as a variable (i.e. starting with

```
/* treat_as_var takes a term and checks whether it is a word that
   starts with an uppercase letter, e.g. X, Y or Foo. */

define treat_as_var(term) -> boolean;
    isword(term) and isuppercode(term(1)) -> boolean
enddefine;

/* set_vars takes a structure and returns a new structure where
   every word starting with an uppercase letter is replaced by
   a "Prolog" variable.  It also returns a list of pairs which
   map the original variable names with the "Prolog" variables. */

define set_vars(structure) -> new_structure -> insts;
    vars database;
    [] -> database;
    set_vars1(structure) -> new_structure;
    database -> insts
enddefine;

/* set_vars1 works its way through a structure and replaces
   all the variables, defined via treat_as_var, by REF objects.  It uses
   the database to keep track of which variables have been so replaced. */

define set_vars1(structure) -> new_structure;
   vars component new_variable;
   [^(for component in structure do
          if treat_as_var(component)
          then
             if present([^component ?variable])
             then variable
             else cons_var(gensym("_")) -> new_variable;
                  add([^component ^new_variable]); /* ADD TO INSTS */
                  new_variable
             endif;
          elseif islist(component) then
             set_vars1(component)
          else
             component
          endif;
      endfor)] -> new_structure;
enddefine;
```

Figure 11-5 Placing Prolog variables inside a list structure

```
/* make_restorative_pairs takes a structure and returns a list of pairs of its
  uninstantiated variables and their contents. */

define make_restorative_pairs(structure) -> pairs;
    vars component;
    [^(for component in structure do
            if is_uninstantiated_var(component)
            then [^(contents(component)) ^component]
            elseif islist(component)
            then explode(make_restorative_pairs(component))
            endif
        endfor)] -> pairs;
enddefine;
```

Figure 11-6 Extracting uninstantiated (though possibly sharing) variables

an upper case letter), it constructs a new uninstantiated REF object (unless that particular variable has already been dealt with). Novel objects are created using the built-in function **gensym**. The **database** is used to keep track of which variables have been dealt with, so that all instances of, say, **X** in the structure are associated with the identical REF object and not given separate values. The function returns both the new version of the structure as well as the list of pairs that map variable names to REF objects.

The function **make_restorative_pairs** defined in Figure 11-6 gets every uninstantiated REF object (i.e. every variable) in a structure and constructs in each case a pair consisting of its contents and itself. This can be used to reset the REF objects to their original values if either unification or the search process fails and an alternative rule is chosen.

We finally come to implementation of the new search function! This is defined in Figure 11-7. It has much the same structure as previous backwards searching functions. In the case where the goal list is empty, the interactive function **top_level_instantiations_ok** (with the variable **insts** having as its value the map of the top level instantiations of variables in the top level goal) is called and its result is returned as the value of the current call. This means that in the case where the user triggers backtracking by typing **;**, the value of the result (i.e. **<false>**) is returned as the result of the *current* call. This ensures that the calling function will go on to try the next alternative (whatever it is), i.e. it ensures that backtracking will take place.

In the case where there are some goals to be searched, the function is able to commence its main activity. First **make_restorative_assignments** is called to obtain the list of pairs which will enable the effects of any variable instantiations to be undone -- should that become necessary. Then it iterates over all the clauses (rules)

```
/* backwards_search_prolog takes a list of goals and set of instantiations
   and returns true if the goals can be satisfied and false otherwise. */

define backwards_search_prolog(goals, insts) -> boolean;
    vars var_map clause clause_goal renamed_clause subgoals
        search_goal other_goals pair pairs;
    if goals = []
    then top_level_instantiations_ok(insts) -> boolean;
    else goals --> [?search_goal ??other_goals];
        make_restorative_pairs(search_goal) -> pairs;
        for clause in database do
            set_vars(clause) -> renamed_clause -> var_map;
            renamed_clause --> [?clause_goal ??subgoals];
            if unify(search_goal, clause_goal) and
               backwards_search_prolog([^^subgoals ^^other_goals],
                                       insts)
            then true -> boolean; return
            else        /* RESTORE OLD VALUES FOR SEARCH_GOAL VARS */
                for pair in pairs do
                    pair(1) -> contents(pair(2))
                endfor
            endif
        endfor;
        false -> boolean
    endif;
enddefine;
```

Figure 11-7 Backwards search for Prolog

in the database. For each clause, the **unify** function is called to find out whether the current goal (the value of **search_goal**) can be unified with the goal which appears in the clause (the value of **clause_goal**). If it can be unified, a recursive call on **backwards_search_prolog** is made. The input is just a list made up of the subgoals of the clause and the goals still left to be satisfied (as well as the inherited top level instantiations). The remaining part of the function is fairly self-explanatory.

Now that we have defined the main search mechanism, we need to define a function which will take the goals input by the programmer and, before presenting them as input in a call on **backwards_search_prolog**, initialise the **top_level_insts** correctly. The function is defined as in Figure 11-8.

The programming "environment" can now be implemented as an interactive loop which reads in a set of goals from the user (using the function **readline**) and then tries to see if (and how) they can be satisfied by calling **satisfy_top_level_goals**. The function is called **toyplog**. The top-level loop involves a single call on **readline** and a test for **[bye]**. The readline prompt is locally redefined so as to make the interaction more Prolog-like. Unfortunately, although **readline** returns a list, it does not cope with input which has internal list structure (an alternative is to use **listread** but this interacts with VED in a different way to **readline**). That is, any list brackets that are read in are simply treated as ordinary characters and not indicators of embedded structure. To get around this, function **makelist** builds the appropriate structure (see Notes at the end of this chapter for a neater way to define **makelist**).

Programming in Toyplog

The machinery that we have implemented above provides a simple Prolog-like programming language which we will call *Toyplog*. Many of the things which can be done with real Prolog can be done using Toyplog. Obviously, it is impractical to try to work through all the possibilities. However, just to give a flavour we will show how a program can be written to perform the basic list-manipulation tasks **member** and **append**.

Before discussing the rules which are required we need to decide on a way of representing list structures. As was argued above, the variable instantiation mechanism provides a way of building and accessing arbitrarily complex (tree) data structures. But in order to deal with a specific type of structure we need to specify what the characteristics of that data type are.

We shall simply follow the Prolog conventions here. A list data structure will be assumed to made up of structures of three elements which for convenience we will call "dot structures". The first element of a dot structure will always be the dot character, i.e. ".". The second element of a dot structure will be an arbitrary item while the third element will either be another dot structure, or the empty list item; namely **[]**. There is nothing special about choosing "dot" rather than some other way of denoting lists; this just follows standard Prolog conventions. Thus a list which in POP-11 we would write:

```
[1 2 3]
```

will be represented under the proposed conventions as follows:

```
[. 1 [. 2 [. 3 []]]]
```

Given these conventions it is quite easy to construct a couple of clauses which in combination will implement a predicate to test whether a given item is a member of a given list. The two clauses look like this:

```
[ [[member X [. X Y]]]
```

```
/* satisfy_top_level_goals takes a list of goals and tries to satisfy them. */

define satisfy_top_level_goals(goals);
   vars top_level_insts;
   1 -> gensym("_");
   set_vars(goals) -> goals -> top_level_insts;
   if not(backwards_search_prolog(goals, rev(top_level_insts)))
   then pr('no'); nl(2)
   endif;
enddefine;

/* toyplog takes a rulebase and conducts a Prolog like interaction */

define toyplog(rulebase);
   vars goals pop_readline_prompt database;
   '?- ' -> pop_readline_prompt;
   pr('Toyplog version 1'); nl(1);
   rulebase -> database;
   until goals = [bye] do
      makelist(readline()) -> goals;
      unless goals = [bye] or goals = [] then
         satisfy_top_level_goals(goals);
      endunless;
   enduntil;
enddefine;

/* makelist takes a flat list possibly containing "[" and "]" and
  returns a correspondingly nested list. */

define makelist(flatlist) -> structure;
   makelist1() -> structure
enddefine;

define makelist1() -> structure;
   [^( until flatlist = [] or hd(flatlist) = "]" do
          if hd(flatlist) = "["
          then tl(flatlist) -> flatlist;
               makelist1()
          else hd(flatlist);
          endif;
          tl(flatlist) -> flatlist
       enduntil) ] -> structure
enddefine;
```

Figure 11-8 The top level of the Prolog system

```
[[member X [. Z Y]] [member X Y]] ] -> database;
```

The first clause is just a fact. It says, in effect, that some arbitrary object is a member of a list if it appears as the first element of that list. The second clause is a rule. It says that an object is a member of a list if it is a member of the "tail" of the list (i.e. the list minus its first element). In some sense these two clauses implement a procedure for testing membership.

We can look at the way the machinery we have implemented deals with a **member** goal by tracing the main functions and calling **satisfy_top_level_goals** on an appropriate input. Thus:

```
trace backwards_search_prolog unify;
satisfy_top_level_goals([[member 2 [. 1 [. 2 []]]]]);

> backwards_search_prolog [[member 2 [. 1 [. 2 []]]]] []
!> unify [member 2 [. 1 [. 2 []]]] [member [$ _1 $] [. [$ _1 $] [$ _2 $]]]
!!> unify member member
!!< unify <true>
!!> unify 2 [$ _1 $]
!!< unify <true>
!!> unify [. 1 [. 2 []]] [. [$ 2 $] [$ _2 $]]
!!!> unify . .
!!!< unify <true>
!!!> unify 1 [$ 2 $]
!!!< unify <false>
!!< unify <false>
!< unify <false>
!> unify [member 2 [. 1 [. 2 []]]] [member [$ _3 $] [. [$ _4 $] [$ _5 $]]]
!!> unify member member
!!< unify <true>
!!> unify 2 [$ _3 $]
!!< unify <true>
!!> unify [. 1 [. 2 []]] [. [$ _4 $] [$ _5 $]]
!!!> unify . .
!!!< unify <true>
!!!> unify 1 [$ _4 $]
!!!< unify <true>
!!!> unify [. 2 []] [$ _5 $]
!!!< unify <true>
!!< unify <true>
!< unify <true>
!> backwards_search_prolog [[member [$ 2 $] [$ [. 2 []] $]]] []
!!> unify [member [$ 2 $] [$ [. 2 []] $]] [member [$ _6 $] [. [$ _6 $] [$ _7 $]]]
!!!> unify member member
!!!< unify <true>
!!!> unify [$ 2 $] [$ _6 $]
!!!< unify <true>
!!!> unify [$ [. 2 []] $] [. [$ [$ 2 $] $] [$ _7 $]]
!!!!> unify . .
!!!!< unify <true>
!!!!> unify 2 [$ [$ 2 $] $]
```

```
!!!!< unify <true>
!!!!> unify [] [$ _7 $]
!!!!< unify <true>
!!!< unify <true>
!!< unify <true>
!!> backwards_search_prolog [] []
yes

!!< backwards_search_prolog <true>
!< backwards_search_prolog <true>
< backwards_search_prolog <true>
```

Toyplog printed out **yes** in response the initial goal. Note that this is the correct answer. One of the problems of the trace is that any REF objects are printed out as the lists that they really are.[3]

Adopting a similar approach we can implement a "function" which effectively appends two lists together. The clauses we need in this case are as follows:

```
[ [[append [] X X]]
  [[append [. H T] L [. H X]][append T L X]] ] -> database;
```

The second and third elements will be used here as "input" variables and the fourth element of goals as a kind of "result" variable. The answer we are looking for (i.e. the append of the two lists) will be the value to which the fourth argument of the original goal is instantiated. Again we have one fact and one rule. The fact says that an empty list appended to a list is just the list itself. The rule says that a list consisting of an initial element **H** and a tail **T** appended to a list **L**, is just a list which has **H** as its first element and as its second element, the result of appending **T** to **L**. Unfortunately, the way in which the search function tries to satisfy even quite a simple **append** goal is quite involved:

```
satisfy_top_level_goals([[append [. 1 [. 2 []]] [. 3 [. 4 [. 5 []]]] X]]);

> backwards_search_prolog [[append [. 1 [. 2 [] ] ] [. 3 [. 4 [. 5 [] ] ] ] _1 ] ]
                          [[X _1 ] ]
!> unify [append [. 1 [. 2 [] ] ] [. 3 [. 4 [. 5 [] ] ] ] _1 ] [append [] _2 _2 ]
!!> unify append append
!!< unify <true>
!!> unify [. 1 [. 2 [] ] ] []
!!< unify <false>
!< unify <false>
!> unify [append [. 1 [. 2 [] ] ] [. 3 [. 4 [. 5 [] ] ] ] _1 ]
```

[3] We have already defined a procedure **prterm** which prints out such objects in a more compact way. In order to make this have a global effect (i.e. even the output of tracing) it is necessary to adjust the way that POP-11 prints lists:

```
prterm -> class_print(datakey([$ foo $]));
```

```
         [append [. _3 _4 ] _5 [. _3 _6 ] ]
 !!> unify append append
 !!< unify <true>
 !!> unify [. 1 [. 2 [] ] ] [. _3 _4 ]
 !!!> unify . .
 !!!< unify <true>
 !!!> unify 1 _3
 !!!< unify <true>
 !!!> unify [. 2 [] ] _4
 !!!< unify <true>
 !!< unify <true>
 !!> unify [. 3 [. 4 [. 5 [] ] ] ] _5
 !!< unify <true>
 !!> unify _1 [. 1 _6 ]
 !!< unify <true>
 !< unify <true>
 !> backwards_search_prolog [[append [. 2 [] ] [. 3 [. 4 [. 5 [] ] ] ] _6 ] ]
                                   [[X [. 1 _6 ] ] ]
 !!> unify [append [. 2 [] ] [. 3 [. 4 [. 5 [] ] ] ] _6 ] [append [] _7 _7 ]
 !!!> unify append append
 !!!< unify <true>
 !!!> unify [. 2 [] ] []
 !!!< unify <false>
 !!< unify <false>
 !!> unify [append [. 2 [] ] [. 3 [. 4 [. 5 [] ] ] ] _6 ]
         [append [. _8 _9 ] _10 [. _8 _11 ] ]
 !!!> unify append append
 !!!< unify <true>
 !!!> unify [. 2 [] ] [. _8 _9 ]
 !!!!> unify . .
 !!!!< unify <true>
 !!!!> unify 2 _8
 !!!!< unify <true>
 !!!!> unify [] _9
 !!!!< unify <true>
 !!!< unify <true>
 !!!> unify [. 3 [. 4 [. 5 [] ] ] ] _10
 !!!< unify <true>
 !!!> unify _6 [. 2 _11 ]
 !!!< unify <true>
 !!< unify <true>
 !!> backwards_search_prolog [[append [] [. 3 [. 4 [. 5 [] ] ] ] _11 ] ]
                                   [[X [. 1 [. 2 _11 ] ] ] ]
 !!!> unify [append [] [. 3 [. 4 [. 5 [] ] ] ] _11 ] [append [] _12 _12 ]
 !!!!> unify append append
 !!!!< unify <true>
 !!!!> unify [] []
 !!!!< unify <true>
 !!!!> unify [. 3 [. 4 [. 5 []] ] ] _12
 !!!!< unify <true>
 !!!!> unify _11 [. 3 [. 4 [. 5 [] ] ] ]
 !!!!< unify <true>
 !!!< unify <true>
 !!!> backwards_search_prolog [] [[X [. 1 [. 2 [. 3 [. 4 [. 5 [] ] ] ] ] ] ] ]
```

```
X = [. 1 [. 2 [. 3 [. 4 [. 5 [] ] ] ] ] ]
? ;
!!!< backwards_search_prolog <false>
!!!> unify [append [] [. 3 [. 4 [. 5 [] ] ] ] _11 ]
          [append [. _13 _14 ] _15 [. _13 _16 ] ]
!!!!> unify append append
!!!!< unify <true>
!!!!> unify [] [. _13 _14 ]
!!!!< unify <false>
!!!< unify <false>
!!< backwards_search_prolog <false>
!< backwards_search_prolog <false>
< backwards_search_prolog <false>
no
```

The above trace demonstrates how much work goes on under the surface in Prolog.

A sample interaction with Toyplog

It is impossible to explore all the ways in which we can get computational behaviour out of the new search function. Since Toyplog constitutes a subset of Prolog most computational strategies which are possible in that language will be feasible in Toyplog. The interaction listed below demonstrates just a few of the possibilities.

First of all we set up an initial rulebase (i.e. "program"). This just contains the definitions of the "member" and "append" predicates:

```
[ [[append [] X X]]
  [[append [. H T] L [. H X]][append T L X]]
  [[member X [. X Y]]]
  [[member X [. Z Y]][member X Y]] ] -> rulebase9;
```

Now we start the Toyplog interaction by calling the `toyplog` function:

```
untrace backwards_search_prolog unify;

toyplog(rulebase9);
Toyplog version 1
?- [member foo [. bang [. foo []]]]
yes

?- [member X [. bang [. ding []]]]
X = bang
? ;
X = ding
? ;
```

```
no

?- [member X [.bang [.ding []]]] [member X [. ding []]]
X = ding
? ;
no

?- [append [. 1 [. 2 []]] [. 3 []] X]
X = [. 1 [. 2 [. 3 [] ] ] ]
? ;
no

?- [append X Y [. foo [. bang [. ding []]]]]
X = []
Y = [. foo [. bang [. ding [] ] ] ]
? ;
X = [. foo [] ]
Y = [. bang [. ding [] ] ]
? ;
X = [. foo [. bang [] ] ]
Y = [. ding [] ]
? ;
X = [. foo [. bang [. ding [] ] ] ]
Y = []
? ;
no

?- bye
```

As a second example we set up a rulebase containing a definitions of facts and rules for building a simple backwards search tree without loop detection, see Chapter 6:

```
[[[rule [. have_smarties []]]]
 [[rule [. have_eggs []]]]
 [[rule [. have_flour []]]]
 [[rule [. have_money []]]]
 [[rule [. have_car []]]]
 [[rule [. in_kitchen []]]]

 [[rule [. decorate_cake [. have_cake [. have_icing []]]]]]
 [[rule [. decorate_cake [. have_cake [. have_smarties []]]]]]
 [[rule [. have_money [. in_bank []]]]]
 [[rule [. have_cake [. have_money [. in_store []]]]]]
```

```
    [[rule [. have_cake [. in_kitchen [. have_phone []]]]]]
    [[rule [. in_store [. have_car []]]]]
    [[rule [. in_bank [. have_car []]]]]

    [[backwards_search_tree [] []]]

    [[backwards_search_tree [. Goal Goals] [. [. Goal Tree ] Trees]]
       [rule [. Goal Subgoals]]
       [backwards_search_tree Subgoals Tree]
       [backwards_search_tree Goals Trees]]
   ] -> rulebase10;
```

This example is rather recursive as we are using our POP-11 backwards search function to implement Prolog, itself conducting a backwards search. Needless to say, this runs a bit slower than doing the backwards search directly:

```
toyplog(rulebase10);
Toyplog version 1
?- [rule X]
X = [. have_smarties [] ]
? ;
X = [. have_eggs [] ]
?
yes

?- [backwards_search_tree [. have_smarties []] [. Tree []]]
Tree = [. have_smarties [] ]
?
yes

?- [backwards_search_tree [. decorate_cake []] [. Tree []]]
Tree = [. decorate_cake
          [. [. have_cake
                [. [. have_money [] ]
                [. [. in_store [. [. have_car [] ] [] ] ] [] ] ] ]
          [. [. have_smarties [] ] [] ] ] ]
?
yes

?- bye
```

In the final example above, we have slightly tidied the printing of the value of **Tree** in order to show its structure (as a solution tree) more clearly. Note that the output matches that given in Chapter 6 for the same problem.

Reading

The fact that Prolog constitutes a general-purpose programming language means that it can be used to *implement* search strategies! It should come as no surprise (now) to find that it is particularly good for this sort of application. Ford provides a user-friendly discussion of this issue (see Ford 1987, Chapter 5). He also covers Prolog implementations of planning strategies (Chapters 6 and 12), probabilistic search (Chapter 8) and a form of concept learning which is related to the focussing algorithm (Chapter 11).

Bratko (1990) provides a general introduction to Prolog programming and gives Prolog implementations for many of the search-related techniques which have been discussed above. The topics of heuristic search, minimax and alpha-beta pruning are dealt with in Chapter 15; basic search strategies are dealt with in Chapters 11, 12 and 13. Chapter 14 is devoted to the topic of expert systems.

Chapter 2 of Ramsay and Barrett (1987) describes the implementation of a sophisticated theorem prover in POP-11. Kowalski (1979) discusses the logical foundations of Prolog and search techniques in general. For a 2-page introduction to Prolog see Rich (1983, pp. 401-402).

Exercises

1. Extend the definition of `backward_search_prolog` so that it can cope sensibly with "extra-logical" goals such as `[write]` or `[assert Y]`.

2. Replace the rather awkward REF objects in the definition by true POP-11 REF objects.

3. Extend the definitions to cover such predicates as `not` and `spy`.

Notes

A neater way to define makelist.

```
define makelist(flatlist) -> structure;
    compile(stringin('' >< flatlist)) -> structure
enddefine;
```

References

Aleksander, I. and Burnett, P. (1987) *Thinking Machines: The Search for Artificial Intelligence*, Oxford: Oxford University Press.

Amarel, S. (1981) On Representations of Problems of Reasoning about Actions. In B.L. Webber and N.J. Nilsson (eds) *Readings in Artificial Intelligence*, Palo Alto: Tioga Publishing Company.

Barr, A. and Feigenbaum, E.A. (eds) (1981) *The Handbook of Artificial Intelligence (Volume 1)*, Los Altos: William Kaufmann.

Barrett, R., Ramsay, A. and Sloman, A. (1985) *POP-11: A Practical Language for Artificial Intelligence Programming*, Chichester: Ellis Horwood.

Bratko, I. (1990) *Prolog Programming for Artificial Intelligence (2nd Edition)*, Wokingham: Addison-Wesley.

Bundy, A., Burstall, R.M., Weir, S. and Young, R.M. (1980) *Artificial Intelligence: An Introductory Course*, Edinburgh: Edinburgh University Press.

Bundy, A., Silver, B. and Plummer, D. (1985) An Analytical Comparison of some Rule-Learning Programs, *Artificial Intelligence*, **27**, 137-181.

Burton, M. and Shadbolt, N. (1987) *POP-11 Programming for Artificial Intelligence*, Wokingham: Addison-Wesley.

Charniak, E. and McDermott, D. (1985) *Introduction to Artificial Intelligence*, Reading, MA: Addison-Wesley.

Clocksin, W.F. and Mellish, C.S. (1987) *Programming in Prolog (3rd Edition)*, Berlin: Springer-Verlag.

Cohen, P.R. and Feigenbaum, E.A. (eds) (1982) *The Handbook of Artificial Intelligence (Volume 3)*, London: Pitman.

Fikes, R.E. and Nilsson, N.J. (1971) "STRIPS: a New Approach to the Application of Theorem Proving", *Artificial Intelligence*, **2**, 189-208.

Fikes, R., Hart, P. and Nilsson, N.J. (1981) Learning and Executing Generalised Robot Plans. In B.L. Webber and N.J. Nilsson (eds) *Readings in Artificial Intelligence*, Palo Alto: Tioga Publishing Company.

Ford, N. (1987) *How Machines Think: A General Introduction To Artificial Intelligence Illustrated In Prolog*, Chichester: John Wiley and Sons.

Forsyth, R. (ed.) (1984) *Expert Systems: Principles And Case Studies*, London: Chapman and Hall.

Gazdar, G. and Mellish, C. (1989a) *Natural Language Processing in POP-11*, Wokingham: Addison-Wesley.

Gazdar, G. and Mellish, C. (1989b) *Natural Language Processing in Prolog*, Wokingham: Addison-Wesley.

Gilhooly, K. (1989) *Human and Machine Problem Solving*, New York: Plenum Press.

Hart, P., Nilsson, N.J. and Raphael, B. (1968) A Formal Basis for the Heuristic Determination of Minimum Cost paths, *IEEE Transactions on SSC*, SSC-4, 100-107.

Hayes, P. (1981) The Frame Problem and Related Problems in Artificial Intelligence. In B.L. Webber and N.J. Nilsson (eds) *Readings in Artificial Intelligence*, Palo Alto: Tioga Publishing Company.

Korf, R.E. (1988) Search: A Survey of Recent Results. In H.E. Shrobe (ed.) *Exploring Artificial Intelligence: Survey Talks from the National Conferences on Artificial Intelligence*, San Mateo: Morgan Kaufmann.

Kowalski, R. (1979) *Logic For Problem Solving*, New York: North-Holland.

Laventhol, J. (1987) *Programming in POP-11*, Oxford: Blackwell Scientific Publications.

Mitchell (1982) Generalisation as Search, *Artificial Intelligence*, **18**, 203-226.

Newell, A. and Simon, H.A. (1963) GPS: a Program that Simulates Human Thought. In E. A. Feigenbaum and J. Feldman (eds) *Computers And Thought*, New York: McGraw-Hill.

Nilsson, N.J. (1980) *Principles of Artificial Intelligence*, Palo Alto: Tioga Publishing Company.

Noble, H.M. (1988) *Natural Language Processing*, Oxford: Blackwell Scientific Publishers.

O'Keefe, R. (1990) *The Craft of Prolog*, Cambridge, MA: MIT Press.

Pearl, J. (1984) *Heuristics: Intelligent Search Strategies for Computer Problem Solving*, Reading, MA: Addison-Wesley.

Ramsay, A. (1986) Computer Processing of Natural Language. In M. Yazdani (ed.) *Artificial Intelligence*, London: Chapman Hall.

Ramsay, A. and Barrett, B. (1987) *AI in Practice: examples in POP-11*, Chichester: Ellis Horwood.

Rich, E. (1983) *Artificial Intelligence*, New York: McGraw-Hill.

Rich, E. and Knight, K. (1991) *Artificial Intelligence (2nd Edition)*, New York: McGraw-Hill.

Scott, P. and Nicolson, R. (1991) *Cognitive Science Projects in Prolog*, Hove: Lawrence Erlbaum Associates.

Sharples, M., Hogg, D., Hutchison, C., Torrance, S. and Young, D. (1988) *Computers And Thought: An Introduction To Cognitive Science And Artificial Intelligence*, Cambridge, MA: MIT press.

Shortliffe, E.H. (1976) *Computer-Based Medical Consultations: MYCIN*, New York: American Elsevier.

Sterling, L. and Shapiro, E. (1986) *The Art of Prolog: Advanced Programming Techniques*, Cambridge, MA: MIT Press.

Stillings, N.A., Feinstein, M.H., Garfield, J.L., Rissland, E.L., Rosenbaum, D.A., Weisler, S.E. and Baker-Ward, L. (1987) *Cognitive Science: An Introduction*, Cambridge, MA: MIT Press.

Webber, B.L., and Nilsson, N.J. (eds) (1981) *Readings In Artificial Intelligence*, Palo Alto: Tioga Publishing.

Winograd, T. (1983) *Language as a Cognitive Process (Volume 1: Syntax)*, Reading, MA: Addison-Wesley.

Winston, P.H. (1984) *Artificial Intelligence (2nd Edition)*, Reading, MA: Addison-Wesley.

Zadeh, L. (1965) Fuzzy Sets, *Information And Control*, **8**, 338-353.

APPENDIX A
Introduction to POP-11

Starting POP-11

To use the POP-11 language on a computer you first have to run the POP-11 system. The way in which this is done will vary depending on the computer which is being used. But let us imagine that we are using a computer which has the UNIX operating system. In this case it is quite likely that the POP-11 system can be run by just typing **pop11** to the UNIX prompt, thus:

```
% pop11
```

Once you have done this some messages will be printed out and then you will see a colon appear at the far left of the screen. This says that the computer is ready to receive input in POP-11. By convention we blur the distinction between the language and the computer and just say that POP-11 is waiting for input.

If you press the <RETURN> key, POP-11 will print a new colon on the next line. This shows that it is responding to you. To make it do something interesting you have to type in some POP-11 *code,* i.e. you have to type in some words in the POP-11 programming language. Note that if you present input which is not perfectly correct POP-11 code, a complaint called a *MISHAP message* will be printed out. This will consist of about three lines of text, each one preceded by three semi-colons. The interpretation of mishap messages is quite a complex business and will not be covered here.

POP-11 as a calculator

At a very basic level, the POP-11 programming language is a bit like a pocket calculator. To work something out on a calculator you type in an expression such as "2 + 2" and then a command such as "=" and the calculator responds by printing out the value of the expression in the display. We can get this sort of behaviour out of POP-

11 by going through roughly the same steps; except with POP-11 you have to type in the command to show that you want the value of the expression to be printed out. If you type:

```
2 + 2 ==>
```

followed by <RETURN>, POP-11 will respond by printing out:

```
** 4
```

Note that when typing in this expression it is necessary to type spaces between the various items. We can actually type as many spaces between items as we like. POP-11 just skips over blanks and blank lines. So we could have typed:

```
2

    +

  2
    ==>
```

and got exactly the same result. Note that POP-11 always puts two asterisks before anything which you have asked it to print out.

The `2 + 2` part of the code we typed in is an expression and the `==>` bit is a command called the *print arrow*; the print arrow tells POP-11 that you want it to print out the value of the expression which appears immediately in front of the command. Typing <RETURN> tells POP-11 to respond to the code that you have typed in. In fact, all POP-11 code consists of commands and expressions. Commands are things which tell POP-11 to do something; expressions are things which have values.

POP-11 understands all the usual types of mathematical expression. Thus we can type things like:

```
2 * 3 / 5 - 0.3 ==>
** 0.9
```

It also allows us to construct expressions using a number of more advanced operators. A useful operator is **rem**. The value of a expression involving the **rem** operator is just the remainder produced when the number on the left is divided by the number on the right. Thus:

```
3 rem 2 ==>
** 1
```

As well as simple commands like **==>** POP-11 also has more complicated commands. For instance we can write some code which says "print out the value of 2 + 2 five times". This code is written as follows:

```
repeat 5 times  2 + 2 ==>  endrepeat;
```

Note that this command has a semi-colon at the end; this just tells POP-11 where the command ends. All commands except **==>** have to end with a semi-colon. If you type the command in and then hit <RETURN> (to say "respond to this"), POP-11 will print out:

```
** 4
** 4
** 4
** 4
** 4
```

The "repeat 5 times ... endrepeat" bit is a command just like **==>**. The difference is that it is a complex command which can have other commands and expressions inside it. In fact, POP-11 allows you to put arbitrarily many commands inside the repeat command. So we could do:

```
repeat 5 times  2 + 2 ==>   3 * 3 ==>  endrepeat;
```

Variables

POP-11 is like a sophisticated "scientific" calculator in the fact that it lets you create *variables*. These are like boxes in which you can keep values of expressions. The command which tells POP-11 to set up a variable is *vars*. To set up a variable called **mine** you would type:

```
vars mine;
```

That is, you type "vars <name of variable> ;". Don't forget to end the command with a semi-colon. Variables always have names; this means that if you want to put a value in a specific box you can tell POP-11 which box to use by giving its name. To put a value in the variable (i.e. box) called **mine** we would do:

```
2 + 2 -> mine;
```

The **->** is a command called the *assignment arrow;* commands using the assignment arrow are usually just called *assignments*. They tell POP-11 to take the value of the expression on the left and put it into the variable whose name appears on the right. If the variable is called **mine**, the value is said to be "assigned to mine".

One of the nice things about variables is that when you just type their names, POP-11 treats it as an expression whose value is just the contents of the corresponding box. This means that we can do something like:

```
mine ==>
```

and POP-11 will respond by printing:

```
** 4
```

It also means that we can copy the contents of one variable into another using the assignment arrow, e.g.

```
vars yours;
mine -> yours;

yours ==>
** 4
```

Functions

Usually, calculators have things like square-root functions. In order to get the square-root of a number you type the number in, then hit the square-root command (i.e. button) and the calculator prints out the answer in the display. POP-11 also has this sort of feature, but to make it work you have to type in the name of the function and then the number to which it is to be applied in brackets, e.g. to get the square-root of 25 we would type in the name of the function (in POP-11 it's called **sqrt**) and then the number in brackets:

```
sqrt(25) ==>
** 5.0
```

The number which goes in between the brackets is referred to as an *input* to the function. The evaluation of a function is referred to as a *call* of the function and the value computed is said to be *returned*. Often, the returned value is called the *result* of the function. Thus, if we wanted to refer to the evaluation of a specific function, e.g.

```
sqrt(8)
```

we would talk about "the value which is returned when sqrt is called on the input 8" or perhaps "the result of sqrt called on 8".

Function calls are types of expression and as such, they have *values*; the value of a given function call is just its result. Thus, we can use the assignment arrow to put the result of a call on the square-root function into a variable:

```
sqrt(100) -> mine;
mine ==>
** 10.0
```

POP-11 has many other built-in functions as well as **sqrt**. Three useful examples are **min**, **max** and **abs**; **min** takes two numerical inputs and returns the one which is smaller. Thus:

```
min(2,3) ==>
** 2
```

max does the opposite: it takes two inputs and returns the one which is larger. Thus:

```
max(2,3) ==>
** 3
```

The function **abs** just returns the absolute value of a positive or negative integer. Thus:

```
abs(-3) ==>
** 3

abs(4) ==>
** 4
```

Defining functions

Of course, POP-11 provides many features which you would be unlikely to get on a calculator. For example, POP-11 has a command which lets you set up new functions of your own. Imagine that we would like there to be a function called **double** such that we could type:

```
double(3) ==>
```

and get the response:

```
** 6
```

POP-11 does not have this function built in, but we can set it up by using a **define** command as shown in FigureA-1. The **define** command shown in this figure provides POP-11 with a script which tells it how to evaluate an expression like **double(6);** by convention the script is called a *definition*. Let us work our way through it bit by bit.

First of all, the word **define** begins the command and the word **enddefine** terminates it (compare "repeat ... endrepeat"). The word which comes immediately after **define** is just the name of the function which we want to set up. The role played by the **(number)** part of the command is quite hard to explain. Basically, it sets up a new variable called **number**. But it is not an ordinary variable. We can always create an ordinary variable using the **vars** command. The variable set up is special because it is the one into which POP-11 will put the input whenever the function is called. Technically, this bit of the command is said to set up an *input parameter* for the function, i.e. a box into which the input to the function (in some given call) is placed.

If we want to set up a function which takes more than one input, then we have to put more than one word in between the initial brackets. For instance, we might type something like

```
define biggest(numa, numb) ...
```

so as to set up a function called **biggest** which might behave as follows:[1]

```
biggest(3, 4) ==>
** 4
```

By putting two words in between the brackets we are effectively telling POP-11 that calls on **biggest** will always include two inputs, so we need *two* input boxes (parameters). By putting the words in a certain order we are specifying which input is to go in which box. We are telling POP-11 that we want the first input to be put into **numa** (the first word) and the second input to be put into **numb**. For functions which take

```
define double(number) -> result;
    number * 2 -> result
enddefine;
```

Figure A-1 Function to double a number

[1] In fact, we have no need to define this function. POP-11 has this function built-in as **max**.

three inputs we would need to include three input parameters, and so on.

The **-> result** of the first line of the definition indicates that our function will produce a single value or result when it is complete. For the purposes of the function the variable holding this *local output* is named **result** in this case.

The middle bit of the **define** command is relatively straightforward. It is made up from the expression **number * 2** and an assignment of the value of this expression to the local output variable **result**. If the input was 5, then the value of the expression would be 5 * 2, i.e. 10. Thus the value returned by the following call is 10:

```
double(5) ==>
** 10
```

Now, in our definition of **double** there is only one POP-11 command inside the definition. But there could be other commands. Suppose we wanted to define a function which doubles and then squares a number. We might use a **define** command as shown in Figure A-2. POP-11 would then produce the following behaviour.

```
double_then_square(3) ==>
** 36
```

Note that in setting up this function we have used a word which is made out of three words joined together with underscore characters. Normally we use the hyphen to join words together (e.g. we would type **double-then-square**). But when talking to POP-11 we cannot do this. POP-11 always treats a hyphen as a minus symbol.

Local variables

The variables which we set up by putting words in between the initial brackets of a **define** command and that following the **->** in the title line have the property of being *attached* to the function. So when we set up a variables called **number** and **foo** by typing:

```
define double_then_square(number) -> output;
    number * 2 -> number;
    number * number -> output
enddefine;
```

Figure A-2 function to double then square a number

define double(number) -> foo; ...

we set up variables which are quite different to the variable which we set up using an ordinary **vars** command. POP-11 treats the **number** and **foo** variables as if they belong to the function we have defined. This means that they cannot get mixed up with any ordinary variables of the same name. We can demonstrate this by setting up an ordinary variable called **number** and then calling the function **double**. The fact that the original value of **number** is not affected by the call on **double** shows that POP-11 treats these as two different variables. If it treated them as the same variable, then its placing of the input 5 into double's **number** variable would change the value of the ordinary **number** variable:

```
vars number;
3 -> number;

double(5) ==>
** 10

number ==>
** 3
```

A good way to think about this is to imagine that the **number** or the **foo** variable belonging to **double** has the word **double** appended as an invisible postfix; i.e. **number_double**. Variables which are attached to a function are called *local variables*. Non-local variables are sometimes called *global variables*. We can set up more local variables if we want by putting a **vars** command *inside* a function definition. Thus:

```
vars temp;
10 -> temp;

define double_then_square(number) -> result;
   vars temp;
   number * 2 -> temp;
   temp * temp -> result
enddefine;

double_then_square(3) ==>
** 36

temp ==>
** 10
```

Boolean expressions

So far, we have only looked at expressions which are made up from numbers and arithmetic symbols such as + and *. In POP-11, the numbers appearing either side of the arithmetic symbol are called *arguments* and the symbol itself is called an *operator*. This sort of expression always has a numeric value but in POP-11 we can also have expressions which have what are called *boolean values*; these are called *boolean expressions* and are constructed using *boolean operators*.

In fact there are just two boolean values; one corresponds (roughly) to "yes", the other corresponds to "no". In POP-11 these values are printed out as follows:

```
** <true>
** <false>
```

where **<true>** corresponds to "yes", and **<false>** corresponds to "no". Expressions which have these "yes/no" values are things like **2 = 2** and **4 > 3**. Any expression involving the = operator has the value **<true>** if the thing on the right is the same as the thing on the left; otherwise it has the value **<false>**. By convention, an expression which has the value **<true>** (or **<false>**) is often just said to *be* true (or false). Thus:

```
3 = 2 ==>
** <false>
```

is false, but:

```
2 = 2 ==>
** <true>
```

is true.

Expressions involving > are true if the number on the left is bigger than the number on the right; otherwise they are false. Thus:

```
3 > 2 ==>
** <true>
```

and

```
2 > 3 ==>
** <false>
```

As well as = and >, POP-11 can also handle expressions involving < (less-than), >= (more-than-or-equal) and <= (less-than-or-equal). Thus:

```
2 > 2 ==>
** <false>

2 >= 2 ==>
** <true>
```

Expressions which just involve two numbers and a symbol like = are simple boolean expressions. But POP-11 provides operators which join boolean expressions together to create more complex boolean expressions. The operators provided are **and**, **or**. These work in exactly the way we would expect: expressions involving **and** are true if the expression on the left is true *and* the expression on the right is true. Expressions involving the or operator are true if the expression on the left is true *or* the expression on the right is true. For example:

```
2 >= 2 and 3 < 4 ==>
** <true>
```

but

```
2 >= 2 and 4 < 3
** <false>
```

Expressions involving or behave differently. Thus:

```
2 >= 2 or 4 < 3 ==>
** <true>
```

This expression has the value **<true>** because one of the two expressions appearing either side of the or has the value **<true>**. In order for an **or** expression to have the value **<false>**, both expressions must have the value **<false>**, e.g.

```
2 > 3 or 3 > 4 ==>
** <false>
```

Finally, POP-11 provides a function called not. Calls on not (e.g. not(2 > 3)) return **<true>** if the expression which appears in the brackets has the value **<false>**:

```
not(2 > 3) ==>
** <true>
```

Conditionals

These boolean expressions may seem a bit pointless. It is usually quite possible to see which of two numbers is the larger (say), so why have special machinery for working this out? The advantages of boolean expressions only really begin to show up when we consider another complex POP-11 command. This is the **`if`** command. Let us consider the function we envisaged above called **`biggest`**. We want to be able to type:

```
biggest(2,3) ==>
```

and have POP-11 respond by printing:

```
** 3
```

We can obtain this behaviour this by defining up a function as is shown in Figure A-3. Note that the function has two local variables in between the brackets on the first line. This is because, as we noted above, calls on **`biggest`** are always going to specify two inputs, so we must set up two boxes (variables) for these two numbers to be put into. The definition we have provided tells POP-11 that the result of a call such as **`biggest(2,3)`** is 2 if it turns out that 2 is greater than 3; otherwise it is 3.

The **`if`** command provides a way of doing something only if some boolean expression has the value **`<true>`**, and doing something else in all other cases. POP-11 responds to an **`if`** command by first testing to see whether the boolean expression which comes immediately after the **`if`** has the value **`<true>`**.[2] If it does then POP-11 does all the commands which come between the **`then`** and the **`else`**; otherwise it does all the commands which come between the **`else`** and the **`endif`**. We can have **`if`** commands which do not have an **`else`** part. In this case, if the boolean expression has the value **`<true>`**, POP-11 does all the commands between the **`then`** and the **`endif`**.

```
define biggest(numa, numb) -> larger;
    if numa > numb
    then numa -> larger
    else numb -> larger
    endif;
enddefine;
```

Figure A-3 Function to choose the larger of two numbers

[2] In fact, it checks that the expression does *not* have the value **`<false>`**.

We can also have **if** commands which, instead of an **else** part have an **elseif** part. This has the form:

elseif <expression> then <commands>

The commands between the **elseif** and the word **endif** are done if the expression which appears between the **elseif** and the **then** has the value **<true>**. If necessary, it is possible to have multiple **elseif** parts. That is to say you can have **if** commands of the form:

```
if <expression> then
  <commands>
elseif <expression> then
  <commands>
elseif <expression> then
  <commands>

  ...

endif;
```

POP-11 also has an **unless** command which works as a kind of *inverted* **if**. We could have used this to write the **biggest** function as is shown in Figure A-4. The way in which POP-11 responds to **unless** commands is effectively, the opposite of the way in which it responds to **if** commands. If the boolean expression which comes between the **unless** and the **then** has the value **<true>** then all the commands between the **else** and the **endunless** will be done. Otherwise, all the commands between the **then** and the **else** will be done. For convenience POP-11 always treats any value which is not equal to **<false>** as being equal to **<true>**. This makes it a lot easier to achieve certain effects as we will see below.

```
define biggest(numa, numb) -> larger;
    unless numa > numb
    then numb -> larger
    else numa -> larger
    endunless;
enddefine;
```

Figure A-4 Function to select the larger of two numbers

Words and lists

We have seen that in POP-11, expressions can have numeric values or boolean values. But this is not the end of the story. We can also have expression whose values are object-like entities called *words*. For instance, if we type:

```
"foobang" ==>
```

POP-11 will respond with:

```
** foobang
```

This is because, in POP-11, a bit of code which just consists of a number of characters enclosed in double-quotes is an expression whose value is a special type of object called a *word*. Words should not be confused with variables. If we had typed:

```
foobang ==>
```

POP-11 would have assumed that the value of the expression **foobang** was the contents of the variable with this name (see above).

Another type of expression which has an object-like value is as follows:

```
[foobang 76 silly wally]
```

In POP-11, a bit of code which consists of a number of words and/or numbers enclosed between square brackets is an expression whose value is an object called a *list*. Expressions of this sort will be called *list expressions*. A list is just a sequence of values (numbers, words etc.) Note that POP-11 assumes that contiguous sequences of characters appearing between the square brackets are words not variables. It does not force you to put in the double-quotes to show that they are words.

Now, the valuable thing about lists is that they have internal structure. That is to say, they are not only objects (i.e. values) themselves, but they have inside them, other objects. But how can we get at these encapsulated objects? For instance, if we type something like:

```
[foobang silly wally] -> mine;
```

so as to put the value of the list expression into the variable called **mine**, is there any way we can find out what objects the list has inside it? (without looking at what we typed!). POP-11 provides a way of writing expressions which lets us dig out components of the list. For example we can type:

```
mine(1) ==>
```

so as to ask POP-11 to produce the first element of the list in **mine**. POP-11 responds by printing:

```
** foobang
```

Other possibilities are as follows:

```
mine(2) ==>
** silly

mine(3) ==>
** wally
```

These expressions look like function calls but in fact this is not how POP-11 treats them. If we ever type an expression which looks like a call on a function but where the function name is actually a variable which has a list in it, POP-11 forms the value of the expression as that component of the list whose position corresponds to the number which appears in between the brackets. Technically, this is called *subscripting* the list.

POP-11 also provides some special functions for digging out the first and the last element of a list. These are called **hd** and **last**. They work as follows:

```
hd(mine) ==>
** foobang

last(mine) ==>
** wally
```

Another very useful function is called **delete**. This works a bit like **hd** and **last**, except that whereas these functions provide a way of accessing a specific component of a list, the **delete** function provides a way of removing a certain component from a list. A typical call on **delete** might be:

```
delete("silly", mine) ==>
** [foobang wally]
```

The **delete** function takes two inputs; the second input is a list and the first input is an expression whose value corresponds to one of the elements of the list. The value of the output is just a copy of the list which has had the specified element removed.

A final list function which we will be making extensive use of is **member**. This function tests whether a given item is included in a given list. The item is provided as the first input and the list is provided as the second input. The function returns **<true>** if the item is included in the list and **<false>** otherwise. Thus:

```
member(2, mine) ==>
** <false>

member(2, [3 4 5 2 6]) ==>
** <true>

member("silly", mine) ==>
** <true>
```

Hats

As was noted above, when evaluating a list expression, POP-11 assumes that any contiguous sequence of non-numeric characters must be evaluated as a word expression, i.e. it assumes that there are some invisible double-quotes around the sequence. But what if we want POP-11 to treat a sequence of characters in the ordinary way? i.e. to treat it as an expression whose value is just the contents of the corresponding variable. We can get this effect by using the symbol ^, which in POP-11 is called an *up-hat* or just *hat*.. For example, if we put the value of a word expression into a variable:

```
"funny" -> yours;
```

and then type in a list expression, we can arrange to get the value of:

```
yours
```

included in the list by preceding the word **yours** with a single up-hat:

```
[this is not ^yours] ==>
** [this is not funny]
```

In effect, POP-11 treats the up-hat as an instruction to evaluate the expression which follows. If the expression is just a single item like **yours** then we can just put it after the up-hat; however, if the expression consists of a series of items (e.g. **2 + 2**) then we have to put it in brackets so that POP-11 can see where it begins and ends. Thus:

```
[adding 2 and 2 makes ^(2 + 2)] ==>
** [adding 2 and 2 makes 4]
```

POP-11 responds to the up-hat by just inserting the value of the following expression into the list. This means that, if we want, we can get lists inserted into lists, e.g.

```
[my old list was ^mine] ==>
** [my old list was [foobang silly wally]]
```

What happens if we want to get the contents of a list merged into another list? For instance, how can we produce the list:

```
[my old list was foobang silly wally]
```

by using the value of **mine**? One way to do this involves using the built-in function **explode**. This function takes a list as input and returns all the elements of the list as output. Thus we can do:

```
[my old list was ^(explode(mine))] ==>
** [my old list was foobang silly wally]
```

But, in fact, we can get this effect more easily just by using a symbol called the *double up-hat* (written ^^). Thus:

```
[my old list was ^^mine] ==>
** [my old list was foobang silly wally]
```

In the case where we have a command which evaluates an expression a certain number of times but never does anything with the values, e.g.

```
repeat 5 times 2 + 2 endrepeat;
```

POP-11 just keeps the values of the expressions stacked-up in the background. This means that we can create a list of five 4s by doing:

```
[^(repeat 5 times 2 + 2 endrepeat)] ==>
** [4 4 4 4 4]
```

For loops

As has already been noted, lists play a very important role in most POP-11 programs. In fact, a lot of the functions which are built in to the language (e.g. **delete** and **last**) do things to or with lists. There are also a large number of commands which are specially designed for using with lists. A case in point is the **for** command. This command allows a specific set of actions to be done to every element of a list. For instance we might do:

```
[1 2 3 4] -> mine;
```

```
vars item;

for item in mine do  double(item) ==>  endfor;
```

POP-11 will respond by printing:

```
** 2
** 4
** 6
** 8
```

POP-11 responds to the **for** command as follows. First of all it looks at the word which appears between the **for** and the **in** and designates it the *loop variable*.

Next it looks at the expression which appears between the **in** and the **do** and checks that its value is a list. Then, for every single element in this list, it does all the commands which appear between the **do** and the **endfor**. But each time it does them, it puts the next component of the list into the loop variable. What this means, in effect, is that first of all it does **double(1) ==>**, then it does **double(2) ==>**, then **double(3) ==>**, and finally **double(4) ==>**. One complete cycle through the loop is called an *iteration* and the command is said to *iterate* over the list.

Since POP-11 has the ability to keep values of expressions stacked-up (see above), we can use the **for** command to build lists, e.g.

```
[^(for item in [7 18 49] do  double(item)  endfor)] ==>
** [14 36 98]
```

There are a couple of special commands for use with these commands which do a set of actions a certain number of times (e.g. **for** and **repeat**). One of these, called **quitloop**, has the effect of making POP-11 stop going around the loop. For example:

```
for item in [1 2 3 4 5 6 7] do
   if double(item) > 8 then quitloop endif;
   item ==>
endfor;

** 1
** 2
** 3
** 4
```

Here, POP-11 happily does the iterations for the 1, the 2, the 3 and the 4; but in the iteration for 5 the call on **double** returns 10. This means that the **quitloop** command is executed and POP-11 stops going around the loop.

A variant of quitloop is **nextloop**. This command tells POP-11 not to do any more of the actions in that iteration but to go on to the next element in the list and carry on from there. Thus:

```
for item in [1 2 3 4 5 6 7] do
   if double(item) > 8 and double(item) <= 12 then nextloop
endif;
   item ==>
endfor;

** 1
** 2
** 3
** 4
** 7
```

A subsidiary use of the **for** command implements an iteration over a range of integers. For instance, we can type:

```
for x from 1 to 10 do x ==> endfor;
```

POP-11 responds by printing:

```
** 1
** 2
** 3
** 4
** 5
** 6
** 7
** 8
** 9
** 10
```

In this usage, rather than binding the loop variable to a different element of a list each time around the loop, the **for** command binds it to the next number in the indicated sequence of integers (e.g. 1 to 10).

Applist

Very frequently, programs need to process the elements of a list using a single function. For instance we might want to take a list of numbers and return a list in which all the numbers are doubled. We could do this by using a **for** command inside a list expression, e.g.

```
vars list;
[1 2 3 4] -> list;

[^(for item in list do double(item) endfor)] ==>
** [2 4 6 8]
```

However, POP-11 provides a special-purpose function for doing this sort of thing. To carry out the doubling process we could use the **applist** function thus:

```
[^(applist(list, double))] ==>
** [2 4 6 8]
```

The **applist** function just has the effect of applying the function which is presented as the second input, to all the elements of the list (first input) in turn.

Syssort

Another useful function which works on lists is **syssort**. This function reorders the elements of a list using a function whose name we have to provide as an input. First of all let us define a function which returns **<true>** if the number given as first input is less than the number given as second input. The definition for this is shown in Figure A-5.

We can use this function so as to sort a list of numbers into ascending order thus:

```
syssort([5 3 8 9 32 1 4 2], smaller) ==>
** [1 2 3 4 5 8 9 32]
```

```
define smaller(numa, numb) -> boolean;
   numa < numb -> boolean
enddefine;
```

Figure A-5 Function to compare two numbers

What **syssort** actually does is make sure that for any two elements A and B in the list which is provided as first input, A will appear before B in the list returned as result if the function provided as second input returns **<true>** when called with A and B as inputs.[3]

Matching

One of the most powerful features of POP-11 is the pattern-matcher. This facility is packaged in the form of a boolean operator which tests whether two lists *match*. The **matches** operator is usually just called the *matcher* and **matches** expressions are just called *match expressions*.

If we want to test whether two lists are exactly the same we can use the = operator, e.g.

```
[1 2 3] = [1 2 3] ==>
** <true>

[1 2 3] = [2 2 3] ==>
** <false>
```

However, if we want to test something a little less categorical like whether or not a list ends with a certain two elements we can use the matcher thus:

```
[2 2 3] matches [= 2 3] ==>
** <true>
```

The matcher assumes that an = in the second list can match an item in the first list, no matter what that item actually is. (Note that you cannot put an = in the first list.) There is another symbol called the *double-equals* which the matcher assumes can match a sequence of arbitrary items in the first list. Thus, if we want to check whether some list of arbitrary size ends in a certain two elements we might type:

```
[foo bang ding 1 2 3] matches [== 2 3] ==>
** <true>
```

As far as the matcher is concerned, the double-equals matches any number of items in the other list. We can put single-equals and double-equals wherever we want, e.g.

---

[3] Technically, since POP-11 treats any value which is not equal to **<false>** as **<true>**, A will appear before B in the result if the function provided as second input does not return **<false>** when called with A and B as inputs.

```
[foo bang ding 1 2 3] matches [== bang = 1 == 3] ==>
** <true>

[foo bang ding 1 2 3] matches [== bang = = 1 == 3] ==>
** <false>
```

Note that by putting two separate single-equals after the **bang** in the second list we have effectively stopped it from matching any list which has **bang** and **1** but only one element in between.

Very often, we will be interested to know what things the single-equals and double-equals matched against. The matcher allows us to find this out by using two variants of the equals signs called the *single-query* (written **?**) and the *double-query* (written **??**). If we do:

```
[foo bang ding 1 2 3] matches [?mine bang = 1 == 3] ==>
** <true>
```

and then print out the value of **mine**

```
mine ==>
** foo
```

we see that, as a side-effect of matching **?mine** against **foo**, the matcher has put **foo** into the variable called **mine**. If we use the double-query, then a list of the elements which have matched is put into the corresponding variable, e.g.

```
[foo bang ding 1 2 3] matches [??mine 1 2 3] ==>
** <true>

mine ==>
** [foo bang ding]
```

Restriction procedures

The single- and double-query can be used to great effect in POP-11 programs for "digging out" bits and pieces from list structures. However, the overall usefulness is increased still further by a feature known as "restriction procedures". The use of restriction procedures can be illustrated by considering the way in which a built-in function such as **isnumber** might be used to influence the result of a match process. The **isnumber** function takes a single expression as input and tests whether its value is a number. If it is, **<true>** is returned; otherwise **<false>** is returned. Thus:

```
isnumber(2 + 2) ==>
** <true>

isnumber(3) ==>
** <true>

isnumber("foo") ==>
** <false>

isnumber([foo bang]) ==>
** <false>
```

Let us imagine that we want to test whether some list begins with a number, ends with the word `foo`, and has an arbitrary number of elements in between. We can implement this test using the matcher as follows:

```
vars list;
[1 ding bong foo] -> list;

list matches [?mine:isnumber == foo] ==>
** <true>
```

By writing `:isnumber` after the `?mine`, we tell POP-11 (in effect) that the first element of the list can match against the `mine` variable provided that it is a number. Note that if it is not a number, the matcher returns **<false>>**:

```
[ding bong foo] -> list;

list matches [?mine:isnumber == foo] ==>
** <false>
```

```
define is_silly_word(w) -> boolean;
   if w = "foo" or w = "ding"
   then true -> boolean
   else false -> boolean
   endif
enddefine;
```

Figure A-6 Function to check whether its argument is foo or ding

Technically, putting : followed by the name of a function tells POP-11 that the variable can match an element provided that, when the function is called with the element provided as input, it does not return **<false>**>. We can illustrate this by defining a new function which returns boolean values as shown in Figure A-6. This function can then be used in match expressions as follows:

```
list matches [?mine:is_silly_word ==] ==>
** <true>

[sensible ding bong] -> list;

list matches [?mine:is_silly_word ==] ==>
** <false>
```

If the function whose name we write after the : returns a result which is not equal to **<false>** but not equal to **<true>** either, then the value is assigned to the variable in the place of the element which was actually provided as input. Thus, if we redefine **is_silly_word** as in Figure A-7 then the behaviour produced by the matcher is as follows:

```
list matches [?mine:is_silly_word ==] ==>
** <true>

mine ==>
** silly
```

As well as function names, we can also put integers after any colon which follows a double-query or a double-equals. The idea here is that the integer forces the matcher to match the given variable against a sequence of a given length. Inserting an integer N makes sure that the variable will only match against a sequence of N elements.

```
define is_silly_word(w) -> boolean;
   if w = "foo" or w = "ding"
   then "silly" -> boolean
   else false -> boolean
   endif
enddefine;
```

Figure A-7 Function to return silly or false, depending on the input

Thus, typing something like:

```
list matches [== ??mine] ==>
** <true>
```

returns <true> and has the side effect of putting a list containing all the elements of the matched list into the variable **mine**. Whereas, typing:

```
list matches [== ??mine:2] ==>
** <true>
```

returns <true> and has the side effect of putting a list containing just the final *two* elements into the variable mine:

```
mine ==>
** [ding bong]
```

Lists which contain symbols which mean certain things to the matcher are usually called *patterns*. Note that, for convenience, a match expression whose arguments are not list expressions works just like an = expression. Thus:

```
2 matches 3 ==>
** <false>

"foo" matches "foo" ==>
** <true>
```

The matcher arrow

As we have seen, the POP-11 matcher can have side-effects. In some cases we may know that a list will definitely match a pattern but want to obtain the side-effects of the match anyway. In this case we can use a command --> which is called the *matcher arrow*. An expression featuring the matcher arrow between two list expressions works just like a match expression except that it does not have a value. Thus we might type:

```
[foo 2 3 ] --> [?mine:is_silly_word ==];
```

so as to get the word **silly** assigned to the variable called **mine**:

```
mine ==>
** silly
```

Alternatively, we could use the matcher arrow to assign values to the variables called **mine** and **yours** simultaneously:

```
[1 2] --> [?mine ?yours];

mine ==>
** 1

yours ==>
** 2
```

The database

As has already been shown, POP-11 is a good language for dealing with list structures. Because, programs will often need to set up and then process many different lists, the language provides a general place in which lists can be stored and accessed. This is called the *database*. In fact the database is itself a list but normally, the lists that are of interest are the ones which are *in* the database list. POP-11 provides simple commands for adding lists into the database, for taking them out and for finding all examples of lists which match a certain pattern. To create a new database from scratch we can use an ordinary list expression and an assignment, e.g.

```
[[1 2 3] [foo bang] [noddy bigears]] -> database;
```

However, the normal way of adding lists into the database list, involves using a special POP-11 command called **add**. An **add** command consists of the word **add** followed by a list expression appearing between round brackets. Thus:

```
[] -> database;
add([Chris Thornton Brighton Sussex]);
```

will cause the list in brackets to be added to the database list (which is initialised to be an empty list). Since the database list is stored in a variable called **database**, we can print out the contents of the database using the print arrow in the usual way:

```
database ==>
** [[Chris Thornton Brighton Sussex]]
```

We can add more lists by executing a sequence of **add** commands, e.g.

```
add([Fred Bloggs Lewes Sussex]);
add([Simple Simon Dover Kent]);
```

```
add([Margaret Thatcher London]);
add([John Smith Brighton Sussex]);
```

We can use the **present** function to test whether there is a list in the database which matches a certain pattern. The value of a call on **present** is **<true>** if there is a list in the database matching the pattern given as first input, and **<false>** otherwise. Thus:

```
present([== Brighton Sussex]) ==>
** <true>

present([== Surrey]) ==>
** <false>
```

If we want to check that the database contains a set of patterns then we can use the function **allpresent**, thus:

```
allpresent([[Chris Thornton ==][Fred Bloggs ==]]) ==>
** <true>
```

Another very useful command is **foreach**. This is like **for** except that instead of iterating over every element of a list, it iterates over every element of the database which matches a certain pattern. Every time it finds a match, it puts the list in question into a special variable called **it**. Thus:

```
foreach [== Brighton Sussex] do it ==> endforeach;
** [John Smith Brighton Sussex]
** [Chris Thornton Brighton Sussex]

foreach [== Sussex] do it ==> endforeach;
** [John Smith Brighton Sussex]
** [Fred Bloggs Lewes Sussex]
** [Chris Thornton Brighton Sussex]
```

If we want the **foreach** command to iterate over the sublists of some other list we can use a command of the form:

```
foreach <pattern> in <other list> do <commands> endforeach;
```

Note that there is version of **present** called **isin** which works for ordinary lists. This is actually an operator like **matches**; expressions involving the **isin** operator have the value **<true>** or **<false>>** depending whether the list (i.e. the value of the list expression) which appears on the right can be matched with one of the sublists of the list which appears on the left. Thus:

```
[= 2 =] isin [[4 5 6][7 8 9][1 2 3]] ==>
** <true>
```

Readline

Another useful function which is built-in to POP-11 is **readline**. This takes no inputs at all. When it is called it prints out a single question mark and then makes POP-11 wait until you type something. It lets you type in whatever you want but when you press the <RETURN> key the function collects up all the words which you have typed and returns them in a list as the result of the original call on **readline**. Thus we can type:

```
readline() -> mine;
? here are a few random words

mine ==>
** [here are a few random words]
```

Quite often we will want to use **readline** in order to find out whether the user agrees to something or not. In this case we can use the function **yesno**. This takes a list as input. It prints out the list, and then calls **readline** to read the user's response. If the user responds either with "yes" or "no", the **yesno** function returns **<true>** or **<false>** respectively. If the user types anything other than "yes" or "no" the function prints out a complaint and goes through the whole process again. It will keep doing this until the user types either a "yes" or a "no". Thus:

```
yesno([do you agree that the world is flat?]) -> mine;

** [do you agree that the world is flat ?]
? what a stupid question
** [please answer either yes or no]
** [do you agree that the world is flat ?]
? I would prefer not to
** [please answer either yes or no]
** [do you agree that the world is flat ?]
? ok, yes
** [please answer either yes or no]
** [do you agree that the world is flat ?]
? yes

mine ==>
** <true>
```

Functions calling functions

In most cases a program will consist not of a single complex POP-11 function, but of a set of functions, where one "drives" the program and "calls" the others either directly or indirectly. In the following example, see Figure A-8 we define the function **makedata** which sets up the database, a function **find_person** which scans the database, and a driving function **find** which makes the others go:

```
find();
? Simple Simon
** [Dover Kent]
? Fred Smith
** [sorry - not in database]
? John Smith
** [Brighton Sussex]
? 1234
```

```
define makedata();
   [] -> database;
   add([Fred Bloggs Lewes Sussex]);
   add([Simple Simon Dover Kent]);
   add([Margaret Thatcher London]);
   add([John Smith Brighton Sussex]);
enddefine;

define find_person(name) -> address;
   unless present([^^name ??address])
   then [sorry - not in database] -> address
   endunless
enddefine;

define find();
   vars name address;
   makedata();
   repeat 4 times
      readline() -> name;
      find_person(name) -> address;
      address ==>
   endrepeat
enddefine;
```

Figure A-8 Functions to find an address, given a name

```
** [sorry - not in database]
```

In this example function **find** calls function **makedata** once and then calls function **find_person** four times inside the loop. Note that **find** and **makedata** do not take any input and return no values, whereas **find_person** takes a single value as input and returns a single value as output.

Recursion

We can sometimes obtain certain useful behaviour by arranging for functions to call *themselves*. This sounds a bit strange but the idea is actually quite straightforward. Let us imagine that we would like to write a function which will enable POP-11 to compute the *factorial* of a number. The factorial of N is defined to be the result of multiplying N by N-1, and that value by N-2, and that value by N-3, etc. all the way down to 1. Thus the factorial of 4 is:

```
4 * 3 * 2 * 1 ==>
** 24
```

Now it turns out (if you think about it) that the factorial of N is the result of multiplying N by the *factorial* of N-1, e.g. the factorial of 4 is the result of multiplying 4 by the factorial of 3. We can demonstrate this as follows:

```
3 * 2 * 1 ==>
** 6

4 * 6 = 4 * 3 * 2 * 1 ==>
** <true>
```

This means that we could define a **factorial** function which works out what the factorial of a number is by multiplying its input with the result of computing the factorial of its input with 1 subtracted from it. This function might be defined as in Figure A-9. Note that the text which appears between the **/*** and the ***/** is a *comment*, i.e. it is just a bit of text which gives some information about the way the function works. POP-11 always ignores any text which comes between a **/*** symbol, (called an *opening comment bracket*) and a ***/** symbol (called a *closing comment bracket*).

We can test that this definition works as follows:

```
factorial(4) ==>
** 24
```

The point to note here is that, given the way we have written this function, POP-11

```
define factorial(num) -> total;
   if num = 1 then
      1 -> total
   else              /* do recursive call */
      num * factorial(num - 1) -> total
   endif
enddefine;
```

Figure A-9 Function to compute the factorial of its input

has to go through quite an elaborate process to evaluate a call on **factorial**. The body of the function consists of an **if** command. The input to the function is put into the variable **num** and the expression in the **if** just tests whether the number in this variable is equal to 1. Now the input is actually 4; this is not equal to 1 so POP-11 has to execute the commands between the **else** and the **endif**.

Now, there is only one command here and it is an assignment. This causes the value of the expression to be returned as the value of the original function. But this expression is actually a call on the **factorial** function! And to work out the value of this expression (i.e. to get the result of the call) POP-11 has to make use of the **factorial** function which we have defined.

Now, of course, POP-11 is *already* making use of the definition which we have provided; but this makes absolutely no difference. Whenever POP-11 tries to work out the result of a call on a function it just uses a *copy* of the corresponding definition. This means that functions can "call themselves" without there being any unfortunate interference effects.

To evaluate the call of **factorial** on the input 3 (i.e. 4 - 1) POP-11 has to go through the same process that it went through to evaluate the call of **factorial** on the input 4. This, of course, means that it is going to end up evaluating a call of **factorial** on the input 2, and another one on the input 1. Now 1 is obviously equal to 1; so this *final* call will not produce any further calls. Given the provided definition, it will just return the result 1. This will enable the call on the input 2, to return the result 2; this result will enable the call on the input 3 to return the result 6 (2 * 3). And this, finally, will enable the call on the input 4 to return the result 24 (6 * 4). This process in which a function uses itself to get a job done is called *recursion*.

Tracing

Note that what really happens in the recursion described above is that the calls of **factorial** get *nested* inside one another. POP-11 has a feature which lets us see this process happening. The feature is accessed via the **trace** command. A trace command just consists of the word **trace** followed by the names of one or more functions. In executing a **trace** command we are effectively telling POP-11 that we would like to be notified whenever there is a call on any one of the specified functions and also whenever that call returns a result. We can demonstrate what this means by first executing a **trace** command on the **factorial** function and then by calling that function with the input 4:

```
trace factorial;

factorial(4) ==>

>factorial 4
!>factorial 3
!!>factorial 2
!!!>factorial 1
!!!<factorial 1
!!<factorial 2
!<factorial 6
<factorial 24
** 24
```

Note that once we have traced a function (i.e. executed a **trace** command on it) POP-11 responds to calls on that function by printing out certain information. When we type:

```
factorial(4)
```

POP-11 prints out

```
> factorial 4
```

The **>** indicates that POP-11 is starting to evaluate a call, the word is just the name of the called function, and any items which appear after are just the inputs which have been provided in the call. If in the process of evaluating the call, a new call on a function is made, then POP-11 acts virtually the same way except it precedes all the printing with an exclamation mark. This indicates that the new call is *nested* inside the original call. For each level of nesting we get one more exclamation mark.

If ever we want to stop POP-11 printing our information about function calls we can use the **untrace** command. This is handled in exactly the same way as the **trace** command: we type the word **untrace** followed by one or more function names. POP-11 then turns tracing off for these functions, i.e. it stops producing trace output every time they are called.

Showtree

The trace feature allows us to display the structure of a sequence of nested function calls. POP-11 also provides a useful feature which allows us to display and inspect the structure of a list. As was noted above, lists can contain lists as elements. These nested lists can contain other lists, which can contain still more lists. If we have such a structure we can see what it looks like by using a POP-11 command called **showtree**. This command simply creates a graphic description in which the nesting structure is shown as a tree structure. For reasons that will become obvious, the tree is always drawn upside-down with its root sticking up in the air. Note that, in most implementations, to make the **showtree** command available we need to type a special **lib** command as follows:

```
lib showtree;
```

A possible interaction using the **showtree** command is shown in Figure A-10.

```
[foo
    [bang [ding dong] bang]
    [one [two three]]] -> list;
showtree(list);
```

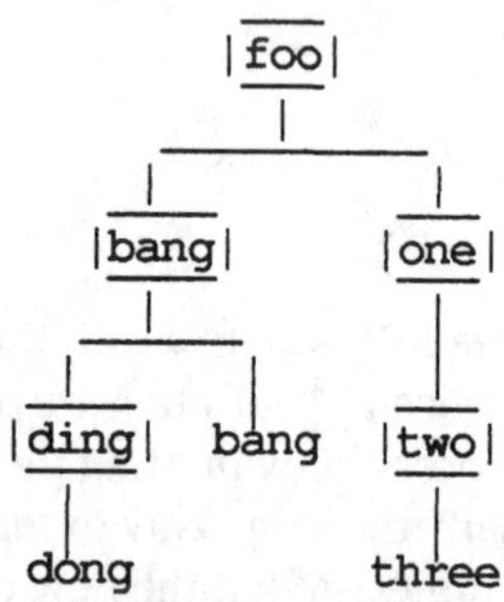

Figure A-10 A simple tree, displayed by showtree

Exiting from a function

Normally POP-11 works through the commands of a function in order and exits from the function when the final command terminates. There are occasions when we require a function to exit prematurely. For this we make use of the built-in command **return**. This has the effect of immediately causing the function to terminate as if all its commands had been properly completed. Function **silly**, see Figure A-11, takes a list and a maximum number as input and returns the first number that it finds in the list which is bigger than the maximum. It does not then search the rest of the list. If no number is found it returns 0. The function also prints out all the numbers that it checks.

```
silly([1 2 3 4 5], 2) ==>
** 1
** 2
** 3
** 3

silly([1 2 3 4 5], 7) ==>
** 1
** 2
** 3
** 4
** 5
** 0

silly([10 20 30 40], 2) ==>
** 10
** 10
```

```
define silly(list, limit) -> wanted;
    for wanted in list do
        wanted ==>
        if wanted > limit then return endif
    endfor;
    0 -> wanted
enddefine;
```

Figure A-11 Function with premature exit from a loop

Partial application

It is sometimes useful to be able to build a specific version of a function from a general definition. Consider the function **silly** given above. Its second argument is used to determine the limit that will cause the function to exit. Suppose we were interested in a specific version of **silly** that had, for example, 31 as the value of its limit. The *partial application* mechanism allows us to build a new function, max_month (say), by fixing its second argument to the value 31 as follows:

```
vars max_month hundred;
silly(%31%) -> max_month;
max_month([10 20 30 40 50]) =>
** 10
** 20
** 30
** 40
** 40

silly(%100%) -> hundred;
hundred([40 80 120 160]) =>
** 40
** 80
** 120
** 120
```

The (%31%) is used to fix the value of the second input of **silly** to the value 31, thus making a new function max_month which expects only one argument.

Concluding comment

The present appendix has looked briefly at features of POP-11 such as pattern-matching, the database, and simple recursive functions. The features covered form a very tiny subset of the complete language so the above should not be seen as a comprehensive review of its capabilities.

To keep things as simple as possible, we have employed a number of "little white lies". POP-11 experts, who have a broad knowledge of the language will probably object to some of these. Anyone wanting the whole truth and nothing but the truth should consult one of the introductory texts on the language (e.g. Barrett, Ramsay & Sloman, 1985; Burton & Shadbolt, 1987; Laventhol, 1987). Ramsay and Barrett (1987) will be of interest to anyone wanting to see a range of possible applications.

Index

APPENDIX B
Where to get the source code

Send the voucher enclosed with this book to the publisher, at the address below. The source will be returned to you on a 3.5" floppy disc, in MS-DOS format.

ORDER FORM

Please send me the *Artificial Intelligence Through Search* source code.

Name (Mr/Ms/Dr)
Organisation
Address

Post Code Country

Date Book Purchased
Place of Purchase

Return to:
Intellect Books, 108-110 London Road, Headington, Oxford OX3 9AW, England